"THE MAISTER"

A CENTURY OF TYNESIDE LIFE

THE MAISTER.

"THE MAISTER"

A CENTURY OF
TYNESIDE LIFE.

Being some account of the life and work and times of
THOMAS HASWELL,—*who for close on fifty years
was Master of the Royal Jubilee Schools at
North Shields,—and of a notable essay
in the education of the people.*

BY

GEO. H. HASWELL.

"He who has found his work is blessed: let him ask no
other blessedness. He has a life purpose."—CARLYLE.

WITH ORIGINAL ILLUSTRATIONS BY
FRANK HEWETT, R. JOBLING, GEO. HORTON, CHAS. J. SPENCE,
HARRY S. CURRY, CHAS. GEORGE, CHAS. DRUMMOND,
ISAAC BLACK, AND S. H. HASWELL.

LONDON:
WALTER SCOTT, LTD., PATERNOSTER SQUARE.
1895.

TO THE MEMORY

OF

MY MOTHER.

PREFACE.

THE story of "The Maister's" life and work would assuredly never have been written but for representations, somewhat urgently pressed upon the author, by authorities whom he could not refuse to regard as competent, that it would furnish a useful, and somewhat novel, contribution to the general history of Popular Education.

Nor is it in any sense put forward as the story of an isolated, individual career—remarkable or otherwise—but merely as typical of the work done fifty years ago in the nooks and corners and by-places of England by hundreds of humble, earnest, and far-seeing, though wholly unseen, unnoticed or unvalued men—the elementary school teachers of early and mid-century.

If any peculiarity—any idiosyncrasy—possessed the Maister in his day, it was an abiding conviction that no child, *of whatever class*, could by any possibility be *over*-educated, or even *sufficiently* educated; that education, as he understood the word, was good for each and all. In which respect, doubtless, he was at issue with most of his generation—though that monstrous expression, "Godless education" (a contradiction in terms), had not then become familiar.

To Tynesiders, the sketch-history of the town of Shields given in Chapter I. may doubtless appear somewhat prolix, because of their familiarity with most of the facts therein set forth (which are taken from the usual authorities), but it was felt that the full significance of the work undertaken by the early educators of the poor, could not be readily apprehended without some account of the conditions under which such work was done. To some extent the summary given in the Introduction must be justified on the same grounds.

The acknowledgments of the author are due to the artists who have kindly contributed original sketches; to Messrs. Cassell, Messrs. Andrew Reid & Co, and the Proprietors of the *Shields Daily News*, for permission to make use of certain engravings; and finally to Sam Timmins, Esq., F.S.A., Mr. Charles Pendlebury, and Mr. John E. H. Burnet for reading the proofs, etc.

G. H. H.

CONTENTS.

INTRODUCTION.

"THE RASCAL MANY."

                                                                               PAGE

The rabble in 1800—A starving people—The "Dear Years"—Artificial famine—A "Pious Pastime"—War for a generation—Moral inversions—To h—— with the French!—Patience preached to the masses—Furious impatience meted out to them—"Example"—Sports of rich and poor—Where brutality found its apologists—A Draconian code—The value of a human life—Death for every lapse—Better hang the wrong fellow than no fellow—The "moral" defensibility of spring-guns—The gibbet—The pillory—Constitutional violence—Warring on the people—No light—Artificial disease and darkness—The outer darkness—The "mortsafe"—Forty-pound crimes—Vagrancy—Combination and conspiracy—Demand and supply—Monopolies and interests—Limiting the vend—Strangling the press—Official corruption—Government lotteries—Society and the *status quo*—Poetic poverty .   .   .   1-15

CHAPTER I.

OF A TOWN WHERE NO TOWN SHOULD BE.

Poverty pursuing her road—The fishers' Sheels—The priors of Tynemouth and the men of Newcastle—Charters and charters—With intent to kill

—A local Cromwell—England's grievance—A tremendous indictment—How charter-right worked—An antient carpenter—"Foreigners"—"Tumbled" by the Scots—An anonymous letter and—a lie—"A poor, miserable place"—The long narrow-street and the life in it—Sailors—Keelmen—Pitmen—Ship-carpenters—A multifarious populace—The "Bar"—A fleet sailing—Foying—Convoy—Privateers and anti-privateers—False alarms—Preparations for resisting invasion—State of the sea-port—A householder's ticket 16-45

CHAPTER II.

WHERE HEZ T' BEEN?

How it fared in 1800 with the British tar—A base institution—Ben Pinder and others—Flogging—The *Susanna*—Spies and informers—The tender-ship—Civil war—Courting an inquiry—Jack's petition—False protections—Repudiation—Stratagem—A dark story—John Babbington Stodart—His letters and his murder 46-64

CHAPTER III.

THE DAY-SPRING

Glory—Plague, pestilence, famine—Battle, murder, and sudden death—Good for trade—*Was fur plunder*—Duty—Repression—Light—Beginnings in culture—*Inter oves*—A benignant people—Lighten our darkness—The old library—"Give the praise to God"—"What do you want with books?"—"Over"-education—Nee sarvints—A jubilee—An "illumination"—May every poor child in the kingdom be able to read his Bible—Lancaster and Bell—The Royal Jubilee School—Its charter—"Directions to the master"—The *curriculum*—Regular and other schoolmasters—Children taken in to *bate*—A Tyne sailor—Running away to sea—Married, and sails next day—Pressed—An effort to escape—A tragic failure—A "perishment" of cold—Air, exercise, and milk diet—The "Three Legs of Man"—Smoking out a philosopher—Foying—Keeling—Cast away—Life in the Low Street—What could a poor sailor do? 65-94

CHAPTER IV.

L'ARNIN'.

Thomas Haswell goes to school—Education in 1815—Writing on sand—Alarm—Leaves school at eleven—Grinding watch crystals—A bone—Bound apprentice—Enters the choir—Thomas Oxley—*Solfeggi* by night—"Where should this music be?"—Thorough-bass—Old ballads—The "late Mr. Harris"—Music *minus* poetry—Choir practice at six A.M.—Joins a band—The "common bugle"—The "plain trumpet"—Who's your leader?—Silencing the horns—The '26 election at Alnwick—The "Battle of Bamburgh"—Arranging for the band—In shirt and candle-light—Learning the organ—A crazy harpsichord—In clover and out—"You can read as well as I"—Organist *pro tem*—At Bamburgh—"Grand musicianers"—The Red Cross Knight in the vestry—The Vicar—Budle Hills—The Bohemian Brothers—The viola—The chord of the fourth and the "p" language—Music and study in London—Two "grand" clerks—Bandmaster again—A musical society—Classics among the pioneers—Passionate abbreviation and ardent capitals—Cupid—A Mechanics' Institute—The British Association—Professor Sedgwick and the basaltic column—The wise-week, 1838—Winlaton Tommy—Becomes a school-teacher—Then master of his *Alma Mater*—Captain John—Marriage—"There was much singing" . . 95-125

CHAPTER V.

IN THE 'FORTIES

Libertas et natale solum—An old newspaper—The spirit of peace—Purging the Statute-book—The railway—The steamship—The penny post—A queer out-of-the-way place—"Nee leets"—Maimed sea-dogs—Picturesque dismemberment—The French feud—Æsthetics—A pantheon of wooden gods—Street cries and street sounds—The evolution of the shipowner—Ship names—The club and the comet-*tee* man—The "laughing man"—Suspension—Luck—Floating coffins—"Ready for sea"—A storm off the Tyne—Volunteers for death—The birthplace of the lifeboat—The pit has "fired"—Rescue—Altruism—"Hardening"—The unruly sons of an unruly people 126-155

CONTENTS

CHAPTER VI.
A BEGINNING.

The Jubilee School in 1839—"Playing the neck"—Deadening influences—Dull lesson-books—Drowsy schools—The "cane"—Wasting time—Idle hands—Tar water—"A craze"—Music—A new emotion—Maps and mapping—Mercator—Globes—Vital geography—A neglected science—The sun without amplitude—Dialling—Equation of time—Newspaper astronomy—Teaching the stars—Geometry with wooden tools—Drawing—Seeking chalk, slate pencil, and Scotch "cam"—A gaunt room—Brightening up—Seeking entrance—Quiet assiduity—An alphabet mill—Spelling—Definition—The newspaper—The subtle music of good prose—A course of reading—Acquiring books—The Mechanics' Institute—Local *Alumni*—Platters and platitudes—The "delightful addition of music"—The annual yawn—Twopenny concerts for working classes—Some respectable gentlemen—Philharmonic *redivivus*—The music of the forties—Some amateurs and some pupils—Early pianos—Tuning—Three diatonic notes—At the old church—Responses—Syncopation—Squabbles—Parochial critics—The Ten Virgins' Solo—A bad job . 156-199

CHAPTER VII.
LIGHTEN OUR DARKNESS.

The Maister at work—Teaching the teachers—Broadening the stream of culture—Magnetism—Electricity—The uncanny—Ruhmkorf and Galvani—Presents from old boys—Wordy formulæ—The (newspaper) deportment of lightening—Educational hurdles—Chemistry—Peripatetic philosophers—The air-pump—Its lessons—Correlation of sciences—Acoustics—Harmonics—Resultant tones—The "roarer"—The "wolf"—Botany and microscopy—Aberration—Land surveying and recreation—Bathing, swimming, and boating—Velocity of sound—Gymnastics—Games—"Leed fardens"—Cockspurs—Declining a holiday—Drill—Gleaning—An examination—Competition—Fair-time—The "Good Design"—A popular banner—The religious "difficulty"—All the tribes—Workhouse boys—"Dinner"—Semi-starvation—Afflictions—Toothache—A benevolent druggist—Impediments—Bereavements—Lighten our darkness 200-235

CONTENTS.

CHAPTER VIII.

ENTER, THE POLITICIAN.

From all climes and latitudes—A museum—Quartets—A *faux pas*—Socrates—The voice of music—Musical classics—The Inner Temple—Vine Cottage—" How va-a-ain is ma-a-an "—Raising the standard of musical taste—D——d symphonies—The new " Mechanics "—Drums and fifes—" Form, form, Riflemen, form "—Ethics for the poor — Mischievousness — Destructiveness — Waste — Habit — Order—Neatness—Care of money—Fagging and bullying—Cruelty—Sports—Pets—Hobbies—Sentimentalism—Old boys—An ice-bound fleet—Musical intervals—Mathematics, music, and science—A testimonial—Leaving the Church and the " Mechanics "—The politician " takes up " Education—A Christmas dinner—Ten-pound patriotism—A respectable boor—No stake in the country 236-262

CHAPTER IX.

BREAKING UP.

A dominie's salary—Financial questions—Enter, the inspector—Getting a certificate—A great globe—Narrowing down—Dialects and dialects—Education and politics—" Views " on education—Baiting the teacher—Bible and Board—Codes—Returns—Regulations—A Scholastic Trinity—Music re-kindled—The "*c e* or the *do re*"—Travelling in deep ruts—Writing on sand again—A noble essay—Mr. W. Jerome Harrison—Letters—Darwin—No time to be ill—A well-filled purse—To Manx Land—Death in the old house—To Bamburgh—A forlorn expedition—Resignation and retirement—Six Sims Reeveses—" A venerable schoolmaster "—Leaving the old home 263-295

CHAPTER X.

VALE.

In retirement—Rest and hobbies—Letters—Hunting animalculæ—Power of music—A sycamore—End of the great globe—Reading courses—Miss Clerke—R A. Proctor—Huxley—and others—A dominant seventh—

xiv   *CONTENTS.*

PAGE

Woolhouse—A draught from Styx—Jack Frost's pranks—"Two old boys and no mistake"—Voyages in a bath-chair—No local magnetic attraction—Among the sea-folk—Leaky weather lore—Failing—A last letter—Eighty-second birthday and the end—"Slates away, boys!" 296-312

CHAPTER XI.

IN MEMORIAM

A record of the Memorial Proceedings—Unveiling the portrait in the Free Library—Presenting the Memorial Medal to the *dux* of the Jubilee School—Unveiling the Memorial Tablet . . . 313-331

APPENDICES

(A.) The Jubilee Foundation 332
(B) Deed of Gift to the School Board . . . 336
(C) Proceedings of School Board anent Memorial . . . 338

LIST OF ILLUSTRATIONS.

		PAGE
PORTRAIT OF THE MAISTER		*Frontispiece*
A TREE OF IGNORANCE	*Frank Hewett*	1
NO LIGHT	,,	15
PEN BAL CRAG	*George Horton*	17
SHIELDS BAR	*J. W. Carmichael*	39
WOODEN DOLLY AND QUAY	*Charles J. Spence*	45
GLORY	*Frank Hewett*	64
LIGHTHOUSE	,,	65
NORTH SHIELDS	*J. W. Carmichael*	76
THE OLD TYNE KEEL		94
INSCRIPTION ON SCHOOL	*S. H. Haswell*	95
THE ROYAL JUBILEE SCHOOL	*Harry S. Curry*	125
AN APOTHEOSIS OF PEACE	*Frank Hewett*	126
AN EARLY RAILWAY TRAIN	,,	129
THAT "SPLENDID" STEAM-BOAT	,,	130
SHIELDS HARBOUR	*J. W. Carmichael*	153
THE LIFEBOAT	*Charles George*	155
THE BIG GLOBE	*Frank Hewett*	156
THE ALPHABET MILL	*Charles J. Spence*	199
THE CULLERCOATS COBLE	*R. Jobling*	200
A LEED FARDEN	*Frank Hewett*	217
A "COCKSPUR"	,,	217
THE "GOOD DESIGN" BANNER	,,	228
PORTRAIT OF W. S. B. WOOLHOUSE, F.R.A.S.		255
THE "OLD MECHANICS"	*Frank Hewett*	262
BAMBURGH CASTLE	*Charles Drummond*	263
THE MAISTER AND MONITORS		295
TYNEMOUTH ABBEY	*Harry S. Curry*	312
MEMORIAL TABLET	*Isaac Black*	313
MESSIS AB ALTIS	*Harry S. Curry*	331

THE MAISTER.

INTRODUCTION.

"THE RASCAL MANY."

"In the multitude of people is the king's honour."

"Shall the clay say to him that fashioned it, What makest thou?"

OF that greater mass of humanity lightly classed, up to quite our own times, as "the rabble," the nineteenth century of grace opened sullen, black, and unhopeful as the portals of Inferno,—black and sullen for what existed; unhopeful for what, over a weary tale of years, was to come.

The "rabble"—or (indifferently) the mob, crowd, lower class, lower orders, common people, and so, on through a great gamut of contempt—comprised the whole toiling population of the nation; nay, on certain arrogant lips the expression confounded in careless indiscrimination all ranks from the pauper to the lower confines of the aristocracy; but, limited to the sense in which it has only of late years ceased to be heard, "the rabble" was yet by far the greatest of the classes, including as it did, not only the vast labouring population and the class below that laboured when it might, but also the entire artisan and operative body and, perhaps, the lower stratum of the feeble middle-class of the time.

"The rabble" was poor—miserably and chronically poor—not seldom indeed spoken of as "the poor", unlettered, of course; superstitious, distrustful, credulous, and, to the mind of some who gave an idle thought to the matter, callous, brutal, and mostly worthless. Wretched undoubtedly in most respects, but, just then, mainly as concerned food.

For this great sub-nation was starving, and no man outside of it greatly heeding. "The winter of 1800-1 was a season of the greatest privation that had been experienced since the days when famine was a common occurrence."[1] Harvest after harvest had failed, and in the dark days of January, 1800, the grain of the previous autumn lay, yet uncut, rotting in the undrained fields. Such food-stuffs as had haply been garnered were disease-smitten, producing at best a sour, leaden, indigestible mass of dough which, though constituting in many cases the sole, and in most the main article of diet, was so utterly unfit to eat that famished children made a grim plaything of the sorry stuff, and in pulling apart the scanty portion, strove with each other to draw out the glutinous strings into which it broke, to the greatest length. When a day old the loaf became as hard as a block of wood, and stank when cut.

And of even this evil stuff there was terribly too little. With wheat at a guinea the Winchester bushel, the quartern loaf could not be bought for less than a ha'penny or two short of a florin; and then the "quartern" loaf was sometimes desperately small—so small as to give point to a poor dejected little joke of the time which suggested as a reason for the housewife laying a cloth that it would prevent the penny rolls from falling into the worm-holes of the table.

These dreadful opening years of the century—" the dear years," as they were pathetically called by the people—had been successively crowned by the "landlords' blessing of a bad harvest;" but in the flux of seasons, bad harvests gave place to seasons of overflowing abundance, and yet through them all—through years of plenty as through the "dear years," in dreary series,—the people of England were to remain in a condition of chronic semi-starvation. The wickedness of artificial famine had not yet been contrived, but it was to come, and to fill the land with such misery and suffering as can never be wholly realised.

Just now, however, in the "dear years," the poor were starving, ill-conditioned and helpless; in a word, the poor were poor; and

[1] Martineau, *History of the Thirty Years' Peace*.

doubtless that stated the whole case to the contentment of the majority of such outsiders as for a moment or two threw a passing thought on the matter. The poor we have with us alway, and poverty is God's affair. Our rulers had other matters to look after.

And truly they had. The monarchs and statesmen of Europe—with hands wholly unfettered and uncontrolled—were busied mainly with the "pious pastime" of war, and England was taking a vigorous hand in the game.

War—ceaseless, reckless, almost indiscriminate; unbroken for almost a generation save in the gasping intervals of hollow Truce or insincere Treaty—breathing times devoted to dogged and savage preparation for renewed strife, and of duration so short and uncertain as to leave sailor and soldier fighting on, in distant parts of the world, unaware or doubtful as the case might be (though never greatly caring) whether a parley had been called or not.

War for a generation! Children born towards the lapse of the past century were to cross the threshold of manhood without once knowing as an experienced reality the meaning of the word Peace. War, on the other hand, so definite in its significance as to be known through the land as *the* War. The nation—lower classes, upper classes, and all classes—believed that it was living, and living highly, on war, and its whole energy was devoted to the work. The scanty, disease-smitten crops, hungrily needed as they were, could scarce be saved, for men were wanted in another "field" than that of agriculture. Privateer and anti-privateer scoured the seaboard destroying what could not be captured; measures offensive and measures defensive monopolised a greater part of the manufacturing power of the country. The mercantile marine—crippled by the enemy and by the visits of king's ships and press-officers—was largely devoted to transport service. There was no pause, no looking back, to count the awful cost, though close in the wake of the miserable business came the inevitable crowd of evils—War's grim camp-followers, debt, poverty, starvation, disease, brutality, and crime. No shadow of doubt, indeed, existed that war was a wholly good thing. Not this or that war, which, perhaps, might be "justified" on its merits or because of its causes, but War—the abstract thing, apart from causes and justifications—the mean, ugly *Wrong* itself, which poets and orators have at all times disguised in *Duessa's* vesture but which no man has yet dared to wholly strip.

Authority—responsible to naught save itself—was ready (as it ever is under such condition) with infernal perversity to invert every moral sentiment and to palliate any wrong; and in this matter of war, as in that of slavery, it had the ready support and countenance of the great mass of the "upper" and "educated" classes: there never lacked an official Christian to prove—in a sermon—how good and needful a thing was war, or how much after God's heart was slavery. The injunction, "Love your neighbour," was truly a beautiful sentiment if you read it aright, but you had only to clear your mind of cant to perceive that it really meant you must more generally hate him. The *duty*, indeed, of hating "the French" was so obvious that it seems strange it required to be so persistently urged by poet, parson, and politician, yet all three were much busied in this matter, and many of the songs, sentiments, and prayers of the day were little better than curses. A common toast in the seaports, drunk with uproarious enthusiasm, was "*To hell with the French!*"[1]

The appalling poverty of the time was in like manner held by many to be God's peculiar work. Some men of light knew and proclaimed that it was His judgment "on the nation" for neglect of this or that duty—a doctrine at once comforting and convenient, as providing that such judgment should fall upon a section of the nation to which under no circumstances these prophets could belong—wherefore, any proposal to get at and, if possible, remove the causes of such poverty must obviously be impious, and the ever-ready epithet, *Atheist*, was hurled at the head of him who had the temerity to suggest such a course. Others again "showed" that a vast body of poor was needed to keep open the springs of charity in the rich, and all (save the poor themselves) were concerned to prove that the one great virtue for poverty was a contented resignation to the lot which Providence had selected for it.

With an inconsistency almost grotesque, this virtue of patience, the virtue after which poor human nature most ineffectually strives, was blandly preached to "the masses" at a time when their worst passions were inflamed by continual familiarity with base surroundings and evil example, and when the shamefullest and most furious impatience was meted out to them for shortcomings born, in truth,

---

[1] With what grim earnestness may be gathered from the case of a poor Scotchman who, having refused to take part in this comminatory rite, was thrown into the fire by a set of infuriated "patriotic" Tynesiders.

of poverty and lack of knowledge, which knowledge, nevertheless, was deliberately withheld. No jot of allowance was made for the hopelessly adverse conditions in which such lives were steeped—pity and sympathy would have been "thrown away."

Regarded with fierce dislike, aversion, or contempt, or with an indifference that was crueller than any of these, they were habitually spoken of as brutal, cruel, ignorant, stupid, and vicious; and yet there was scarce an element of brutality, of cruelty, of stupidity, it might even be said of ignorance, in "the rabble" which had not its counterpart among those who so bitterly despised them.

If the sports and pastimes of the poor were in the main cruel and mean and cowardly—and the majority were detestably so—those of the rich were no better. Each squalid town had its Bull-ring where, in the eyes of even children, a poor infuriated animal secured by a rope was torn by dogs amid the shouts and cheers of the crowd. Possibly the rich man was rarely a spectator, but the shameful ' sport" had its appropriate defenders among his class in the House of Commons, where a Windham, a Sheridan, and a Courtenay in 1800, and again in 1802, successfully opposed a bill for its abolition; and on such high ground as this—"That it is a combined effort of Methodism and Jacobinism, in itself totally *unworthy the dignity of the House,* and a portion of that spirit of intrusiveness which was being exerted in depriving the common people of their few remaining amusements."

The same children might see—nay, could not fail to see—their fathers busied in cock-fighting, dog-fighting, ratting, ferreting, and the meaner cowardice of coursing;[1] might see disgusting eating competitions, man and dog fights, furious prize-ring encounters, with "the gentry" in full force hounding on the brute-like champions.

Violence and savage selfishness formed the narrow horizon surrounding the hapless populace. No glimmer of a sense of duty towards the people manifested itself. The irritation caused by chronic hunger and hopeless immersion in poisonous surroundings; the evils flowing from the darkest ignorance and lack of

---

[1] So late as 1891 a Right Honourable, speaking at a meeting of the Gimcrack Club at York, referred in jeering terms to "the canting cry" which had lately been got up in different parts of England about the barbarity of rabbit coursing, which he described as "a humble form of sport." This remarkable individual went on to urge that "*all* brutal and *all* unsportsmanlike pursuits *should be discouraged!*"

chance for betterment, met with neither tolerance nor consideration. The "social disorders occasioned by poverty were treated with the harshest methods the Constitution could be made to yield;" nay, the sacred Constitution itself—the Constitution which to attempt to alter by jot or tittle was accounted the rankest treason—was openly manipulated by the men in whose hands its conservation lay, to subserve any political move against the people. Amid a crowd of neglected duties one alone did Society manifest any zeal in performing—the duty of protecting itself.

And though, as was said with equal truth of a later period, "most of the evils from which the country was suffering arose from misgovernment," it was determined that no complaining voice which could be stifled should be heard, a state of alarm and of distrust of the people being created to justify repeated suspensions of the Constitution. Just now, indeed, the series of repressive measures was complete, and all popular liberty suspended. The nation was in fact muzzled, and by a mere handful of politicians, who, furious at the crowd of disorders arising out of their own mismanagement, met the "brutality" of the masses with a still greater brutality

A ferocious penal code, under which a crowd of offences involved the death punishment, was passionately clung to, defended, and vindicated by the united mass of the so-called educated class, and administered with merciless precision by a harsh and intolerant judicature. A monstrous disregard for the sanctity of human life, and an insensate passion for its destruction on grounds of incredible triviality, possessed alike the highest and the lowest in the land. Death was there for almost every lapse. Death for picking a pocket of five shillings, for pilfering five shillings worth of goods from a shop, or forty shillings worth from a dwelling-house; for stealing from ships in the river; for horse or sheep stealing; for wounding cattle; for firing a rick, for forging a will, a bank-note, or a money order; for petty forgery; for sending a threatening letter; for being found disguised in the Mint; for injuring Westminster Bridge, for stealing with a blackened face at night. A gipsy for venturing to reside a year in England, or a thief for living in Northumberland, could be hanged! In the convict cells, under capital sentence, lay women who—destitute and distracted, mayhap, from having a father or husband dragged from them under a press-warrant, or for debt—and with the cry of helpless and famished infants in their ears, had madly ventured on a paltry theft, nay, even children of tender years, for stealing bread, lay under sentence of death. Every punishment of the time was degradation for the lawgiver, as it was debasement for the culprit. Amid all the distressing horrors arising out of the wide-spread prevalence of crime and violence and sin, nothing was so utterly repellent, so hopelessly barbarous, as the passion and scorn, and as often blasphemy, with which any suggested amelioration of the savage death code was met by England's rulers—Lords and Commons. Romilly had not as yet opened his chivalrous crusade against legalised savagery, but when he did!—what a slough he had to wade through. Three hundred years earlier a great Englishman said, " I think it not right nor justice that the loss of money should cause the loss of man's life, for mine opinion is that all the goods of the world are not able to countervail man's life." [1]

How stood it as to this with "great" Englishmen, now?

A Lord Chief Justice "laments that any attempt is made to change the established and well-known criminal law of the country,"—to change it, that is to say, in the way of mitigation. There was no jot of hesitation to alter it in the opposite direction.

A Chancellor is equal with him in declaring that "he saw the wisdom of the principles and practices by which our Criminal Code was regulated."

And when, in 1808, Romilly carried in the House of Commons a bill for the abolition of capital punishment for picking a pocket of five shillings—a first step which had to be retraced again and again, the bill being thrown out by the Lords—a gentleman, the brother of a peer, was not ashamed to declare himself in terms such as these—" I am against your bill. I am for hanging all. There is no good done by mercy I would hang them all up at once." What poor brute in gaol was capable of a baser utterance? The spirit of the "debilitated cousin" was indeed rampant in this diseased society—this society of " men slowly and painfully emerging from

---

[1] A noble lord, years after this (in 1820), was "alarmed" at the proposal that men should no longer be put to death for blacking their faces when stealing by night. It cost him and his neighbours £200 a year to check deer-stealing on the borders of the forest, and if men, already deer-stealers, were no longer to be hanged for blacking their faces, the practice, he claimed, would be universally resorted to. This "noble" savage was supported by the Lord Chancellor, and actually succeeded in thwarting the suggested reform.

a state of barbarism " " Far better hang wrong f'ler than no f'ler," said Society, and, alas! the law was being administered on that very principle. Judges, irascible from the drinking customs of the time, hurried men off to slaughter, for in the bloody haste of those days, certain convicts—murderers, to wit—were hanged next day but one after sentence. Many wretched prisoners at the bar were to all intents and purposes undefended, for counsel was yet denied to felons. For a score or more years to come men and women were "brought out in batches and hanged in rows," and the revolting butchery found its last defence in the august presence of the Lords among whom it took sanctuary long after it had become intolerable to even the privileged representatives of the people in the Lower House.

To some extent the very licence with which human blood was legally spilled, provided its own check, for juries drawn from the people shrank—to the grave displeasure of judges and counsel—from participation in the guilty business, and not seldom, in the face of the clearest evidence, refused to convict. In this way the death-laws became largely inoperative, and felons who, in the interest of the State, should have received adequate punishment, deliberately played on the chances of acquittal.

Turning aside from the lurid track of the capital laws, elements of ferocity and barbarism are met with in all the dealings of the legislature with the people—some incredible in their wanton cruelty; others depressing because of their disgusting absurdity. The mangling of the suicide's corpse by pinning it to the bottom of the grave with a wooden stake, the coarse mummery of the midnight burial at cross-roads, the desire to wreak a posthumous vengeance by withholding religious rites; the continued toleration of a right to challenge "wager of battel," with its preposterous inversion of right and wrong,—these perhaps arouse sentiments of contempt rather than aught else. But graver matters were as closely defended.

The condition of the law as concerned women was scandalous, nay, was pronounced by a high legal authority to be "atrocious." For yet a generation or more, rich men were allowed to "protect" their property from trespass with weapons of murderous intent, with spring-guns and man-traps. And inevitably —as a matter of course—three English judges are found, shortly before the legal prohibition of such murderous contrivances in 1827, delivering an opinion that the "setting and charging of such implements is lawful and *morally* defensible."

What were the chances for the poacher charged with trespass after game, or with assaulting armed keepers, when even judges were not ashamed to indulge in sentiments of such atrocity?

The land was indeed filled with cruelty, oppression, evil example, and wrong; and Society was demoralising the masses. If the gibbet, on every hand, like some hideous tree of ignorance, dangled its dead-sea fruit in the face of a people rendered callous, the pillory was there too, with its object-lessons in spite and malice, depending for half its efficacy on the vicious cruelty of the onlooker.

Hemmed in on the one hand by poverty, ignorance, and base example; on the other by a savage passion for repression of the cruellest type, the masses returned the unconcealed hatred and contempt of their "betters" with open hatred and distrust. The Government was waging war on the people, and the social condition of the nation was therefore mainly one of confusion and violence. The main roads were filled with ruffianly and desperate highwaymen, and thieves and foot-pads infested the streets. Smuggling, encouraged *sub rosa* by lawgiver, magistrate and parson, was fought against by the Preventive Service with the bloody persistence and determination of a *vendetta*. Impressment by the Crown had its muddy reflection in unchecked crimping and kidnapping. Flogging in the army and navy of unimaginable severity engendered and was matched by atrocities perpetrated by pirates and privateersmen. The outrageous Game Laws, crowding the gaols with victims, filling the villages with mourning women and children, and involving the destruction annually of millions of pounds sterling worth of food, brought their heavy return in awful murders by returned convicts. The life of a man and the ruin and misery of a family weighed as naught against the value of a pheasant or a hare in the eyes of the great landowners, who in this guilty business pushed their "rights" to extremes beyond belief. Hopeless and endless imprisonment for debt raised paupers by thousands and filled the streets and by-ways with mendicants as "the war" covered the land with crippled beggars. The darkness and horror of the time when contemplated rise upon the imagination like some hideous nightmare. The filthy streets and the unsanitary kennels which formed them were as yet, practically, unlighted, and in the long winter it was unsafe to be abroad after nightfall. Save in a few of the largest towns, a pall of Egyptian darkness came down upon the land and peopled the outer world with terrors real as well as undefined for a superstitious and ignorant people. No light! no light! Darkness mental, the work of man, and darkness physical, also of his making Darkness artificial in window taxes and candle taxes; filth and disease artificial in iniquitous salt taxes. No light! no light! and no hope of light!

The violence of warfare, the oppression of class legislation, and the barbarities of judicial murder were demoralising the nation and leading it into deeper depths of degradation, and the passing away of war left a new horror behind it. For years the incredible spectacle of a people unable to protect its dead was to sicken and disgust successive generations. While yet the century was young, and until it had run more than a third of its course, "the resurrectionist," or body-snatcher, added to the pathos of death a harrowing concomitant. It is well-nigh impossible to realise the anguish of those who, newly bereaved, were compelled to watch by the dead through the night in the horrible graveyards of the period. The resolute government of the day, fiercely swift to harry and kill and avenge, was to the last degree perfunctory in the performance of any duty of protection it owed to the people, and the safe-guarding of the dead was left to the mourners practically unaided by law. A starving child might be hanged for a petty theft of food, but the brute defiling and rifling a grave escaped with a short term of imprisonment! To protect their dead, the people were obliged to organise watch clubs, whose members undertook, in turn, to hold melancholy guard—with lanthorn and blunderbuss—over the newly-formed grave. Churchyard walls were raised and spiked like those of gaols, to keep *out* the night thief. Heavy iron contrivances, gruesomely called "*mortsafes*," laid over the grave, or bars of iron passed across the coffin and bedded in the earth, were used to defeat the body-snatcher; but even these failed at times, and the grave was, in the early dawn, found plundered. Ghastly stories come down from those evil times, all bearing their weighty proof of depravity. It will be enough to quote one In a town of northern England a resurrectionist had secured the corpse of a woman, and, having put it into a sack, was hoisting it over the graveyard wall when, his foot slipping, he fell with the end of the rope, noose-like, round his neck, and hung counterpoised by his ghastly quarry. The wretched creature, when found by a watcher going his rounds, was still alive, but died on being released. Nor were the attentions of these degraded beings confined to the dead. The impunity with which the obscene traffic could be carried on led to the swifter and less troublesome method of finding "subjects" among the living, and one of the besetting terrors of the black night was the silent and remorseless mercenary whose object was robbery, not *from* the person but of the person itself.

Nothing of all this squalid vice, of all the profligacy and indecency that was ever *en evidence* in every considerable town in the kingdom, was more shocking than the methods adopted to deal with it. "The revolting cruelty and disgusting absurdity of the criminal laws were in perfect harmony with the system of police which (in 1816) had arrived at its perfection of imbecile wickedness." The clumsy and dangerous device of offering heavy money rewards for its detection was being perverted to the very purpose of inciting to and fostering crime, and raw recruits in the great army of vice were nursed and encouraged and protected by the thief-takers until ripe for the commission of such an offence as would enable these guardians of the public peace to claim a lucrative reward.[1]

There was not, nor could there be, any faith in the capacity or even the desire of governments to promote any mitigation of these crying wrongs. The working artisan, face to face in his daily labour with the operation of natural physical law, and nurtured in the stern school of fact, found his distrust deepen as he reflected upon the lawless means by which the most reasonable of his aspirations were crushed. In this matter of distrust, indeed, his rulers had been beforehand with him, for all government known or experienced by him was deliberately administered upon a policy of distrust of the people. No demagogue preached a fiercer hatred of the upper classes than did the governing bodies of the lower. No radical rag libelled more violently or unscrupulously than the government press. "In every outbreak the government were beforehand in provoking the people;" but the elements of provocation were rarely absent. He heard of "secret committees," of spies who, if not directly employed by them, were equally listened to and remunerated by governments. Government informers infested him in his workshop or at his club, and tempted him to justify, by violence, a greater violence in repression and a blank refusal of

[1] A "forty pound crime" was one for whose detection the State adjudged a reward, to be paid on conviction, of £40. In 1816 three police-officers were detected in a conspiracy to induce five men to commit a burglary.

any jot of concession to his legislative necessities. Of special legislation devoted to him there was indeed an abundance, though hardly of a sort to win his gratitude. Old vagrancy statutes—aimed at rogues and vagabonds—brought out and refurbished, to prevent his free movement to better markets for his labour, were supplemented by Combination and Conspiracy laws administered by the very class with which he was at issue as to his remuneration, and rendering it dangerous for him to talk over his affairs with his fellow-workmen: the doctrine of "demand and supply" perverted and misapplied, and driven over him like some mental *Juggernaut*, crushing without convincing him; manipulated, in fact, by political economists and others, so that it was never for him to demand at all, but to supply what was demanded of him on terms never by any means his. "Monopolies" and "interests"—the twin darlings of great statesmen — quoted against him and his, and calling for perpetual and unrequited sacrifice from him. His wages, at best wretchedly small, were irregularly paid and not always in cash, nor could he compel such payment; his working hours ran from early morning until night for six days of the week, and after finishing on the Saturday he was, in most instances, obliged for hours to hang about his workplace for the money he had earned, and, mayhap, take a large proportion of it in "truck." While his masters might enhance prices by combination, he was exposed to the risks of *penal servitude* for taking the same course to increase the value of his labour.[1]

So, half-starved, coerced, furious at times with a sense of burning injustice, moody at others from a conviction of utter helplessness, he had only a glimmering sense of the direct responsibility of his superiors for much that was amiss with him, and they saw to it that no full light should be vouchsafed him. There was strife incessant between the Government and the young but growing Press. Not for half a century or more was this struggle to end in the victory of liberty and light and truth. Instinctively recognising the issues involved, successive groups of statesmen closed with and, by every desperate artifice, strove to strangle, the young giant that was just beginning to feel his strength—and for long the issue

---

[1] "The Limitation of the Vend," as practised by coal-owners, enabled a few wealthy men to dictate to consumers the price of so necessary a commodity as fuel; yet a group of Dorsetshire labourers for striking were sent, under an obsolete statute, to penal servitude for *seven years*.

appeared doubtful. But, dim and doubtful though the light, might be, there was enough to reveal to the observant workman, now and for years to come, a mad king bent on having his uncontrolled way, and many evil counsellors to abet him. To show corruption, bribery, and nepotism naked and by no means ashamed, open villainy and dishonesty of every kind among Corporations and Trusts. To show a Public Debt which, rising like a gathering wave and threatening to submerge the Empire itself, was yet enriching crowds of aristocratic and official adventurers. To show men who were hanging women and children for five shilling crimes, sharing in a general robbery of the State. To show the Departments scandalously mismanaged and deliberately jobbed; soldier and sailor starved and robbed to enrich a noisy and clamorous horde of "patriotic" placemen. To show taxation spreading like a plague and blighting every peaceful and honest enterprise, and—in the place of an inducement to thrift among the people—Government lotteries to debauch and demoralise rich and poor alike. To show, amid this hurly-burly of oppression, wickedness, and wrong, an exalted scorner of his countrymen—with God's name ever in his mouth—wondering "what is to happen if the people do not continue to think a king something more than a man." To show a House of Lords deploring the "lack of all reverence for authority." Other Lords—those of the Admiralty—marvelling that "the Navy is unpopular," and yet another lord publicly "regretting" that a public opponent had done nothing he could be prosecuted for. To show a judge, with Christian formulæ on his lips, refusing an undefended prisoner before him on a "press" charge a few minutes to arrange his papers. A duke whining "may I not do what I like with my own?"—his own being the votes of his tenants, which he claimed were his as much as any property that he held. To find one nobleman writing to another that "every meeting for radical reform is an overt act of treasonable conspiracy," and a solemn Chancellor declaring that "numbers (of his countrymen) constitute force, and force terror, and terror illegality." To show prime ministers and statesmen fighting duels without a whisper of remonstrance from a bench of bishops, and a poor commoner sent to prison for twelve months for *challenging* a peer.

And again, for all the dimness of the light, he saw that these wondering, deploring, marvelling, distrusting, duel fighting superiors, while pledging over their cups "our" glorious Constitution, were ready at any issue to suspend or alter it to suit their own political necessities, always in the sacred name of "our" country; which, however, for them meant merely a few thousands of courtiers.

He found his own conservative distrust of change, his crass notions of what was "good" and what was "not good" for trade—(the savage growth of inherited and enforced ignorance)—intensified in the stupider and less excusable distrust of his "betters." Did he hate the introduction of labour-saving machinery, and with an unfounded though not unnatural dread that it might take from him the work that came to him so precariously; his representatives were even with him in the dull arrogance and flippancy with which they assailed all such innovations. Gas-lighting was denounced as menacing the navy, and threatening to ruin the whale fisheries—not by the lower classes but by the earls and aldermen of the day.[1] Members of parliamentary committees and counsel "ridiculed" Murdoch on his "light without a wick," as they bantered and patronised Stephenson. Great landed proprietors scrupled not to use physical force in an attempt to beat off their estates the pioneers of the railway system. Financial schemes of idiotic character met with the ready support of the "classes," and many of the "educated" believed that the huge unmanageable Public Debt was a source of public wealth, and railed against the cessation of war and the establishment of peace, as menacing the trade of the country. A Lord Carnarvon gravely urged his peers to reflect that a return to a metallic currency would bring the highwaymen again upon the roads.

And to this ignorance and folly was joined an indifference which amounted to heartlessness. In times of acute distress, governments reported commerce and manufactures to be in flourishing condition. This minister "denies" that there is much amiss. That minister "asserts" that the people are in an enviable condition of comfort. A Castlereagh girds at the "ignorant impatience of taxation," manifested by an overburdened people, and a fellow-statesman declares, at a time when wages were so low that it is well-nigh impossible to state them in a way to be credited, that he did not see how the labouring man needed pity for having to pay *twenty* to *twenty-five shillings* a year for salt !

[1] At a time when the Lancashire mobs were breaking machinery, the noblemen, magistracy, and gentry of the county of Lanark, assembled to consult upon the wretched state of the operatives, threw the blame for the condition of things on the invention of machinery.

PICTURESQUE POVERTY.

The two great classes into which the nation was cleft—the ruling and the ruled—were indeed separated by an impassable gulf of passion, distrust, and hatred; and in the main, the only enthusiasm manifested by the one was to crush and keep down the other.

No sense of wrong-doing, of injustice, of dishonour in all this. Nay, it was right. War was good; Slavery was good; Ignorance was bliss—for the poor; Poverty was of God, and called only for small charity on the one hand and large patience on the other. The awful reality was kept out of sight, and a counterfeit—which poets and philosophers, daintily shrinking from contact with the vulgar thing, could trick out in the garb of the picturesque—was, in sober truth, made mock of.

Yes! of God—for Society piqued herself then, as now, on her Christian-like ways, and was ever ready with text and parable to justify the *status quo*. No barbarity of the law existed but could be excused by the dread risk of sparing the rod. The doctrine of vicarious suffering enabled Dives to fast—vicariously, while leaving a vicarious dinner for Lazarus. Labour being a curse, and the touch of barter defilement, Society would have none of either; though with a levity and affectation which had just brought down upon France all the horrors of "the Terror," she was wont in powder and paint to sing, over her lute or harpsichord, the charms of simplicity, of morality, nay, even of poverty!

"Let me pursue the steps of fame,
Or Poverty's more tranquil road."

CHAPTER I.

OF A TOWN WHERE NO TOWN SHOULD BE.

"They are all Danes, these people; stalwart Normans; terrible sea-kings:—are now terrible drainers of morasses, terrible spinners of yarn, coal-borers, removers of mountains; a terrible people from the beginning."—CARLYLE.

MONG the many places in the England of 1800 where Poverty was pursuing her road in aught but tranquillity, probably none displayed the poorer life of the time within narrower limits or in more varied phase than the twin seaport towns of North and South Shields.

Lying on either side of the Tyne, close by the grey North Sea, and in the very eye of the rough Nor'easter with its sea-fret and salt rime; harried successively from the earliest times by Norseman, Dane, Scot, moss-trooper, pirate or privateer, and harshly oppressed, always, by the haughty Mistress of the Tyne up-stream; the two small communities, separated by a broad and swift tidal river, and united in naught save a common experience, hatred and defiance of oppression, maintained for centuries, in the face of hostile man and element, a dogged struggle for existence, and in the process developed a community in many respects curious, peculiar, and picturesque.

Newcastle, yet girt with her town wall and many of its four-and-twenty gateways, and strong in privilege, monopoly, and charter-right, warred incessantly upon the contumacious amphibia who, centuries before, had fastened on the littoral, and, in imperious jealousy of the puniest attempts at founding rival townships, made law for herself when that provided by statute failed her. The struggle had its early beginnings long before the little cluster of fisher's "sheels"[1]

---

[1] Shields = *le sheels, sheel, shiel, shield, scyld*—shelter.

PEN BAL CRAG.

which sought protection, however precarious, under the walls of the Priors of Tynemouth Abbey had taken to themselves a common name.

Standing out in the face of the broken and restless waters of the North Sea, and almost surrounded by them, the bluff and precipitous promontory known to the Britons as Pen Bal Crag is, in virtue of its commanding position, pre-eminently suited for the purposes of watch and ward, and the ubiquitous Roman, with eagle's eye for an eyrie, was not likely to overlook the advantages it offered him. Here, accordingly, only three miles away from *Segedunum* (Wallsend), the terminus of Hadrian's great wall, he pitched the easternmost camp of that great line of defence.

Centuries flowed and ebbed, and Time swept away Roman and camp alike, leaving for King Edwin a *tabula rasa* on which to build a Christian church and convent of timber, in which (*circa* A D 630) his daughter Rosella, the Abbess Virca, took the veil, and, some say, gave to St. Cuthbert himself, while yet he lived, a "rare winding-sheet." The Saint-King Oswald, having replaced Edwin's wooden edifice by one of stone, "a small colony of monks who followed Scottish rule" was established round it, and here, in 651, the bones of King Oswin, friend of Aidan, were laid.

Towering high above the shore-line, and forming the northern boundary of the estuary of a great river, the Crag with its band of holy men could scarcely fail to catch the eye of the predatory Norsemen. Nor did it. Plundered and devastated by them again and again,[1] at intervals quite extraordinarily short, the church at length lay abandoned in ruins, and so remained until Tostig built a monastery, which after being re-founded A.D. 1090 by Earl de Mowbray, was given by him to the Benedictines of St. Albans. Here, in 1093, it is alleged (and denied) King Malcolm of Scotland and his son were buried. The red King Rufus, in suppressing the rebellion of Robert de Mowbray, for twelve months besieged, and in 1095 stormed the position, converting it into a castle, and down to the present day the names Tynemouth Priory and Tynemouth Castle are used indifferently

Early in the thirteenth century the Prior of Durham was exhorting and promising to those who would contribute to the building of

---

[1] First recorded Danish descent, 789. Tynemouth plundered by Danes, 800; again in 832. In 866 destroyed utterly In 876 and 937 plundered

a cathedral "the benefit of three hundred masses and two hundred recitals of the psalter, to be said and sung by the prior and monks of Tynemouth," and, at length, the noble promontory was crowned by the magnificent Early English convent church, whose beautiful ruins to this day stand

"Nodding o'er the silent deep."

With the erection of this, the last of the priory churches of Tynemouth, the history of the Shields may be said to begin, for they are first mentioned as inhabited in 1259.

Men of action as of meditation, the priors and monks had already begun to develop and make the most of the great natural advantages presented in their unique position at the mouth of a fine river, from which the dominating influence lay at no less distance than nine miles by water, and seven direct inland. Briskly there sprang up a busy little port with wharves, quays, ovens, breweries, shambles, and a lucrative salmon fishery, which attracted the ships of the Norsemen, not now on plunder bent, but the doubly-blessed errand of commerce.

But the wolf up-stream complained that the lamb was troubling the waters In the jealous spirit of the time this development was regarded by the rich burgesses of Newcastle as an invasion of their "rights," and with the adroitness which has ever characterised the "Quaysider" they sought to identify a claim to the whole of the resources of the river with the rights of the Crown itself. Seizing the opportune advantage presented in the dark misgovernment of Edward I., they set about pushing home their claims, and that there was no mincing matters, may be seen from their plea.

The petition set forth and complained that "the Prior of Tynemouth had raised a town on the bank of the water of Tyne at Sheles on the one side of the water, and that the Prior of Durham had raised another town on the other side of the water, *where no towns ought to be*, but only huts for sheltering fishermen, and that fishermen sold fish there which ought to be sold at Newcastle, to the great injury of the whole Borough, and (mark the 'cuteness) in detriment of the tolls of our Lord the King at the Castle. . . . That the said Prior of Tynemouth had also made a brewery at Sheles—that he had large fishing craft where there ought to be only boats. . . . That the Prior of Durham on the other side of the water had made a brewery, and had ships where boats only ought to be—that the aforesaid

Prior of Tynemouth caused other people's bread to be baked in his proper oven which ought only to have been baked at the Borough of Newcastle, whereby the Borough lost its furnage, amounting to 4d. in every quarter." That, in short, Newcastle was the most grievously misused borough in the realms of her "Lord the King."

The sullen Edward, ever ready to strike a blow at the rival power of the religious bodies, decided against the Priors, and in 1303 judgment was given that henceforth South Shields and Tynemouth must not hold fair or market, or expose for sale meat or drink, or bake bread. The ovens were to be closed, the wharves destroyed; ships were not to be laden or unladen save at Newcastle—nine miles away from the coast, and only to be reached by navigating a river filled with shoals and sand-bars—and wrecks of the sea were to fall to the lot of the king and his heirs for ever thereafter.

In common with many of his predecessors and successors, Edward scattered charters and favours as freely as the *post obits* of a spendthrift, and exclusively with an eye to present necessity. The struggle between Newcastle and the Shields was indeed a battle of conflicting charters, the last heard petitioner apparently ever obtaining the craved favour, for which unquestionably a consideration was always forthcoming. In 1292 the Bake Houses had been suppressed, yet seven years later certain free customs were restored to the Monks by the King In 1300 he himself is offering at the Shrine of St. Oswyn a clasp of gold with six marks. In 1303 his queen is residing with the Priors at Tynemouth during his Majesty's journey into Scotland. In the same year—the year of his cruel decision against the Priors—he grants a fair to Tynemouth, but revokes it in the following year on the petition of the town of Newcastle.

The irrepressible Priors, however, were not readily discouraged, and sadly perturbed the spirits of their Newcastle neighbours, so that again, in 1306, a judgment in Parliament is given that the Priors must remove the quay at North Shields. Stephen, Henry II., Richard, and John[1] had successively granted and confirmed charters to the Priors, giving them freedom from toll, the right to

[1] A remarkable letter of King John, in Latin, refers to certain Norwegian ships which had then frequented Tynemouth, and granted something very like free trade to these Norsemen and the Prior, "et permittatis eosdem mercatores vendere alias mercandisas suas ubi voluerint, et cum navo suo sine impedimento ire quo voluerint."

"sell their merchandise where they please," and entirely emancipating them from the effects of any claims on the part of Newcastle. Yet Edward, while accepting for himself and his queen the hospitality of the monks, never hesitated to set aside all such charters in the interest of the party with the longer purse.

Such conflicting decisions appear, however, to have been disregarded by both parties to the dispute in so far as they were adverse to the one or the other, hence, though the struggle was an unequal one, it ran fitfully on, the Priors sometimes gaining an advantage, at other times the "men of Newcastle"

In 1311 Edward II. and Gaveston are at the castle, where too the queen is, nearing her confinement. In 1316 Sir Gilbert de Middleton, of Mitford Castle, commits great depredations on the Priory. In 1334 Edward III. is by writ restraining the Mayor and Bailiffs of Newcastle from hindering the mooring of ships on the south side of the river, and again, in 1384, Richard II grants a charter to the Bishop of Durham permitting the mooring, loading, and unloading of ships in the Tyne *without molestation from the men of Newcastle.* In 1389 the Scots under the Earl of Murray plunder Tynemouth.

So, amid the "depredations" of neighbouring noblemen, the "plundering" of Scots, and the "molestations" of the Newcastle folk, the poor townships push their precarious way, the Priors appearing, nevertheless, to sustain these repeated assaults without any significant loss of dignity or importance. In 1462 the queen of Henry VI., with an army, landed at Tynemouth, and in 1503, when Margaret, daughter of Henry VII., was making her stately progress northward, the monks of Tynemouth made a gallant show.

"Thre mylle forethens cam to her the Prior of Tynemouth well appoynted and in hys company xxx. horsys. Hys folks in hys liveray. At the bryge end apon the gatt war many children revested of surpelez; syngyng mellodiously hympnes, and playing on instruments of many sortes"[1]

In 1447 the Priors are found to have set up, upon land gained from the tide, taverns, shops, shambles, herring-houses, and staiths (coal-loading wharves), large quantities of wheat are being baked in

[1] The Fyancelles of Margaret, daughter of Henry VII., by John Younge, Somerset herald.

their common ovens, and two thousand quarters of malt brewed, the rents amounting to 1500 marks.

Too much to be borne is this; wherefore, in 1510, the first year of the reign of the English Blue-beard, "a great number of the people of Newcastle, headed by some of the aldermen and principal townsmen, assembled at Jesmond *with intent to kill the Prior*," but having failed, straightway proceeded to crave the protection of Henry, from whom they obtained an Act prohibiting the "loading or unloading of any merchant's goods within this kingdom or elsewhere, to be sold from any ships or vessels at any place within the port and river of Tyne between Sparhawke and Hedwin stream, but only at the said town of Newcastle, and not elsewhere."

This Act, rendering it illegal for a ship captain to cast ballast or take in cargo without either navigating nine miles of river, or having the ballast and cargo conveyed at ruinous cost in "keels," and compelling the owners of a coal-pit in the town of North Shields[1] to have all their sea-sale coal carted away from the river and harbour to the little fishing village of Cullercoats, two miles up coast, would probably have proved as ineffectual as the conflicting decisions of the Edwards, Richards, and Henries but for the sudden culmination of the struggle between King and Church. With the dissolution of the monasteries, the powerful protection of the sturdy Priors at once passed away from the busy little community which had grown up under their walls, and in the early days of January 1539 the bewildered monks were compelled "of their own free will" to yield up to the king the Priory, with all its lands and belongings.[2] The bold headland, which for centuries had borne aloft the beacon-light kindled by Cuthbert and Bede and Aidan, now reverted to its condition under the Romans. The monastery fell into ruin, and the Priory buildings were converted by Henry to the uses of the castle, which, strengthened with fosse, dyke, and rampart, was "conveyed" to the Crown, and thenceforth became variously a Royal stronghold and a state prison.

Bereft of the protection hitherto vouchsafed them by the monks, the hapless harbour-towns saw their growing prosperity stricken by

---

[1] This coal-pit stood on ground which afterwards became Union Street, the site being precisely that on which the theatre was built.

[2] On January 12th, 1539, Robert Blakeney, prior, with fifteen monks and three novices, surrendered to Henry VIII., a pension of £80 being paid to the prior.

a more ruthless enforcement of the claims of their big neighbour. Trade languished, and the towns, though never yielding a jot, but rather holding fast like the limpets on their rocks, grew but languidly, poor and sparsely peopled, and the history of the time became mainly the history of Tynemouth Castle. Here, in 1544, the Earl of Hertford, invading Scotland, embarked ten thousand men. Here lived the unfortunate Sir Harry Percy, governor of Tynemouth, until his arrest in 1571. Here, in 1633, Charles I. having sailed down the Tyne with a brilliant retinue, including the Duke of Lennox, the Earls of Northumberland, Newcastle, Suffolk, Cumberland, Pembroke, Salisbury, Cleveland, Southampton, Northampton, Holland, and others, rested on his progress to Scotland to be crowned.

Nine years later, King and Crown getting into jeopardy, Rupert sailed into the Tyne, and measures were taken to put the castle into a posture of defence—to some purpose, it would seem, for Colonel Curset reports to the Parliamentarians that "the greatest matter next unto the taking of Newcastle town is Tinmouth Castle," this next greatest matter being accomplished on the 24th October, 1644, when the castle capitulated "with 38 pieces of ordnance, 50 barrels of powder, and 500 muskets, the garrison suffering from the plague."

In 1648 it became a prison for Royalists, and there, in the same year, Colonel Lilburne was executed, his "head being stuck on a pole." Passing scatheless through the time of the Commonwealth, the venerable ruins were, in the days of the "blessed restoration," largely demolished, to provide for the Royalist governor stone wherewith to build barracks and a house for himself.

While yet the larger strife between the nation and its law-breaking king was being pushed to bloody extremity, the meaner struggle 'twixt Newcastle and the harbour-towns kept its course. Claiming not only the exclusive jurisdiction of the river, but the very soil and bed over which the stream flowed, the oppressive proceedings of the Newcastle corporation eventually led to the ultimate emancipation of the whole of the Tyneside communities from a wicked and unfounded monopoly—but not yet. The Priors had long passed away, and in the weakness of the unchampioned townships Newcastle thought she saw her opportunity; but vaulting ambition o'erlept itself, with the proverbial result. It chancing that, in 1631, a Lord Chief Justice of Common Pleas—one Sir Robert Heath—having land at Shields, set about building thereon a ballast wharf and saltpans, the burgesses of Newcastle had the temerity to attack the project, and, first, trying and failing to obstruct him by force, then appealed to the King and Council. Repeated trials, invariably resulting in the success of Sir Robert, at length brought a final decision that "Sir Robert Heath's ballast wharf now a-building shall be built, go forward and be quite finished and backed with ballast to make it fit for the salt works which, for his Majesty's service, are begun and intended to be performed." A few years later the waste land recovered from a wide shallow expansion of the river known as Jarrow Slake—close under the church of the Venerable Bede—was in like fashion claimed by Newcastle; and this claim like the other failing, the Crown was craved to *sell* the land; but a higher price offered by "two London gentlemen" being accepted, the sale was confirmed under the Great Seal of England.

While these cases, mere skirmishes in a long and desultory war, were being prosecuted and discussed—for the general question of monopolies was now stirring the nation to its heart's core—there was growing up in the town of Newcastle a youth who, like another Cromwell, was presently to smite the abuses of the time with more than the spirit of the old priors.

Ralph Gardner, son of Devereux Gardner, gent., a writing-master in the Grammar School at Newcastle, and born in August, 1625, entering the lists against the great monopoly, put on record in his powerful *England's Grievance Discovered*[1] an overwhelming indictment of the incredible abuses to which the Corporation and Companies of Newcastle were systematically subjecting the Tyneside communities. The story of his intrepid, single-handed encounter with the agents of a great chartered wrong is a remarkable record of sturdy endurance and perseverance on the one hand, and of utter licence and lawlessness on the other.

Ralph, who received from his father an excellent education, had in 1650, at the age of twenty-five, set up a small brewery at Chirton,

[1] "*England's Grievance Discovered in relation to the Coal Trade*, with the Map of the River of Tine and situation of the Town and Corporation of Newcastle. The tyrannical oppression of those Magi-strates, their Charters and Grants. the several Tryals, Depositions, and Judgments obtained against them, with a Breviate of several Statutes proving repugnant to their actings: with proposals for reducing the excessive Rates of Coals for the future: and the use of their Grants, appearing in this book. By Ralph Gardiner of Chriton in the County of Northumberland, Gent. London · Printed for R. Ibbotson in Smithfield and P. Street at the White Horse in Giltspur Street without Newgate, 1655."

near North Shields—within a stone's-throw of the mansion which 150 years later became the residence of the brave Lord Collingwood —and was brewing beer in defiance of charter, which charter, he contended, was contrary to the common law of the land. Promptly he is warned by the Bakers and Brewers of Newcastle to "surcease," and the "warneing" being disregarded, a series of actions are brought against him, fines piled up and costs accumulated, until his assailants, growing impatient, determine to arrest him. In August 1652 he is seized and thrown into prison, his treatment being described in the thirty-seventh chapter of the *Grievance*, wherein

"Tho. Salkeld, gent, upon his oath saith that he knew a gentleman (Gardner) cast into Newcastle prison, upon a bare arrest, and laid actions upwards of nine hundred pound, where twenty pound could not be recovered; and kept him lockt up in a prison from all comforts, in a tower above 36 foot high. . . . He offered good bayl, freemen of Newcastle, who were accepted, and entered in the book, and two daies after rased out again, and he still kept there He desired to be admitted to defend his own cause, in their own court, but they refused it. Desired to go with a keeper to counsel, which was also denied, his friends and servants often not admitted to come to him

"Proffered good bond to be a true prisoner, to the end he might have the benefit of the freshe aire for preservation of his health, but at the jailer's house; which the sheriff granted at the first, but presently after refused, saying that the mayor, aldermen, and himself had a meeting and resolved that he should have no liberty, *being an enemy against their privileges*. The said gentleman offered them, that what any could recover against him by law, they should have it without law.

"No tryal ever against him; they disobeyed two or three *habeas corpusses*, which the sheriff received, and his fee, and was proffered to have their charges born, but never returned them

"Refused substantial bond, to appear at London before the Judges, and after five months' imprisonment *he brake prison* in February following.

"He further affirms that on the third of February 1652, one John Cuthbertstone being imprisoned upon an action of £5 debt, but no tryal ever had against him for the same, was upon this gentleman's getting away, cast into the dungeon, by command of the magistrates of Newcastle, where they laid fetters of iron upon him, to force a confession from him, whether he did not help the said gentleman out; where he lay upon the cold earth, without either bed, straw, or any other thing to keep him warm, or firing, and fed him onely with bread and water, and refused comfortable subsistence to be brought unto him The poor man being not worth in the whole world forty shillings, and two children a-begging, and himself kept in prison, after this impression begging for food.

"And that he was certainly informed that some of the officers of Newcastle had counterfeited a letter, and set the gentleman's name to it, and read it to the said prisoner, thereby persuading him to confess he helped him out of prison."

As Thomas Salkeld deposes, then, Ralph brake prison in February 1653. Proceeding to his home at Chirton, he at once set about gathering material for an attack upon the authority, which in his very soul he felt was acting outside of all law and justice While so engaged, and within three months of the time of his escape—

"A great number of men belonging to Newcastle, with swords drawn and pistols, environed" Ralph—"who was peaceably in his house, and shot at some of the said gentleman's servants, and beat his wife, and much blood was spilt, they pretending they came by warrant, and produced a warrant from the Mayor and Sheriff of Newcastle to take him and carry him away to prison, under pretence of debt ; but the seamen got ashoar, fell upon the said Newcastle men, wounded and disarmed them, and relieved the said gentleman."

Notwithstanding this drubbing, the Newcastle men contrived shortly afterwards to re-arrest Ralph, and he was again thrown into the "loathsome prison," where his tremendous indictment, depositions, and petition—in a word, his *Exgland's Grievance* was written.

Setting forth in singularly clear and powerful terms the particulars of his and all England's grievance against the Newcastle Corporation, he appeals to the Parliament to place the trust of the river in "faithful Commissioners' hands," and further—and there lay the rub —to have the charters upon which all these inroads upon the common rights of "the freeborn of England" were justified, produced, exposed, and examined.

The book is dedicated to " His Highness OLIVER, Lord Protector of the Commonwealth of England, Scotland, and Ireland," to whom, in a manly address (in which he declares he "will not presume to use arguments, but present collections of records, proving thereby general wrongs and insupportable burdens "), Ralph unfolds his charges.

"First, forcing people to lose their lives, others to swear against themselves, others to cut purses in their courts for gain, and all to themselves, illegal and false arrests and imprisonments; refusers of bail, and disobeyers of *habeas corpuses,* great and usual impositions, and arbitrary fines, contemners of your law; judges, jurors, and witnesses in their own causes; converting all fines, felons' goods, and wrecks to their own use; destroyers of that famous river of Tine; forcing ships and boats to sink, and imprisoning those that dare to succor them; ingrossers of all coal and other commodities, into their own hands, from the inheritors by pattent; with other irresistible oppressions like to the Spanish inquisition, and practise of the high commission, and star-chamber; being put in execution at this day, in that town, by command of the magistrates, and other their officers, and what they cannot do by force of their charter among themselves against any private person opposing, then, by combination ruin them at law, by their dilatory plea and out-pursing them; to the high dishonor of God, and your highness, and tending to the people's undoing."

He then proceeds humbly to beseech that certain changes be made to bring the powers of the local authority into harmony with statute law, and in those pleas contrives to cover an indictment even heavier than that just quoted.

"That Sheriffs and their substitutes may be *liable* to the punishment of perjury, for breach of their oath, in denying bail to such as are capable; for not returning writs of *habeas corpus,* and other their false returns, as others in other nature."

In his address to the "Courteous Reader" he says—

"I set not out the map of the river of Tine for ships to steer their course by, but for a demonstration to such judges as may be appointed regulators of the great abuses done thereto; nor the effigies in my book for other Corporations to act the like by, but that the cruelty of this Corporation of Newcastle may the plainer appear . . . The thing I aim at is a right understanding between the free and the unfree men of England. A perfect love, every one enjoying their own, and to be governed under our known and wholesome laws, and not by hidden prerogative alias charter. . . . *I appeal to God and the World.*"

Then in a series of chapters he goes on to quote the several charters granted to Newcastle, and to show in a luminous comparative criticism, that many of them contain no reference whatever to the rights claimed to be conferred by them, and that others, and the majority, are inconsistent with statute law. In this examination he manages to give many keen thrusts at his oppressors —as for instance, in a charter granted by Edward I., licensing the authorities of Newcastle to build a wall about their town, he adds in parenthesis, "on which wall one of the Mayors of Newcastle was hanged."

The whole indictment is drawn with extreme skill, and grows in vigour and precision as it marches on. He cites cases where the authorities are called to account for having "slighted and neglected" the duty of preserving the river, for having sought to avoid paying the cost of cleansing it, and being ordered to pay "by reason they receive the profit." Gives particulars of the fining of the Newcastle Hoastmen, or coal-sale monopolists, for selling bad and unmerchantable coal—a peculiarly galling thrust! Cites the whole of Sir Robert Heath's successful action, and the failure of Newcastle to establish a claim to the bed and soil of the river at Jarrow Slake, and then, in his twenty-eighth chapter, sets out in full his famous "Heads of the Charge exhibited by Ralph Gardner, of Northumberland, Gent, to the Committee for Trade and Corporations, against the Mayor and Burgesses of Newcastle, 1653."

After his masterly examination of the charters and powerful "Heads of the Charge," perhaps the most curious and interesting portions of his "case" is the series of sworn depositions with which he sustains his piled-up charges. The social lawlessness revealed in these quaintly-worded statements and their queer old-world woodcuts is well-nigh incredible. It is impossible to give more than a mere outline of the tremendous assault upon the Newcastle authorities contained in these chapters, but it may be worth while to quote one or two of the depositions in full.—

"John Mallen, master of a ship, upon his oath, said,—That the Mayor and Burgesses of Newcastle do deny to load any ship, nor suffer any others to load them with coals, who refuse to sail up that dangerous river seven miles, to cast out ballast upon their shores, which compulsions causeth the loss of many ships in that river, amongst sands, shelves, and sunk ships, it being merely for the gain of eightpence per ton of ballast. That he was in company with one James Beats, of Aldborough, who was a master of a large ship being compelled to sail up the river to cast out his ballast, and in returning to Shields to take in her loading of coals, in the middle of the river, his ship sunk and none durst help to save her for fear of being imprisoned, as others were for the like, nor to weigh her up again. The freemen came and required a greater sum than she was worth, so the poor master was forced to leave her upon small terms; but soon after they (the freemen) got her up and set her to sea for their own use, which the said Master Beats might have done the like, if those at

Newcastle would have tolerated the unfreemen to work, who were as well able to perform the service."

"Henry Harrison, master of a ship, upon his oath, said,—That in April 1646 a ship sailing into the Tynemouth Haven by storm was cast upon the rocks near Tinmouth Castle, the master got ashore with all expedition and obtained the present help of an antient ship-carpenter, by name Thomas Cliff, of North Shields, with three of his men, to save the ship from perishing, which ship had been quite lost if the said master should have run to Newcastle to have agreed with the free carpenters, whose excessive rates and demands often surmount the value of the ship in distress, and their tediousness in coming and going that distance, that often the ships in distress are quite lost. The said Cliff and his men saved the ship, and got her off and brought her to the lower part of North Shields, and laid her upon the sands to mend her, where the three carpenters were at work, and Ann, the wife of Thomas Cliff, and Ann Wallice, his daughter, standing near unto the ship to see their servants work, the Mayor and Burgesses sent Thomas Rutter and John Hall, two sergeants, with Thomas Otway and other free carpenters of Newcastle, to Shields, to seize upon all the aforesaid workmen, for daring to save any ship from sinking in that river, with command to carry them to prison. The two women seeing their servants trailed away, railed against their evil practices, for which Thomas Rutter with a club, by several blows upon Ann Cliff's body and head, knocked her down to the ground; the other sergeant, John Hall, by several blows with a rule or truncheon, broke Ann Wallice her arme, and then perceiving souldiers coming from Tinmouth Castle, both the said sergeants fled to Newcastle, where they were protected from the hand of justice. The said Ann Cliff was taken up, carried home, got to bed, and in a few weeks dyed thereon, for which the said Rutter was indicted and found by the jury guilty, yet did not suffer. The said woman required her friends, as they would answer for it at the last day, they should require her blood at the hands of Rutter, he being her death.[1] The poor men kept in prison, and Cliff kept in suit of law for his working by Newcastle, and his men, and they forced to give bond never to work again."

This time the Corporation was hoist with its own petard; the suit brought against the "Antient Carpenter" by them, and which lasted five years, resulted in a verdict in Cliff's favour, and the judgment was that "the Mayor and Burgesses ought to be severely fined for their unjust claim, in that part of the River Tine, and shall pay £30 and costs."

---

[1] "Ann, the wiffe of Thomas Cliffe, of Shieles, was buried the 14th of August 1646."—Extract from the Register of Burials of Christ Church, North Shields.

"Gawen Potts deposes that no stranger's ship, though she be in never such great distress and sinking, must be pylotted into the river by no other than a freeman of Newcastle, in the interim one is sent for (being sixteen miles forward and backward) often either she is lost or driven by storm away."

Instances of fines and imprisonment inflicted on workmen for working, and of compelling them to take bonds not to work again, of making it unlawful for any tradesman to work or live in "any port adjoining the river of Tine but only at Newcastle," charges of "witch-finding," forcing people to "swear against themselves" and to cut purses in their courts for gain, of plundering strangers on the pretence that their goods "were foreign bought and foreign sold, and therefore confiscate (all people not being free of that town are reputed foreigners)," of openly defying a Judge's warrant and tearing it up, and of repeated violations of Acts of Parliament, follow *pêle-mêle* in overwhelming number. A perfect reasonableness in all that is stated and claimed, and a genuine solicitude for a just and legal decision on the points at issue, are obvious throughout the book. It effected Ralph's purpose. On the 5th October 1653 the petition was referred to the Committee for Trade and Corporations, and the Newcastle authorities were duly notified that it would be taken into consideration on the 15th November. Profoundly fluttered and perturbed, these gentlemen petitioned for a delay of fourteen days to prepare their defence, which however was not ready in time, their solicitor humbly begging for a further postponement of ten weeks, " by reason they were not ready nor prepared to answer the charge, for it struck at all that was near and dear unto them . . . the Scots having tumbled their records" The Committee, evidently becoming convinced that these pleas for delay were mere shuffling attempts to stave off all investigation, peremptorily ordered the authorities to be ready for the 13th of December, beyond which date "further time they would not give in a matter of so high concernment."

Unhappy Gardner, and unlucky Tyneside! On the 12th, Cromwell strode into the House of Commons, and, dismissing the Parliament, swept away all present chance of an investigation which must instantly have broken the fetters in which the men of Newcastle held all the smaller Tyneside towns.

Not until some two hundred years later was it definitely ascertained that the original charter upon which all this mischievous work was founded *did not exist*,[1] though the consternation evinced wherever there was a prospect of its production being enforced, was too genuine to be misunderstood or explained away; the truth being, in fact, all along shrewdly suspected. Howbeit, although the Committee of the House had drawn a report which confirmed and supported Gardner's prayer, no immediate effect could be given to it, and the old work speedily recommenced. Straightway, too, did the resolute Ralph gird up his loins for a renewal of the struggle, and there is little doubt that for the remainder of his life he continued to trouble the peace of his oppressors. Not much more is known of him. His name appears frequently in the lists of Churchwardens of Christ Church, and "he seems, notwithstanding occasional incarcerations, to have been quite a pillar of the Church from 1651 to 1659—his name generally standing next to that of Sir Ralph De Leval, of Seaton Delaval, in the place of honour."[2] It is certain that his antagonists failed utterly to dompt the spirit of this intrepid champion of free rights, that they dreaded the results likely to flow from his exposure of their legal nakedness, and that they rancorously hated the man himself.

In 1662-63 a notable entry was made in the books of the Bakers and Brewers of Newcastle, the significance of which was not foreseen or most surely the books had never contained it.

> "Item.—Paid at Shields and other places for discovery of Mr. Gardner's brewing, with wherry hire, and given to Peter Easterby for his pains touching same . . . . £1 2s."

In an anonymous letter, dated 1677—probably after Ralph's death—a "nameless alderman of Newcastle," emulating his forerunners who went out to kill the prior, gave currency to, and quite probably concocted, a vile story intended to blast Gardner's work and reputation. The letter, which was characterised by a Newcastle writer as being "a more bitter libel on the Corporation than anything that Gardner in his grievance ever wrote," gives so curious a picture of the times that it is worth quoting in its entirety

---

[1] The charter of Henry II., it was admitted on behalf of Newcastle in 1850, *did not exist*, and as to John's, which merely confirmed Henry's, there was but "an office copy"! The Tynemouth charters, on the contrary, were original, extant, and legible.

[2] *Ralph Gardner and the Tyne.* T. T. Clarke.

"I believe you are well content you have no share amongst us in our feastings and jollity. We are like a drunken man, who feels not his wounds and weakness; high in our loyalty, low in our faith. You need not wonder we damn you fanatics, for it is come to pass, a man is not thought to speak modishly, without wishing his own damnation. We all pretend to love the king; and we curse, swear, and drink for him. You can expect no justice, much less favour from us. The tendency of things in the government of the town may be discerned by any that is not blinded by prophaneness. The perquisites of place are more minded than the duty of them. 'Once an alderman and never poor afterwards' is grown a proverb. Bakers shall furnish the market with half that size of bread required by law, and be connived at, if they be customers to an alderman who is a corn merchant.

"If there be a vacant spot of ground that belongs to the city, an house without lease, without rent, is presently built upon it. Our artificers learn to drink instead of learning their trades This will fill the town with dunces and blockheads, who, because we can employ none but freemen, will impose their own price, and botch our work, and we must submit to scoundrel rascals, and give double money for that which is neither well done nor half-done. Apprentices grow gentlemen and get full liberty before their time is out, that they quickly break when they come to be their own masters, and then, to keep up their pride, some place in the king's army, some office in the revenue, or a stewardship under some man of great estate must be had; and attorneys and ale-houses are like to be the only standing traders. Our bench, which now shines with knights, will shortly be filled with what I shall not name; and our charter, which was granted for the good of the town, will become a barr to keep everything good out of it. *There was one Gardiner writ a malicious invective against the government of Newcastle, but he got his reward, being afterwards at York hanged for coyning.*"

Subtly avenged Ralph Gardner, in every line of this bitter philippic, for the poor slander with which it closes! The story appears to have been based upon an entry in a certain record or "Criminal Chronology of York Castle of the Criminals capitally convicted and executed at our County Assizes for a period of 279 years," and a mere similarity of names. It runs thus:—

"March 30, A D 1661.
Peter Hall and R. Gardner both for Coyning, they was executed at Tyburn without Micklegate Barr."

The cowardly lie, long unchallenged, was passed round and repeated by men who took the short method of denying everything alleged against them—men who had sworn by charters which they knew did not exist—by other charters which contained no tittle of reference to the claims and "rights" based upon them; but significantly, it received its *quietus* from the official books of these same people,—the little entry in the records of the Bakers and Brewers touching the expedition to Shields for the "discovery of Mr. Gardner's brewing" being dated 1662-63, or two years later than the time of Ralph's reputed hanging.

Gardner was never answered in his lifetime, nor for long after, a "Plea and Defence of the Mayor and Burgesses of Newcastle-on-Tyne against the malevolent accusations of Gardner and his adherents," though dated 1653, being—like the mythical charters—discreetly kept out of sight until 1849, when it was "published." On examination, however, it was found to contain nothing whatever that in any degree confuted Gardner's charges—nay, rather it confirmed their accuracy in every essential particular.

Cromwell, busied with mightier affairs, had by his dismissal of the Parliament unconsciously swept away for the Tyneside towns every chance of emancipation from abuses upon which he would have been first to put his iron heel, hence for a century or more the two Shields struggled on, literally "between the devil and the deep sea," as in uncompromising terms a son of the Tyne described the position—barely worse off from the coasting rover than from the harsh and haughty authority up-stream. Newcastle, systematically misapplying the greater portion of the large river revenues, took no account of any interest save her own, and with incredible short-sightedness so disregarded all obligation to the noble stream, to whose exclusive guardianship she so tenaciously clung, that in the latter half of the eighteenth century Lord Mulgrave, an experienced sailor and competent and unprejudiced witness, declared that he considered "the river Tyne to be capable of becoming one of the finest rivers in the world, but ignorance, inattention, and avarice had converted it into a cursed horse-pond."

. . . .

Described at the time of the accession of George III. as "a poor, miserable place, consisting in the main of a narrow street along the river margin," North Shields was nursing and training in her great fleet of colliers, keels, and cobles that incomparable school of blue-jackets which was presently to take so prominent a part in creating the naval supremacy of England, and giving to the British flag the renown associated with the names of Nelson, and Rodney, and Collingwood, and, at the close of the century, was sending to the fleet its smartest and most dare-devil fighting men.

The narrow street along the river margin still constituted the essential Shields, and was filled with curious life and character. Shut out from all but the most limited communication with other parts of England by the almost impassable roads, intense local jealousies, and precariously uncertain vagrancy laws of the time, the population, wholly seafaring, or drawing its means of subsistence from the sea, knew less of England and its people than of countries across the main and their multifarious inhabitants. Even the twin-town could only be reached by sculler-boat across a broad river up which surged heavy seas from "over the bar"; while a journey to Newcastle involved for most people the use of a craft quaintly called a "comfortable"—a mere rowing boat, over the stern portion of which a shelter fashioned somewhat like the hood of a carrier's cart was fixed.

But if access to inner England was barred for the Shieldsman, he had his compensation in the extraordinary and ever-changing variety of sea-borne folk bearing up for the shelter, or trade, or protection, as it might be, of his almost natural harbour of refuge. The birthplace and home of the early trade in sea-coal, colliers arrived and sailed in fleets, bearing to London, Hamburg, the Baltic, the Euxine, and elsewhere, across the most treacherous and wrathful of seas, deep burthens of coal and salt and glass.

The Dutch lugger, with green painted deck-houses and varnished side-swapes (like the *elytra* of some glorified beetle), the smart Norwegian; the poor little French coaster, the stately East Indiaman with black hull and painted "ports" (and some not merely painted through which to point the muzzles of her carronades); timber-ships from Quebec or the Baltic with pine battens or Stockholm tar, collier pinks, barques, brigs, schooners, brigantines, sloops, snows, of every shape, size, and rig;—all lay vast in number, moored in tiers just off the long "narrow street," from the balconies of which rude Doric conversation could be carried on with the men aboard.

The long "narrow street" was narrow indeed (lack of width compensated for, however, in vast and tortuous length), made up of a double row of oddly jumbled red-tiled houses with high-peaked gables—the one built against the high banks of the river and far over-topped by them, the other sheer on the water's edge and propped up by wooden piles slanting out into the stream like stilts. Here and there at short irregular intervals an "entry" pierced the line on one side or other, and afforded access to a squalid landing-place, where a broken set of wooden steps led precipitately down from a rotting wharf to "the shore"—"shore," however, only at low tide—or to narrow break-neck stairs running from the Low Street to the top of "the Banks." Broader quays afforded unexpected peeps at the busy harbour, and on the foot-worn steps of these the noses of sculler boats, waiting a turn, gently bumped with the lipper of the tide like dull fish that had been hooked on mooring lines. Much argument, sarcasm, and horseplay was indulged in here by chewing and spitting loungers, keenly though quietly enjoyed by the observant scullerman—the river "cabby" sitting on the gunwale of the boat, waiting, boat-hook or mop in hand, for a turn, and showing cheery interest in the business of every soul that came down the quay, whether good for a job or not. He possessed encyclopædic knowledge of the name, rig, and whereabouts of every craft, of whatever flag, afloat in the harbour, and was ready to "put y' aboard, sur, for sixpince."

Scarce a house on the river side of the street but had its ruinous wharf, supported on half-a-dozen green weed-grown piles, or its tumble-down, gaudy-painted balcony on which a few "fresh herring," split and peppered, were hung out to dry, among the newly-washed "duds" which bellied out in the wind. Here and there a ship's bowsprit, reaching across the street from a vessel in one of the graving docks, might be seen hospitably accommodated by an opened window into which it projected, the good woman at her housework or toilet chatting nonchalantly with the sailor who, busied with some mending of its gear, sat astride the spar.

Public-houses leaning side by side or lurching towards each other across the street, like half-drunken men seeking a quarrel, were open at all hours, and from the crazy tap-room with its sanded or saw-dusted floor came the scratching rhythm of a hornpipe, the discordant uproar of a sea-song with tipsy chorus, or the clamour of a drunken fight. Jack Tars with bared hairy breast, pig-tail, and long pipe in hand, capered to wretched fiddle or hurdy-gurdy with poor flaunting, bare-headed, ribbon-bedecked girls, or leant out of crazy casements to squirt the well-churned succulence of a sapid quid at the bumboat woman, who, with broad-beamed craft stacked up with brown earthenware, apples, tobacco, nuts, chimney ornaments, long glass feeding-bottles bearing endearing legends and sentiments in gilt lettering, smuggled salt, chap books, keepsakes, and broad sheets of doggerel vaunting the deeds of some recently hanged cut-throat who died game, was chaffering below with a mate or stevedore, or bandying unfeminine compliments with a sister craftswoman whose blandishments have been more, or less, prosperous than her own.

Away among the tiers lay the craft of that essentially indigenous creature, the keelman, who, in flannel shirt, blue woollen stockings, loose flannel jacket, and generously coloured neckerchief, navigated his perilously over-charged but magnificently sea-worthy keel up the squally river in the face of a half gale. Give him but the tide, and so "Weel may the keel row," or rather *sail*, under her extraordinary press of canvas, that "Geordie" could give odds to any craft of his time Bringing the coal from the staithes (*steeths*, he called them)— long wooden jetties with shoots down which the coal from the colliery waggons was shot, he and his "marra" had to "cast"—that is, shovel—every ounce of it from the keel into the hold of the vessel being loaded. Such of the colliers as did not cast their ballast at sea were obliged to have it taken out by keelmen and conveyed up the river to the Ballast Quays of Newcastle, not a little of it consequently being conveniently lost overboard, and so contributing to the gradual conversion of the river into a "cursed horse-pond."

The "Kelers" of Tynemouth were a recognised class away back in the days of the early charters, and, in the year 1700, numbered some sixteen hundred, with a fleet of four hundred keels. The pursuit of an arduous and dangerous calling through so long a period developed a highly characteristic and strongly differentiated human being, and there exist few more genuinely interesting personalities than "Geordie." To the brawny strength of a Hercules he unites the gentleness and *bonhomie* of an Uncle Toby. He speaks a strong guttural dialect of which many of the words are pure Anglo-Saxon. Quaintly humoured, strongly domesticated, and with a passionate regard for children, he has conferred upon a few words of the local folk-talk a loving tenderness that cannot be expressed by any other. No man born away from Tyneside can enter into the full sense of his "hinny" or "canny." It is, of course, not at all the "canny" of the Scotsman—nay, the quality expressed by the Scots "canny" is one that would rouse his strongest distaste and contempt. "Maa canny bairn" is the *ne plus ultra* of affectionate address to a child. The "hinny," though undoubtedly the "honey" of other places, conveying a delicacy of tender fellowship and regard otherwise unutterable; and when the two come together, the power of verbal endearment is exhausted and only a "cuddle" and a kiss can follow. His songs are full of altruistic disregard for self and love of kin. His wife, a shrill-spoken, hardy, but "muthorly" woman, croons over the little one in her arms, as she sits on a cracket in the doorway of her cottage in the "raa," in words full of the deepest meaning for her, but untranslatable and *caviare* to the multitude born away from Tyneside.

Near akin to this Geordie is the other—the pitman—though in the early eighteens he had not yet been rescued by the Primitive Methodists from the semi savagery into which the almost brutish nature of his work and the scandalous character of his domestic arrangements had plunged him. Living with his invariably large family in a cottage of one or, at most, two rooms, buried under ground from early morning till night, working in a state of nudity with women toiling like beasts of burden in a condition scarcely more decent, he sought the roughest and rudest relaxation in the few hours of leisure that were his. Fighting, drinking, racing, gambling, cock-fighting, dog-fighting, all through Sunday, it was scarcely safe, and certainly not pleasant, for a respectably-clad stranger to pass through one of his pit villages. So nearly a serf was he that it would be difficult to shortly express in what respect he differed from one His children, kept below in the workings of the noisome, ill-ventilated pit, shut away from heaven's light from Monday until Saturday, were, in sober truth, savages.

It was only on a Saturday night, therefore (apart from a rare holiday), that he could be away from his village, but then the narrow street was sure to find him boisterously, exuberantly "happy"; gay in a neckerchief of excruciating colour, and more often than not having on his arm his wife or his "lass," arrayed in greater chromatic variety than the spectrum itself

Pouring, at meal-times and after working hours, into the long narrow street come troops of ship-carpenters, rough, lawless, fiery-tempered men and youths, foremost in revelry, row, and riot, or, what was equally dreaded, public jubilation,—these were the terror of the populace and the irresolvable difficulty of the town authorities. Not even the press-gang, strengthened by a strong escort from the war-ships in the harbour, might face these dare-devils, who never missed an opportunity of rescuing any miserable wight who had been captured, and of soundly drubbing the gang, to the shrill delight of the women.

Here and there along the river margin, right in the midst of the dwelling-houses, were the forges of the chain and anchor makers, brawny giants who, long before the days of the steam-hammer, forged by hand the huge anchors of his Majesty's Line-o'-battle ships. Here, too, and again in the midst of a teeming populace, were butchers' shops, vast in number because of the needs of hundreds of sail, in which at all hours were conducted and openly displayed before the eyes of children the whole of the disgusting processes of slaughtering and dressing cattle and sheep, the offal and filth being cast out into the street and left there to be eventually kicked into the river. Block and mast makers, riggers, sail-makers, and rope-makers had their places, in which they were seen busily at work all day among the living houses of the town. Marine store dealers too, and ship "chandlers," where was sold mahogany junk and flinty biscuit, weevled-flour for dough-boys, mouldy pease-meal, hair-oil, candles, gunpowder, spun-yarn, and rum; every article of commerce strongly impregnated with the searching odours of Stockholm tar, oakum, and naphtha.

Whalers' crews, Greenlanders—men who afterwards went up into the Arctic seas with Ross and Parry—sauntered along the narrow street, telling yarns of hair-breadth 'scapes and showing scars from frostbite and scurvy. Smugglers and preventive-men jostled 'gainst Russian, Norwegian, Swede, Dutchman, Spaniard, Maltese, Greek, Portuguese, Dane, Italian, Lascar, Malay, and John Chinaman. Such Frenchmen as might be in the street were being led in chains from the landing-places to the Castle at Tynemouth. Rough North Sea pilots—mottled-faced men in pea-jackets, standing no nonsense from owner or skipper, and brooking contradiction from no man, standing back to back when conversing, and keeping their keen puckered-up eyes always upon "the offing." Soldiers from the high-perched castle-yard, where now Oswin's Church stood in ruins, or from Clifford's Fort, which, prone on the sandy shore at the mouth of the river, was ready—or was expected to be (perhaps not the same thing)—to give good account of any cruiser or rover on mischief bent. Blue-jackets, marines, and powder-monkeys from the buxom-bosomed frigate lying in the very jowls of the harbour, still as a spider in its web, but as keenly on the alert for any stray prize. Watchful Customs officers—wary crimps—fussy ship's-husbands, pompous shipbrokers, shrill-voiced fisher lasses from the little bay of Cullercoats, away up coast—sturdy wenches in short multi-pleated petticoat of dark blue, revealing much strong-ribbed stocking of like colour, and stooping under the burden of the heavily-laden fish-creel; lame men, deformed men, wooden-legged men, armless men—every third person making up this phantasmagoric scene deeply pitted with small-pox scars, or seared with king's-evil, or gashed, hacked, maimed, or marked in some way Faces tied up because of "sore" ears, "sore" eyes, or "sore" heads.

All these crowded the long "narrow street" from end to end, busily threading its lanes, entrys, quays, stairs, or courts, and in a babel of diverse languages and dialects carrying on the drama of a strange community's quaint every-day life.

No other seaport—in the whole world possibly—presented so bewildering a variety of folk and character and speech and costume in so concentrated a form; the harbour with its vast fleets, its multifarious affairs and busy, palpitating life being over-looked, and seen as it were in bird's-eye view, from the walk "along the Banks," on which paced gravely and argumentatively the shipowner, the broker, the pilot, and the ship captain, each man of them pointing his talk with glances at the crowded tiers, or at the "narrows" through which vessels were being "foyed," or at the distant horizon, on which specks known to them as the *Mary Ann*, or *Betsy*, or *Lovely Jane* passed in or out of sight.

The "bar," since become so entirely a thing of the past that old Shieldsmen differ and dogmatise as to where it precisely lay, was then as potent as any contrary wind in governing the movements of the fleets sailing to and from the Tyne, nay, more so, and it contributed by far the greater of the perils of "making the harbour" in a storm. Where now, at any time, there is a safe thirty-feet bottom, the "bar" was at certain tides so near the surface as to be visible, and it is a matter of faith with Shields folk, repudiated, it must be admitted, by the men of Newcastle (nine miles away), that a man once waded from one side of the harbour to the other upon the nearly exposed summit of the dreaded sand ridge. However that may have been, the "bar" undoubtedly ruled the sailings of the Tyne fleets, and as the depth of water due to the

SHIELDS BAR.

state of the tide was in its turn modified by the amount of "sea"— *i.e*, the height of the waves or rollers breaking outside, there was at all times some uncertainty as to when a ship might safely leave or come into the harbour.

Locked in by an adverse wind, a bad tide, or "too many feet sea on the bar," there was nothing for it but to wait for a change and wile away the time in frolic and revelry among the squalid drink-shops and crimping dens ashore. When, however, the wind veered and the big dial at the Low Lights showed a good bar, a scene of extraordinary bustle and gaiety broke out. On the decks of hundreds of vessels the tramp of men at the windlass was heard, and the rattle of the cable coming home resounded over the harbour. Men and boys, swarming up amid the forest of spars, shook loose the canvas, or with chanty and chorus hauled upon warps, hoisted boats, and made all snug. Crowding down the river, beset by the craft of vociferous and gesticulating chandlers, hoarse bumboat women, mendicant fiddlers scraping a last hornpipe, or keelmen strenuously lifting the last bit of cargo aboard, the fleet passed through "the Narrows,"[1] each vessel becoming transfigured as she nimbly donned her beautiful vesture and took the wind. On the northern side of the "narrows" stood the Look-out or Hailing House, whence a searching string of interrogatories was hoarsely administered through a brazen speaking-trumpet to every in or out-going craft. The steam-tug had not yet appeared, hence, as in certain winds it was not possible to *sail* out of the harbour, ships were "foyed" out into the offing. Foying, though always an arduous occupation, was at times a lucrative one, and the foymen of the Tyne constituted a very important class. In foying a ship the foymen rowed ahead in a small boat, and at a warp's length dropped a small kedge, which, being hove upon by the ship's windlass, brought her up to a position nearly over it. The kedge was then weighed, carried ahead again, dropped and hauled upon, the process being repeated until sufficient sea-way had been attained by the vessel.

A gay, exhilarating scene, then, was the sailing of a weather-bound fleet, each craft bent on shaking off the land as quickly as might be. Scrambling foymen hauling up the kedge and rowing as for life, roaring pilots, chanty singing tars, creaking and shrieking

[1] A narrow neck formed by the sharp approach of the north and south shores just at the entrance to the river, and separating it from its broad estuary.

blocks, the fresh green water of the North Sea, crisped by the lively wind, filling the harbour up to the verge of overflow, bringing the boats on the shore up to the very level of the quays and wharves, and covering up the squalor and filth of the shore No smoking funnels, no clouds of steam, but from the narrow embouchure of the river, spread fan-like over the sea, hundreds of sail, handled as only the old trained men of the Tyne knew how to handle a ship.

It was always "war time" then, and an escort of man-of-war ships was needed to protect these sheep of commerce from the sea-wolves The perils of the rude navigation of the day, great as they were in the ill-found colliers on that savage East Coast, were overshadowed by the barbarous warfare carried on by illegitimate cruisers, which, taking advantage of a general condition of hostilities wrested from commerce the ready profits of direct plunder.

In such wise, then, on the 11th of May 1800, a fleet of one hundred and forty-four colliers sailed from Shields for the Baltic, carrying 11,600 chaldrons of coal. Not this time, however, because of a good bar or a fair wind, but under convoy. One other dominating influence governed the movements of merchant fleets and compelled them to sail in clusters. "Like gnats round the tap of a wine cask" the predaceous sea-rovers of the day flitted about the coasts of the Tyne, taking here and there a collier even from under the guns of the Castle, and there was not a seaman among all that crowded the "narrow street" but had his experience of a brush with the busy privateers in the offing.

And, notwithstanding the unhandiness of his fighting equipment, his clumsy breech-fastened carronades, his handful of flint-locks, pikes, and boarding pistols stacked round the interior of the skipper's cabin, he not unfrequently beat off and escaped from his quick-sailing and well-armed assailant, but sometimes even captured him at the point of the cutlass. Many incidents, told in a mere line or two in the local records, are full of the romance of unconscious heroism.

In 1757 the *Ann*, Richardson, of Shields, carrying five guns and eight men "engaged" ([1]) a French privateer of fourteen guns and one hundred and fifty men for four hours and "made him sheer off." On board the *Ann*, in addition to the crew, were nine miners, passengers, who "assisted and behaved gallantly"

In 1758 a French privateer of six guns took a brig and a sloop off Tynemouth, "but soon afterwards the brig's men rose upon the

French, threw one overboard, made the rest prisoners," and ran into Blyth.

In 1759, about two o'clock in the morning, a French frigate of twenty-four guns, two cutters, and a schooner, appeared a little to the southward of Tynemouth, where they fell in with a large fleet of laden colliers from Shields, several of which they took. A small brig, the *Mary*, mounting only three guns, fought her way through and escaped. The Spanish Battery was silent on this occasion, owing to a "shameful want of ammunition." In September of the same year the redoubtable Paul Jones fell in, near Flambro' Head, with the Baltic Fleet, convoyed by H.M. frigate *Serapis*, of forty-six guns, and the armed ship *Countess of Scarborough*, of twenty guns, and after a severe fight captured the two British war-ships, the convoy, however, escaping.

In 1795 "a small French privateer landed its crew near Seaton Delaval, which they plundered, carrying everything off."

Early in 1781 "the redoubtable sea-wolf," Daniel Fell, who, in his cutter *Fearnaught*, armed with eighteen four-pounders, had scourged the North Sea coasts, fell in with and encountered the brig *Alexander and Margaret*, of North Shields, commanded by a brave young Shieldsman, David Bartleman, who, after beating off his assailant three times, losing his mate, and being severely wounded himself, was compelled to strike. The incident is quaintly described in the inscription upon a tombstone erected to his memory in the churchyard at Yarmouth,[1] where he died of his wounds. But the "privateering" was by no means confined to the "other side." Privateers and anti-privateers—equipped by Newcastle and Shields owners, and manned by the sea-dogs of the Tyne—were

[1] "To the memory of DAVID BARTLEMAN, master of the brig *Alexander and Margaret*, of North Shields, who on the 31st of January 1781, on the Norfolk coast, with only three three-pounders, and ten men and boys, nobly defended himself against a cutter, carrying eighteen four-pounders, and upwards of a hundred men, commanded by the notorious English pirate FALL, and fairly beat him off. Two hours after, the enemy came down upon him again when totally disabled. His mate, *Daniel Macauley*, expiring with loss of blood, and himself dangerously wounded, he was obliged to strike and ransom. He brought his shattered vessel into Yarmouth with more than the honours of a conqueror; and died here in consequence of his wounds, on the 14th of February following, in the twenty-fifth year of his age. To commemorate the gallantry of his son, the bravery of his faithful mate, and, at the same time, mark the infamy of a savage pirate, his afflicted father has ordered this stone to be erected over his Honourable Grave."

sent out in numbers to cruise against "the enemies of Great Britain;" some of them, to all intents and purposes, war-ships, as the *Anti-Gallican* and the *Heart of Oak*, each of thirty-three guns, the *Dreadnaught* with four. The *Ferret* and *Weasel*, made out of five-men boats, lengthened, with two lug sails, were very swift sailers The *Wrights*, the *Pomona*, the *Good Design*, and sundry others (anti-privateers) were built and equipped specially to chase and run down the enemy's privateers.

Of all grades, sizes, power, and swiftness, legitimate and illegitimate, the North Sea saw these fighting in every possible combination. Privateer taking collier; collier beating off privateer; privateer taking frigate, or anti-privateer capturing both.

A strange being the Shields tar, then! On this voyage sailing in a peace-seeking collier, on that, one of the crew of an outlawed-privateer, with the assured knowledge that a noose from the yard-arm of a frigate might be his fate, or, again, in the swift, heavily canvassed privateer-chaser seeking for an enemy with whom he must fight to the death; sailing in every case on the most savage coast and treacherous sea in the world, with no clear notion as to who was or was not his "enemy"—now Spain, now Holland, now America, to his mind invariably France, and in general terms "foreigners" of all sorts—*when afloat*, for ashore, he greeted, danced, got drunk, and wrangled with them in the friendly roughness of the time. The harassing prospect of invasion, never absent from the minds of the shore-going people of the East Coast during the great war, gave him no definite concern. For him, war was omnipresent, an inevitable concomitant of his work-a-day experience. At sea it was always on his horizon, hence, to have the French ashore behind him could never greatly move him.

A strange place, too, the Shields of that day. Shut out from England itself, but in intimate touch with most of the stirring events occurring outside of it. Hearing to-day of this or that collier being taken by a Frenchman in the offing, seeing next day the *Anti-Gallican* beating up after plundering a score of sail. Scurrying down to the "Banks" to watch the frigate under tremendous press of sail mark down some unlucky foreign cruiser; to be mystified by the sudden apparition of *five hundred* Schaeveningen fisher-boats, which prove to have been chased into the river by privateers; or to witness, as in November, 1799, the landing of General Sir Ralph Abercrombie and his suite, accompanied by a Russian General, and followed a few days later by seven transports carrying upwards of a thousand Russians and Cossacks—a remnant of the Duke of York's abortive expedition in Holland. These transports, bound for Guernsey, put into Shields under stress of weather, and landed the outlandish-looking troops, who were described by their rough, though not unfriendly, critics as "a loosy set, but very religious, strong and robust" They came ashore in droves, and soon had troops of gaping children at their heels. "The Cossacks, these wild men of the Steppes, were objects of great interest, particularly to the female part of the population, who were quite captivated by the splendid green uniform of the officers, their red boots, silken sashes stuck full of costly pistols, silver-hilted Turkish sabres, and enormous cocked hats with gold lace, as well as by their formidable moustaches, light blue eyes, fair ruddy complexion, and merry (?) national songs which they sang in the evenings to please their hosts."

What astounding reports, rumours, and *canards* each day must have brought to the folk of the seaport, all *viva voce*, of course, unsifted, and unauthenticated! Small wonder that an insatiable passion for gossip was hugely developed

News travelled at best but slowly, and as it was deemed neither necessary nor desirable that "the people" should know anything of the affairs of the nation, the most momentous events passed long before any tidings percolated down to their stratum. Just then the whole English people was agog for news of Buonaparte, whose threatened invasion absorbed the public attention to the exclusion of most else. It was recognised that if the French should succeed in effecting a landing on any bit of English coast, days must elapse ere the news could be brought to the knowledge of the country at large; and, as for the coast-folk, with the noise of heavy guns ever in their ears, they could not possibly know from hour to hour whether the enemy was or was not upon them. They did know full well, however, that to themselves they must mainly trust for the efficacy of the defence should the brunt of the ever-impending assault come particularly upon them Vigorous measures, therefore, were taken by the Tynesiders to ward off the blow which they had no manner of doubt was fated to fall. To prevent a night attack on the shipping, and the drifting of fire-ships into the harbour, a huge iron chain, made by the forgemen at Swalwell, was conveyed to the mouth of the river, and arranged for stretching across "the Narrows," from shore to shore, a heavy winding crab, with ropes attached to each end, being fixed on each side of the river to pull the chain taut. To facilitate the passage of troops from North to South Shields "a line of keels was moored, end-on, across the river, joining the sand-end at the Beacon to the Lighthouse point near Clifford's Fort, with a platform of deals placed upon them so as to form a temporary bridge. This extraordinary highway was inspected on the morning of the 2nd October 1801 by Lord Mulgrave."

The Government, on its part, had filled the forts with soldiers and militia, and drafted large bodies of ill-regulated recruits into the seaports, or sent them into camp on the shore Incessant disturbances broke out between these men and the populace, the younger officers leading the van in disorderly revelry and outrage in the streets, and the older ones shielding them from civil punishment. Such affrays at times grew into bloody tumults, in which bayonets on the one side, and extemporised weapons of the ugliest kind on the other, were freely used.

The unrest and misery of the ordinary inhabitants, and particularly of the women and children, were distracting and distressing Exposed to the unrestrained rowdyism of their "protectors," they were peculiarly the subjects of the repeated "alarms" which, one after the other, proved to be "false," but each one of which was reality itself while it lasted.

Misery and ruin stared in the face all but the rich, for, with evident distrust of the value of their shore preparations for defence, the authorities arranged that on the landing of the enemy the non-combatants of the seaward towns should be conveyed into interior and remote parts of the country. For the Tynesiders, Alston Moor in Cumberland was fixed upon; farmers being ordered to be prepared to provide long carts for the purposes of transport; and—to prevent confusion—elaborate regulations and instructions were issued to the local authorities. Here is a copy of a "householder's ticket":—

"Ticket No. 196. John Wilkinson, you and your six children, belonging to Cart No. 1011, driver Anthony Butler, Station No 106 As soon, therefore, as the Alarm is given, do you pack up your Blankets, and a Change of Cloathes for yourself and Children, in the coverlid of your Bed, and fix upon the Bundle this direction.—No 106, John Wilkinson and Children, of the Township of North Shields, in the Parish of Tynemouth Carry also what Meal, Meat, and Potatoes (not exceeding one Peck) you may have in the House at the Time; but on no

Account will any Article of Furniture or heavy Baggage be allowed to be put into the Carts. *One Hour only will be allowed for Preparations,* and then set out. January 23rd, 1803."[1]

There was, without doubt, a grim conviction, all the more strongly entertained because of being by general tacit consent left unexpressed, that upon the navy must rest the duty of preserving inviolate the British shore-line; and that should it by some mischance fail, the issue must be darkly uncertain.

How then was England (or rather the men who monopolised the right to speak and act for her) treating the sea-warriors upon whom she put so tremendous a trust?

[1] Brockie's *History of Shields.*

THE WOODEN DOLLY AND QUAY.

CHAPTER II.

WHERE HEZ T' BEEN?

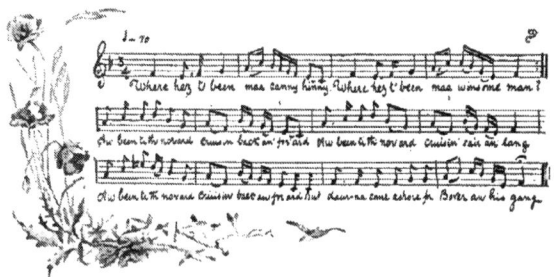

O man born on Tyneside in the first half of the nineteenth century can fail to find flickering up at times among the fading memories of his early childhood and haunting them with a tender, ineffable sadness, the sweet reminiscences of the lullaby with which every mother and every nurse softly sang her little one to sleep. The quaint old air, in which the stately grace of the *Minuet* is strangely mingled with the wailing plaintiveness of Northumbrian melody, had attached to it but a few poor lines—a mere fragment of a "song" written by some forgotten poet of the people,—but their sentiment was burned by tragic experience into the heart of every woman who sang them.

> "Where hez t' been, maa canny hinny,
> Where hez t' been, maa winsome man?
> Aw's been ti th' nor'ard, cruisin' back an' for'ard,
> Aw's been ti th' nor'ard, cruisin' sair an' lang,
> Aw's been ti th' nor'ard, cruisin' back an' for'ard,
> But daurna come ashore for Bover[1] an' his Gang."

[1] Captain Bover, sometime Regulating Captain of the Press-gang.

A BASE INSTITUTION.

Cruising *sair an' lang*, and *daurna* come ashore!—so it was with the "bold British tar," the "heart of oak," the "brave sailor-boy," about whom patriotic sea-song writers were weaving their tissue of tawdry boastful falsehood, to be bawled in the streets and by-ways of inland towns by sham "disabled sailors." Brave, reckless, fearless and manly he was, truly, but brave and manly and fearless and reckless though he might be, one harassing anxiety beset him on all hands by day and by night, and made him, as it made the hardiest of his comrades, when at sea, cast wistful glances round the horizon, or when ashore slink and crouch under cover like a hunted slave. Never Sallee rover nor Levantine pirate inspired in the heart of the merchant sailor the dread and detestation that seized upon him when one of his Majesty's ships hove in sight. No storm that littered the foreshore with the chafed and splintered fragments of broken wrecks checked the heart-beat of a sailor's wife and her children with so sudden a chill as did the apparition of the prowling cruiser that sneaked round the coasts to intercept the crews of English home-faring ships.

A base institution, worked by the basest of instruments, was in full operation, and the British sailor of 1800 had no more share in the "liberty" about which pot-house poets so lustily bellowed than any black villager in Mid-Africa.

Short-sighted and stupid, like the crowd of miserable unconstitutional processes by which England was being "ruled," there can be no doubt that the feeling of intense detestation entertained by the whole seafaring class for the navy was mainly the fruit of the iniquitous system known as "Impressment", mainly, but not wholly For the "service" was universally unpopular among those who best knew it, and for other reasons. With the gross corruption that ran riot among the administrative classes, nepotism of the most daring kind prevailed, and men were appointed to command whose incompetence in sea-craft exposed them to the bitter contempt, as their drunken ferocity gained for them the hatred, of their crews. It was no fear of danger or of death that made the sprightly Shields tar turn with disgust from the thought of serving his king and country—unbounded proof of *that* lay on every hand—but the knowledge that every element appealing to the instincts of a brave and free man must be outraged the moment he put his foot on the deck of a British man-o'-war. The merchant service brought him as much, perhaps more, danger, perhaps greater risk of violent death. It was a hard, cruel life, but at all events it left him at the end of each voyage a free man, and with some of the privileges of an Englishman In the navy, as he knew it, the short story was one of bondage, of harsh intolerance, of mutilation, and not seldom of a convict's death. In the meanest affairs of every-day life there was overbearing wrong to be silently borne; and it was common experience that under even the bravest and best of commanders a system of chicanery, in nowise their work, but that of the official class ashore, was universal. How could sailors hearing day by day a hundred stories such as that of old Benjamin Pinder trust themselves voluntarily to the tender mercies of the Admiralty? Ben's experience, shortly told, was this:—

"In the year 1793 he was impressed at London and draughted on board the *Agamemnon*, 64 guns, Captain Nelson, lying at the Nore; was made captain of the fore-top; sent out with the fleet under Lord Hood to the Mediterranean, and remained there three years and five months. Was in two general actions with the Toulon fleet (war 1794 and war 1795), engaged in 1793 with three 44-gun French frigates, a 32-gun frigate, and a brig of 18 guns, which after a long engagement were beaten off. During the time he was in the *Agamemnon* in the Mediterranean, was in sixteen various actions with the boats of the ship in attacking batteries and cutting-out vessels in harbours. Taken prisoner at Genoa along with the boat's crew commanded by Lieutenant Chatham, and marched, 360 miles, into the province of Languedoc with Austrian prisoners, he escaped, got to Toulon, and was sent, by a cartel of prisoners, to the Isle of Corsica, and there taken on board of H.M. frigate *Meleager*. He was a month on board this vessel, taking three prizes during the time, and was then ordered back to the *Agamemnon*. Came home to England in the *Agincourt*, Captain Smith, and thence was draughted on board the *York*, 64 guns, and sailed to the West Indies, where he remained five years and seven months. On that station they buried three hundred and sixty men in ten weeks. Ordered to England, and sent with a flotilla of flat-bottomed boats to Boulogne. Came back to the Nore, and was paid off April 7th, 1809, at Woolwich. He is now seventy-five years old (says the writer, telling the story in 1851), and has *never received his share of any prize-money*. In 1849 he made his claim for the medal ordered for the above services and actions of the years 1793, 1794, and 1795, but has not received it"

These experiences, however, were as nothing to others to which the host of men joining the navy were exposed, nay, could scarce escape from. The flogging was incessant and of inconceivable severity, and the dark iniquities perpetrated by African slave raiders fail to outmatch the "regulation" punishments of the time. Lashes were given by *hundreds*, and often enough for lapses of ridiculous triviality. "I have seen," said an old Shields salt, "a man tied up to the gangway and flogged for spitting on deck,—flogged for neglecting to salute a middy, flogged because a hammock did not look white or a deck clean, flogged because the captain had drunk too much wine," and it was no fancy flogging! the boatswain's mate being threatened by the ruffian in command that he should himself be flogged if he did not flog to the pitch of his utmost strength. Jack knew that he must put off his manhood and become a veritable slave in word and deed to avoid outrage and possible death at the hands of uncontrolled tyrants. He knew too that there was no appeal, no redress, no certain escape from the floating Hells into which many of the men-o'-war were thus converted by the furious bullies in command.

But with it all, it is doubtful whether the frenzy of detestation which possessed every English merchant sailor for the navy could have existed but for the despicable institution known to him as "the press." The war-ships that cruised round the British coasts to protect them were regarded as the worst enemy known to the people of the seaports. Hovering about in the vicinity of harbour mouths like kites, they pounced upon the poor little merchant vessel slowly beating up for the port after an absence of possibly two or three years, and overhauling her, took on forced service the pick of her crew, leaving not unfrequently a number insufficient to safely navigate her into port. Or beating about in the track of home-bound fleets, king's ships depleted the merchantmen, wholesale, of their hands, leaving to those on board the business of coping with the rude dangers of a savage sea, and of facing the risk of plunder by the swarming privateers that hung about in their wake.

"It was the regular practice the day the fleet made Flamborough Head to bring the convoy to and board every vessel. Mr. Somers stated before a Select Committee of the House of Commons that he was once lying in the Cowes roads bound to the West Indies during the war in 1812. He was armed with 12 guns, and carried 20 men. His ship's company was taken away *three successive times from him* by impressment, and at last he was obliged to appeal to the Admiral at Portsmouth, who ordered the men back the third time they were taken; but he knew resistance was out of the question, it was frequently offered ashore, but seldom or never afloat, it being so severely punished."

Not only home-faring vessels, therefore, but ships at the moment of sailing on a long voyage had their "hands" taken by any navy captain chancing upon them. Resistance being "out of the question," the men made extraordinary efforts to avoid capture, by hiding themselves away in remote out-of-the-way holes and lurking places, contrived by arrangement with the captain and owners. Too often, however, such stratagems failed and the poor fellows were ferreted out like escaped felons by the press-officers, who searched for them, gimlet in hand, with which to bore into likely places in the timber work of the ship

The prospect of incarceration in a French gaol was not one whit more dreaded than that of capture by an English officer carrying a press order, and, incongruous as the notion may now appear, it is unquestionably true that the merchantman which had dared a stand-up fight with some quick-moving, heavily-armed privateer, would crowd sail and, if he could, run away instantly on perceiving an English cruiser coming up to his rescue.

A few months before the descent of Paul Jones upon the Northern coasts, two privateers of eighteen and twenty-four guns respectively, and crowded with men, fell in with the *Content*, a Government armed ship of twenty guns, in company with a Greenland-man, for whose hands he was on the look-out. "A sharp engagement ensued, which lasted near two hours and was visible all the time to the inhabitants ashore. At last the *Content* compelled the Frenchmen to desist and stand off to sea with all sail they could spread. Had the Greenland-man (the *Freelove* of Whitby) stood to the *Content*, the privateers would probably have been taken, as she mounted fourteen guns, but the crew having the fear of a French gaol on the one hand, and of forced service on board a man-of-war on the other, ran close in shore with a view of escaping both."

Sometimes the English frigate dropped in at the close of a dogged fight between a merchantman and some powerful but beaten assailant, but she was equally unwelcome to the sailors. The following spirited account of an encounter of the kind was given by one of the hands aboard, and is a good specimen of the style of narration common among Shields seamen.—

"The *Susanna*, 314 tons, mounting eight guns and manned by eighteen hands—one of them a boy—was homeward bound from the Mediterranean with returned ordnance stores, bound to Portsmouth. We made the Bill of Portland, and saw a large three-masted lugger standing off, the wind westerly at 2 P M. He was on the starboard side, about a pistol-shot off, with a red English ensign flying; we with a white one with red border. Our master had given orders for every man to 'off jacket.' Our carronades were loaded, and had we not taken him for English we could have, perhaps, sunk him at that time, but he hailed us in English, 'Ship a-hoy, what are you?' Our master answered, 'One of his Majesty's armed transports' The mate, who had just made his escape from a French prison, says to the master, 'He is a Frenchman.' At that instant he down English colours and up French, and many of them took up their muskets and fired at us. They hard-a-starboard their helm and tried to grapple us; but our ship having a good deal of way he could not hold on, and we having a quarter-boat and spars over the quarter, he could not board us. There he was, a long time under the stern. We trimmed sails and kept her N.E., the wind then on the larboard quarter. He then set a large stay-sail and came up on the weather quarter. We took to muskets and fired from under the quarter-board, but finding our few nothing to his many, we dropt One of his shots stuck in the mizen-mast, just above the man's head at the wheel he let it go; he was a foreigner. The ship came to, and the sails shaked in the wind; but Mark Thompson and I hove the helm up and she filled again. The mate, thinking he was fast to us, called out for us to take our cutlasses, give them three hurrahs, and at them like bull-dogs, which we did. We then again shore off from him, and when at a fair distance we let fly our double-charged 18-pound carronades at him, but the shot sometimes went over him and sometimes under him. The ship had a good deal of motion, and they were fixed breech-ends, that is, they did not slide in to sponge and load, therefore there was a risk of them picking us off during the time we were over the rails. But having a breeze we kept away the time of loading, and by manœuvring so a few times the contents of the gangway gun went into his midships at the water's edge. That was about 5 P.M. He hove her about and nailed a sheet of lead over the hole; then we saw a sloop standing off with no colours up. We thought it might be a partner of his Sometimes we were for running over him, so he hove his vessel right in the way of the French, and was sent over to France with five hands of the privateer. It came on hazy and foggy. About midnight the fog cleared away, the moon got out, and a frigate that had been three days after him, hearing the report of our guns, came so near that we were all three within the reach of his guns, and nearly calm. The next day we all three brought up on the Mother Bank, and after getting clear of quarantine we went into Portsmouth harbour, where the ship was refitted by Government. The main-shrouds, back-stays, and gear about the mizen-mast was shot away, also the sails much riddled, but *we were pressed and sent on board a man-of-war to fight for our king and country, as they told us.*"

The Frenchman had fourteen guns and eighty men.

The whole seafaring class was truly kept in a state of feverish uncertainty and dread from the moment of sighting the English coast-line—a dread that never for a moment left them until they had once more seen the shores sinking under the horizon. This sentiment—manifest in all the genuine records of the time—may be read in the following letter, dated May 1799 : —

"DEAR MOTHER,—My brother George is going out to the Cape of Good Hope. I hope he will be enabled to keep from the Press I think he had better try a foreign voyage than run the risk of being pressed in the ship he was in; he will stand a better chance of keeping from a man-of-war You will not let any one know where he is gone.

"THOMAS STODART."

Thus harassed and worried, his faculties always on strain to avoid the lynx-eyed cruisers which kept unremitting and relentless watch for him at sea, Jack's case was even worse on shore, for here the greater brutality of the press-gang awaited him. Slinking from his ship, if he could, while she was yet in the offing, he would land at some unfrequented part of the coast, and get him away inland, to hide; often to be tracked and run to earth by the wretched spies and informers, who, to earn the blood-money paid them by the Naval authorities, resorted to the basest and most cowardly artifices Escaping detection perhaps, he would presently be tempted by the prospect of meeting wife, children, friends, or comrades, or be driven, by the necessity of again taking ship, to face the risks of going into town, where at every step in the "narrow street" he was menaced with capture and personal violence at the hands of the gangs of blackguards to whose tender mercies "those in authority" had confided the lives of the poorer classes.

For it was not only Jack who was pressed, though mainly he; but when, in the parlance of the time, an "impress *broke out*" (as though it were some blasting pestilence or scourge), artisans, labourers, and even petty tradesmen were chased through the streets, dragged out of their houses, or torn from their work, hustled, beaten, and ill-used and, under circumstances of revolting humiliation and degradation, haled off to one of the jetties by the river, and thrown into a boat to be conveyed to the tender. Once there, a word of indignant remonstrance or expostulation exposed the hapless wretches to the chances of being loaded with irons, or even chained down to the deck, and finally, of encountering that *ultima ratio regum*, the "cat."

It is not difficult to realise that the system was regarded by the populace with hatred and detestation, but it is impossible now to appreciate the loathing and abhorrence in which its instruments were held. Recruited, as they deliberately were, from the most degraded and, not seldom, criminal class—for even in that dark time the work was too base to be touched by any other—no man, woman, or child living within the scope and ken of their operations hesitated to accredit them with any crime, however cruel or treacherous.

Throughout the greater part of the eighteenth century the popular mind was kept excited and inflamed by repeated tumults arising out of ferocious encounters between the gangs and the classes upon whom they preyed. The shocking nature of the punishment inflicted upon those who failed to effect an escape did not deter pressed men from rising upon their captors and carrying a struggle for freedom to the bloodiest extremity, and the populace, or the rougher portion of it, was ever ready to join in any affray arising out of such encounters. The desperation which led men to face the terrible odds, and to risk the frightful consequences of failure, was intense, but again and again the chances were grimly taken.

Down in "Peggy's Hole," a deeper portion of the river just inside the harbour mouth, lay at all times a tender,[1] one being relieved by another as the cargo of captives was gradually accumulated. Kept for an indefinite time below decks in the hold of the vessel, amid foul stench, darkness, and discomfort, the miserable beings at times took heart to rise upon the sentinels or, with greater daring, proceeded to the extreme course of capturing the vessel from their custodians when at sea, and running her into port somewhere whence they could make a dash for freedom.

"On February 6th, 1755, a smart press broke out at Shields, when sixty or seventy hands were taken by the *Peggy*, sloop of war.

"Next year, war having been proclaimed against France, a very hot press was made for seamen at Shields and in the Tyne generally, and *no regard paid to protections*. Several hundred men were taken. On March 30th, 1759, a press-gang went to Swalwell in quest of men, but the inhabitants making head against them, they came off with a severe drubbing. Part of them laid hold of one William Moffat, a barber, and Mr. Bell, one of the chief inhabitants, interfering, received five stabs

---

[1] One, for many years on the station, was appropriately named the *Lynx*.

with a sword in different parts of the body, in consequence of which he died. Some others, on both sides, were dangerously wounded, including the midshipman who headed the gang. In January of the following year, a tender having sailed from Shields with sixty pressed men on board, the men found means to release themselves, and taking possession of the vessel, took her into Scarborough and made their escape

"On March 3rd, 1771, the impressed men on board the *Boscawen* cutter lying at Shields found an opportunity to over-power the watch on deck, and fifteen of them got clear off—an officer was desperately wounded.

"On February 12th, 1777, about eight o'clock in the evening, the impressed men on board the *Union* tender at Shields rose upon the crew and took possession of the ship and, *notwithstanding the fire from the other tenders and from Clifford's Fort*, carried her out to sea.

"On the 13th February, 1783, the sailors at Sunderland having got liberty to go on shore, and having a list of persons who had informed against them and their mates to the press-gang, assembled in a great body and went to the informers' houses. Those whom they found they mounted upon poles and carried through the principal streets, exposed to the insults of the populace. The women, in particular, bedaubed them plentifully with rotten eggs, soap-suds, mud, and other dirt Some constables interfering had their staves taken from them, and were soundly beaten. The mob was reinforced from every lane and alley in the town, and by the time it grew dark in the evening the numbers had so increased that the military had to be called out The drums of the North York Militia beat to arms, and the regiment paraded the streets, which had the effect of clearing them.

"In February 1793 the seamen at Shields, Newcastle, and Sunderland, and all along the eastern coast, entered into a resolution to resist any attempt to press them, and invited all the seamen in the kingdom to join. On Tuesday, the 19th, they got hold of the press-gang at North Shields, and reversing their jackets, conducted them, accompanied by a numerous crowd, to Chirton toll-bar, where, dismissing them, they gave three cheers, and warned them never again to enter Shields, or they should be torn limb from limb.

"On the 18th of March, 1793, the sailors, to the number of five hundred, assembled in a riotous manner, armed with swords, pistols, and other weapons, and made an attempt to seize the *Eleanor* tender, in order to rescue the impressed men on board. Their design, however, was rendered abortive by the activity of the officers

"On the 26th of April, 1793, the most extraordinary preparations for impressing were made by the crews of the armed vessels lying in the harbour. That night, the regiment lying at Tynemouth barracks was drawn up *and formed into a cordon round North Shields*, to prevent any person from escaping. The different press-gangs then began, when sailors, mechanics, labourers, and men of every description, to the number of about two hundred and fifty, were forced on board the armed ships."

Nay, not men of *every* description! No man of wealth or position was found inside the trawl

This disgusting and almost incredible occurrence, like many others not quoted—the infamy of the whole of which lay solely with the governing bodies of the day—provoked outbreaks which could only be repressed by military force, and made the condition of the seaport more resemble that of the seat of war in an enemy's country than a portion of His British Majesty's dominions; and the wicked selfishness of the whole business was only equalled by the quiet complacency with which it was regarded by those who, secure in the knowledge that such outrage could never possibly reach them, denied, defended, or palliated it all

For, of course, the system was defended and its injustice denied Slavery was defended and flogging was defended. What monstrous iniquity, benefiting one small class at the cost of others, is not defended by those profiting by it? In 1827, Sir James Graham, First Lord of the Admiralty, "courted an inquiry" into the practice of impressment. It was a safe proceeding—a safe challenge. Poor Jack had no representative whose vote was wanted, or whose silence might need to be purchased. Not a man at the Admiralty was ignorant of the horrors being perpetrated in every seaport in the kingdom, and yet they "courted an inquiry"! The noble Lords, too, were wondering at the unpopularity of the Navy. Unpopular! with its hundreds of lashes, not a single cut of which would "my Lords" abate. Unpopular! with its slave-raiding methods. Unpopular! with all its chances for its victims of falling into the hands of some drunken tyrant holding, unchecked, the power of life and death. Unpopular! while evading every obligation to the sailor, withholding his prize-money on this pretence, defrauding him of his pension on that, "feeding him like a dog, treating him like a dog, flogging him like a dog" (though it is doubtful if a savage would so flog a dog), ill-treating, starving, and swindling him, and finally turning him adrift, hopelessly crippled, to shift for himself,—truly a marvellous thing the Navy was unpopular!

Here is the petition which, in March 1827, the seamen of Tyneside sent to the Honourable the Commons of England, at the instance of some active men in Shields. They represent—

"That they are liable, whenever it pleases the Lords Commissioners of the Admiralty to issue press warrants, and even sometimes it pleases the captains of his Majesty's ships to collect a stronger crew, to be hauled out and seized, or like the vilest criminals, to be forcibly carried away from their employment, their homes, their parents, their wives and their children, and be kept close prisoners on board His Majesty's ships for an undefined period. They are liable to be thus treated merely because they are seamen, and because some persons, possessing more power than wisdom, have imagined that so to treat them was advantageous to the country They humbly solicit the attention of your honourable House while they point out in detail the injustice of impressment to your petitioners, all the enormities of which cannot be known to your honourable House, and while they endeavour to demonstrate that it is not less injurious to the country than unjust to them

"Your petitioners have sometimes been surprised by night in their beds, sometimes their peaceful homes or ships have been invaded by day, sometimes they have been carried off from amidst the revelry of the evening, and sometimes they have been arrested in the public streets, but in all cases personal violence is used towards them. They are surrounded by armed men and threatened with blows or wounds if they resist, not respecting (as it is impossible they should respect) such violence, they seek to escape or resist as may be practicable or prudent; strife and bloodshed ensue, and some of your petitioners have witnessed, as all have heard described contests between the seamen and press-gangs which resembled civil war. Such scenes are always disgraceful, but when they are actually caused, as in this case, by the power which is instituted to protect the rights of all, and preserve the peace of the country, the violence is base as well as unjust: it adds treachery to outrage, and appears to your petitioners revolting and atrocious.

"The increased dangers of your petitioners' profession during war are compensated, as they ought to be, by increased wages; but the Admiralty, disdaining to have their services while it can impress them, makes no advance of wages corresponding to the danger, and compels your petitioners to serve His Majesty for 28s to 32s. per month, while the Merchant would readily give them from three to five pounds.

"The labour of your petitioners is their chief property, and to exact that without adequately paying for it is a species of plunder which can never be excused by a government that in many cases punishes a less fraudulent appropriation by the penalty of death.

"After suffering this personal violence and plunder your petitioners are sometimes pinioned for security, and they are always stowed like slaves in the hold of a tender to be transmitted from port to port, or in the gloomy dungeon of a guard-ship till their spirit has been sufficiently subdued, when they are sent on board some man-of-war. Here they are still further maltreated. Having been injured, they cannot be trusted, they live continually under the bayonets of an armed body of soldiers, and a host of officers useless for every other purpose but to compel their obedience, and to them a man-of-war is in reality a floating prison. So inevitable is the mistrust arising from ill-treating your petitioners, that even when the exigencies of His Majesty's service require them to be sent on shore, they are generally accompanied by some stripling midshipman, and soldiers, to prevent their deserting. Their hearts are not in unison with their constrained duties, and they do not exert themselves with that alacrity which distinguishes voluntary labour. Hence has arisen on board His Majesty's ships a system of compelling them to exert themselves, by flogging, which differs not in principle, and is worse, your petitioners honestly believe, in degree, than the slave flogging of the West India Islands, except the gross barbarity of flogging women And your petitioners submit to your honourable House that a system of discipline founded on this principle, though it is perhaps the necessary consequence of the first flagrant injustice practised towards them, adds greatly to its enormity.

"Your petitioners know that owing to the decided reprobation—expressed by the public and by some of their eloquent representatives in Parliament—of military flogging, some feeble efforts have of late been made by the Admiralty to control the excessive severity to which some individual captains are prone; but the oldest among your petitioners remember numerous instances of seamen having been unmercifully flogged, for no other reason that they could discover than because their captain had drunk too much wine, they have seen their comrades scourged, by dozens, to the backbone, because a hammock did not look white or a deck clean, the captain continually threatening the boatswain's mate, who inflicted the punishment, that he should be tied up and flogged if he did not flog to the pitch of his utmost strength; and knowing as they do from long experience that they cannot procure the punishment of any captain, however he may behave, who has what is called interest at the Admiralty, they can have no confidence, exposed as they must be to his irresponsible caprices, that the feeble efforts which have been made to check severe flogging will secure them in future against the tyranny of which they complain, as long as they are forced into service, and as long as the Mutiny Act authorises any and every captain to punish them according to the laws and customs observed at sea,—those laws and customs being the very laws and customs of those captains who are so tyrannical and cruel

"Thus, forced from their homes and confined to a floating prison in which they are subjected to a terrific system of punishment, your petitioners are liable to be sent abroad for many years, to be exposed to the dangers of an unhealthy climate, often aggravated by pestilence in a crowded ship, and they are forced to contend in murderous battle against men, strangers to them, with whom they have no cause to quarrel; nor has it been unusual when your petitioners have returned from one foreign station to send them immediately to another, not allowing them even the poor boon, but delightful recreation, of spending in a dozen years one single day in freedom in their native land; and your petitioners have seen some of their comrades so maddened by this continued constraint, that they burned the (to them, under these circumstances) worthless bank-notes, which were all they received for years of toil and privation."

Poor Jack! thou mightst better have spared thy pains. The result was *nil;* and so late as 1833 a majority of the House of Commons voted against even an *inquiry* into the possibility of finding a better means of manning the Navy than by impressment.

And so the Navy was unpopular and remained unpopular, and the Government cozened and cheated its tars as basely as any crimp in the slums and alleys of the long "narrow street." Jack had no friend aloft—in society, at least—to watch over his interests, and his poor wits were sharpened by the necessity of coping with ever-menacing danger. False "protections" could be purchased, which (if they passed muster with the keen and suspicious Press-officer) enabled him for a time to possess his soul in peace. Nor must he be blamed if he availed himself of the use of such fraudulent scrip, for had he not the high example of the noble Lords themselves—his final court of appeal—the Admiralty? Their "protections" were more detestably "false" than his, as many a poor fellow who, having honourably gained, won, or bought one, found to his cost. When "men were wanted and men must be had," the Admiralty took the short course of what was euphemistically called "suspending" the "protections" they themselves had issued; in plain terms they dishonoured their own bonds, and in so doing made the re-capture of their dupes the more facile. Surrounded by treachery such as this, Jack took sanctuary with the fierce ship-carpenters, who—always ready, nay eager, to try an issue with authority of any kind, and to push it home with the ugliest of weapons—were the particular dread of the gangs who hung back as they saw them escort the hunted seamen to and from the docks. When convoy of this sort was not to be had, stratagem was resorted to, and many are the stories of tricks played by Jack and his always sympathising town-fellows.

On one such occasion a sailor named Bell was impressed and safely lodged in the house of rendezvous. In the evening, his sister, a young woman under twenty, resolved to attempt his rescue, and to that end went to take a "long farewell" of her brother, who was to be sent off to the tender in the morning. She was readily admitted to an interview, but, in order to prevent any possibility of escape, brother and sister were bolted and barred in a room by themselves for a few minutes. During this short interval they managed to change clothes, and on the door being opened, the young man, apparently snivelling and piping his eye, walked off unmolested in female attire, while the sister remained to face the consequences. "It would be difficult," says the writer who tells the story, "to describe the rage and disappointment of the gang on discovering how they had been duped." The heroine, who was soon restored to liberty by order of the magistrates, received several pounds from the crowd of people who went to see her, as a reward for her intrepidity and affection.

Cool audacity sometimes served to rid a sailor of the consequences of being pressed, or saved him from capture. "A sharp old South Shields 'salt,' on being impressed and taken on board the tender, ran up against the lieutenant on deck and instantly begged pardon— 'he couldn't help it, he was so short-sighted.' As a consequence he was ordered over the ship's side and got off."

A smart young sailor sauntering one day "along the Banks" was seized by the chief of one of the gangs, who, pointing a pistol at his head, pressed him in the king's name. "I have a protection," said the sailor, putting his hand into the breast of his jacket "Let me see it, then," demanded the other. "Now, you thief—the first to H—ll," retorted Jack, as he drew out a pistol and pushed the muzzle of it into the face of his discomfited captor, who was thus obliged to relinquish his prize.

It is only fair to say that the system was almost as cordially hated by officers of the Navy, save perhaps those of the higher ranks, as by the people whom it so cruelly oppressed.

The reflective observer scarcely knew whether to marvel more at the supercilious complacency with which the abominable injustice of the system was regarded by the responsible authorities, or at the fatuous indifference which closed their eyes to the enormous damage it was working to the State. Abstract justice rarely commands the attention of governments, but it may be supposed that the stolid self-sufficiency of even the Circumlocution Office would have been stirred by the fact that the merchant marine was being denuded of its best material and the very flower of English sea-craft driven abroad to man the fleets of the enemies of England, and, in the bitterness of hatred engendered by ill-usage and outrage, to fight, under the flag of America or France, against her "wooden walls," or 'neath the colours of the privateer to prey upon her commerce. The daredevil crews sailing with Paul Jones, Daniel Fell, and other sea-wolves of a century ago, were largely trained and brutalised in the British Navy.

Of its overwhelming cost, it is not to be thought the administrators of the Navy, in such an age, cared a candle-snuff—yet it was enormous. Numbers of fighting ships were permanently diverted to press work, a fleet of smaller craft was constantly employed in it. The fleet itself was kept in pay and victuals throughout the winter to avoid dispersing the crews, who certainly would not voluntarily return. Merchant ships lay in harbour for long periods at vast cost because of depleted crews. Wages lost, ships lost, ships damaged, cargoes destroyed through undermanning—all this was directly and indirectly involving the waste of millions of money.

Of the demoralisation it worked among the people, they certainly took as little account, yet that *too* was enormous. A rank crowd of evils sprung up and flourished under the shadow of the accursed institution Kidnapping, robbery, and murder dogged its steps in security; for there was nothing to discriminate the ruffians engaged in the one ugly business from those busied in the other Magistrates on the bench of justice offered to thieves and blackguards the option of joining a man-of-war as an alternative to imprisonment, unconscious, apparently, of the bitter satire upon the service involved in their action. Strikes were "settled" by hustling off, to the tender, men who had "conspired" to obtain an advance of wages. Crews refusing to "proceed to sea"—no matter for what reason—and it was too often terribly adequate—met the same fate. A huge wrong was being done the mass of the people, and the "constitution" was systematically invoked to bless, justify, and enforce the work.

But nothing could justify, could reconcile, the ugly business to Jack. He recognised its gross unfairness. Conscription, he knew, was a comparatively all-round matter—*this* was not so. This was no affair of facing a draft and of faring luckily or otherwise. He was never for an instant free from seizure. In his ship,—in the streets of every seaport,—on his return from long voyages of inconceivable monotony and irksome circumstance,—in his home with his wife and among his children, he was ever subject to arrest and outrage, and, when being dragged off and beaten, his heart was filled with the bitter conviction that neither wife nor little ones could be sure of ever more hearing of him—that the ending of no voyage, however long, would certainly restore him to them; that voyages of years might be followed by voyages of years; and that, if he escaped death, or degradation by infamous punishment, the chances were more than equal that he would eventually be cast ashore a broken cripple, far past the age for helping himself.

Well might the whole body of the people—the "rabble"—execrate the name of the Navy, well might the poor women of Shields tremble with the agitation of a bitter hatred at the sight of the scoundrel gang slinking along the "narrow street," and peeping up its alleys, lanes, and entries. Well might the wistful, semi-incredulous wife and mother, tearfully looking into the face of the altered and much aged man standing before her, whom she knew years before as her husband, ask in tones of troubled uncertainty, "Where hez t' been, maa canny hinny?"

. . . .

The dark story of this ugly blot on the history of the early eighteens finds its fitting culmination in the crowning shame of John Babbington Stodart's deliberate murder by the instruments of a British Government. A bright, smart young sailor, a favourite with his captain, the well-beloved of a widowed mother, sisters, and aunt, this poor boy's untoward career and ultimate fate is an epitome of the chicanery, outrage, and ruffianism with which the best of England's sailors were only too familiar. His letters, in their very unconscious simplicity, are at once a bitter satire on, and a damning indictment of, the system which, while he lived, robbed him of all peace, and, in the end, filched from him life itself.

"LYDD, *August 9th*, 1802.

"DEAR MOTHER,—I am happy Manners has got safe home. You may tell him for a truth that he need not be the least afraid of any of the officers nor any one looking after him, for that villain Frazer that we had tormenting us for two months is suspended, and Lieutenant Bennet is going away. Frazer dowened the heart of the ship's company very much. First, he lets us have no fresh provisions; in the next place, if two or three people were playing or amusing themselves, he said they 'were upon some mutinous designs'—he even called a guard of Marines and took the men from their play (which Captain Bennet always allowed), and told the ship's company he was jealous of them, which did not become the captain of a man-of-war. He wrote to the Board of Admiralty and told them we were the most mutinous set of men ever he was with in his life We suspect this is the reason of our being kept here. . . . When he left us he descended the ship like a rat and hissed like a cat, and brave Captain Hardy took command. He exceeded Captain Bennet for everything that is good, but that is no excuse for to say if the application had been made sooner that I might had some chance to get clear, for I asked him before the draft was made, and he told me I should be cleared of the ship as soon as the ship came from Cook's Haven; but at the same time, he cannot get his own servants clear until the ship is paid off."

"*From the Ship Amphion, Sept. 20th,* 1802.

"The truth of it is I get quite tired of writing, since I see there is no chance of our getting clear of this miserable life . . . There have been mutiny on board different men-of-war, which makes me think it will be worse before long, but we must weather it out as well as we can. It greaves me to think of leaving what I have due, but if we are not paid off shortly I mean to get liberty on shore and leave the ship."

"STROMNESS, *April 2nd,* 1803

"We arrived at Stromness on Tuesday, and we are waiting for a fair wind to sail to Greenland. We got down to Shields last Friday night, and on Saturday morning at daylight the frigate's boat came on board and pressed seven of our men, which stoped the ship from going to sea that day, and as soon as the boat was gone there was nine of us went to Hartley[1] and stopped till Sunday forenoon, and the ship came out and we got safe on board, and we got all our hands clear, which was a lucky chance."

"*Great Nore, His Majesty's Ship Lynx,*
January 20th, 1804.

"Mr. Bishop informs me that he has employed a person to get my discharge, at the same time I got one from the person employed, who says he thinks there is no doubt of me getting clear after he is in possession of my indentures, which I shall hope for every day. . . If I do not get my clearance in the course of a short time I will give up all hopes. Here was another thing Mr Bishop wished to know, if he could not get me clear by that means—if I wish to go to the expense of one or two substitutes, if they would accept of them I told him that if they would give me a discharge, and not to be impressed during the war, that I would willingly go to the length of forty or fifty pounds. But I doubt it will be all in vain, the officers being at me at different times to enter. I would thank you if you would write to Sir Tom Swinburn, and ask him if Captain

[1] Hartley-Pans, some five or six miles up the coast.

Bennet has got a ship, for sooner than stay on board this disagreeable thing as a presst man, I would enter for Captain Bennet or Admiral Collingwood. I hope, dear mother, you will not put yourself about, for they will never keep me so long as they did last war. I expect to see you in less than three months at any event.—I remain, your affectionate son, "J. B. STODART."

"*His Majesty's Ship Lynx*,
Great Nore, January 28*th*, 1804.

"DEAR MOTHER,—I am sorry to inform you that I had the misfortune to be presst yesterday for want of my indentures for my servitude of a carpenter. So if you please to send my indentures and bond to Mr. Bishop as soon as possible, he will do his endeavours as far as lays in his power. . . . I told Mr. Bishop if it was twenty pounds he was not to mind the expence. Mr Bishop asked me if I would have the money sent home immediately, or keep it in his own hands until he saw if he could get me clear. I told him to keep it in his own hand till he saw how things turned out; he is a very honest man; but please send my indentures up to Mr. Bishop as soon as possible."

"LONDON, *February* 8*th*, 1804.

"DEAR MOTHER,—I have been here at Aunt Gowland's since the thirtieth of January, and have not got another ship. Mr. Bishop says it is a long time for me to be out of a ship and little astir in the river at present, and the ship being light and not taken on for any cargo, she won't protect me on board, or I would have been at work ever since I got my discharge. I keep close quarters at present I go very little out except it is with my aunt, who goes out purposely to give me a walk. I expect, in the course of three weeks, to be with you again *It has been an expensive job*, but I don't much mind it, as I have got my clearance of them."

Poor lad! got his clearance, indeed! Pressed again and again; buying with his hard-won earnings a discharge from the Noble Lords, he arrived in the Tyne in April, 1804, and, it being Sunday, straightway proceeded to Newcastle to see his mother and sisters. Dining on board ship, he was watched by the press-gang, who, on his landing, instantly gave chase Hunted along the Quay, and seeing no other possibility of escape from his old enemies, he jumped into the Tyne and struck out for the opposite shore. Infuriated at the prospect of so losing their victim, the ruffians threatened to fire upon any one who should attempt to go to the swimmer's assistance. "When he had neared the opposite shore he was shot in the head by one of the gang."

NO RETRIBUTION.

The bloody business brought in its track no retribution. The horrible penal code, furiously swift to shed human blood on every trivial pretence, had no vengeance for this murdered boy. The poor, ill-starred lad, who had paid for his "clearance"; who had not even been re-captured and broken arrest; who was fleeing, as any wretched negro might flee from Arab slave-dealers, was done to death in the face of English people, in an English town, on the day consecrated to God's service, and his murderers left unmolested to sneer at the execrations of the excited "rabble."[1]

---

[1] A coroner's quest, *held with closed doors* on April 23rd, 1804, gave a verdict which was not officially published, but the statement made by the press authorities —of course untrue—was to the effect that Stodart, being ordered to yield under a threat of being fired at, lost his presence of mind and was drowned. This version, having recently (1888) been repeated in the local press, a niece of Stodart's wrote giving the facts as she received them from her mother, a sister of the murdered boy. Desirous of seeing such documents as might be in the possession of this lady, the author wrote to her early in 1891, and received the following reply, together with copies of her ill-fated uncle's letters :—

"CLIFF COTTAGE, JARROW, *January 12th*, 1891.

"DEAR SIR,—I am in receipt of yours this morning, and beg to say that I have to-day concluded [copying] the letters on the subject of the Press-gang. It was a terrible time both for sailors and their friends. It was a trouble to my mother to her death fifty years after. I beg to crave your indulgence for all imperfections in my writing, as you will perceive my hand is very unsteady.—Yours sincerely,

"ELIZA HUTCHINSON."

Miss Hutchinson, who had long been an invalid, died within a fortnight after making the copies. The original letters then passed into the possession of Mr. T. A. Clark, who kindly allowed the author to photograph them.

CHAPTER III.

THE DAY-SPRING.

"The Walkers told Sarah Spence that she would get to Paradise when she came to Shields! She thought of their words when she was in the Low Street, which is more likely to resemble the lower regions, I should think."—*Records of a Quaker Family.*

A CRUEL, sordid time it was, and though, looking back through the softening mists of a century, it may appear in a nimbus of glory, this is but a meretricious glare produced by the imperfection of the medium.

So busied indeed with "glory" were all who in any degree controlled the flow of events, that there was neither opportunity nor desire to count the fearful cost. The grimmest horror and misery falling, as they did, upon the voiceless poor were regarded with an indifference amounting almost to unconsciousness. Unconsciousness, and not complacency, mayhap it was; nay, it is scarcely possible on any other supposition to reconcile the fantastic contradictions that have to be faced in studying the social phases of that dark time.

Sunday after Sunday, throughout the land, in the drowsy, humdrum churches to which worshippers were beat-up out of shops and public-houses, by patrolling Warden and Beadle,[1]—men mumbled a petition that the good Lord would deliver "us" from plague and pestilence and famine, from battle and murder and sudden death; yet all these were, day by day, dreadfully at work, and scarce a man who cared to lift a finger to stay them. Storm-strewn shores were close at hand on which, at intervals short and unfailing, bread-winners were cast up by the retreating tide; pestilence invited by every crazy artifice to dwell among the people; famine fastened upon the land, and cramping its swarming thousands. Battle omnipresent; murder —criminal and judicial—before every man's eyes, and sudden death in every cruel and shameful form, the commonest of experiences

While, therefore, in church, petitions against visitations such as these might take the form of a mechanically-uttered prayer, it was elsewhere quite another affair, and 'twould have been a brave man who, in the club, the bar-parlour, on 'Change, or at the festive board, should have ventured to advance such "unpatriotic" sentiments. Money was to be made out of tempest and famine, and, above all, out of "battle." War was an undoubtedly good thing, everybody said so. And good in so many ways. Good, for instance, for trade,— particularly good for trade, and the factitious "prosperity" flowing from it in seaports such as Shields was sufficient not only to blind those whose interest it was not to see, but—in the dense ignorance of the time—to half convince the poor wretches on whom its heaviest burdens, sacrifices, and miseries fell, that, in some inscrutable way, it was "good" even for them; for the only trade they knew in their generation was that which came directly out of warfare.

And, therefore, while much glory was current in the gossip, the conversation, the songs, the speeches and the sermons of the time, the "main chance" held a steady course all through, and ran her showy sister a close race. There was high example for it. A general scramble for plunder,—an eager desire to wrest from misfortune as much as she could be made to yield,—a universal rush to help "Old England" on the highest possible terms, was seen to lie at the bottom of much of the windy patriotism that men were shouting themselves

---

[1] "Il-y a vis-a-vis de nos fenêtres une boutique à moitié ouverte; deux hommes, en habits galonnés, et avec des chapeaux retroussés comme on les portait il-y a cent ans, viennent la fermer de force. le marchand qui paraît être un quaker les laisse faire, mais rouvre sa boutique aussitôt qu'ils se sont eloignés. On nous dit que ce sont de beadles qui veulent faire observer le dimanche."—*Voyage en Angleterre, 1810 et 1811.* Ls. Simond.

hoarse with. Lavish honours went hand in hand with huge pensions, lucrative honorary posts and fat commissions. Fine Admirals, with a keen eye for prizes, sailed a course which, never for a moment shirking the enemy, yet gave golden chances of meeting treasure-ships in convoy. *Was für Plunder* lay in the hearts of crowds of star-bedecked warriors, if not precisely on their tongues. No marvel then that in the small society of a seaport town, where possibly three-fourths of the population lived upon the war, a baser sort of social ascendency was fostered, and that, in the neglect of every art save the poor blundering one of destruction, all desire was stifled, as opportunity was destroyed, for culture and learning. Nay, a contempt, in itself sordidly vulgar, for both was never concealed, but rather obtruded, and any suggested movement for the advancement of the Arts and Sciences, by a large majority, heavily frowned down

The dark violence of England's higher rulers was reflected in the acts of the lower, though not less despotic, officials who exercised authority in the smaller affairs of life, and in dealing with an ignorant and helpless people a cruel, harsh impatience was universal. Just as the landowner held in the hollow of his hand the liberties—and not seldom the lives—of those who refused to cringe to him in obsequious and unmanly deference, or who displayed any stubborn resistance to his edicts; just as he might drive poaching into murder, gleaning into theft, trespass into vagrancy, and all into penal consequence; so too the ship-owning magistrate wielded over the "hands" who manned his vessels, monstrous and unnatural authority. He knew, as they knew, that for them there was no appeal against his sentence of months of imprisonment (or the detested alternative of forced transfer to a king's ship), in the event of their refusing to "proceed to sea" in a vessel for which the crimp had drugged them into signing articles, but which they had come to learn was a mere crazy, leaking death-trap.

Never was lofty sentiment so profuse; never was so much lip-service to king, country, glory, duty! "Duty, duty, duty," cried out statesman, judge, and magistrate. "Duty, damme, duty," snapped the flogging martinet. "Duty, my brethren," urged the patience-preaching bishop. Never was "duty" so much in men's mouths, so lauded, so unquestioningly worshipped, and surely never so entirely a *fetish!* "Duty" faced but one way, and that never by any chance towards the people

And so, the merciless law which stooped to kill even children, vouchsafed them no protection. The pathos of the child's life was indeed unutterably touching. Every element and circumstance surrounding his existence made for misery. The father was pressed, imprisoned, transported, drowned, killed in the pit, killed in the war, "missing," his ship "given up," or "not heard of." The goad of famine incited him, even as an infant, to petty crime, as it tempted his forsaken mother to risk the gallows. Hired out by foster-parents to unscrupulous middlemen, and given over in tender years to drudgery of hideous duration, which crippled and deformed him; coerced by masters, unconsciously but not the less effectively brutal, surrounded from infancy by horrible superstition, subjected to barbarous methods of "cure" for the hundred ills flowing from chronic starvation, ignorance, and filthy habits—truly the child of 1800 was in hapless case. More hapless the fatherless and motherless little ones immured in the dreadful workhouse, and exposed to the cowardly violence of the brutes to whom thoughtless or niggardly Poor Law Guardians abandoned the helpless. Passing, if his enfeebled constitution enabled him, through the sordid hope-quenching miseries of workhouse existence, he was sold by the overseer to some small collier-owner, or master chimney-sweep, to work through long years of so-called apprenticeship, with no human hand to shield or human heart to bestow a kindly thought upon him.

At best, life was cruel and unsympathetic for the young. No healthy amusement was tolerated. Relaxation of every kind was frowned upon as an evil thing. Repression was preached and practised by authority, however ignoble, and—like some quack panacea—prescribed for every human ill.[1] A mental darkness covered the face of the social world, and the wail of the children was drowned in the clamour of sordid strife and cruelty.

Yet in the deepest depth of the universal gloom, the lamp of culture, of purity, and of humanity was being tended and kept alight, its sweet radiance flowing out over the darkness with the promise of brighter days. Thoughtful men there were of all ranks and classes who, standing aside and looking on despondingly at the wrong-headedness of all the methods of dealing with a people and the seething corruption arising from it, in very hopelessness sought refuge from the sorry business in study, all the while wistfully scanning every suggestion or proposal for the betterment of things

---

[1] It was an era of flogging, and fine ladies, whipping their naked maids, thanked God that they knew their duty.

Of such, a small social group, a little band of Quakers, drawing to itself, by the subtle influences of unostentatious simplicity of character, singleness of purpose and intellectual and moral beauty, all that was best in the local society of the river-side, was already by brave example and dauntless advocacy leading the way to a higher plane for England's people. Quaintly in contrast with all that was going on around, these people were also unconsciously helping to found the taste for that newer and broader culture which, overflowing the narrow boundaries of "the Classics," deemed it no condescension to take some account of the great outer Universe. And so, the mild science of the century's first decade was placidly, and perhaps a little complacently, pursued. Geology was then passing through its early stage of mockery and ridicule, too much a weakling as yet to be anathematised. It was perhaps too early also, in the provinces, for chemical text-book wonders—for the "deflagration" of phosphorus or steel-filings in oxygen, or the "detonation" of fulminate of silver or mercury. Carbonic acid was still fixed air, and "phlogiston" had not yet been dislodged from the schemes of provincial amateurs. A "Tree of Diana," however, growing downwards in its blown glass decanter, might perhaps be seen on a parlour table; or a wire basket in unsymmetrical coating of alum crystals, or a collection of birds' eggs, or mosses, or autumn-fired leaves, be found on the side-board. Specimens of seaweed, floated out into extension on sheets of foolscap, and coaxed, with infinite trouble—and a pin—into symmetry, lay waiting for the advent of some profounder brother or sister, who would gravely pronounce and affix the generic, and, if he could, the specific names. Botany, with its limitless terminology and facile methods, yielded endless interest, as the close adjacent shores furnished the small beginnings which developed into systematic collections and studies in conchology. Cook's voyages, to what was yet by readers called Terra Australis, still excited wonder or scepticism, and Mungo Park's travels had yet to be written.

Pleasant and healthful the "reading parties" at which, from the rare magazine, the latest phase of philosophy, science, or *belles-lettres* was recited and afterwards sedately discussed. Being held in turn at the several houses of this gentle, cultured folk throughout the district, the Book Club and "Reading Party" promoted a community and breadth of interest and of sentiment which were precious indeed in their action on the northern community. No light matter at times was it to make attendance at these meetings, for in stormy weather the open sculler-boat, or the tilt-covered "comfortable," were alike unsafe on the squally Tyne, and intercourse between the harbour-towns was only possible by long circuitous drives over roads dangerously bad. Diligent correspondence with other groups of thoughtful men widened the knowledge and broadened the sympathies of these pioneers, as the wide humanity of a simple and generous creed facilitated intercourse with all who, from that higher bravery than the mere animal quality so profusely *en evidence* on every hand, had the courage to say and to do the right. And so the Reverend this, or Doctor that, the Unitarian minister, an army captain even, might be found *inter oves*, contributing his modicum of special knowledge to the general store.

The sweet serenity of this little community betokened no selfish— no epicurean indifference to the outer strife. The cry of poverty had long before called forth the benignant and healing charity of this people, who put out the hand to raise, not to degrade, the poor. Not for them the humbling dole or indiscriminate pauperising gift— indiscriminate, because lazy and careless; often the mere barter of an unneeded surplus for a period of salved conscience—but the sympathetic, sustained, and, above all, patient succour which fosters self-respect and promotes self-help in the recipient. The societies founded in that early day by "the Friends" are yet the model of all that is best in the systematic relief of the poor.

But men cannot live on bread alone. Out of the depths came, with a pathos all the more touching because not wholly articulate, the cry of the people, "lighten our darkness," and, with sweet sagacity, these thoughtful men and women saw that only in *that* light lay secular salvation.

But the time was inauspicious—the soil uncongenial. Sentiments about the "people" which in these latter days dare not be suggested on the platform or in the press, but which are reserved for the safe seclusion of the drawing-room, were then openly avowed and as tenaciously clung to as the utterances of the man of "common sense" ever are.

It was an open question among the war magnates of Shields whether education was a good thing for anybody, nay, rather the question was not open with the majority Let one of those cocksure gentlemen speak for himself In the autumn of 1802 a "respectable meeting of gentlemen and tradesmen (mark the careful differentiation) was held at the 'White Hart' for the purpose of establishing a public Subscription Library." Four years later, one thousand pounds having been subscribed, the foundation-stone of the building "was laid with great solemnity by William Linskill, Esq., High Sheriff of Northumberland," on a site overlooking the harbour, and anciently known as St David's Mount. "This structure," the local scribe quaintly goes on to say, "is placed in such a situation as to command one of the finest marine and *rural* views in the kingdom. A highly-gilt copper-plate enclosed in the first stone bore a Latin inscription, of which the following is a translation: 'Give the praise to God.' A special committee superintended the laying of the foundation-stone of this building *sacred to learning and the liberal arts*, on the 5th day of June 1806, in the 46th year of George the Third, King of Great Britain and Ireland. 'What is more grateful than Literary leisure?'"

The Library, known lovingly in after years as the "Old Library," replaced a mountebank's stage which had occupied the site so late as 1788—a change regarded, however, by no means universally as being for the better. The frowning, half-toleration bestowed upon the time-wasting clown turned to scowling distrust, nay, detestation, when the shelves of the edifice "sacred to learning" were being charged with their blessed freight.

"Men of Shields," bellowed one of the war-pagans, entering the room, "men of Shields! what business have *you* with any books but your ledgers?" What, indeed! echoed many of the *élite* of the day.

But if there was doubt as to the virtue of education for anybody whatever, there was no shade of doubt as to its being absolute poison for the "poor"; and there the coarse philistine who wanted no reading save that afforded by his ledger found himself on common ground with his "betters." Society, the governing class, Church and State, from motives variously stated, but always having the element of selfishness as a component, preached unceasingly against what was grotesquely called "the over-education of the lower classes"; *over*-education, forsooth!—and the bishop,[1] the judge, the minister, the diplomat, the lord, courtier, squire, and parson were as assured of the folly of this teaching of the "rabble" as—why, as of the absurdity of abolishing State lotteries, perpetual imprisonment, the law of *deodand*, or the pillory. Eloquently, and of course with

[1] One bright exception was to be found in the Bishop of Chester

unanswerable logic, its unwisdom was demonstrated as often as needed; but, reduced to its elements, the logic all came down to the *naive* retort made by the Shields shipowner when asked for a subscription to a charity school: "Eddicashin! eddicashin? Noa! we'll syun hev nee sarvints."

Yet none of these luminaries could plead that the opposite view, with its beneficent possibilities, nay, certainties, had not been fully set forth. When Whitbread, in 1807, called upon the country to support a plan of general national education, he proclaimed "that nothing can possibly afford greater stability to a popular government than the education of its people. . . . In the adoption of the system of education I foresee an enlightened peasantry; frugal, industrious, sober, orderly, contented, because they are acquainted with the true value of frugality, sobriety, industry, and order. . . Your kingdom safe from the insults of the enemy, because every man knows the worth of that which he is called upon to defend."[1]

But the government and the "classes" had no word to say on behalf of the education of the people; "it was left to go on as it might without a grant for more than a quarter of a century."

Some there were indeed—the clergy, notably—much busied with popular education; but all their busy-ness was to restrain, to hold back, the hand of the educator. They stood by the schoolmaster as Bumble stood by the porridge-cauldron, to control and limit the outgoings, and how effectively they worked may be appreciated when it is remembered that so late as 1829 Harriet Martineau could truthfully utter this grim sentence—" To this hour men are disputing about the order of religious education that shall be given, and insisting upon the right to communicate exclusively his own views while one generation after another passes off into outer darkness, and beings called human are, after leading the life of devils, dying the death of brutes."

The core of cores, the heart of the whole phenomenon, was the

---

[1] Canning, in 1816, said he "was satisfied that the foundation of good order in society was good morals, and that the foundation of good morals was education."

Mr. Peel, secretary for Ireland in the same year, said "it was the peculiar duty of a government that felt the inconvenience that arose from the ignorance of the present generation to sow the seed of knowledge in the generation that was to succeed."

Brougham, in 1835, spoke of "the intense *animosity* to education that was manifested when his proposals of 1818 were brought forward ' dread conviction that education would emancipate the great suffering class, and enable it, in some of its units here and there, to compete for the good things so tenderly cherished and conserved by the "educated." Hence, while Society and authority held an attitude of dead opposition to popular enlightenment, the great body of the *bourgeoisie* was either distrustful or heavily indifferent.

But brave men and women were at work leavening this dull, inert mass and, in the face of social inquisition, protesting what, like Galileo of old, they felt in their hearts,—that the world *must* move, that it *does* move, and perhaps no question ever more sharply divided a community into two hostile camps than this one of "lighting the darkness" of the poor. The one party, active in sympathy and invincible in the conviction of right, drew to it what there might be making for light; the other, armed with the crushing power of authority and of class-privilege, rallied the eternal forces of prejudice, selfishness, indifference, and stupidity.

The time was at hand for a trial of strength. The jubilee of his august Majesty George III. was approaching, and throughout England that monarch's dutiful subjects, with the two-fold object of displaying their loyalty and of finding for themselves the infrequent experience of a little relaxation, were bestirring themselves betimes to celebrate the event in the historic, that is to say, the customary, and therefore correct, way.

Whether for a victory, a royal birth, an accession, a jubilee, or, *mirabile dictu*, for a treaty of peace, public rejoicing found invariable expression in what was called a general illumination. Not a jot did it concern the heedless mob to whom for a time the conduct and control of the festivities were handed over, what the occasion might be. A time of unrestrained frolic spiced with mischief and destruction, with the charm of comparative impunity thrown in, was too good to be missed, and always met with a ready response from the rowdy element for whose delectation it appears mainly to have been devised. King Mob, indeed, constituted himself Master of the Revels, and rude and rough were his manifestations of displeasure for all or any who had the temerity to shirk what was deemed to be "duty to the king"

Athirst for a break in the hideous monotony of their lives, early morning saw toilers of every grade pouring in their hundreds into the long "narrow street"—each squalid alley and lane yielding its tributary stream—and filling every room of the shambling public-houses with a surging, striving, and shouting crowd, bent on the first business of the day, to wit, that of getting generously and gratuitously drunk as a preliminary to more serious manifestations of loyalty. Abundant to overflow is the provision of liquor; barrels of strong ale and kegs of rum being broached and emptied with magic celerity.

Jostling in dizzy confusion are morris-dancers, jugglers, dancing-bear men, fiddlers and hurdy-gurdy players, discordant brass bands, tipsy sailors, strident rogues bawling coarse ballads, quarrelsome pitmen, keelmen and carpenters, bands of rowdies charging through the crowded street, cheering, hurrahing, and shouting defiant imprecations mingled with noisy commonplaces of "loyalty" Banners and streamers dangle from clothes-lines stretched across the narrow-way; busy groups of men hurry over the preparations for roasting an ox or barbecuing a pig. From every crazy gallery or wharf overlooking the river; from every anchor-smith's, block-maker's, or boat-builder's quay wall is belched forth the din and smoke of small culverins and stumpy wide-mouthed cannon, rammed to the muzzle with double or treble charge, and fired with a red-hot iron rod. Off, on the river are hundreds of colliers with every scrap of coloured rag on board hung out and festooned from mast to mast; keels and wherries made smart with fresh paint, and decked out, like pitmen's brides, in all the gaudy bunting that can be begged or stolen; gilded barges bearing important river-side magnates off to civic banquets; pleasure-boats carrying enormous spread of white canvas, and pressed down to the gunwale with struggling freight of merry-makers. Down in Peggy's Hole, stately and complacent, is the big-bosomed frigate at her smartest, arrayed in a perfect nimbus of colour and breaking the panes of the adjacent houses with her heavy royal salute. Close by her, the narrow-waisted, wasp-like, tender-sloop, for once relaxing the chase, is in holiday garb, and fussily burning gunpowder. The press-gang to-day must lie low, and not even the preventive-service dare face the inflamed devilry waking up ashore Away, up on Pen Bal Crag Oswin's ruin is wreathed in white mist rising from the thudding ordnance in the castle-yard, and Clifford's Fort is lost in a bank of smoke from her pounding guns.

Din and clamour, fire and stench, increase the hurly-burly hour by hour, and manifestly the volcano, which is rapidly getting into full play, cannot be controlled but must burn itself out.

Up in the town householders are busily at work indoors preparing what is, in perhaps the majority of cases, an involuntary contribution to the day's crazed doings. In every window looking upon a street or lane—some say in *every pane* of each window—must be fixed and displayed ere nightfall a lighted "dip" or a smoking whale-oil lamp—a matter of no small expense in those days, though nothing to the cost involved in a failure to comply with the imperiously imposed rite. A fiery, excited mob, jealous of the slightest infraction of the rules and rites of the "King's day," parades the streets, and with angry zeal calls upon the dilatory or belated or rarer recalcitrant, on the pain of having every window in the house smashed, or even the dwelling itself fired, to "light up." And, as no manner of excuse or explanation is accepted, it may well be believed that very diligent solicitude is manifested to secure the safe working of the illuminating arrangements by an early hour. Nor is this outward sign of allegiance and loyalty demanded of the "better class" only. Every glazed aperture, whether of house or hovel, runs the chance of having thrust through it the end of a pole if behind it the smoking flickering token of deference is not seen. Glass being costly, almost a luxury, only the cheapest bottle-green quality was found in the poorer houses, and of that mostly the portion bearing a virid wart-like excrescence known as the "punty-mark."

As the day wears and evening comes on, lights by the thousand swarm out like fire-flies and gradually link themselves in long chains, lining out the terraces on the banks on either side of the river. The ships in the harbour reveal in stippled gold their spars and rigging, and the swirling tide glances and glitters with myriad-fold reflections. Huge bonfires, with screaming gangs of lads beating clouds of red sparks out of them, fill the sky with a lurid glare. And now King Mob is ready to beat his boundaries.

Down by the Docks the mad ship-carpenters have secured a booty of empty or half-emptied tar-barrels, crammed with shavings, chips and pine-knots, these are fired, and when ablaze, frantically and recklessly kicked along the narrow streets, down hill, up hill, it matters not, followed by a dense crowd of hoarse men and boys madly beating each other with flaming torches and, in the frenzy of excitement, dancing in the very flames. Street by street the procession passes on, the pole-men executing prompt vengeance on unlighted windows, amid the shrieks and howls of the drunken mob.

Here and there two gangs meet and fight wildly for possession of the flaming cask which promises to burn longest. New groups come up with fresh material, and so the mad orgies proceed until the supplies begin to give out, and the influence of unstinted drink gradually overpowers the noisiest of the revellers. The long filmy lines of light are breaking into ill-defined patches; the bonfires give out only pungent smoke; the scratch of the fiddle and drone of the bagpipe are silenced; the dancing, singing, fighting, and revelry in the drink shops has died down; here and there a few drunken celebrants stagger along, trying in a confused way to account for the irresistible depression that has overcome them, and which manifests itself in the melancholy howl with which they attempt the chorus of some sea-song they erewhile heard. The "Illumination" is at an end. Naught remains but candle-snuff, an evil odour of burnt oil and stale drink, and an intolerable burden on the air of sulphurous smoke. To-morrow the excesses of the "rabble" will be punished with a severity that would startle the world of to-day, and which owes some of its stringency to a certain irascibility manifested by the authorities, and born of an excess of the good things met with at the public dinners of the time

Such was an "Illumination," and in some such wise was celebrated the *Peace* (or armistice—for it was rather this) *of Amiens;* and possibly the experience was too fresh in men's minds to allow them to view with complacency any revival, in so short a time, of the Saturnalia.

Howbeit, in the Tyneside communities the wisdom of so celebrating the impending Jubilee was called in question by a few of the bolder advocates of education for the poor, who indeed went so far as to suggest that, possibly, it might be a better thing to devote the money, which was being subscribed, to the purpose of founding *Public Free Schools* for the people. Mark well —as was hurriedly explained in the same breath—it was to be education with a condition, perhaps more correctly, with infinite conditions; education limited and hedged in by a hundred safeguards and precautions; education, as it were, with the smallest possible "e."

With a quaint unconsciousness or unrecognition of the derivation of the word (not wholly absent in later days), education was regarded, not as an agency or influence directed to the out-bringing and development of qualities existing in the subject, but as a dangerous

NORTH SHIELDS.

potion, of potent though unmeasured toxic properties, needing to be experimentally administered in cautious doses; and, even among the friends of the movement, there was no full agreement as to how much of the active principle the prescription might safely contain.

At best, the "how much" could be but little, warm debate, all to the advantage of progress, however, being engendered between the advocates of little and of none. Probably no man had any honest objection to the abandonment of an "Illumination," nay, doubtless the counter scheme met with a certain gruff toleration as providing a respectful extinction of its rival,—but—"Eddicashin, eddicashin, what about our sarvints?"

While then, the question as to how much (or rather how little) of the poison might be adventured upon was being incessantly debated, GEORGIUS REX himself came to the aid of his disputatious lieges and decided the issue for them. His gracious Majesty signified, or was said to have signified, his desire that "*every poor child in the kingdom shall be able to read his Bible.*" Adroitly availing themselves of the spirit of patriotism and loyalty, the friends of popular education, holding fast by this expression of the Royal will, were enabled to carry their proposals at a public meeting of the inhabitants of the town, and the victory of "Light" over "Illumination" was won. Not, however, without much head-shaking and grave warning on the part of the men of "sound common sense" of the day.

Early in the year 1810 a committee of subscribers was elected, and on the 10th of June following the foundation of the *Royal Jubilee School*, North Shields, was laid;[1] and, a year later, the pale starveling "free education" made its small beginnings.

The scheme of the institution is set out in a poor, high-shouldered, narrow-margined circular, from a copy of which, now faded and yellow, it may be curious and instructive to quote.—

---

[1] "June 10th, 1810.—The foundation of a new Charity School, near the church, North Shields, was laid with great solemnity by John Scott, Esq, one of the magistrates for the county, assisted by William Linskill, Robert Laing, Esqs., and others The Rev. William Haswell (afternoon lecturer) then stood upon the stone and pronounced a benediction suitable to the occasion, after which he delivered an elegant oration. A brass plate with an inscription and several coins of the reign of George III were deposited in the stone."—*Sykes's Local Records.*

"JUBILEE SCHOOL.
"NORTH SHIELDS, *Sept.* 30, 1811.

"At a General Meeting of Subscribers towards the Establishment of a School for the Instruction of the Children of the Poor of this Town, and its Vicinity, held pursuant to public Advertisement, from the Committee appointed to superintend the building of a School in Lieu of an Illumination on the 25th of October, 1809,

JOHN SCOTT, ESQ., in the Chair,

"Resolved I. That as the School is now complete and ready to open; and this Meeting being convinced of the facility and economy of the improved British system of education on the plan of Mr. Joseph Lancaster,[1] concludes that the same be adopted"

Wise and well-weighed the resolutions that follow:—

That brave John Scott and other men of light—among whom are Spences, Richardsons, Taylors, Fosters, and Proctors—shall be president, vice-president, committee, treasurer, and secretary, as the case may be. That the "maintenance of the school shall be provided for by annual subscriptions," which, "however small, will be thankfully received and applied to the benevolent purposes of the institution," that "annual subscribers of half-a-guinea shall have the privilege of recommending one scholar; of one guinea, two, and so on in proportion," but that "for the present, subscribers are desired to recommend only one scholar each"—notwithstanding which, the first list of annual subscribers, printed in honest alphabetical order regardless of the amount subscribed, contains one hundred and fifty-eight names at a guinea each, nineteen at two guineas, one at five pounds, and ten only at the amount conferring the privilege of nominating a single scholar. That the committee shall attend on certain prescribed days for the purpose of receiving the children recommended. "These must be accompanied each by a parent or friend, who shall be informed that the children must attend the school regularly at the hours appointed, viz., nine in the morning, and two in the afternoon, and be always sent clean and decent, with hair combed, and face and hands washed; and that they will be required on the Lord's day, regularly to attend the

[1] The Joseph Lancaster and Dr. Bell systems were rival plans for "educating the poor," and respectively typify the aims and desires of the "how much" and the "how little" parties. Lancaster, identified with the Nonconformists, broadly speaking, advocated *more*, Bell, with the Church, *less*.

place of worship *which such parent or friend shall appoint.* Also, that when any boy leaves the school, due notice of it must be given by the parent or friend, on the Monday morning previous to his being taken away, when the committee will present him with a Bible or Testament, at their option, provided his conduct has been satisfactory and such as to merit approbation," etc., etc.

The combination of simplicity and formality in the phrasing of the prospectus is instinct with the sedate, quiet, and effective sympathy of the Quaker, and with his sterling recognition of the right of parent and friend to an unfettered choice in the matter of the higher influences under which the child is to be placed.

"That before the children proceed to learn in the morning, silence shall be observed, when a chapter in the Old or New Testament shall be solemnly and audibly read by the master, or, at his discretion, by one of the elder boys and the same practice shall be repeated at the close of business in the afternoon"

"That the school shall be *daily visited* by one or more of a Committee of six Governors,"—the qualification, evidently a privilege, "being an annual subscription of one guinea or upwards"

That an annual exhibition or examination shall be held, and prizes be distributed "to such of the children as shall have made the greatest improvement during the year, and whose conduct, attendance, and orderly conduct at school may have entitled them thereto"

That strangers "can only be admitted on Fridays from eleven to twelve o'clock, but for a short time after the school is opened it is particularly requested that strangers will postpone their visits to it until the *plan of education is somewhat matured* N B —Strangers visiting the school are not required to give anything, but should any person incline, a box is provided to receive whatever they may choose to give, the sums contained in which shall be strictly applied to the purchase of rewards for the children whose conduct renders them deserving of it."

Other resolutions provide, in the most guarded manner, for the proper government and conduct of the institution, and then come the "*Directions to be observed by the master.*"

He must attend punctually; must cause to be entered daily in a book kept for the purpose an account of the lessons performed by each class, and of the absentees from school, or from their respective places of worship on Sundays. To this end he must make out distinct lists of the children who are to attend each particular place of worship, and appoint one boy out of each list as an "*inspecting monitor of worship,*" who is to report to the master every Monday morning. He is to make a monthly report of attendance, work, proficiency, and of the rewards distributed, but—"fifthly, the committee do not desire to receive a similar account of punishments, in the ordinary course, but"—only of cases of incorrigibility, when they will—" cause a representation and remonstrance to be made to his parents or other friends, and in cases of great delinquency will expel him from the school."

And now for the *curriculum* :—

"*That the following Books be used in the School:*—
Lancaster's New-Invented Spelling Book.
. . . . Dictionary   do.
A Spelling Dictionary.
Watts' Hymns.
Scripture Instructor.
History of Christ in the Words of the New Testament.
Miracles of Christ.
Parables   do.
Discourses do
Sermon on the Mount.
Testament.
Bible.

And the Committee are recommended to cause some of the elder boys to be instructed in the art of navigation before they leave school."

From all of which it may be inferred that the Royal wish and its implied limitations, had received most loyal recognition from the majority of those responsible for the framing of the constitution of the new institution. The combination of the "art of navigation" with the slender "store of learning" arranged for in the meagre scheme perhaps grew out of a feeling that in such a town as Shields

" . . some are bred for service of the sea,
Howbeit, their store of learning is but small
For mickle waste he counteth it would be
To stock a head with bookish wares at all,
Only to be knock'd off by ruthless cannon-ball."

The educational course contemplated by the founders may, it is true, have been more ample, but, very clearly, any extension of the field of operations would have to depend upon chance, and upon the qualifications and aspirations of the dominie, which perhaps came to the same thing From him, at all events, no great danger of "over-education" was to be feared, for avowedly it was "not the intention of this institution to interfere with that useful class the *regular* schoolmasters," and as for their *irregular* brother, why he constituted a most innocuous class, whose qualifications, as varied as they were slender, cannot be more appropriately described than in the suggestive observation of a worthy and high-souled Tyneside Quaker,[1] himself one of the boldest of advocates for national education: "The only education I ever had in my youth was from a man whose sole qualification for keeping a school was that he was *lame*, and therefore disabled from making a livelihood in any other way." It is much to be doubted, though, that such was his sole title to the office; another he doubtless had, in virtue of which men could say of him—

> "He never spoils the child and spares the rod,
> But spoils the rod and never spares the child;
> And so with holy rule deems he is reconciled."

For probably the qualification regarded as most essential was that of the strict disciplinarian; the universal faith in punitive, and nothing other than punitive influences, inspiring even the teacher himself with the conviction that his principal function was that ingenuously avowed by gentle Tom Hood's "Irish Schoolmaster"—

"CHILDREN TAKEN IN TO BATE."

As for *educing* any good from human nature men, in the name of religion and experience, scouted the mere idea, and acted as though they believed that a tree instead of being allowed to grow because of the inductive effect of sunlight, should be forced out of the ground by a screw-jack.

On the 7th October 1811 the doors of the Royal Jubilee School were opened to a little, huddling flock of innocents, and, one Nicholas Jowsey having been appointed chief-flagellant, the small beginnings of a dubious experiment were adventured upon.

---

[1] George Richardson, of the Low Lights, whose ancestor, John Richardson, in 1766, "brought his wife and three children from Seghill to their new home near Shields. It is credibly reported that one horse carried the family! John Richardson had his eldest son Isaac on the horse before him; his wife Margaret on a pillion-seat behind him. His coat, probably still one of his mother's spinning, had long and capacious pockets. In one of these pockets was snugly ensconced a little John, and in another a little Margaret."—*Records of a Quaker Family.*

Some four years earlier, that is to say in 1807, was born—in one of the river-side houses of entertainment, which, forming a corner of one of the broader openings to the river, looked as to one of its gables into the busy, long "narrow street," and from the other on to the quieter but not less characteristic quay—the subject of this memoir. The child who was destined as a man to extend and expand the royal charter of this jubilee institution so as to cover a system of education for the children of the "town's poor," so beneficent, humanising, and effective, that his fellow-townsmen have thought the story of his life-work worth the telling The work was indeed all his own; for if he had not, at the outset and long after the active opposition of his patrons, the School Committee, he assuredly had little more than their good-humoured though hesitating toleration For years the sympathies of the general public— of even the parents of the children—were adverse, almost hostile, to the general scope and quality of the training he made it his duty to give to his young charges, and it was long before time brought them on his side. As for the equipment with which he set out, let us see what it was

His father, George Haswell, was a sailor, whose career, being in the main an epitome of the life of the Tyneside seafaring class, it may be worth while giving some short account of. Born in 1765, in the upper reaches of the river, he, at an early age, ran away from home and engaged himself as a carpenter at Sunderland Discovered by his father, he was taken back, only to adopt the course so common with Tyneside lads of running away again—this time to sea—and being sorry for it. "After a while," said he when an old man, "I set off again and travelled to Thorn, port of Hull, and bound myself to sea for six years with Robert Gildersdale, merchant and farmer, and traded between Thorn and London. Before my apprenticeship expired I once more ran away, and shipped on board a vessel bound for St John's Island, and in this vessel traded for three years from St. John's to New York."

In his twenty-eighth year, while "delivering" at Liverpool, mate of the *Friendship* of London, he married Alice Corlet, a native of the Isle of Man, and, sailor-like, shipped *next day* for Riga. On the passage home the vessel fell in with the frigate *Lizard* off the Mersey, and, in deference to a shot fired across her bows, was obliged to throw main-yards aback and heave to Soon a boat was seen to leave the frigate carrying an officer and a number of armed men, and it became obvious that the king was about to abridge the liberties of some of his subjects. The prospect of being pressed so near the end of their voyage, and only a few hours from their homes, so exasperated the crew that they declared to a man that they would not be taken out of the ship, and going below decks they set about arming themselves with cutlasses.

On arrival alongside the officer in charge of the frigate's boat requested the ship-master to muster all hands on deck, but being told that they were prepared to resist, ordered his men to draw their swords, go below, and bring up every man they found. The attempt was no sooner made than it failed, for as there was room only for one, or at most two, to descend at a time, the blue-jackets were quickly beaten back, and the officer saw that by persisting he must in any case lose a number of his men, and not improbably the whole of them, while he could not hope to carry off any of the crew. He therefore sent the boat back to the frigate to explain how matters stood, the ship-master protesting the while that it was illegal to take men from the ship while at sea. The boat soon returned bringing a carpenter's crew and tools, and the captain's order to "cut open the deck, all hands jump down at once and take the men dead or alive"

The work of cutting a way into the hold was set about with a will, whereupon the poor fellows below, recognising the hopelessness of further resistance, and having by this time reflected upon the prospect of being flogged, signified to the officer that they would "give in." Telling them that he could promise no terms, the officer carried them off to the frigate and there informed Captain Williamson of the ship-master's protest. To the surprise of all concerned not a man was flogged; a result due, it was suspected, to the doubtful legality of the proceedings.

But the ship hailed from Liverpool, and Liverpool was an important seaport, and the Liverpool shipowners, a powerful and influential body, were not prepared to brook such an outrage upon one of their number. An action was brought against the captain, and he was heavily cast in damages. Government also being appealed to, he was brought to court-martial and dismissed the service, and there the matter rested. In thus vindicating the claims of outraged justice one thing was strangely overlooked. The sailors who, in high-handed fashion, had been taken from their ship and transferred to a man-o'-war, were left there without redress or compensation, no explanation being tendered, no mention of them made save during the trial, when their evidence was required to secure the disgrace and punishment of the captain, who in this instance was clearly made a scapegoat of, his offence being simply that of venturing to deal out to a powerful body of shipping magnates the same treatment that he might with impunity have extended to less influential people. The impressed men, however, were left in the war-ship from which Williamson had been dismissed, and Rodney succeeded, for a time, to the command.

For three years George Haswell was in the *Lizard*, communicating, on the rare occasions that presented themselves, with his young Manx wife in long letters worked out laboriously in printed characters lest his cursive hand should be illegible to her. A thoughtful, humane, and intelligent man, he found much in the condition of his shipmates to set him pondering over the iniquitous circumstances under which their country demanded service of them. He found that an intense, unmitigated hatred of the navy was shared by every tar aboard, and that the one sleepless aspiration which animated each soul was to seize the first chance of escape from a dreary round of cruelty and inhumanity. A sense of unappeasable wrath smouldered in the breasts of men who yet dared not manifest the slightest sign of discontent, for a man might be flogged for even wearing a sullen expression, though it might be the outcome of some foul personal insult or outrage perpetrated upon him.

With wits sharpened by the extraordinary precautions taken to prevent escape, and by the not infrequent experience, as spectators, of the horrible punishment inflicted upon the miserable beings who made, and failed in, an attempt, the most unheard-of expedients were in desperation adopted by men attempting to regain freedom Prize-money, long overdue, was allowed by the authorities to remain due in the hope that the prospect of some day receiving it might induce those whose it was to stick by the ship; yet though the amounts were sometimes very large, they were always joyfully left behind when they might be successfully run away from

During the three years that George Haswell was in the *Lizard*, she took a number of valuable prizes, and a considerable sum thus became due to him; but, much as it was needed in such times as those, his heart, like that of all his mates, was set upon liberty, and he knew that some day he must stake more than his prize-money upon a desperate venture to gain it

The day came, and with it the venture. The story, often related in after years, and always exciting keen interest among the little circle of seafaring men who listened to it, was to this effect:—

The frigate, for some reason unknown to the hands, was anchored close in shore, on the coast of Ireland, on the outlook, it was thought, for a French privateer reported to be hanging about. Now, it entered the heads of George and a messmate that, the weather being fine and calm, it should not be an impossible thing for them to swim to the shore if they could but once get clear of the ship; and the more they thought of the enterprise the more feasible it appeared. From morning till night sentries paced the deck with loaded muskets ready to shoot down any one who should attempt to leave the ship without permission, and after dark the guard was doubled. If this threatened death, the flogging ensuing on failure was worse than death. Yet against all the fearful odds the two men made up their minds to take their chance. The plan of escape was to select a very dark night when there would be no moon, wait until midnight when all but the sentries should be asleep, then to lower themselves slowly and gently without noise or splash, from the port side into the sea, strike for the shore and, on reaching it, hide in the mountains (which could be seen from the deck) until the ship left the coast.

A favourable night coming they made the venture, and getting clear of the vessel, struck out for the shore. So far all had gone well, and they swam doggedly on, encouraged to hope that land would soon be found under their feet; but in time they began to wonder that they had not reached the sandy beach to which they had so often cast longing glances from the frigate's deck. No trace of it, however, could they find, though they swam on until the dread of exhaustion began to beset them. At length George told his mate that he could go no further, but must take his chance of regaining the ship, or be drowned, for he doubted whether his strength would hold out for many minutes. The other, being a stronger swimmer, strenuously urged him to persevere as they could not, he was persuaded, be far from land. George, however, turned, and with the little strength that remained to him made for the far-distant frigate, swimming alternately with one arm and resting the other. In a short while his messmate came tearing after him, swearing at their failure, passed on, and was soon out of sight of his comrade, who was too far gone to be able to speak. Striving on, however, he managed to get alongside the ship, but so "perished" with cold and exhaustion that he was just able, as a last effort, to seize the rope by which they had lowered themselves into the sea and hold on to it with his teeth. After resting a little time, he managed to climb unnoticed into the port-hole and get to his post undetected. What he suffered in his struggle to swim back was beyond his power to describe, but for the rest of his life he could not think of it without pain and horror.

Notwithstanding the risk and suffering and deadly disappointment, the other poor fellow tried hard to induce George next night to venture "once more," but nothing could persuade him to do so, nor did he, but his comrade made the attempt, and it was only after he had gone on his forlorn hope that George discovered what had brought failure the previous night, and what must of necessity bring it again.

Ships at anchor in roadsteads and tidal ways swing with the ebb and flood, and consequently present opposite sides to the land at each change. Now, none knew this simple fact better than these two A B seamen, but so full of their plan of escape had been their heads and hearts that this natural result of tidal motion, daily witnessed by them, wholly escaped their attention. Between dusk and midnight the frigate had swung with the flood and so brought her landward side round to the open sea, hence the poor fellows had been swimming out into the ocean instead of towards the sandy beach as they fondly imagined. No wonder the second attempt failed as the first had—though more tragically; for that the solitary swimmer perished there could be no doubt The two men had pre-arranged that whichever should first reach home must at once communicate with the friends of the other; but though George did so when he himself afterwards escaped, his unlucky comrade was never heard of after that fatal night.

After spending three weary years on board the *Lizard*, anxiously watching all the while for a chance to get away, he at last succeeded in effecting his escape at Portsmouth, leaving behind prize-money, kit, and all else that belonged to him.

Shortly after this he shipped on board a transport, sent to the Netherlands to bring home the defeated troops of the Duke of York. The winter was a severe one, offering in this respect certain advantages to the French army, enabling them to cross the frozen rivers and canals with great facility, and, ultimately, to drive the Duke and his men out of the country. In conveying the troops home George took what the doctors then called "a perishment of cold" which secured for him a written discharge, a document running thus:—

"*The bearer, George Haswell, A.B. seaman, has taken a perishment of cold, and must be landed in England as soon as possible for the benefit of air, exercise, and milk diet.*"

He was accordingly landed at Yarmouth, as the fleet passed along the East Coast, and left to find for himself the air, the exercise, and the milk. The two first he found in making his way, on foot, from Yarmouth to the Tyne, and the rest came when he gained his father's house whence he had, so many years before, run away. There is nothing very striking or amusing in the wording of the discharge, yet somehow, in after years, when an old man, the subject of it was wont to quote it so frequently, and in such sententious fashion, that the words "air, exercise, and milk" could never be heard by any of his family without causing a recital by one or other of the young folk of the whole passage. Giving one of his quiet smiles, the old man would say, "None of you would have thought it a joke had you been in my place."

"My next voyage," continues George's narrative, "was to Archangel, after which I wrote to my wife in the Isle of Man to come to me in Shields, which she did, but so great were the difficulties and obstacles to be encountered at that time in travelling, that the journey, made mainly in a carrier's cart, occupied no less than three weeks. I had already purchased a false protection, and by its means—though in constant dread of being discovered—succeeded in evading the Press-gang for the remainder of the war."

So it came that, three years or more after their wedding, the married life of the young couple began. A handy, industrious man, and a skilful "hand" in a boat, George took to the business of "foying," and soon was in possession of a few foy boats, in which much money was adventurously made when a good tide and a safe bar released the penned-up fleets of colliers, and created a sudden demand for the services of the hardy kedge-men who shared among them the work of towing ships to sea. Sometimes quite a golden harvest was gathered in a tide or two, and, though the life and habits of the time made against thrift, George presently saved sufficient to take one of the better-class taverns in the long "narrow street," and in honour of his Manx wife put up the arms of her native Isle as his signboard.

Under the roof of the "Three Legs of Man" came to him, all too quickly, a large family, demanding from him hard and incessant toil on the stormy reaches of the river; for he found the "Three Legs," as he jocosely put it, incapable of supporting them. Here in the midst of the strange medley of folk that surged about in the low town, his thoughtful, studious, and observant nature made him the friend and adviser of the harum-scarum tars who, not altogether to his advantage, sought his society. Self-educated above his class, he found companionship too of a better kind, as a little sketch from a letter written by one of his sons, nearly ninety years later, indicates.

"My father was always reading books on astronomy whenever he had the chance; moreover, there was an old-fashioned schoolmaster named Marshall, one of the mathematical teachers of that day, a *cangey*, cross-tempered, clever old man; in grey wig, grey small-clothes, and grey stockings. Well, this be-wigged old ill-twist was wont to come to the 'Three Legs' to visit my father, who was always glad to see him, and in a short time after his arrival the table between them would be covered with ellipses, parabolas, solar systems, comet's paths, ship's lee-way, plain sailing, departure, etc., etc.; a group of sailors looking on in wonder and amazement. When my mother wished to get quit of the 'old scorpion'—as she was used to call him—she would get a candle, light it, and when the wick was red, blow out the flame and allow the stinking smoke to rise up and fill the room. With a hasty 'Ah d—mn!' the old fellow, who had a peculiar detestation of the odour, would jump up and get outside of the house as quickly as possible, not looking in again for some days."

The old lady had accidentally discovered how she might smoke out the philosopher, who never suspected that he was the victim of a premeditated plan for getting rid of him.

Writing again in 1887, his son Thomas says:—

"On December 8th our club room was nearly filled with old and young friends of mine, met to celebrate my eightieth birthday I gave them an account of some of the many strange things which had taken place in my earlier time and, among other incidents, mentioned that I could remember being carried up the Ropery Stairs on my father's shoulders from the 'Low' Street to Dockwray Square to see the great comet of 1811, and that, though I was not then four years old, I could now draw its shape as then seen by me."

Thus early was the Shields sailor—not altogether consciously perhaps—training and fostering the most precious faculty of childhood—observation, and in his small way laying the basis of that better education which not a century's lapse has made universal. In after years, when he was old and infirm, children sought him as he sat in his arm-chair by a little round table—which always stood at his elbow to carry his book, long pipe and 'bacca—knowing that after a little interval of genial fun (he was an expert in the making and use of all kinds of toys) he would draw one of them to him, lift him or her on to his knee, and then taking from his pocket a piece of chalk, sketch out on the black surface of the table, in white lines, the concentric circles of the solar system, showing the earth and attendant moon, Jupiter and his four satellites, and Saturn with his tilted ring. Sometimes Jupiter, sometimes Saturn was the outermost planet, but he always explained that there was yet another, which, sweeping out his arm and looking round the room, he said would be "out there." The phases of the moon, the phenomena of solar and lunar eclipses, all had their turn, described in a style of delightful lucidity and interest. Sometimes the *séance* treated of Navigation, Geography, Natural History, or other subjects of boy-curiosity, but, invariably, it ended in a ravishing series of sketches of the incidents of *Æsop's Fables*, or the *Thousand and One Nights*, carrying the child-mind away on the wings of imagination and fancy.

The cares of motherhood and an unconquerable distaste for the business of an innkeeper on the part of his wife, led George to leave the "Three Legs," and also to abandon the fluctuating and uncertain avocation of "foying" for that of wherrying. The towns of North and South Shields were then supplied with coal brought in "keels" from the "staithes" to suitable landing-places on the river-side, and thence retailed by the cart-load or smaller quantity. On the north side were but three such places, the "Scarfe," the Limekiln Shore, and the Low Lights Shore, on which, besides the business of vending coal and other commodities, vessels were beached for small repairs, caulking, scraping, tarring, or "smoking"—the latter a summary process for ridding old colliers of rats and other vermin, by means of the fumes of sulphur burned in the hold after the hatches and other outlets had been hermetically closed.

"Now, my father," says his son Thomas, "had two such keels, and I have heard him say that he made a very comfortable living at this employment. The work though was rude and dangerous. One day, in taking an empty keel up to Wallsend Staiths to reload, the wind being unfavourable, he and his mate were compelled to use the oars, of which two are used in propelling this craft, one at the stern called a 'swape,' and the other at one side, a little for'ard of midships. The man helping my father on this occasion had only been a short time at sea, and for nearly all that short time on board a man-o'-war, from which he had been discharged as being of no use. They were just rounding Whitehill Point when the ebb came away, and with it a furious gale from the West, and, to complete the disaster, the man lost the swape overboard, thus, at one stroke, rendering them helpless. Having no anchor, the keel rapidly drove down midstream, through the 'narrows,' over the bar, and out to sea. As darkness was fast closing down upon them, it was unlikely they had been seen from the shore, and, as my father well knew, the chances of rescue were practically *nil*.

"The Tyne keel is decked only for a short length at bow and stern, and as the gale was hourly becoming more terrific (it was noted in the calendars many years after for its unusual violence), the danger of being swamped by the water breaking bodily over the craft was imminent, but they hoped they might be able to keep her afloat by means of a small hand-pump which they had on board.

"On the second day of the gale several tiers of ships in the Tyne were torn from their moorings and many small craft overwhelmed and sunk in the tideway. Every man on the river had his energies taxed to protect his property, and Shields was fully preoccupied with the work of salvaging the wreckage going on before its eyes. At length, however, some pilots informed the authorities that from the 'Lawe'—a point on the south side of the river's mouth—a keel with two men aboard had been seen by them to be driven out to sea two days before, and nothing, they believed, had been heard of them since. Of course this was long before the appearance of the steam-tug on the Tyne; however, the captain of the revenue cutter was applied to and, on being apprised of the facts, volunteered to put out to sea (if the gale had sufficiently abated) as soon as it should be daylight, and try to pick up the missing men.

"The cutter was out all the next day, and in the evening, just before dark, came into the harbour with the news that, although they had sailed fifty miles in various directions, nothing had been seen of the keel, indeed, the captain said, no vessel of the kind could possibly live with such a sea running as he had encountered, and he had no doubt whatever that she had foundered, and the poor men with her. But those who know the qualities of the Tyne keel will readily understand that in good hands she can weather almost anything at sea. To go back to my father; after driving helplessly out into the open, it became sharply necessary to find some means of preventing the craft from falling into the trough of the sea, in which case she would instantly fill and sink. Discovering two or three slabs of wood on board, they placed these first at one and then at the other side, and so in precarious fashion contrived to keep her head to the wind Well knowing the first-rate qualities of the keel when under canvas, my father gave his whole attention to the problem of stepping the mast and shipping the rudder; but the grave risk involved in making even an attempt in such a tearing sea was again and again made plain to him. It was a heavy task for two men, even in the smoother waters of the river, and an apparently impossible one under present circumstances; yet, attempt after attempt was doggedly persevered in, my father realising that the salvation of his man and himself from starvation or drowning depended wholly on an early success of these efforts. So, toiling on in unending essays, during which almost the whole of the second day had passed away unnoted, they suddenly, and to their great surprise (in one of the lulls which occur in the heaviest gales) succeeded. My father goes on to say, ' Having got the sail set I felt easier in my mind, but now gaunt hunger commenced its torments, neither of us having touched food for over thirty hours. My man Friday, poor fellow, was suffering severely, indeed he declared he could not live much longer, and I tried to cheer him by telling him I hoped to sight the land in the morning. I said this merely to revive his spirits, for he seemed like dying, but I had no means of knowing how far we were from the shore. I had seen, in the early morning of the second day, the Castle lights dipping in the horizon, which would make us about twenty miles from the land, but how far we had since driven it was impossible to judge. Presently we sighted to leeward a Scotch sloop going south, and I at once bore away for him Hailing him, I asked him to give me the course I had been steering, and to tell me how far we were from the coast His reply conveyed no comfort to us. He "did not know how far we were from the land, our course being no better than N.W. by W., but from the distance we were off we could make no land." Then in few words I made known to him our case, telling him this was our second whole day without food, and that in all probability another night and part of a day must pass before we could hope to land,—begged he would heave-to and give us something to eat and drink, for that we were suffering from thirst as much as from hunger. But he made no answer, filled his sails, and was soon out of sight.

"'All next night the wind neither shifted nor abated; clouds concealed the sky, so that I only saw the Pole Star two or three times, however, in the early morning, at daybreak, I had the joy of seeing land low on the horizon, and I called up Friday to look at it The sight caused the poor fellow to shed tears and exclaim that he had thought he should never see it more. Our hunger, thirst, and exhaustion had now become so unbearable that I resolved to run the keel ashore under the first human dwelling I could discern, and presently getting close in-shore near to a long stretch of sand I ran into a small creek, and, pulling out the plug in the boat's bottom, beached her. It fortunately happened that it was just past the flood, spring tide, so the keel was safe without other mooring for a fortnight.

"'Soon there came to us a farmer-like gentleman, to whom I related our circumstances. Desiring us to leave everything and try to walk up to his house, which was not far off, he went on, we with difficulty following him. Soon there was set before each of us a basin of warm soup, which we disposed of as by magic and asked for more. This, he said, would not be safe, and taking us to a room in which there was a good fire, he advised us to lie down for a while when he would give us some solid food After a night's rest under warm rugs I thought we might make an attempt to reach home. Driving us to Morpeth, this generous and hospitable man put us in the way to walk to Shields, and, giving me a few shillings to help us along, wished us God-speed I never saw him again.

"'The place where we landed is called Druridge Bay, some distance north of Cresswell Hall. The reaching of this spot from some thirty or forty miles east of Tynemouth Castle, almost in the teeth of the wind, justifies the high opinion entertained of the good sailing qualities of the keel; few ordinary vessels could have made such a course. The Scotch skipper, who said we could not make land at all, of course knew nothing of the vessel he was speaking of.'

"We had, indeed, given my father up as lost, though I, being a little fellow of but five or six, scarcely realised what this meant. On the fifth day of his absence, towards evening, while playing with some boys in the street, I was caught up in his arms, and he was soon kissing away at a fine rate; but he had soon to put me down, for a crowd had got round him, struggling to get a shake of his hand and of Friday's too. They both had a hungry, tired, and altogether strange appearance, and seemed glad to get away from the warm welcome of their many friends. When at home, my father commenced to change his clothes (which had not been off for five days), but so sluiced and saturated had they been with sea water, which the wind and sun had again and again evaporated, that the whole was incrusted in a thick coat of salt. He wore the ordinary costume of a Tyne keelman, namely, a longish cloth jacket and knee-breeches, and I remember that when, after many trials, he and I pulled the latter off, I set them up on the floor and they stood, of themselves, unsupported—which made us all laugh."

The little fellow of but five or six who played in the long "narrow street"—playgrounds for children were then undreamt of—could not fail to see much of the strange life of the busy seaport, of its violence, cruelty, pathos, and tragedy. His father, though an overworked, scantily paid, and therefore much occupied man, steadily gave him such l'arnin' as he himself possessed, no "schooling" being available; yet there were long intervals in which this education was suspended and when there was only *play* in the Low Street for the boy. And in the Low Street, therefore, he saw much that sunk into his young heart, and in after years gave him the key to many things that sorely puzzled others who had not themselves lived with and among the very poor. It was a precious seed-time, a time in which was sown and nurtured a wise sympathy for, and a deep, broad, loving comprehension of the lives of the humble, and of the inexorable limitations by which such lives are conditioned.

Some of his reminiscences afford a glimpse of the circumstances in which the seafaring class found itself early in the century.

"For long before I was born, and for many years after that important event, there always lay, moored close to the Sand-end, only a few yards from where the Fish Quay now is, either a frigate, a cutter, sloop, or tender. The cutter (Revenue) was supposed to be looking after smugglers and other such *amphibia*. It was not at all known what the frigate was after She was an imposing-looking vessel, always of a beautiful model, smartly rigged, with not a slack line to be seen, every rope as taut as a fiddle-string, decks as white as snow from frequent scrubbing and washing. No vessel of any kind was allowed to lie near her. On each side was an accommodation ladder with knotted coloured ropes, a marine or sentry standing at the head to present arms to all who went ashore or came aboard from the officers' gig. These gangways were for officers only; ladies, when they came, being boussed up in a chair with a tackle from the main yard, hauled on by the tars on the main deck and governed by the boatswain's whistle. On board, in most cases, was a fine full band, whose chief duty was to play on the quarter-deck while the officers were at mess.

"Every evening, a few minutes before sunset, the boatswain's whistle would be heard, when on all the masts was instantly seen a crowd of tars racing up to the top-gallant yards which had to be struck and sent down before dark; and keen rivalry was manifested between the different sets of men to accomplish this the smartest and quickest.

"On a fine summer's evening hundreds of people assembled on 'the Banks' to witness this evolution No sooner was the sunset-gun fired than, to the sound of the boatswain's whistle and the rattle and piping of drums and fifes, the three top-gallant yards would, in an instant, be seen to change from a horizontal to a perpendicular position, and in less than half a minute be on deck, sailors as well and, just as before the flurry began, not a slack line to be seen,—the whole thing being done as by magic The band in fine evenings played for an hour or so afterwards.

"No one understood the movements of the frigate. She would leave the port suddenly, and sometimes not return for a long while; at others she would come back after a day or two and remain in harbour for several weeks.

"The cutter was a small, one-masted craft, carrying an enormous amount of canvas for her size, which enabled her to chase and overhaul the smuggler or other vessel suspected of cheating his Majesty of the duty on a cigar or bottle of Jamaica. As to the tender,—

> 'The tender-ship, said Sally Brown,
> What a hardship that must be,'—

she was more obviously concerned with the press-gang; and of the press-gang I can just remember a dozen or fifteen fellows, armed with heavy cutlasses,—which they were free to use,—skulking about the Low Street, looking up entries and passages for sailors hiding in the so-called Englishman's 'castle.' If any poor tar were caught out of his ship these fellows would pounce upon him and away with him to the tender, whence, after a sufficient number of captures had been collected, he was, with them, sent off to the navy. And it might be years ere any of them were seen or heard of again by their families, if at all. Masters, mates, and apprentices were said to be protected from impressment when ashore on ship's business; but then, masters and mates had no business on shore at the same time, and 'How do we know that you are a mate at all?' In case of doubt, away to the boat with him and off to the tender! Men were often dragged out of their homes, which, of course, could never have been legal; but what could a poor sailor, in such case, do?"

THE OLD TYNE KEEL.

CHAPTER IV.

L'ARNIN'.

N 1815, when the long war was about to culminate in the throes of Waterloo, this small boy of eight, the future dominie, found his way to the Jubilee School, there to stay for the short term of two and a half years, and thence go out into the world to work. Let him in his own way describe what he knew and what was taught him.

"I could read the Bible very well for a boy of my years, which, indeed, was all that was then deemed necessary to constitute a scholar. Nothing else, at all events, had been attempted. No writing; no arithmetic; no grammar; no geography had I ever heard of. But about this time the two first were added, the three subjects (the renowned three R's) being driven forward at a pretty rapid rate, followed closely by, not a Manx cat, but one with the orthodox nine tails, which seemed to have discovered the long-sought perpetual motion. For it never ceased during school-hours, but indeed made itself evident to all our five senses; and we could see, feel, hear, taste, and even smell it from morning till night.

"Scripture lessons, such as the miracles of Jesus Christ, the parables, and some of the psalms of David, printed in large type and pasted upon flat wooden boards about two feet square, hung from pegs on the walls, and round these standing, hands behind back, in a semicircle, the class of a dozen or more boys, turn by turn read a portion, or, failing, were helped by the monitor (himself only one of the older boys), who, pointer in hand, stood at the head of the class.

"A few Bibles and Testaments, and some easy spelling-books, constituted the whole of the reading stock.

"Writing was taught to beginners on *sand;* wooden styles, or the finger, taking the place of pens, and a 'smoother' being used by the monitor to efface the rude efforts of the learner and prepare a fresh surface for him.

"More advanced pupils had ruled slates, but writing-paper was never seen The 'four simple rules' of arithmetic were all that it was deemed advisable to teach the classes, though it was supposed that the monitors were privately advanced to the compound rules.

"At each 'opening anniversary' was held a public examination of the scholars, which, however, was rather an exhibition of the method by which a hundred boys could be taught by one man. On one occasion, I remember, after some chapters of the Bible had been read by the barefooted, ragged little lads in that sing-song, monotonous way familiar all over the world to teachers of children (but at that time not unpleasing, by reason of its novelty), we showed our writing on slates, which was very good indeed, and then proceeded to work sums in the simple rules So quickly and correctly were these done that some of the assembled company openly expressed alarm, and the chairman was obliged to explain that these boys were to be advanced no further, and that, in fact, they were on the point of leaving school to go to work, having *finished their education*. Only this qualifying assurance prevented certain of the half-hearted patrons from withdrawing their subscriptions"

It is a strange picture of hesitation, doubt, and apprehension; all being done, as it were, with bated breath. At these anniversaries the town's-people attended in numbers, some of them "friends of education," some not friends, many avowed enemies; but all drawn irresistibly to look on with something of fascination at an experiment which might develop a hundred fateful results.

Getting then such "education" as was afforded by this meagre *curriculum*, the little fellow was taken from school—the common case—ere he was eleven years old, to go to work; first to help his father in his boat on the river, then, at twelve years of age, with a man who in a small way was a maker of watch-crystals

"My business was to grind the roughly-formed glasses on a metal plate with emery and cold water, not a warm job in winter time.

"One day while the master, two men, and an apprentice two or three years older than myself, were all grinding away making a humming, and not unpleasant sound, though loud enough to drown the sound of conversation, my master called out—

"'B-o-y!'

"At once the wheels ceased, and with them the noise.

"'B-o-y! go and tell your mistress (never "Mrs." in Shields) to put a bone in the fire'

"Now I had not long before become acquainted with the hoax played upon unsuspecting lads of sending them into a chemist's shop to ask for a pennyworth of the 'oil-of-hazel,'—hence I at once came to the conclusion that this was a joke of the kind, and of which I was to be the victim; so I stood still, looking at him. Happening to turn his head, and see me still standing inside the door, he bawled out at the top of his voice, and with a volley of oaths (for he was a fearful swearer), 'What the —— are you standing there for?'

"'Did you say *bone*, sir?'

"'*Bone, sir* (mimicking me), I'll bone you!' cried he, reaching forward to some glass globes, seeing which I slipped out of the shop, and, pausing outside, heard him remark to the man who worked next to him—

"'By G—, Smith, it's amazing the amount of ignorance there is in the world. Here's a boy close upon twelve years old, and he doesn't know what a bone is!'

"There he was entirely wrong; I was much better acquainted with bones than with flesh, for, being war-time, every article of food was heavily taxed, great destitution prevailed, and flesh meat was seldom seen in the homes of the poor. However, my first impulse was to give the job up and go home, but reflecting that this would be cowardly I resolved to risk the mission and run for it should the mistress manifest any intention to apply the oil-of-hazel. Away therefore, I went across the street, up two pairs of stairs, and listening for a moment, heard the good woman taking up the cinders. 'Now,' said I, 'she has the coal-rake in her hand ready to let fly as soon as I play my joke': so I put my head a very little way into the half-opened door and shouted rather defiantly, 'Master says you are to put a bone in the fire,' and then sharply drew back. But instead of the coal-rake there came, in mild tones, 'Very well, hinny; all right.'

"This confounded me more than ever; however I got back to the shop, slipping quietly in without being noticed.

"When the men went to dinner I said to the apprentice—

"'William, why did that madman send me to his wife with such a foolish message, and what made her reply "all right"?'

"'There was nothing foolish about it, and it *is* all right.' Then he explained that the last process applied to the crystals was to polish them with calcined bone, reduced to powder by first heating and then crushing it to dust,—'to-morrow you will have a chance of seeing why you were sent to ask the mistress to put a bone on the fire.'

"The grinding business not lasting long, I was next employed as errand-boy at a grocer's, and for some two years enjoyed the privilege of working excessively long hours for eighteenpence per week.

"In 1823, at the age of fifteen, I was bound apprentice for six years to Mr. John Park, Master Painter."

His life now became one of extraordinary activity and application;

for, with an insatiable longing for the acquisition of knowledge—a passion which never abated up to the last hours of his long life—he had the work of acquisition all before him. Chances and opportunities were few indeed, but never chance nor opportunity was missed Every clue, however slender, leading into the labyrinthian paths of knowledge was seized and followed up with an eagerness and tenacity of purpose that nothing could shake.

Entering the choir of Christ Church, he acquired a complete knowledge of vocal music The choir-master, Thomas Oxley, a fine old worthy with an unquenchable passion for music, took an immediate interest in the young recruit, and gave him every opportunity for pursuing his studies that a scanty leisure afforded. Oxley, himself a *quondam* journeyman painter, combined the duties of parish clerk with those of choir-master. "He possessed the most charming voice I ever heard—a baritone of unusual compass, its quality of surpassing sweetness, power, and expression." It was, at that time, the custom at funerals for the clerk to sing two or three verses of a psalm, and music being a sacred matter with the old teacher, it was a delightful thing to hear his beautiful voice swelling out in devotional fervour as he sang the "Old Hundred," or "Rockingham," or some other of the lovely old "tunes" that the modern hymn has disfigured or displaced, and wayfarers, seeing him, left their present purpose to follow on into the quiet and empty church, where in rapt silence, and not seldom with tears in their eyes, they listened to the echoing strains of his lonely requiem In his little, heavily-eaved cottage near the churchyard gates, long after the day's work was done and far into the night, Oxley coached his young pupil in the mysteries of the *Sol-fa*, their vigorous *Solfeggi* ringing out on the night air, and bringing the passing and marvelling stranger to a pause as, looking uneasily over towards the dark, uncanny graveyard, he wondered—

"Where should this music be? i' the air, or the earth?
It sounds no more. . . .
       . . . 'tis gone.
No, it begins again"

"Soon after entering the choir I commenced the study of harmony, at that time called 'Thorough Bass.' Mr. Oxley presented me with a copy of 'Corfe's Thorough Bass,' an excellent work, and one which I so much delighted in studying that, for years after, I carried the book about with me on all my journeys to London and elsewhere."

But long before this unheard-of, overwhelming present (the book cost half-a-guinea) was made, the young pupil had copied out, in a beautiful, fluent hand, the whole of the contents of Corfe's work, and noted a number of errors into which its profound author had fallen. The old book still exists, a long folio published at ten shillings and sixpence, its florid title-page, embellished and ornate with flourishes and scrolls, running thus:—

"Thorough-Bass Simplified, or the whole Theory and Practice of Thorough-Bass *laid open to the meanest capacity*. . . . With exercises from the compositions of Handel, Corelli, Geminiani, Tartini, Sacchini, etc., etc., by Joseph Corfe, Gentleman of His Majesty's Chapels Royal, etc., etc."

Bound up with the volume is a queer old set of Ballads (graced with as many flourishes as the specimens of a writing-master) by Santi, Anfossi, Paesiello, Kozeluch, Sacchini, Sterkel, and others, associated with the nakedest of accompaniments for "*piano*," or "*piano e cembalo*," consisting of the melody, a thinly "figured bass," and a very occasional third to the treble furtively peeping in —in the smallest and timidest of character. There is also a collection of Sonnets called the "Hours of Love, containing Morning, Noon, Evening, and Night, composed by Joseph Hook, properly adapted for the Voice, Harpsichord, Violin, German Flute, or Guitar." Nothing could more surely indicate the feeble character of the general musical taste of the time than these quaint, tinkling, inept old things. Most manifestly they were arranged with an eye to the "old rule given to Thorough-Bass players," quoted approvingly by Mr. Corfe, and running thus—"the right hand should be kept as much as possible in one position, but if an agreeable and elegant melody can be gained," he goes on to say, "by sometimes moving the right hand not more than a fourth, I see no reason why such a liberty should not be taken."

On an early page, treating of *Consecutives*, is written in a youthful hand, "the author has fallen into the very error he wished to avoid; in proof of this observe where this mark occurs," and in two places in the same exercise are seen flagrant infractions of the rule there expounded by the author. Here and there are marginal discussions of the true nature, root, or derivation of some of the remoter chords, as to the propriety of the use of which, in any case, the gentleman of his Majesty's Chapel is in sore doubt, protesting in a perturbed way against over-indulgence in them by "modern writers," such as Haydn! "This terrific chord," says he, "is often introduced by modern composers in their Instrumental Music, particularly by Haydn, Mozart, etc.; but as it expresses no sentiment, and only causes a GREAT SHOCK, the mind is by no means so satisfied as when in vocal music it heightens the idea. *For, as the late Mr Harris observes, Music when alone can only raise affections which soon languish and decay if not maintained and fed by the nutritive images of Poetry, for here a double force is made to co-operate to one end.*" A passage sadly lacking a Q.E.D. !

How the mighty Beethoven had fluttered the souls of these precise old square-toes could they but have crossed his path !

"It was during my connection with the choir that I first became acquainted with the compositions of the fine old English anthem writers, with the immortal 'Messiah,' 'Israel in Egypt,' 'Judas Maccabæus,' and the delightful 'Creation.' In the study of these classical works we were encouraged by the Vicar and his family, who were devotedly attached to the music of the Anglican Church. Two of his sisters had been pupils of Dr. Greatorex, whose anthems were on our list, and one of them was a fairish organist."

Oxley's standard of excellence was an exacting one—his training rigorous and stern. In summer-time the choir practice was held in the church at six o'clock in the morning, and as the organist could not be induced to attend at such an unheard-of hour, the singers had a hard and wholesome drill at the hands of the testy old master. The whole of the music was manuscript, for at that time the heavy cost of printed anthems and oratorios placed them entirely out of the reach of all but cathedral and other leading choirs Pilgrimages, therefore, were made—piously and laboriously—to Durham, or York, or Beverley, where the privilege was craved of being allowed to copy out some treasure in the way of a new anthem, or service, or kyrie, or chant, by some noted contemporary composer; and the veneration in which such copies were held may be estimated from the perfect state of preservation in which they came down to later years, notwithstanding their continual use at the numerous choir practices and services of the church.

At the age of sixteen, young Haswell joined a "military"[1] band then being formed in the town. Such bands were then something of a curiosity in country places, and their instrumental equipment of

[1] *I.e.*, "Brass" and "reed" band, not necessarily connected with the army.

a very elementary kind,—such, indeed, as to confine within extremely narrow limits the range of their operations.

"My first instrument was the 'common bugle' with a compass of *five* notes!—from middle C to G above the treble stave. Soon, however, I was promoted to the 'plain trumpet,' compass ranging from gamut G to G in alt.

"After playing this instrument for some time we acquired a complete set of new instruments and obtained the services of a retired army bandmaster who had lately settled in Newcastle, one of the most accomplished musicians I ever knew. At his first lesson he appointed me to the 'keyed bugle,' just then invented and soon after a favourite solo instrument. I now felt a strong desire to learn some of the others, the trombone in particular, and after a while experienced little difficulty in attaining proficiency on all the 'brass,' though I had not yet attempted the 'reeds.'

"About this time there appeared in the streets of our town a well-dressed stranger, playing very finely on the clarionet. Though he neither spoke to any one nor asked for alms, he took with a silent bow anything that was offered to him. At Eastertide it was customary to hold races on Tynemouth Sands, and a 'hoppin' in the village. On one of these occasions, our band, followed by an enormous crowd of people, marched down to Tynemouth, playing most of the way. On arriving at the tents on the Sands we laid down our instruments and went for a stroll on the beach. Returning after a while, we were surprised to see walk in among us the strange clarionet-player, whom, by the way, I had observed among the crowd when we were marching.

"'I would like to speak to your leader,' said he.

"'I am the leader, sir,' responded our recognised chief, stepping forward. The stranger looked at him for a moment, shook his head, and replied—

"'Indeed, you are not;' then turning round and taking me by the shoulder he continued to address Scott—'I daresay you think you have been leading the band, but this young man has, and without the leading instrument. I advise you members of the band, without hesitation, to appoint him at once.' Then to me—'You must begin at once to learn the clarionet, you will soon master it, and then will be in your proper place, and the band all the better for it,—Good day,'—and we saw him no more.'"

A few weeks later Haswell, by unanimous choice, was made bandmaster, and setting about the task of learning to play the clarionet in a short time overcame most of the difficulties, and eventually became an accomplished player. The conquest of the bassoon and other reeds was also undertaken and achieved.

"Mr. Totton, our teacher, came down from Newcastle once a week, and, when introducing a new piece, brought each man's part in manuscript on a slip of paper. The music was then copied into the band-books, and the slips being considered useless were thrown away. But I carefully collected them, and found that in studying the art of arranging they were of great value to me, as the following incident will show.

"On one occasion the French-horn players came to me and said they had lost the slip containing their part, could I write another? I told them I would try. Got on very well until within a bar or two of the end of the march (a fine slow march), when I found the harmony such as to require notes not to be found on the horns. In vain did I try all the inversions of concords and discords; nothing would do—and the next bar was in the same case. Here then, for two bars I was unable to give these poor fellows a single puff! There was nothing for it but to await the next visit of our teacher. But to make matters worse a note reached us saying we were not to expect him until the following week as he was going from home. Nearly a fortnight's suspense for me to endure! Well, the day of his visit at length arrived and he came. After the usual greetings I told him that the horn parts of the new march had been lost, and asked if he would be good enough to write another copy. I had a piece of music-paper ready for him. 'With pleasure,' said he—'bring me the bass part.' Sitting down he commenced writing away as fast as he could make the pen go. I had my own arrangement in my hand, and was delighted to observe, as he went on, that what he wrote was note for note identical with it. As he approached the mysterious two bars I could feel my heart beating with excitement. I watched him eagerly as he reached them, and saw him without a moment's hesitation dash down—*two bars rest!* Now, although I was proud to find that I had been right in my conclusion that the horns could not play in the two bars, I was not a little vexed with myself for having overlooked the simple expedient of making them rest. Of course I was quite inexperienced in the work, but still it chagrined me greatly to have missed so obvious a solution of my difficulty. I told Mr. Totton how puzzled I had been, and showed him my arrangement with which he was much pleased, for knowing I was studying the subject he often gave me valuable advice. He then said that to know when to silence an instrument was a highly important element in the art of arranging—not merely when the instrument could not take the passage, but when it could and might be employed—for to silence some of the parts for a time added much to the general effect, and he cautioned me not to forget this.

"Two years before I was out of my time—that is to say, in 1826—

Parliament was dissolved, and the business of a General Election fiercely entered upon. Northumberland was then represented by two members. The polling took place at Alnwick, and ran over fifteen successive days Railways had not yet been dreamt of, and the work of conveying the voters to and from the remote little county town was not the least of the difficulties that beset the committees. From Shields, the usual plan was to send them by steamboat to Alnmouth, a small village on the coast some six miles away from Alnwick The candidates were four, two Whigs and two Tories—Lord Howick, son of Earl Grey, T. W. Beaumont, of Bywell; H T. Liddell, son of Lord Ravensworth, and Matthew Bell, a colliery owner[1] Each candidate had his band or bands, and ours was engaged in the interest of Mr. Liddell We had been playing in Shields each evening from 7 to 9 for some weeks past (finishing with a nice little supper) when, one day, the committee sent word to us that a steamer was going next morning to Alnmouth with voters, and that if we cared to take a holiday—returning in the evening—it might be a treat for us; the boat in any case was to be paid for. As we had quite recently acquired a rather startling uniform and were anxious to display it, we gladly accepted the offer. The costume consisted of a bright scarlet Turkish jacket brought down in two points in front ending in long tassels, braided with white cord down both lapels, the seams of the back, and round the cuff; a scarlet belt secured by a large brass star in front; white trousers; a Turkish turban—also scarlet—with a black feather, the leader as a mark of distinction showing a white one. It may easily be conceived that the townspeople hailed with exuberant manifestations our martial and oriental appearance, as with waving plumes and brass instruments shining like burnished gold we marched down to the quay. The committee were in raptures and thought the election won. After a pleasant run down the coast we landed, and were received by the landlord of the inn, who announced that the committee had ordered dinner for the band and voters, and that it was 'quite ready if we were.' Running down the centre of a long dining-room was a table decorated with large bouquets and resplendent with cut-glass decanters, cutlery, china, etc. There were many kinds of wine, bottles and tankards of ale, stout, etc; hot and cold joints, fowls and game, and to this unwonted feast we were pressed by the landlord to sit down. We had brought with us but three or four voters and these had gone to dine with friends, so that we were left alone in our glory. Our seats we took, indeed, but opposite no dish cover was a man to be seen, nor at the head or bottom of the table could any one of us be induced to post himself, notwithstanding the polite expostulations of the landlord. At length one of our older members spoke up and explained that we were none of us accustomed to deal with

---

[1] 1826. An exuberant joiner, for disturbing the congregation of St. Nicholas Church, Newcastle-on-Tyne, by shouting "Bell for ever," was *put into the stocks*.

joints such as these; that though we could play upon musical instruments it by no means followed that we could venture to carve—would he therefore kindly take the head of the table himself and allow one of his waiters to take the bottom, and so relieve us? If so, we should be grateful to him. He consented, and we made an excellent dinner. While strolling afterwards on the beach the landlord, who was with us, called our attention to two carriages, each drawn by four horses, coming dashing up to the village. In the first was our candidate and friends; the second was empty. Drawing up in line to receive them we played our election tune, for each candidate appropriated to his interests a particular one, which, during the election, was recognised as sacredly as his colours. Ours was 'Because he was a bonnie lad'; Howick's, 'Buff and Blue'; Beaumont's, 'The White Cockade'; and Bell's, 'The bonnie pit laddie'

"Complimenting us highly upon our playing and appearance, the gentlemen went aside in consultation, and then one of them, approaching, said that the Hon. Mr. Liddell would be much gratified if we would consent to go to Alnwick for a few days, and that, as no voters were going that day, we might have the use of the carriages. We pointed out to him that the committee in Shields had stipulated for our return that same evening, to which he responded that the candidate would take the responsibility. In the end we jumped in, went off at a gallop, and in half-an-hour were playing away at our hardest in front of the hustings, amidst crowds of shouting and struggling people. The hustings was a rough wooden structure with four rostrums projecting from the front, from which the candidates spoke. Each day the poll closed at four o'clock, and a statement was at once posted by the returning officer showing how the numbers stood. The candidates were then expected to address the mass of people surging and swaying in front of them, priority being allotted to him who that day happened to stand highest on the poll This matter of speaking every day for a fortnight was nothing to those with the 'gift of the gab,' but a bitter affair to those who had it not Liddell was eloquent and powerful; Beaumont jocose; Howick sulky and taciturn; but Bell—poor fellow—was nothing;—had next to nothing to say, and never knew how to say it. A burst of derisive laughter from the crowd greeted every sentence, and it was painful to look at his face and note his mental suffering.

"Though there were but four candidates, there were many more than four bands, some having as many as three or more Now, at the close of the poll each day the whole of these bands met at the hustings and with one accord played their candidate's tune as noisily as possible. Sometimes ten or more bands were thus engaged in the work of creating an uproar, the drummers in particular appearing to regard this part of the proceedings as specially theirs, and making the din as outrageous as possible.

"But if the music was not altogether harmonious, no more could be said of the speeches of the candidates and their friends. Discourteous and insulting passages were hurled from one to the other in unstinted quantity, and greeted with yells of delight by the one party and groans and execrations by the other. The pleasure of seeing not one but three or four regular 'mills' going on at the same time was always to be indulged in without payment, and, as the people at large invariably manifested infinitely more interest in these 'little events' than in the hustings twaddle, it became a recognised matter of *etiquette* for a speaker to stay the flow of his discourse until they were satisfactorily pulled off. Those on the hustings were no whit better than the mob in front of it. Mr. Beaumont one day passed his card to Lord Durham with a request for his lordship's in return This was immediately given, and both gentlemen at once drove off to their respective committee-rooms to be seen no more that day.

"No morning papers at that time! A hand-bill was issued during the forenoon of the next day stating that Earl Durham and T. W. Beaumont, Esq, had, at an early hour, had a hostile meeting in a field near to Bamburgh Castle. Neither gentleman had sustained any injury, but the honour of both had been perfectly vindicated. Furthermore, having shaken hands, both would appear on the hustings as usual. The thing produced nothing but mockery and derision on the part of the people; it, however, gave ample employment for days to the squibsters and cartoonists, who poured pitiless ridicule upon all concerned. Whether, as is probable, they unduly exaggerated the circumstances does not greatly signify, but it was securely ascertained that both Lambton and Beaumont were more dead than alive when on the field of honour. Beaumont braved the ridicule of the mob at his first appearance after the fray, taking a pinch of snuff and laughing heartily at some uncomplimentary reference to the 'battle of Bamburgh Castle'; but Durham, who was a proud, overbearing, though sensitive man, suffered so severely from the coarse jeers and banter of the crowd that he seldom afterwards came to the front of the hustings."

After a week's exciting experience of the uproar, horse-play, riotous extravagance, and shameless bribery to be witnessed on every hand, the band left the scene of the contest, and got back by steamer to Shields.

Up to this time scarcely anything beyond a plain quickstep or slow march was available for bands and orchestras away from the greater centres of population, and, though not a few of the provincial amateurs, here and there, excelled in execution and style—being carried off to take part in competitions or contests between professionals of the army bands—little else had been written for them. "I therefore arranged several of the standard glees of the day, such as 'Hail, Smiling Morn,' 'Life's a Bumper,' etc., choruses and airs from Handel's and Haydn's oratorios and Mozart's masses, a class of music hitherto played only by the crack bands of the Line; and the zest and interest displayed in them, not merely by the public who listened, but by the performers, was of the greatest service in promoting and encouraging the practice and study of the different instruments, and in improving the execution of the band as a whole."

"During his apprenticeship," says the grandson of the master-painter to whom he was bound, "young Haswell was often engaged in work in the country, and then for convenience lodged as near to 'the job' as possible. Lodgings not always being easy to obtain, the gang of painters were sometimes obliged to occupy a single large room. On one such occasion the son of the landlord of the house in which Haswell and his fellow-daubers stayed was such another musical enthusiast as himself. Never was a pair better met,—music their perpetual theme! The twain lay in the same bed, and even there carried on, far into the night, an animated discussion of the eternal topic, to the great annoyance of the others in the room who wished, and were trying, to get to sleep. Sometimes, after language was exhausted in the praise of some piece, nothing would suffice,. forsooth, but they must get out of bed to *try it over;* and, as one of the party used afterwards to say, to see the pair in their shirts playing by candle-light with unspeakable delight, wholly unconscious of the severe objurgations showered upon them, was an experience not to be readily forgotten. No day's work, however long and hard, was long and hard enough to keep the student from his beloved music."

But a new craving was beginning to assert itself.

"During my apprenticeship, and while one of Mr. Oxley's choir, we met, during the summer, every Sunday morning at six o'clock for practice. Organists then were few, numbering in Shields only one, a fairish amateur—an indolent man, rather too fond of his tipple. Our official organist was a professor living in Newcastle, who walked from that town on the Saturday evening, finding his way back in like manner on the Monday morning, for the costly alternative of hiring a gig from the Bull Ring was not to be thought of Like his amateur deputy, the professor was fond of tippling, and took inordinate pains to gratify this fondness Rarely indeed did he fail to afford the lads of the choir optical, nasal, and aural proof of his love for the fragrant Jamaica, for his grimaces were extraordinary, the aroma of rum spread generously throughout the organ gallery, and his opening 'voluntary,' bidding defiance alike to common, triple, simple, and compound time, was an unfailing indication of the mellowness of his condition, though (to our unceasing delight) it was ever received with absolute seriousness and 'acceptation' by the unconscious congregation. The principals were Matilda Henzell, a little girl about a year in her teens, who had a fine, powerful voice, and who, like the rest, could read the most intricate music at sight; myself, alto; young Archer, tenor; and Mr. Oxley himself, bass. Some dozen others formed the chorus.

"One morning—there was no work at the time—happening to be in the churchyard just after six o'clock, and seeing old Jemmy Pye, the sexton, open the tower door, I went up into the organ loft, and gazing at the noble instrument—wondering whether I should ever be allowed to put my fingers upon, or become able to play it—thought the lock seemed but a poor one Taking out my knife, I pushed back the sprint and the door flew open ! To draw two soft stopped-diapasons, run round the gallery to the bellows handle, fill the chest with wind, and hasten back to the keyboard was the work of a moment A very few chords exhausted the windchest, the sounds dying away in a ghost-like wail, which had a most uncanny effect in the empty and, at that hour, almost dark church"

And so, in this fashion, running between keyboard and bellows, a distance covering the whole length of the choir gallery, making the very utmost of the delirious intervals, the first attempt at organ-playing was made.

"At length the question as to how the organ was to be locked up again without my being detected came upon my mind, and with it the conviction that condign punishment must certainly be meted out to the miscreant guilty of so sacrilegious an act as mine. However, I discovered that I could lock the door as easily as open it, and so I escaped This method of learning to play was by no means to my taste, but I could not help myself I knew of no other way in which to secure the chance of touching the grand instrument, and my desire to learn was so great that I could not overcome it."

Many, therefore, were the stolen interviews with this sombre-situate king of instruments on dark mornings up in the tower gallery of the ghostly old church, his sister sometimes going with him to "blow." Those alone who have experienced the mental exasperation involved in that most dismal of occupations, bellows-blowing, can appreciate the self-sacrifice of the sister, who, stationed in a dark well in a corner of the tower, one hand on the toilsome lever, the other groping after the leaden tell-tale, maintained the divine *afflatus* for the young learner.

Being now out of his time, and having before him no prospect of employment for some months, he resolved to ask the organist to take him as a pupil. A strange, ingenious creature was this official. He had a crazy old harpsichord to which he had added or attached an old windchest with a flute stop upon it, and both harpsichord and flute could be played together, or either separately. On this queer combination instrument the overpowering privilege of practising whenever he felt disposed was offered the student.

"Now, I thought, am I in clover!—but, alas for the vanity of human hopes, the clover only lasted for a week. As I practised one day, while waiting for my teacher to come and give me a lesson, he entered the room, and walking up to me, said, 'I'll not give you any more lessons; you can read music as well as I can, and want nothing but practice—good-day.'"

But practice was precisely his difficulty, for he had nothing on which to exercise it. "However, I worked away whenever the chance came to me of getting my fingers on either piano or organ," and fortunately he was able in a little while to save a small sum of money—"I forget whether it was £3 or £5"—and still more fortunately to fall in with a piano which could be, and was, purchased for this modest amount.

The organist at the church not long after took suddenly ill during morning service, and was carried out never to return. "I finished the service that day, and was appointed organist *pro tem.*, and continued to officiate for three months 'at the usual salary,' when a permanent official assumed the duties. The post was open to me, but I had no thought of applying for it, as I had determined to go to London every summer for four or five months, and regarded this as being so important that I would not give it up, even to become an organist."

It might naturally enough be assumed that all this while the interests of the master-painter received but scanty, pre-occupied attention, especially as in addition to, or rather concurrently with, these manifold musical studies, books on all available subjects were greedily ransacked, and the pressing work of self-culture, only possible in the short intervals afforded by the long working hours of the time, never relaxed. A common enough bit of cant is often heard to the effect that the culture of what may be termed the emotional arts unfits a young man for the business of life; but it may securely be doubted whether the idler who excuses his neglect of ordinary duties on the plea of devotion to some æsthetic study ever gives a moment's honest work to the latter. At all events the young band-master and organist did his master's work as he did all else, with his whole heart, and had attained a position of confidence and trust with him As an apprentice he was made charge-man of the most important "jobs," and when his indentures were returned to him, he was as his employer's right hand. In 1829 he was entrusted with the charge of painting and decorating a magnificent East-Indiaman built—in avowed competition with the Government shipyards—by Thomas and William Smith. This splendid vessel, the *George Green*, was, on her maiden voyage, cast away on the Hasbro' Sands, and miserably wrecked in a calm sea, though in charge of two pilots

The same year saw him at Bamburgh, superintending the painting of the church, the castle, and also Belford church, just then rebuilt. Here he lodged in the cottage of the sister of the (afterwards) celebrated Grace Darling, and founded a friendship with the family, to which it always gave him delight to refer in after years. Here, too, he somehow discovered a well-informed old gentleman, master of the boys' school in the castle, who had some special knowledge of astronomy, and from whom he got a sound course of instruction in the use of the celestial and terrestrial globes. "He never tired of explaining and working out interesting problems for my information, and created in my mind an intense desire to learn as much as possible of this wonderful science "

The Vicar of Bamburgh happened to be an excellent musician, and though an old man, had still a fine bass voice. His wife was also musical, and the family, among themselves, were able to do what then must have been somewhat unusual—namely, perform the whole of the " Messiah."

The old sexton tells the vicar, to his great surprise and delight, that "the painters are grand musicianers." Straightway to them goes the old gentleman to bid them come when they can and let him hear their music.

"So John Stewart, bass; his brother and I, sang to him, in the vestry, 'The Red Cross Knight,' the old clergyman joining in grandly—Stewart leaving some of the tit-bits of solo to him. So delighted was he that he went off and brought Mrs. Vicar and some other ladies to hear us. The lady of Budle Hills sent her compliments to us, with a request that we would allow her daughters and self to hear us sing a glee or two, so we went and sang Dr Callcott's beautiful prize glee, 'Peace to the Souls of the Heroes,' Lord Mornington's 'Here in Cool Grot,' and several others."

This brought to the painter-lads an invitation to visit Budle Hills. The Vicar lent them a volume of old Elizabethan madrigals and catches, some of them pretty and most of them somewhat difficult. Also a volume, folio size, and quite new, containing the music, "uncommonly beautiful," "then being performed in London by the Bohemian Brothers."

"In a day or two we told Mr. B—— that we should like him to hear us sing some of the compositions, and the Vicar, who had heard the 'Brothers' at the Argyle Rooms, was charmed with the unexpected performance.

"I afterwards arranged some of the airs for our band, and they became great favourites in the town."

He does not mention, though, that while this music was in his possession he copied out the whole of the Bohemian pieces—a laborious work, but more than half a century later the manuscripts in his beautiful hand, carefully stitched and bound with calico, and *sol-fa'd*, were in existence.

"In the printed copy I observed in the bass part a *double A*, and asked the Vicar if it were true that the human voice could produce so low a note, a minor third lower than the 'cello. He replied that it was really so, but that it could only be taken on the syllable *la*, which occurred in the piece, and that, of course, no singer could articulate a word at such a pitch."

After three or four pleasant months at Bamburgh he took a journey by coach to Edinburgh, and there for the first time met his only two first cousins, John and Thomas Miller. There also he met for the first time a musical instrument entirely new to him, though the fact was not noted until some sixty years later.

"I well remember that during our Bamburgh campaign in 1829 we went down to Edinburgh for two or three days, and that one night in the Theatre Royal, between the acts, the orchestra played a slow, soft piece, in which I detected a peculiar and novel effect for which I could in no way account. Creeping round the gallery, which was but thinly filled, until I could see the whole of the band, I soon perceived that the sounds referred to were produced by two fiddles larger than the ordinary violin —tenors, in fact. This was my first introduction to the viola, an instrument which never fails to delight me when I hear it."

Before leaving Bamburgh a letter reached him from a companion and town-fellow, W. S. B. Woolhouse, the afterwards distinguished mathematician, astronomer, and writer on the theory of music. Addressed "Mr. Haswell, Painter and Musician, North Sunderland," it runs:—

"NORTH SHIELDS, *August 14th*, 1829.

"Now you are at a distance I shall not say anything about the chord of the fourth, but I may be allowed to say a little of the chord of friendship between us, which I hope will always be a perfect chord, even better than the sweet fourth . . . I have lately very much missed you, and concluded you are a gentleman out of your time, left us never to return. You may be assured that I feel very great pleasure in the expectation of again enjoying your concordant company. I intend to remain here until the beginning of next year, when I mean to set off to the South. But I hope to see you long before that.—Believe me to be, yours truly,

"W. S. B. WOOLHOUSE.

"P.S.—Thpe B flpat fpife wpill tpake thpis npote cponcpert-ppitch."

Writing again in 1890, some sixty-two years later, Mr. Woolhouse threw some light on this queer epistle

"In my early days your father and myself were very frequent companions, and often indulged in interchange of thought. We sometimes talked in the *p* language, which consisted of putting the letter *p* before each vowel. Your father on almost every subject was imbued with a keen spirit of intelligence, and, as you know, possessed an unusual fund of humour, always entertaining. It is curious you should come upon any correspondence so far back as sixty years! I well remember our thrashing out the question whether a perfect fourth is a concord or a discord. We came to the conclusion that absolutely it is a concord, but relatively a discord when its resolution is taken into consideration. And this result is in strict accordance with the best books on harmony of the present day.[1]

"In 1833, being in my twenty-sixth year, I sailed in the well-known old

---

[1] In respect to the "*p*-language," the following curious note on a similar practice occurs in A. R. Wallace's *Travels on the Amazon*:—

"In two days more we reached the village of São Pedro, where Senhor L—— borrowed another canoe. . . . The owner was a young Brazilian trader. . . . He and Senhor L—— were old cronies, and began to talk in a language I could not understand, though I knew it to be some kind of Portuguese. I soon, however, found out what it was, and Senhor L—— afterwards told me that he had learnt it when a boy at school. It consisted of adding to every syllable another rhyming with it, but beginning with *p;* thus to say '*Venha ca*' (come here), he would say '*Venpenhapa capa*,' or if in English, 'Comepum herepere.'"—Chapter VIII.

Liberty and Property—a collier with 'pink' stern; the last of her race, I believe—for London, and was at once engaged by the firm of Robinson & Skipsey, Carey Street, Lincoln's Inn Fields."

For several years he made this voyage, thereby enlarging his experience of men and things, and here, as elsewhere, his musical attainments secured for him access to people much higher in social position, and helped him signally in the beloved quest for knowledge.

"One day, in the year '33 or '34, I am not sure which, while busy in the shop in Carey Street, I was told by one of the labourers, an Irishman, that I 'was wanted in the affis.' Going there I found the master and his clerk waiting for me

"'Haswell, do you know anything about music?'

"'Yes, sir,' I replied.

"'Can you play any instrument?'

"'Several.'

"'So Taylor tells me. Well, we have a rather large job at Admiral J.'s, at Maidstone. The family are going on to the Continent, and the whole of the vineries, greenhouses, and conservatories are to be overhauled and painted; it will be a "strong" job, and last some time. We have a number of men there now, but when down yesterday I arranged to send ten or a dozen more In coming away the steward said that if I had any men who could play a musical instrument I was to be sure to send them. Now, Taylor tells me you are the very man for him and, as we like to please these people if possible, you must get ready to go down there on Monday with the rest' No railway to Maidstone at that time, nor for long after; so we had to coach it all the way. When the coach stopped in the market-place, a tall, gentlemanly man came up and said, interrogatively—

"'Painters from London?'

"'Yes, sir.'

"'One of you named Haswell?'

"I was pointed out to him, when he approached, shook hands and said he was glad to see me—where was my trunk? Called one of the ostlers to him and said, 'John, send this gentleman's trunk up to the hall as soon as possible.' Then walking towards a stylish trap, said to me, 'Jump in—have a cigar?' and, lighting up, turned the vehicle round and dashed off past the group of putty-men who stood gaping at us and wondering what it meant. I raised my hat to them, at which they laughed, and we were soon out of sight. Admiral J.'s residence lay some three miles out of Maidstone, in, or rather on the side of, a beautiful vale containing a number of paper-mills at which were employed a great many hands, and I was much interested in the novelty of all that we were passing, but my friend would talk of nothing but music. What instrument did I play? Could I play the flute? Delighted when told I could. Did I know 'Wragg's Preceptor'?—more delighted when I hummed over one or two of Wragg's airs

"He told me that he played the flute himself, and had a copy of 'Wragg' and two eight-keyed flutes, also that he played the violin. The bandmaster at Maidstone barracks was one of his musical friends, and, of course, a fine clarionet player, another friend was a fair second violin, furthermore, that though they possessed a 'cello, they, unfortunately, had no one to play it

"When I told him I thought I could manage to do that, he gave me a curious sort of look, which, to my mind, implied, 'Suppose this man is only fooling me'; however, by this time we had arrived at the hall, where he at once took me to his sitting-room, poured out a glass of wine, then, producing two beautiful flutes with eight silver keys, and placing 'Wragg' upon a music-stand, said, 'Which will you take—first or second?' 'Either you like.'

"Off he went with a pretty *rondo* in C, which, I was glad to note, he played very well. As I well knew everything in Wragg by heart I walked about the room playing 'seconds' to him. He seemed delighted That same evening we had a meeting— 1st vio, 2nd do., clarionet, and 'cello, and played some pretty music, manuscript, of course, by Haydn, which I had not before heard. As they had been for some weeks without a 'cello-player my advent was warmly welcomed, and many an afternoon the steward came to the 'cod' (*i e*, the charge-man or foreman)—a 'real Newcastler'—and said, 'Now, Armstrong, I want Haswell about four or five o'clock; we have a musical party this evening a few miles away.' 'Ay,' replied Armstrong, who never refused, probably having had instructions from our master, 'ay, aw wish *aw* wiz a musicianer'"

Such is but one out of a crowd of instances in which his music, at that critical time, afforded him the opportunity of meeting with educated men on terms which enabled him to seize all the advantages their society conferred. He read an enormous mass of matter at this period, getting books and manuscripts from such friends as the steward and his musical chums, and being allowed to dip into great libraries in the halls and mansions where he worked. Long walks were made to different parts of the "great city," where access to books and museums yielded gratuitous sources of knowledge, and, with all his passion for music, it never for a moment diverted him from the steadfast pursuit of study and self-culture. Wages were small, and even the scanty savings he managed to wring out of them he was not able to devote to the acquisition of books; hence laborious tasks, self-imposed, of copying out the contents, or essentials, of whole volumes of precious matter, perhaps the most thorough and certain of all methods of learning a subject, yet not undertaken with any consciousness of this, but purely as a matter of economy. His parents were living, and he knew them to be in very straitened circumstances, for trade was bad and much destitution and privation existed

"One day, walking along the Strand—it was in 1834—I was accosted by a man selling almanacs, or rather pocket-books with an almanac in them 'Only sixpence,' said he. I saw they must have cost more than that, being made of leather, so needing a pocket-book I bought one. Opening it, I read that a certain bank in the City forwarded small sums of money to the country 'free of charge.' Now I had long wished to send some money down to the old people, but could never find how it might be done; but here was the way if the book were correct. I had been at a country job for some weeks, and had about £6 to take for balance of wages due. Mentioning the matter to a fellow-lodger whose parents lived in the same street in Shields as mine, I told him I was about to send home £4, as I had the certainty of constant work for some months to come He begged me to send also £2 on his account, and I promised him I should try At the first opportunity I set out for No — Lombard Street. Behind a wide mahogany counter were two grand clerks, each with a large quill behind his ear, one with his back to the counter, arms crossed, talking briskly to the other Attracting his attention with some difficulty, I pointed out the paragraph in the almanac which had brought me there, and said I wished to send home some money

"'Where to?'

"'51 Stephenson Street, North Shields.'

"'Whom to?'

"'George Haswell.'

"'How much?'

"'Six pounds'

"Keeping up his conversation, which indeed had not ceased, he swept the six sovereigns into a drawer, put the quill behind his ear again, went up to his chum, crossed his arms, and took no further notice of me I waited some time for a receipt for my money, but no sign of any forthcoming I spoke up and said—

"'Pray, sir, do you give no acknowledgment?'

"Looking over his shoulder he replied, quite politely—

"'Oh, no Write down to your friends and tell them to go to the bank in Shields and apply for the money. There will be nothing to pay'

"Well, thought I, when I got outside, I've made a pretty mess of my first banking transaction; who will believe a common workman's statement that he paid £6 into a bank without any acknowledgment? However, I wrote home that night requesting my father to go to Mr. Spence's bank, give his name and address, and ask for £6, and then let me know as soon as possible how he fared; for, to tell the truth, I had my doubts as to the entire success of the enterprise.

"After some days of anxiety I received a long and warm-hearted letter from home, in which my sister said it was impossible I could realise what a relief my timely assistance had been, they seldom saw many shillings, and here unexpectedly were four sovereigns!—the old people could only shed tears Ellen said I must have taken to Turpin's trade, and that they would next hear that I was to be hanged at Tyburn. My father was not two minutes in the bank, the money being paid at once. There was misery and suffering on all hands (resulting from the frightful and wasteful wars on the Continent), lack of employment and scarcity of food, intensified by a succession of bad harvests, and consequent failure of crops"

The adventure ended more prosperously than might have been anticipated, but a certain shrinking lack of self-assertion, which always characterised him, is manifested in the philosophic resignation with which he leaves his money, without a struggle, in the hands of the "grand clerk."

These excursions to London only occupied the summer months. In the autumn he was back again in Shields, where he stayed over the winter and spring

About this time the high quality of the "arrangements" he was providing for local bands induced the "Glass Makers" band of South Shields to apply to him to become their teacher. He accepted the office and held it for a long series of years, during which he steadily raised the standard of quality of the music, arranging from the old church manuscripts most of the choruses and solos of the Handelian and later oratorios. The band performed in the market-place once a week, and drew hundreds of people, on summer evenings, from both of the harbour-towns to listen to the strains of the Immortals. A prime favourite with the *al fresco* audiences was "The Marvellous Work" from the *Creation*

"The cornet-à-piston had not long been invented, but already had completely displaced the beautiful keyed-bugle—as indeed all the new instruments fitted with pistons did those with keys. The ophicleide was a great improvement on the old bass horn and serpent, but the euphonium with its pistons superseded it, taking first place, which it holds to this day. In arranging 'The Marvellous Work' I gave the solo part to the cornet, which was beautifully played by a young fellow named Hart, who was also our best 'piccolo' He had a fine musical ear and taste."

The delicious softness of the copper keyed-bugle was lost in the new brass instruments, and those who remember the choruses of Handel as they were played forty years ago by an orchestra of picked buglers, can understand the regret with which the young bandmaster regarded their extinction. He had indeed an extraordinary delicacy of perception for the finer shades of quality in tone, which perhaps the range of orchestral writing, at that time familiar to him, scarce gave scope for; but he always hoped that the tender-voiced copper bugle might be re-introduced Possibly it may be. It is difficult now to believe that the perfectly indispensable *timbre* of the French horn could be spared from the orchestra, yet in some way, this beautiful instrument fell into neglect, and for quite a considerable period was disregarded by writers of orchestral arrangements Haswell always persisted in having the full quartet of horns, writing the parts himself, and predicted with absolute conviction that they must be employed in modern orchestras. The great symphonic writers had not then been heard away from the greater towns, but in after years the loving grace with which Mendelssohn and his compeers were found to have *suffused* their harmonies with the tender warmth and wistful mystery of the horn tones always brought an expression of absolute delight into the eyes of the humble disciple.

"There now chanced to be several good amateurs—vocal and instrumental—in the town. Mr. Jonathan Cockerill, a local solicitor, was a violinist of exceptional excellence, well versed in classical music; his brother Charles, a fine player on the viola—an instrument rarely heard out of the large orchestras; John Jowsey, regarded as a prodigy on the piano and organ; and sundry others With a view of giving a series of subscription concerts in the town, the gentlemen above named formed a society called the 'Tynemouth Amateur Musical Society,' and soon had as many recruits as they desired. We met for practice weekly, and gave a full concert every month during the winter. Each member subscribed a certain sum annually, for which he received tickets for the concerts In many respects the rise, progress, and success of this institution was remarkable. In the large town of Newcastle they had nothing to approach it, yet in a few years, owing to a great and universal depression in trade, subscriptions fell off to such an extent that it became necessary to entirely suspend the meetings, with a hope, however, that in a year or two it might be possible to resume them. Mr. John Tinley—a warm and enthusiastic supporter of the movement—undertook to stow away the stage or platform, music-stands, etc., and the music and grand piano were placed in my keeping, which was a *grand* thing for me."

Much of the music exists to-day, and it proves how strongly the influence of the classics predominated with these pioneers. Handel, Haydn, Mozart, Bach, Spohr, Schubert, and Weber, in arrangements for piano and small orchestra, overtures from the grand operas, and here and there a *morceau* by some then unrecognised German composer, make up the bulk of the volumes. Yet probably these were then, as to some extent now, tolerated merely as filling up short intervals between other meretricious items. Even to-day it is not altogether unusual to have a grand orchestra sit silent through four-fifths of a programme while Signor A., Madame B., or Signorina C. mouth at a *scena*, or give some debased "royalty" song as an *encore* to one of the divine melodies of Schumann, Schubert, or Gounod.

The thin, wire-drawn old ballads of the century's earlier days, with their sparse harpsichord accompaniment and "figured" bass, their florid garniture of trills, shakes, graces, flourishes, and *appoggiature*, under which the poor starveling melody was almost buried, were fading away out of public ken, and only came faintly out upon the air, with the dusty withered fragrance of an old *pot pourri*, in the parlours of romantic spinsters and faded *belles* of the previous century (where yet lingered the "Battle of Prague" and other "descriptive" horrors of the kind), passing away with the "gentle" nymphs, "fleeing" shepherdesses, and "pursuing" swains who—in passionate abbreviation and ardent capitals—sung of "flames," "fonder wishes," "warmer fires," "gay desires"; of "fav'rite haunts," "murm'ring doves," "op'ning flow'rs," "flow'ry bow'rs"; of "blest retreats," "sequestered vales," and "untrodden glades." Of lovely LAURA's, cruel SYLVIA's, gentle PASTORA's, and sweet MA-R-IA's.

People were becoming ashamed to ask their hearers to

"Let the declining damask rose
With envious grief look wan and pale"

Still, there was much that was mean, common-place, and false in sentiment, in the songs and pieces that found most acceptance with the "concert-goer," and the following sketch shows that the young musician was not entirely satisfied with the taste of his audiences.

"Our solo flute was a Mr. Hawks, a youth of independent means, whom, somehow, it had never been possible to teach the art of reading music. As a consequence, he was not of much use in the concerted pieces, yet, in the eyes of the young ladies—and of the old ones too—he was the gem of the orchestra. Whenever he was down for a solo the delight and excitement of the audience knew no bounds; their applause commencing long before he sounded a note. The cause was not far to seek: he was a handsome lad with a somewhat effeminate face, a winning smile, and a perfect Adonis in figure. We generally addressed him as 'Cupid,' and, though most men would have regarded this as an insult, he never resented it, but giving one of his pretty smiles, seemed rather to like it.

"Well, having plenty of money, he had gone to one of the crack flautists in London, whom he somehow induced to coach him in the execution of a few of the showy solos of the day, without learning to read —a disagreeable duty for a teacher, and one which would have to be well paid for. Nevertheless, it was managed, and he played his pieces well, had a good tone, and if he did take unwarrantable liberties with the time, was there not a Jowsey at the piano, ready and able to accommodate all such eccentricities? A bar too quick, a bar left out, it signified not—no one was aware, not even 'Cupid' himself; and the applause was tremendous. When, on the concert night, the flute solo fell due, a flutter and buzz arose among the audience, quickly subsiding into dead silence. Then my lord would emerge from the 'wings' with flute and music, both of which he would lay on the piano while he leisurely looked round for a music-stand. This he'd place at one end of the platform sideways to the auditorium, then taking up his flute—a beauty it was, cocoa-nut with eight solid silver keys—and a position some three or four yards from the stand, raise his arms and begin. Nicholson's flute solos were then the rage, in general they opened with a long flowery *cadenza* running from the lowest to the highest note on the instrument (a proceeding which, it seemed to me, mainly served the purpose of warming up the flute), the piano meanwhile putting in an occasional chord. An *adagio* followed, and then a brilliant *allegro*, which never failed to produce tumultuous applause."

This sort of thing has long been abandoned by instrumentalists, but it is yet paralleled in the antics of some of our modern pampered "public singers."

Not, however, alone, or even mainly, was he engaged with the delights and eccentricities of music. His handicraft had to be closely pursued for the support of his ageing father and mother, and his exacting, rigorous regimen of mental athletics, to be stolen from hours that should have been devoted to sleep. The demands of an unenterprising public for all that made for light and improvement fell upon quite a small band of self-sacrificing men, of whom he, though yet but a workman, was one of the most energetic.

A "Mechanics' Institute" had been founded by this little group, and he was secretary for a long period. After the first few years of its existence it got gradually into financial difficulties, and presently had to stop. Two good and enlightened men, Matthew Robson and William Greenwell, paid the debts and took charge of the precious volumes, placing them in a room in Church Street, where they remained until 1832, when the institution was revived. This institute was the subject, over a long succession of years, of all the fostering care and attention which his ardent love of culture enabled him to devote to it. In this same 1832—one of the pregnant periods of the century—the fiery William Cobbett visited Tyneside, and in the records of the proceedings is this passage—"At Tynemouth the address presented to him (Cobbett) contained no fewer than 835 names, among which figure those of John Carr, William Haswell, Thomas Haswell, Robert Pow, J. R Procter, etc, all men of local mark and consequence." The men of mark and consequence were large manufacturers, magistrates, and "gentry"; yet among them, at the age of twenty-five, the young painter was thought worthy of inclusion.

As a matter of fact, however, every movement for the advancement of his town's-fellows had his energetic support, often his initiative; at re-unions of all kinds he was indispensable, and all this, naturally enough, brought him into contact with what was best in the local society of the harbour-towns, while his wide range of reading and knowledge of the sciences of the day secured for him the cordial friendship of many of the cultured men of the northern districts. He was a born teacher, and the yearning for some other mode of life was now strong in him, though an extraordinary diffidence and modesty restrained all conscious manifestation of it, without, however, concealing it from those around him; and it was at the pressing instance of his more intimate friends that he began, slowly and doubtingly and hesitatingly, to seriously contemplate the idea of throwing aside his handicraft and taking up the ideal work of teaching. The growing influence of Natural Science among thoughtful men unquestionably moved him strongly towards the new mode of life, and inspired him with a conviction that in *that* direction lay light. One of the outward evidences of the intellectual ferment at work in the minds of the new generation was the establishment of the famous British Association, and the scattered flock of students of Nature, isolated and cut off from each other by a great ocean of popular ignorance and indifference, took courage when they saw what a brilliant retinue Science had called round her. The first meeting of the Association was held in the city of York in 1831, and it is impossible now to realise the intense interest and enthusiasm it excited among the amateur "natural philosophers" of the day Neither the patronising toleration of the "press," the unconcealed contempt of the mass of literary and classical scholars in the great seats of "learning," nor the uneasy dread and hostility of the bulk of the "cloth" availed to stem the broadening stream of wonder and curiosity that was sweeping among the people and stirring them to offer a half-fearful welcome to the "wise men" who proposed to come among them and hold parliament. In 1838 the Association met in Newcastle-on-Tyne, and on one of the days of the "Wise-week" the Geological Section had an expedition on the coast stretching northward from Tynemouth.

"In the castle-yard, under the Abbey ruins, a tent was erected in which luncheon was laid for the party, but, unfortunately, a sudden and violent squall of wind overthrew the tent and almost blew it, and the section with it, over the 'cliffs of Old Tynemouth' into the sea. As it was, the company had to clear out in double-quick time, and lose the luncheon as well as the grand speeches which had doubtless been as carefully prepared.

"It had become known that the section would, early in the afternoon, meet in the haven, and then, walking round under the cliffs, proceed by the Short Sands along the beach to Cullercoats, thence to a colliery some little way inland. I therefore went down to Tynemouth and found some hundred or more people assembled near the Castle waiting for the wise men. Presently we saw approaching a group of fifty or sixty gentlemen, led, apparently, by a tall, noble-looking man, whom I afterwards ascertained to be Professor Sedgwick—certainly one of the most eloquent speakers I ever heard.

"They made for the north side of Prior's Haven, when, getting close to the Professor, I heard him exclaim, 'Ah, here we are Let me introduce you, gentlemen, to an old friend of mine, whom I have not seen for fifteen years'—he referred to the basaltic column in the castle cliff—'and a finer specimen of this natural wonder is nowhere to be seen in England.'

"It—the column—was very much disfigured in making the pier, and quite recently—in 1887—was entirely plastered over with cement by the

Goth-like war authorities, under the pretence of protecting the cliff from the wearing action of the sea

"We then passed on round the Short Sands, the Professor all the way having much to say, and keeping the party both interested and in good humour by mingling genial joke with instruction, mounting now and then upon a seaweed-grown boulder to hold forth, and laughing at some of his friends who slipped from time to time from a treacherous green-carpeted rostrum. After a delightful walk we arrived at the *ninety fathom dyke*. The Professor said that just where we stood was a seam of coal not many fathoms below the surface, and yet that a yard or two to the north the same seam lay ninety fathoms lower. The colliery owner had sunk a small shaft to the upper seam, and we might possibly get some fossil fish. He could not, of course, assure us of this, for if there chanced to be no fish just where we sought them, none would be brought up However, when the blast had been made and the corfe was drawn up, a rich booty of fossils was displayed I obtained a nearly whole herring in perfect condition and two or three other specimens, the scales being beautifully preserved After a brilliant concluding speech from the Professor the company dispersed, the 'Geological Section' returning to Newcastle in the conveyances by which they had come.'

Quite another affair, the following incident of

"THE WISE-WEEK, 1838.

"A rather singular circumstance occurred during the week My father was coming up the Wooden Bridge Bank, and being tired, had put his back against the wall to take a rest, when an oldish-looking workman with a kindly but eccentric expression of countenance came up to him and, without preface or introduction, said—

"'This is 'n awful heavy bank, canny aad man'

"'Yes, it is that, indeed.'

"'Aa belang ta Winlaton, 'n aa cam doon to Newcassle ta see tha Wise-men—but nee Wise-men cud aa see Thor's a man i' this toon aa's lang wanted ta see, se aa thowt aa wad cum doon tha day 'n try ta fin-d *him* Mebbies thoo can tell us wheor aa can fin-d him, but thoo mun cum inside this hoose 'n' we'll hev a drink o' beeor.'

"Before he could be stopped he had pushed my father inside

"'Ivvorybody knaws me i' tha North iv England. Aa'm the *greet batten[1]-makor* a' Winlat'n. Ask onybody ya like if they knaw Tommy Haswell tha patten-makor a' Winlat'n 'n' ye'll heor w'at they'll say.'

"'Why, they call *me* Haswell,' father said

"'Man! d'ya say se?'

"'Yes—and I have a son called Thomas'

---

[1] Women's *pattens*, then much used by housewives

"'God's wons! wey that's tha varry man aa's wanted ta see se lang!'

"'Well, come along then, and I'll take you to him.'

'But so astonished was the old fellow at the singular turn of events that it deprived him of the power of speech. Father brought him up to Stephenson Street, where we then lived, but nothing would induce him to come into the house, though only a constitutional bashfulness prevented him; however, he begged that I should be sent to him at an inn close at hand, where he would wait, and, my father promising, they shook hands and parted. I was at dinner when my father came in and told us of his strange meeting with Winlaton Tommy, and did not feel much inclination for an interview. He insisted, nevertheless, that having made a promise on my behalf I must go and see the old fellow—so I went. When I entered the room he was eating his dinner, but instantly left it, and, taking hold of my hand, led me to a chair, telling me, the while, that he was the best patten-maker in England. However, he did not want to talk about patten-making, but about band-music, for he believed he was the best sarpint-player in the country.

"'Thoo'll think aa's nowt but a braggor—but aa's nee braggor. If thoo'll ask ony o' tha band-maisters if they knaw the Winlat'n sarpint-player, thoo'll hear. Aa wish aa had hor heor noo; aa'd let thoo heor the sarpint!' And placing his hands in the appropriate position he worked his fingers as, in imagination, he played his favourite instrument. I learned afterwards from a trusty informant who had known him all his life that he was, as he said of himself, 'nee braggor,' but really an extraordinary fellow in many ways. It was quite true that in patten-making, though often matched for large sums, he left his rivals far behind for quickness, neatness, and finish. In like wise his tone on the serpent far surpassed that of any player he came across, and had gained for him a reputation among the army bands, for he had been taken to York to some contest and had carried all before him. I remember I pleased him very much by showing that I knew the scale of his instrument. He said he had been told that I could play every instrument in the band, and would like to know if that were true. I told him I could play any of the band instruments, though not equally well; that I could not play the violin, though I could the 'cello. My father had told him that I was organist at the parish church, so poor old Tommy was quite overpowered. It was now getting time for him to be moving homeward, so I went with him to the steamboat at the new quay. On parting he begged I would some Sunday go and dine with him, when he would have the 'largest leg of mutton that could be bought in Newcastle or Gateshead'; but I never saw him again, nor did I ever hear of his death, for I continued to go to London every year, so had no opportunity. Altogether the incident was a strange one, for ours was the only family in North Shields named Haswell, and I was the one man in the town this stranger wished to see, and saw without trouble or enquiry.'

After much earnest reflection and consideration he at length finally decided to devote himself to the work of a school-teacher, and early in 1839 entered the Westoe Lane Schools, South Shields, under the mastership of Francis Mason, to study the *system*, as it was then called, of teaching in the National Schools. The other and rival system was the *Lancasterian*, taught at the Borough Road institution, London.

"At the completion of the course under Mr. Mason I received the appointment of master to the Trinity Church School, South Shields, and held it under the Rev. Thomas Dixon for some eight weeks, when the mastership of the Royal Jubilee at North Shields fell vacant. I became a candidate and, against some thirty-eight applicants, received the appointment."[1]

In a circular to the subscribers, dated "Jubilee School, May 1839," tendering "sincere thanks for the honour" conferred upon him, the new dominie most earnestly assures them "that the whole of my time and ability shall be devoted to the improvement and proper deportment of the children who may be placed under my superintendence and care"—a promise assuredly most amply discharged.

Woolhouse appears to have been wholly unaware of the step his friend was taking until after the change was made; indeed, from the following letter, it would seem that he had been advocating the claims of one of the rival candidates:—

"LONDON, BELVEDERE ROAD, *October 20th*, 1839.

"MY DEAR TOM,—I was both surprised and pleased to hear that the schoolmaster was at home, and shall be gratified to hear that he continues so in every sense of the word. When I recommended young Gourley as Jubilee man, I was not aware that so worthy and deserving a candidate as yourself was in the field (over by the soldier's pond I suppose). I could not imagine a more suitable person than yourself, and would have at once felt the utter absurdity of backing any one against you; and in addition to this there are the strong *chords* that bind us, and such as no one, I hope, 'can break asunder.'

"I should think your new position is an improvement on your former profession, and it gives room to hope that you will now have opportunities at command of preparing your mind for another stretch upwards;

---

[1] "LOCAL INTELLIGENCE —Mr Thomas Haswell, Trinity School, South Shields, has been elected to the Royal Jubilee School, North Shields."—*Port of Tyne Pilot*, April 27th, 1839

and it would afford me much pleasure indeed if I could ever have an opportunity of contributing to your advancement. . . . This is only an apology for a letter, and I hope will suffice to prevent you from giving me a good damn'd blowing up —Yours ever truly,

"W. S. B WOOLHOUSE."

"Mr. Thomas Haswell, etc , etc

Some time in 1830 he became acquainted with a retired ship-master who, with his wife and family of three daughters and a son, lived in a cottage near the Barracks in Percy Square. The head of the family, Captain John Collinson Armstrong, was a queer, brown, dried-up, fiery-tempered but kindly-natured little man, very proud of the aquiline turn of his features ("aristocratic" turn, he called it), and immensely lordly and punctilious in manner and address; qualities, however, always comically at issue with, and breaking down under the stress of an irresistible sense of humour and propensity for waggish joking. In his earlier days he had been well known in the long "narrow street" for the daring pranks he played upon the press-gangs, who made unceasing attempts to capture him. Being a spare, light, active man, and extraordinarily swift of foot, he was much given to indulge in the excitement of leading the gang a chase after him, when he would repeatedly stop short, close under their outstretched arms, to

" Put his thumb unto his nose
And spread the fingers out,"

to the screaming delight of the women and boys. Many narrow escapes he had, but somehow he invariably succeeded in dodging his exasperated pursuers.

Captain John took warmly to his young friend, and over their long pipes—for he insisted on "my boy Tom" smoking one, to the excessive discomfort of the young fellow—reproved him for lack of reverence, angrily swore at him for venturing to express a different opinion, or cried with laughing at the humour of his stories.

The acquaintance of the young musician with the family ripened into a warm friendship, and on his appointment to the Jubilee mastership, "Tom," feeling that he was now settled in life, decided to take a wife.

"Dr. Huntley, of Howdon, married Sarah Hannah, the eldest daughter, and on the 21st September 1840 I married the youngest, Matilda Preston, at All Saints' Church, Newcastle-on-Tyne After the ceremony we proceeded to Corbridge, dined, and spent the day at the village, returning home to the Jubilee the same evening."

He never took a better step in his long life. His bright, cheery, busy, happy, and musical wife was the best companion and help-mate the studious, retiring, unassertive teacher could have wished for.

Writing in 1890, an old friend, and favourite ballad-singer of the old days, says:—

"Concerning your father; of his painter-days I know little, as he was appointed to the Royal Jubilee School when I was a scholar there myself. I have a vivid remembrance of his marriage and of being with Dr. Huntley, my father, and my mother. *There was much singing*, and the room and faces are still in my mind's eye."

"There was much singing!"—much singing and much music were there in the Jubilee School and school-house for forty years or more to follow.

THE ROYAL JUBILEE SCHOOL.

CHAPTER V.

IN THE "FORTIES."

"What a howling blast is here, and oh how it blew in the night!"

"LIBERTAS ET NATALE SOLUM. Freedom and our Fatherland. The spirit of Reform has since the peace —the long, blessed peace—awoke the thinking faculties of the Nation and left men 'leisure to be good.'"[1]

To such effect the *Port of Tyne Pilot*, a four-page weekly newspaper, dated April 1839, bearing the red impress of the Government newspaper-stamp, and sold at 4½d.

For close on a quarter century the peace—the long, blessed peace—had run its healing course. The war with its evil memories was fast sinking back into the limbo of the forgotten; its accursed shadow was lifted, and men were trying with some hope of success, to work out long-delayed and frustrated schemes of self-elevation.

But the terrible legacy of misery and poverty and demoralisation remained. England, like some fever-wasted patient, was even now but slowly emerging from the pangs and perils of a grave crisis: to weak and reduced to bear with aught but the wisest treatment; yet her case was largely in the hands of ignorant and selfish quacks who,

---

[1] "One blessed result of the peace has been the leisure and opportunity it has offered for the cultivation of the popular intelligence."—*History of the Thirty Years' Peace.*

in all the arrogance of dulness, clung to the methods of their fore-runners,—leeches (in a double sense) who had faith in nought but cupping and bleeding.

Trade was still harassed and crippled by insane restrictions imposed by the crowd of dull country gentlemen who had, until now, made up the bulk of England's law-givers, and who neither understood nor cared to understand the simplest principles of commerce, and the shocking "Starvation Laws"—greedily hugged by men who, ever talking of patriotism, were nevertheless prepared to risk the infliction upon their country of revolution and civil war—were year by year crushing the lives out of tens of thousands of men, women, and children, and making hideous and infamous for ever the memory of the time. An incredible proportion of the people was on the borderland of absolute starvation,[1] and a brisk trade in opium was being done among operatives to relieve the misery of hunger between Saturday night and Monday morning! The poor was still the greatest of the "classes," and upon them in every form that ingenuity could contrive the burden of taxation was piled

Yet something had been done. The process of repair and regeneration truly might be slow, desperately slow, but the blessed spirit of peace was abroad, and the thinking faculties of the great broad mass of the English people were being aroused. The great middle-class had, in a political sense, just been created, and more was doing and to be done for the "rabble" in the next generation than had yet been accomplished in any like period in the history of man

How close upon this time of day-spring the dark reign of violence touched may be realised by considering a few of the laws and customs repealed and abolished within a mere few years.

The gibbet was gone; the last erected in England being set up on Jarrow Slake, close by Bede's Church The crimes punishable with death were reduced in 1837 from a horrible total of *thirty-one* to ten. In the same year the pillory was struck out of legal existence Government lotteries had been allowed to demoralise the people until 1826, and bull-baiting to brutalise them up to 1835. In 1832 it was possible for an English parliamentary candidate to be asked whether "you will advocate the speedy abolition of the

---

[1] "In Carlisle the Committee of Inquiry reported that a *fourth* of the population was in a state bordering on starvation, actually certain to die unless relieved In Devonshire a man and his wife had for wages 2s. 6d. *per week* and three loaves."
—*History of the Thirty Years' Peace.*

slave-trade?" and for another at the same election to need to announce himself "a stern opponent of the systems of slavery and impressment"; and not until the year 1834 could a meeting of Quakers thank the "Author of all good, that the cause of slavery throughout the British Empire is this day ended." Another and crueller sort of slavery was also now ended—child-slavery in factories. In some smaller things too there was progress to be noted. The window-tax had been reduced in 1835, and in the Budget of 1833 no fewer than *thirteen hundred and seven* "places" were abolished

These purgations, however, were by no means the spontaneous work of the nation's representatives, but in the main had been advocated and pressed to solution by the classes newly enfranchised. "Society"—the "old" element—as a body, dreaded, detested, and opposed every such movement with rancorous bitterness.

And there was yet terribly much to do. Impressment and military flogging remained; "blasphemy" prosecutions and church-rates persecutions remained, the "mournful romance of the Game Laws"[1] remained to shock and dishearten the thoughtful—mournful truly, yet perhaps not more so than the spectacle of a noble lord[2] using his high position in an endeavour to make those laws still more stringent and oppressive Chartists were meeting to enforce their "five points," Rebecca and her children meeting to "burn and destroy," gentlemen meeting to settle affairs of "honour" by violence, and politicians meeting to babble about it all " Freedom and our Fatherland" was the war-cry of reformers, Freedom, our Fatherland, and much else of the kind, the staple of patriotic toasts, drunk, with all the gravity of conviction, by men who voted for the maintenance of slavery, of impressment, and of the shame and horror of the death laws. But freedom was, after all, becoming a reality for the mass of Englishmen, and the Fatherland *theirs.*

And while politicians babbled and statesmen in their arrogance tried to change the course of natural laws, a new and unsuspected agency, yet the subject of patronising ridicule on the part of many

[1] "Between 1833 and 1834 forty-one inquests were held on slain gamekeepers. In some rural counties nearly half the total commitments to gaol were game cases. The convictions in England and Wales for breaches of the Game Laws were *four thousand five hundred and twenty-nine.*

"In 1845, before a Committee of the House, evidence was given that so many of the commitments (under the Game Laws) were illegal that the Home Secretary made an extensive gaol delivery."—*History of the Thirty Years' Peace.*

[2] Lord Stradbroke in 1844

THE RAILWAY.

of the "cultured," was gathering strength—an agency which, in a few years, was to burst all the artificial bonds in which meddlesome legislators had cramped the people, and to set the many-headed free to raise himself, which was almost all he asked for. George Stephenson's mighty and beneficent giant was as yet but in leading strings, scarcely strong enough to be hated, dreaded and opposed with the dead earnestness that must have been manifested had its stupendous influences been foreseen or suspected.

On the water, *Vaporfluens* had secured a beginning; the first steamer on the Tyne appearing, to the amusement of the crowd, in 1812; but he was still only half tolerated as a very doubtful acquisition, and few men had any doubt that he must always play second to the wind. In 1842 the first iron screw-steamer—the *Q.E.D.*—was launched from a shipyard at Walker-on-Tyne, and though a wonderful advance upon anything that had been accomplished in marine architecture (having water-tight bulkheads and water ballast), she received the usual baptism of objurgation and was greeted as a very ugly duckling indeed.

Glancing again at the little *Port of Tyne Pilot*, a quaint announcement is seen among the advertisements; one which, perhaps as well as anything could, shows to what a slight and unpretending position the great railway system had then attained.

"TO THE PUBLIC.

"THE STANHOPE AND TYNE RAIL-ROAD COACHES have commenced running five times a day between SOUTH SHIELDS and the DURHAM TURNPIKE (Sundays excepted), from the 1st of March 1839 until further notice.

TIMES OF STARTING.

From Shields.	*From Durham Turnpike.*
6 o'clock in the morning.	7 o'clock in the morning.
9 ,, ,,	10 ,, ,,
12 ,, noon.	1 ,, afternoon.
3 ,, afternoon.	4 ,, ,,
6 ,, ,,	7 ,, ,,

Coach Office, 31 King Street, South Shields."

 "The Proprietors of that splendid Steamboat, The Twilight (the fastest Boat on the River Tyne), return thanks for the unprecedented support which they have received from the Public, and respectfully announce that, having had her fresh painted and decorated," she is ready, as heretofore, to carry passengers to and from Newcastle at a fare of sixpence. The old *Comfortable* was already nearly forgotten.

 A passage to London in that "large, splendid, fast, and commodious steam-ship, the LONDON MERCHANT, 600 Tons burthen, with very superior and elegant accommodations," might be had—Best Cabin for two-and-forty shillings, Second Cabin for thirty, and even a " Dog, with food," for an additional half-sovereign,—the " splendid " steamer and " splendid " tug having their claims on public patronage and favour enhanced by the same feeble wood-cut.

"The great North of England Railway," says the *Pilot* of January 4th, 1840, "it is thought, will be opened in the autumn between York and Darlington. The journey from Newcastle to the Metropolis will thus be made to occupy but one day."

Travelling, withal, was not as yet for the million, and the great process of convection by which the well-nigh countless units making up the great English community were presently to be set in ceaseless motion—to find in such incessant change of environment, experience and moral atmosphere, a bracing, health-giving exaltation—had not yet set in. It was the vivifying currents initiated amid the lower sections of society by facility of movement that, more than any legislative influences, were to give strength, tone and direction to the aspirations of the vast artisan and labouring class, whose present condition, however, was as stagnant and vapid as a lagoon into which no cleansing stream could come.

Another great and beneficent agent of popular elevation, equally unsuspected as to its possibilities, was also being set afoot. The *Pilot*, just quoted, says " A Treasury Minute relating to the Penny Postage scheme, and bearing date December 26th, 1839, has been published. The new postage will commence on Friday, 10th of January, and the charge will be one penny for half an ounce," etc., etc.

. . . .

Shields was still a queer, out-of-the-way place, wholly identified (except as to its small beginnings in steam shipping) with the past, and scarcely touched by the spirit of innovation and progress now sweeping over the land; still a place cut off, as to the mass of its population, from England; still finding its communication with an outer world wholly in that grey uncertain sea which beat in every varying mood on its sable rocks.

And in this lesser world there were not wanting appropriate defenders of the faith in darkness and stagnation. "*Nee leets! nee leets!*" shouted these when, in 1817, it was proposed to adopt gas-lighting.[1] "*Nee eddicashin! nee eddicashin!*" they had roared in the year of the Jubilee. "*Nee farries! nee farries!*" they cried later when steam communication between the harbour-towns was mooted. "This," said one of them, as he watched the steamboat cross the river—"this is begun in ignorance and folly, and it will end in disappointment and loss." "*Nee Custom-Hoose*" and "*Nee Incorporation*" again they bellowed when the harbour became a port and the town a corporate one, and yet again when the Augean filth of the Low Street was first attacked by sanitarians.

The French feud was burning slowly out and the incidents of the long war, in the slow process of transition to the traditionary stage, were taking on the inevitable mythical character. "Glorious" victories, described by pressmen and other writers, so filled the popular imagination that the incidents of occasional defeat—the fact that the French marine fought a wonderful fight—that English frigates had now and then been captured and British crews taken prisoners, were lost in the glitter of the picture, and a thoughtless and ungenerous contempt took the place of the old rancour and hatred. Ballad-mongers, writers of sea romances and sea songs, framers of patriotic toasts and sentiments—mostly men who had never seen either sea or Frenchmen—might stir to the dregs that mean compound of swagger and selfishness so generally miscalled "patriotism," and draw complacent pictures of an ignoble and contemptible foe, whom, all the same, it had been found well-nigh impossible to overcome; but such sentiments were never entertained by the men who did the actual fighting

[1] "On Monday last a number of freeholders and inhabitants assembled for the purpose of presenting Mr. John Motley with an elegant silver snuff-box" (appropriate *snuff*-box!) "bearing the following inscription:—'Presented, Nov. 5th, 1817, to John Motley by the inhabitants of North Shields for his conduct when chairman at a meeting held Sept. 11th, 1817, to oppose the *innovation of lighting* the said town.' The night was spent with the greatest harmony."—*Tyne Mercury*, Nov. 11th, 1817.

And of these—the sea-dogs of Camperdown, of the Nile, of Trafalgar—scores were to be found on the quays, the wharves, the landing-places, and lower streets of old Shields, in every stage of picturesque dismemberment—one arm, one leg, one arm and one leg, one arm and no legs, or a mere trunk, with neither arms nor legs, drawn about on a little trolly, to be propped up against the corner of some quay or entry; the lack of legs, however, curiously exceeding the lack of arms, and grimly suggestive of the peculiar horror of 'tween-deck fighting.

Hardy, patient, long-suffering fellows, whose bronzed faces spoke in every line of hardship and privation; cheery and good-naturedly responsive when addressed, but mostly reflective, taciturn, and observant,—those to whom the fortunes of war had spared the more precious *arms* and hands, manned the sculler-boats, and waited a turn at the quay landings, or swept a crossing, or lent a hand at any honest job that could be had; no one of them all begging save always the poor armless and legless hulk who had no choice. These men who had "served their country," and to such purpose that the glories of the victories they won were ceaselessly vaunted wherever Englishmen met, yet for whom the virtue of soundly beating the "enemies of England" was left to be its own reward. Whether he had legs or arms or neither, "Jack" had to work his passage through life unaided of Britannia, who had spent all she could spare (and more) in remunerating, with monstrous pensions and grants and honours, so many of those who had the privilege of voting them to each other.

Among these silent men, the poor disfigured remnants of the long war, never one could be found to cast an ungenerous epithet at the foe against whom they had so bravely fought;[1] but deep and hot was their indignation at the treatment meted out indifferently to the best of them, whether while abroad in the service, or after discharge. Let no man speak of England's glory in the early eighteens until he has well considered the treatment of those who won her laurels. It is a chapter of shame, and they who saw face to face the human wrecks thus chucked aside after being put to the fullest possible use, and who heard from their lips the unvarnished story of needless wrongs,

---

[1] Bands of sturdy rogues with ostentatiously bandaged arm and leg stumps infested the inland towns and, bawling braggart sea-songs as they limped along, begged for charity under the guise of poor disabled tars. But such rarely ventured into Shields.

can take no full pleasure in contemplating the events which in so many ways have been lauded and sung.

Here on the quays, about the stairs, or in the sculler-boats was to be seen, and talked with, Jack Crutwell of the *Bellerophon*, who read the Bishop of Durham a lesson on the matter of Christian patience; John Hunter, too, who'd been with Nelson, and who waxed warm in denunciation of the press-gang and the cat-o'-nine-tails when apologists affected to justify either; Gideon Dodgin of the *Amethyst* and *Metis*; William Hall, 11th gun on the *Victory*; John Eldon of Lord Howe's *Victory*; John Stewart of the *Circe* at Camperdown; John Morris of the *Leda*, and many others.

Hearty, sincere, uncompromisingly frank old fellows they were, facing day by day with placid resignation the privations in which the service of their country had involved them, but tormented out of all semblance of dignity by boys who ran away with their boats, stole their mop or boat-hook, hid away a needed crutch, or made fast the painter to an inaccessible mooring-post, and then—after the sudden storm so raised had subsided, came and, sitting beside their victim, looked lovingly on the beautiful model three-decker—presently to be mounted with real brass cannon—that was gradually taking shape under the cunningly handled pocket knife of one of the old scullers.

Not a boy in all Shields was there but could pull, scull, sail, and generally handle a boat, and no manner of threat or prospect of punishment availed to deter the hardy urchins—war-orphans many of them, or orphans of the sea—from gratifying their passion for aquatics in however illicit a way. Stealthily scrambling down a slimy wharf-pile, or floating down on the "timmers"—rafts of baulks being unloaded from timber-ships—or pulling off the rags that barely veiled them, and swimming to the craft of some dozing or pondering Nile hero, they would "cut out" his *Betsy Jane* or *Nil Desperandum*, trusting to chance for a bit of floating scantling or board to swape the vessel out into the river for a roistering afternoon. A "ducking" being the penalty for such piratical doings, the boat was rarely taken back to the owner, but usually was moored close in-shore in some inaccessible place whence its owner tried to reclaim it, amid the growling sympathy of his fellow timber-toes.

The "long-narrow" street, with its quays, jetties, wharves; its multifarious trades and strange motley of nationalities; its frowzy drink-shops and dancing-rooms, still teemed with life—still formed the main artery of the town's commerce, but respectability was shrinking from contact with it, and Shields had spread away, up, over the high banks and across the plateau, from almost any point of which the gleaming sea might be seen. And here the retired sea-captain, part-owner, or chief mate, the chandler, dock foreman, or steamboat man gave expression to such æsthetic emotion as possessed his soul, in the decking of his modest residence. Whether from the impracticability of ground landlords, or the insularity of sentiment so intensified in this introspective community, "no thoroughfare" seemed to be your only code of respectability; and formal little houses built in rows formed funny *culs de sac*, into which, on Sundays, groups of foreign sailors lounged and lost their way. Queer little houses they were, with cobble-stone paved pathways, wooden pallisading, prim little doors carrying slim brass knockers. A single lower-storey window in front displayed inevitably the same small table covered with a Berlin-wool mat, on which lay—square with the four walls—the family Bible, and again on that a beaded basket containing wax fruit or flowers highly toned in the primary colours. A narrow strip of "garden"—along the front of the house—not more than two yards wide, had yet a practicable path of broken oyster shell running round it, bordered with a feeble edging of Virginian stock: in the centre a solitary flowering currant, which, however, never flowered. Sometimes instead of the flowering currant, there stood in staring surprise a ship's figure-head bought cheap at the ship-repairer's, and plenished with a thick coat of white paint. But, usually, treasures such as this were reserved for the "gardens" further up town, where on Sundays, after one o'clock dinner, Shields withdrew to enjoy the long clay pipe in the trellised and nasturtium-clad summer-house.

Here was a veritable Pantheon of wooden gods and heroes—the Elgin Marbles of the retired mariner, ravished from the indiscriminating hands of the marine store dealer, or "long-shore man." Minervas, Britannias, Neptunes, Nelsons, liberal-busted mermaids, black-eyed Susans, and cheerful admirals, in the greatest profusion and confusion. Here too, in every garden without fail, was a tall mast and top-mast, in full rig, often with main and upper yards —again all painted a dazzling white—on which a bit of bunting could be hoisted when any ripple of interest stirred the calm, not to say stagnant, surface of the town's life. Faint reminiscences of the war betrayed themselves in the battlemented ornamentation of the arbour, and in the rusting four-pounder with rotting, moss-grown tompion, standing on its sun-cracked carriage and wooden wheels in the middle of the "grass plat." The water-butt in acutely virides cent paint—the heavy lignum-vitæ locker forming a garden-seat—the thick planks dividing the borders, and showing at intervals a tree-nail hole, were all treasure-trove from the beach. "*Messis ab Altis*"[1] was presently to be the motto of the town, and a certain suggestive appropriateness was perhaps overlooked by the authorities when they made the selection. "Our harvest" was truly "from the deep." The portals of most of these sylvan retreats was of ponderous Gothic character—the jaw-bones of a whale

Here and there throughout the town, ingloriously plunged, muzzle down, up to their trunnions in the ground, stood groups of disused cannon marking a boundary, or lending dignity to the gates of a terrace, but serving mainly as vaulting posts for the heedless school-boy whose unfailing daily flight over them kept the breeches of both in a state of high polish,—a true apotheosis of Peace! These old cannon were the armament of the colliers in the by-gone privateer-ing days and, thrown aside like the discarded salts who had handled them, they found humble service as gate-posts, or down among the quays and wharves of the Low Street as corner or mooring posts.

Boxes of scarlet geranium or trailing nasturtium might be seen on the toothless ramparts of Clifford's Fort, the frigate in Peggy's Hole had her spars "housed" and, like some prosperous tabby slumbering in the sun, lay with her claws carefully concealed. Away up on the heights overlooking the bar, the little cottages forming the Barracks glistened in whitewash, and the garrison at the Castle fulfilled purely decorative functions, rarely parading in public save to attend Sunday service at the parish church—to follow, in measured tread to the chill strains of the "Dead March in Saul," some comrade to the burial-yard, there fire a volley over his grave, and march back in ostentatious heartlessness to the jaunty lilt of a quick-step, or now and then to delight the nurse-maids and urchins with a march-out. Truly the spirit of the peace—"the long, blessed peace"—was abroad!

Away from the noise and stir of the Low Street—for 'twas there only

---

[1] November 1st, 1849. The common seal of the Borough of Tynemouth. The shield bears the arms of the former Priors of Tynemouth. On a field gules three crowns in pale or, to which was added a ship for a crest, with a miner and a sailor for supporters, and the motto, "*Messis ab Altis*"—"our harvest is from the deep."

where the life of Shields found any considerable manifestation—a certain sedate repose hung over the town, its cobble-paved streets, grass-grown in many cases, being steeped in a silence so palpable that from early morning until evening the murmur of the blended river sounds, and the strangely musical crepitation of the thousand caulking hammers down at the docks, was heard through every open window and door. In such silence, the quaint, characteristic street-cries of the town became invested with an interest, and in some cases a beauty, which lingers in the memory of all on whose ears they fell.

How delightful the clarion-like ring from the strong, clear larynx of the Cullercoats fisher-lass as she strode on her way, bearing on her broad haunches the mighty "creel"—giving the difficult interval of a major seventh with a precision quite amazing; or sending through the morning air, with limpid purity of tone, the equally strange—  or again, making the welkin literally ring with her

In the herring season, when, as often as not, the market was glutted with a big take—there being no outlet by rail to the greater world of England—the sleepy thoroughfares would be stirred by the tumult of a horde of fish hawkers carting the shimmering booty away to inland villages, or to farmsteads where it could be used as manure; but, usually, the relation of supply to demand found vocal statement in this strange phrase; strange in its broken rhythm, in the weird defiance of tonal relationship in its final note, and not less strange in the persistence with which it haunts the memory of a Shieldsman.

Endless, almost, the variety of old-world snatches of spontaneous song which echoed through the streets and by-ways—most of it, as in the case of all natural music, invested with a strain of melancholy, the plaintive minor third of the rubbing-stone girls, to wit, chalk to whiten the hearth flags, or rubbing-stone, a soft, brownish sandstone used to colour the door-steps of "respectable" houses.

Perhaps the most beautiful of all the street-cries, "lingering on the summer air like a breath from scented orchards," as an enthusiastic Shieldsman said of it, was this—

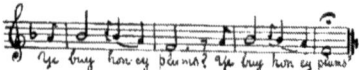

But not alone by vocal manifestations was the sleepy stillness broken. The sputtering *fanfaronnade* of the scissors-grinder as he took up his post after trundling his wheel into another street, and deliberately and with something of a faded kind of pride raised his old, battered and tarnished trumpet to his lips, is perhaps a thing entirely of the past, but it was an elaborate ceremonial, faithfully performed, and as necessary to the destruction of a good razor or the production of serrated edges on a pair of scissors as the working of the treadle. Far different the poor, broken-spirited monotonic *toot* of the "candy-man" on his tin horn—surely the most colourless and dejected of all musical emanations; but this was heard only in back lanes and alleys, whither urchins furtively conveyed a booty of rags, or bones, or bits of old iron, to be exchanged for a smear of "claggum"—a horrible sticky sweet-stuff so called—or a bit of jaundiced-looking candy; or—when larger business was being negotiated—a paper mill, flimsiest of toys; or deceptive paper kite, incapable of a rise by very nature and structure (and thus early carrying doubt and distrust into young hearts); or a monkey-up-a-stick, or what not, from his frowzy oilskin-covered basket. Such sounds, however, stirred the sluggish town-life no more than does a stone dropped into a stagnant pool; they came, passed away, and remained unnoted as the things of every-day experience are wont.

The process of segregation which was slowly cleaving the community into an up-street aristocracy and a down-street—anything, had not long set in, and the lines demarcating the several strata of social position had not been definitely drawn. The professional man, the lawyer, the magistrate, betrayed in errant locutions the thinness of his educational veneer. The well-to-do shipowner had hardly cast off the manner and bearing of the skipper and, despite his wide-skirted blue surtout, was recognised by the altogether un-awed populace as Captain So-and-so, who had lived not long ago on the banks of the river, or in the long "narrow street" itself. The shrill-toned, energetic-spoken matrons assembled for vigorous gossip by the ha'penny pant and—in bared arms, pattens, rolled-back skirts, a "weaze" in the gesticulating hand; and in the other, akimbo, an empty "skeel" resting on the hip—discussing with a monthly nurse or the "lady-wife"[1] their neighbours and neighbours' affairs, well knew the Mary this, or Jane that, who had "merried" Captain Jacks when "ay — he wiz on'y mate i' the *Jemima*" (with high inflection on the *i* of the ship's name), "an' when *hor* mother selled coals in the Laa Street, 'n' *his* kept a staall,"—dearly cherished such reminiscences, and volubly expressed when any subject of them gave him or herself airs on a rise in life. And so the poor rubbing-stone lass had a half-friendly, half-defiant, but wholly familiar nod for the new owner as he strolled a-mornings down to the "Banks," and the fishwoman held the most friendly, and even intimate, terms with his "missus" as they chaffered for fish on the door-steps.

The concentrated life of the Low Street, now passing quickly away, had gone far to produce this curious intimacy, but it was also very much due to the terrible frequency with which the bread winner was swept away, and his wife and children thus plunged from any position of comparative prosperity down into the depths of poverty and squalor. There was little opportunity for the play of refining influences, then, the urchins in the street foregathered with, and naturally took their tone and habits from, their poorest and lowest associates Perhaps nowhere were rougher men, or ruder or more unruly lads. The harsh code of sea life, the hardness of the lives of their parents, the hopeless indifference of the greater portion of the classes above them, the cruelty, the neglect, the contempt, mingled with absolute dislike, which they had to face on all hands, conspired to develop in children the fearless, unruly lack of deference so strangely manifest to the puzzled onlooker.

Down on the Banks, overlooking the "narrows" and the broad estuary of the river, paced as on quarter-deck the gruff, old collier-owners, every man of them a Jack Bunsby in his wooden, unimpressionable obstinacy, in his dogged, opinionated self-sufficiency. Brave, hardy, ponderous, unlettered men, moving in the narrowest sphere of experience, intolerant of innovation and contemptuous of any "interest' but that of the mercantile marine, they growled in unison at the state into which the river was lapsing.

[1] "Lady-wife," a woman who conveyed to seamen's wives information of the arrival of their husband's ship at the Shields *Bar*.

More of a "cursed horse-pond" than ever, they declared that a man could walk across the bar at low water without wetting his hips. In the very effrontery of incompetence and neglect, the men whose exclusive claim to the revenues of the Tyne had not yet been destroyed made a yearly "progress" from Hedwin Streams (a locality mentioned in an imaginary charter, and as shadowy as Mrs. Harris herself) to Spar-Hawk in the sea, where the "rights" to misappropriate were claimed. "Barge Day" was one of humiliation for the Shields shipowner, and symbolised his wrongs. He still had to "enter-out" his vessels at Newcastle (no Custom House having as yet been established nearer home), and it is likely he must have indefinitely continued to do so had not fellow-townsmen of brighter wits come to his assistance and broken the indefensible monopoly which oppressed him. For even in such a matter as this his deep-rooted distrust of the word "reform" rendered him half doubtful of the wisdom of bringing about any change.

Down on "the Banks," then, or on the "Library flags"—a broad space also overlooking the harbour, so called from its nearness to the Old Library on St. David's Mount, now known as the "Lit. and Phil."—he pondered in his heavy way on wrongs such as this; casting his eyes mechanically to the horizon at each turn on his short beat till, seeing a speck in the offing, he, with the faintest suspicion of animation in his manner, says—

"There's the '*Your-a-dice!*'"

"Not hor!" pointedly returns his collocutor (perhaps a stranger), unregardful of pronouns, but intent on his point.

"Not hor? That's the '*Your-a-dice*,' I tell ya."

"The '*Tarpsey-cor*,' more like."

"The '*Tarp-sey-cor*.'" (Scornfully drawing the word out.)

Whether *Eurydice* or *Terpsichore*, both sides will hold doggedly on until there is no room for further argument.

A rich anthology might be culled from the quarter-boards of these old Tyne ships, a reminiscence of the war, maybe, when the resounding though uncomprehended names of classic gods, goddesses, and heroes (after whom H.M. battle-ships were called) were always at hand to be copied straight from gilded bows or quarters. And roughly over-ridden were such names by their altogether unconscious adapters!

The "Airey-adden," the "'Roarer," the "Veenis," "Sarse," "Chair-on," "Cally-oap," "U-tarp," "A-chills," "Ni-oab," "'Polla,"

"Juner," "Mark'ry," and "Dinah" (not she popularly associated with Wilkins, but the Huntress),—all these were literally household words in the homes of Shields, on the quays, in the docks, on the library flags, in the insurance clubs—and uttered with a good faith sufficient to disconcert a university don. The *Euphrosyne* and *Mnemosyne* rhymed, of course, with *Auld Lang Syne,* and *Psyche,* the ethereal *Psyche,* had as many aliases as though she'd been " up " for her " hundred and second appearance."

But such names expressed nothing more than an undefined, superstitious regard for the unknown or ill-understood. Of a totally different class those that lay nearer the heart, pet names which, if only in a shadowy way, nevertheless to some extent defined the evolution of the shipowner himself. What were the "James and Jane," the "Thomas and Mary," "Daniel and Rebecca," "Robert and Ann," "William and Deborah," etc., but tokens of that union of hearts (or means) which had led the pushing, thrifty mate to win the hand of the cap'n's daughter (he invariably pronounced it *doubter*), and to put his savings and services into a little venture so "christened" or re-registered. The penny novelist had not yet poured his flood of Gladyses, Muriels, Veras, not even his Ethels, Ritas, or Florences, into the minds of the great serving class, hence these duplicated names, in addition to symbolising the fruition of a tender sentiment, furnished an easy means of extending a somewhat inconveniently scanty nomenclature. Sometimes the new owner, under the influence of a gallant altruism, sunk self absolutely and devoted the whole expanse of the name-board to his "Mary Ann," "Charlotte Jane," or "Sarah Margaret" or, with a higher sense of the dignity of the wedded state, swept away all evidence of pre-marital separateness in "The Dixons," "The Robinsons," and so forth. Other and older men might speak of and hail the "Brotherly Love," the "Pride of the Ocean," etc.; but these were too wide, too indefinite, altogether too inexpressive of the great fact that property and a partner had been acquired at one stroke.

And by diligence, hard strife, the relentless pursuit of one idea in life, and by luck (always by luck), more and more property accumulates, until the mate, skipper, master, captain comes finally and permanently ashore to don the blue broadcloth and take his saunter on the Banks as far as the High Lighthouse, hold argumentative converse with others of his class, spit defiantly over the iron pallisading and then wend slowly off to "the Club."

No social or society club this!—but the office of the Mutual Ship Insurance Association—say "The Eligible," which he knows only as the "Illegible" and in which his ships are "part" covered, and of which he now is probably one of the "Comet-*tee*."

Entering with a "Hi Bo-or-y!" he asks in a single sentence, "Where's the *Shipping Gazette?*" and "What news?"—opining in turgid sententiousness, as he swings into the sanctum overlooking the river, that "noh nuze is gudd nuze." Not to the "leader," nor to the intelligence columns does he pay the scantiest heed, but with accustomed eye runs down the apparently interminable columns of "arrivals and sailings" at and from every port in the world, noting keenly the position of every vessel afloat. He knows where they are to-day, remembers where last week, where on any previous voyage you like, and predicts with confidence where at any future time—barring accident! Nay, not accident! No mishap is "accident" in these latter censorious days of his, but "shee-or carelussness, sur" A golden haze is gradually metamorphosing his past sea-life and he is often heard to say, with an earnestness betokening his distrust of being believed, and perhaps a shade of doubt as to the *absolute* reliability of his memory in *this* particular matter, "Aw nivir lost a spar, sur; no, sur!—nivir 'n me life"

In this terrible "Comet-tee" room he is a fearsome autocrat, holding inquisition with fellow comet tee men into the doings of some unlucky devil of a captain who has lost, or perhaps worse, not quite lost his ship. Never in the daily round of his life getting outside the shrunken horizon of his experiences; having every prejudice clinched and riveted by perpetual association with his own class, he yet wields tremendous authority over captains and mates— nearly equal, in fact, to that he holds over the mere crew in his magisterial capacity, and, uncontrolled by any authority trained in the work of weighing and sifting evidence, he "suspends" the luckless skippers who appear before him for periods very much at his discretion.

On such judicial occasion the Comet-tee foregather somewhat earlier, and in larger number, than when it is a mere question of a "Sorvèy," or the adjustment or approval of an "average statement," and pace heavily up and down the room, pausing sometimes to gaze steadfastly out of the great bow-window at some "bottom" (a ship is ever a "bottom" to the Insurance man) newly come into harbour or being towed out, but pausing never a moment in his long loud discussion of the, as yet, unsifted evidence, for every man is talking, each unheeded of and heedless of the other, and forcibly urging "M1 opinion, sur," with ponderous gesticulation. And the tumult may be heard by the head-clerk and the office-bo-or-y, cut off though they be by double doors covered with green baize.

To them presently comes a faint knock, and then, in response to a careless "Come in," a seafaring-like man timidly enters, and instantly stumbles down the two steps leading into the office. The head-clerk glances for a moment over his shoulder and is already looking away when something arrests his attention and impels him, after another look, to saunter along to the bo-or-y and whisper him. Then both turn round, lean back against the long desk, face the new-comer, and regard him steadily. He approaches the long wide counter, already has his hat in his hand, hesitates, then stops in the centre of the room, and fumbling with a roll of charts, drops it; then, with nervous precipitation, picks it up. As he does so the head-clerk and the boy respectively exchange a wink and a grin. Mark you, this is a fine brave English master-mariner; a man accustomed to face storm and peril and death; sadly out of feather to-day surely!

With a strange, almost pathetic, mingling of propitiation and defiance, he asks for the secretary, is demanded his name, and replies, perhaps, Cap'n Blews. The young man and boy this time quickly regard each other and then the captain. Told to sit down and wait, he coughs, looks into his hat, and says he'd rather stand. Meanwhile the head-clerk passes through the green baize doors, leaving the boy still gazing with unconcealed interest at the other, who, quite unconscious of him, is now working in a pained way at some knotty mental problem. Why does the lad stare at this? He has seen many a captain come up for suspension. Is it because on that strange face, standing out beyond the knotted perplexity in the brow and the furtive anxiety in the eyes, a broad unchanging grin, as of a man who has made a good joke and is enjoying it, never for a moment disappears? Ay, truly! Yet the boy's young eyes see that there is no more mirth in the grin than in that of a skull, and he is so puzzled by the changing and indefinably incongruous expressions that seem to flicker over the face like a phosphorescence, that he makes a pretence of going to shut the outer door in order to pass the man under closer scrutiny. In a moment all is obvious and understood. From some terrible old wound the mouth has been twisted and distorted so as to fix for ever a facial expression wholly at variance with the natural expression of the poor creature—a serious, thoughtful man—who has ever to bear with him this horrible, mocking contradiction. A broad grin truly and, in the twitching nervousness now fluttering over it, so awful and uncanny that the boy shrinks away to his post and looks no more.

Until his fellow-clerk, returning from the committee-room, is beckoned to him to listen for a moment to a hurriedly whispered communication. Then both face round, and the head-clerk once more leaning his back against the desk thrusts his hands deep into his trousers pockets and whistles softly as an amused smile spreads over his face This grows more and more pronounced, until he is obliged to turn away and laugh. He puts his head to the boy's and, after a muttered word or two, both laugh and try so to smother the sound that naturally their mirth becomes uncontrollable, and they are still struggling with it when the baize doors abruptly open and the secretary comes down into the office, flushed and impatient—stands with his back to the fire; pushes the big green eye-shade up on his forehead, and, looking severely towards the clerks, sharply asks—

"Where is—— Is this Captain Blews?"

"Yes, sir"

The poor fellow turns his mask appealingly to his interlocutor. The two clerks see the grin grow more ghastly and a nervous convulsion run over the face as the men look at each other; seem to feel rather than see the secretary's distrustful frown deepen into a scowl, and then they hear in tones of choking indignation—

"Damme, sir, you look as though you thought you'd done a clever thing!"

As the double doors slam upon the retreating figures the two clerks give vent to their pent-up feelings and dance about, as the elder, smiting his leg again and again, shrieks, "Ha, ha, ha, I felt sure he'd think he was laughing."

An hour after the captain plunges out of the committee-room. not timid now, nor nervous; but with a white passion of resentment on his face that makes the grin look horrible. He takes up his hat and says bitterly, "Too bad, too bad." Then looking at the head clerk, he nods, and hurries towards the door.

The clerk regards him, and then raises his eyebrows interrogatively.

"Ah!" grimly responds the captain, as he disappears.

The green doors are presently held open, the court-martial is over, and a tumult of boisterous talk bursts out. "Laughin', sur, laughin';" "He'll laugh on the other side o' hez face, noo!" "Aa nivir lost a spar in me life, sur, nivir," etc., etc. The meeting is lumberously dispersing, and the "Comet-tee" will be smoulderingly indignant for the remainder of the day.

So it is that the captain and mate regard "luck" as ruling their lives, and submit to such tribunals with a resignation which is more than half fatalism. 'Tis a rough-shod time and rough-shod methods are the vogue; and if captain or mate were given to philosophising—which under no circumstance they are—they might come to reflect that to the crew, the apprentice, and the cabin-boy, they again, on their own part, represent as harsh, unreasoning, and inexorable an authority. The absolutism of captain and mate when aboard was tremendous; the knock-down blow with belaying-pin or marling-spike, and the brutal kick with heavy sea-boots being common and ready means of emphasising an order. Power of life and death lay in the hands of cantankerous skipper or ill-natured mate, and the crew knew it full well. A grudge was to be avoided at all cost, and gross ill-usage cringed under, else an order aloft on some furious night when the craft was staggering under heavy hail-laden squalls and jerking her spars in mad disorder, was like to settle the affair finally and for ever.

The poor apprentice—new to his duties, more than half sea-sick, his fingers frozen and almost useless—as yet clumsy at climbing, had to scramble aloft, grope his way along the dipping and reeling spar, hang over it, and pull at the freezing sheet until his benumbed hands could no longer hold. Smart, bright, alert sailors were so made, it was said, and it is true that a fearful kind of "selection" operated to produce the result, but it was at a shocking cost of human life—a cost that can never be fully estimated. Scores of poor urchins—mere children—weak in physique, and in all ways unfitted for so coarse a vocation, sailed out of the Tyne in her colliers, to drop from the crazy spars into the toiling waters of the North Sea—a mere note in the "log" stating that "the boy" was missed in the night being the last trace of him in this world.

Crazy, ill-found, rat-ridden craft many of these colliers' were; leaky as baskets, and only kept afloat in a heavy sea by slavish labour at the clanking, ill-contrived pumps. Foul with bilge stench, vermin and dirt; cramped, dark, and comfortless in "accommodation" for the hands; known to every sailor, sailor's wife, and Low Street lad as "floating coffins"—there was naught but "luck" in the way of a man finding himself compelled to sail in one of them, with the fullest conviction at his heart that the chances were dead against her living through any stress of weather. Drugged by the prowling crimp, driven by necessity, or cozened by some glib-tongued ship's husband, a handful of ill-assorted "hands," sleeping off the fumes of drink as gratuitously, as mysteriously provided, would discover that they'd "signed articles" for the *Betsy Ann*, or some sister coffin, and find themselves aboard a creaking hulk, leaking already on the smooth waters of the river, though, in sardonic phrase, said to be "ready for sea." The ship in most cases was already under weigh, slipping out of "the Narrows" towards the "bar," and a few kicks, a sullen growl, an invocation on the "luck" which had brought them to such a pass would end in a mechanical assumption of the hundred duties that lie on every hand about the sailor. If not; if the prospects of safety were too shadowy; if the portents, speaking from every vital part of the overladen hulk, were too obvious and the men refused to face the chance of "settling" with it, then the facile aid of the law was invoked, the crew was hauled before the magistrates—many of them shipowners, and most in the shipping "interest"—and three months' hard labour allotted as the alternative to the hazarding of a life against a North Sea voyage in a floating coffin.

In the "forties" a not uncommon spectacle in the long "narrow street" was that of a file of sailors—the very "boy" among them—chained in couples and being shuffled off like criminals to the police court, whence, unprotected and unrepresented, they were summarily ordered back to their ship or sent off to gaol. On one such occasion—the poor folk of Shields believe, and there is nothing improbable in the story—a crew accepted the worser alternative, sailed that day, and ere next morning's dawn were drifting lifeless among the wreckage of the miserable craft on the harbour rocks. Earlier in the century the Government offered yet another alternative, hated more intensely than either of the other—the privilege of transfer to a king's ship, but the honest and humane course of referring such matters to an impartial and disinterested authority was not adopted for many years to come. The "law," therefore, in respect to seamen, was deeply distrusted and women, girls, and children might be seen clinging to the gyved men, begging them to refuse at all hazards to go to sea—rather to prison, the crowd meanwhile hooting the representatives of authority, and giving rough but well-meant encouragement to the unlucky wretches, whom they recognised to be unfortunate rather than wrong doing.

And is it possible to wonder at this when, year after year, with a certainty that was frightful, this people—mothers, wives, sisters, brothers, children—saw those crazy death-traps by ones and twos, by the half-dozen, nay, sometimes by the dozen, or more, beaten to pieces before their eyes, and cast at their feet in matchwood?

All through the savage winter of this latitude—from early autumnal to late spring equinox—the sudden wrath of the North Sea was wont to rise in a night and strew the ragged shore-line with the broken remnants of helpless craft, huddling, like affrighted sheep, into shelter. In so busy a waterway, with the coal trade at its zenith, ships arrived, sailed, or lay off, in fleets, hence " bad weather" never " came away," as it was expressed, without swooping upon material in plenty for havoc.

At best 'twas a difficult harbour to make. On the one hand, the deadly ridge of jagged semi-submerged rocks known as the Black Middens, lying right out in the fair-way to the "Narrows"; on the other, the long treacherous shoal called "The Herd" (pron "Hard"), and, spanning them, the dreaded, uncertain "bar." It needed a brisk-witted, dauntless skipper to run such a gauntlet. No fabled *Charybdis* and *Scylla* this, when the roaring Nor'-easter, or the fell and perhaps more dangerous Sou'-easter broke loose!

Let the gale but blow for eight-and-forty hours, and such a scene of wrath fills the horizon to the very verge, as only this coarse, hard coast can yield. All night the wind has shrieked with a myriad voices, and the burdened and oppressed ear recognises that the air is vibrating with notes of every pitch and interval, from the deepest bass to the shrillest treble—all commingled in overpowering dissonance, and suggesting amid a crowd of nameless sounds the wailing and crying of human voices, the mocking of devils, the splitting shock of thunder, and the sobbing of children, and above it all, screaming up and down the mighty gamut in restless pitch, the death-song of the fiercer squalls.

At early dawn the mouth of the river, like the fabled viper's jaws, is filled with foam; out on the "Black Middens," over the

"Herd," and away on the "Bar," ceaselessly and toilsomely rise and writhe in shapeless mass unending breakers. Not a speck of green or black can be seen on the water as far as the eye can reach; all is a savage waste of dirty, blurred white, from which come hurtling and swirling on the wind, gyrating clouds of foam. The boom and roar of the breaking waters is swallowed up in the ear-splitting scream of the wind, and the din close at hand so cuts off all sound from the outer strife that the mighty breakers rise and wrestle unheard,—in an outer unreal silence that is weird and awful.

The smarter craft—the East Indiaman, the timber-bark—have long ere this run for shelter, or have stood out far to seaward, away from so perilous a lee-shore; but poor little colliers are known to be out in that white waste; perhaps also a tug or two, and a few Cullercoats fisher-boats; and already groups of men stand under the lee of the Lighthouse, or the Beacon, or a house corner, peering out in the face of rain and hail squalls, and, in quelled tones, comparing views as to the chances of comrades and mates known to be in peril. Very early in the morning ill-clad, anxious-faced women join the look-out, and as the morning wears townsmen come down in heavy coats and oil-skins to stand for a while and ask sympathetic questions of the oracles of the hour—the North Sea pilots.

Down at the club windows are owners and committee-men, with something of the old sense of a captain's responsibility and risks restored to them. Less assertive than usual, and a touch more tolerant of another man's mind, they confer and exchange opinions gravely and with shaking heads. Frequent and familiar as this old, old scene may be, it has a resistless fascination for every Shieldsman, and there is no heart in the business of the day. The lawyer is found by his head-clerk at the window of the private office, trying to make what he may of that heaving world out there through a long telescope, and even asks him to take a look. The doctor tells his dripping coachman to drive round by the river so that he may snatch a hasty glance at the great strife. The shopkeeper is pre-occupied, reflective, and errant of purpose, the shop-boy, scurrying over his rounds with a celerity wholly unwonted, and which has in it the set purpose of looking at the storm, takes the lighthouse in his course, and finds his master there, too engrossed in the tragedy of death now being played to an awe-stricken audience to express any surprise or disapprobation.

For the time the old comradeship of the "narrow street" is renewed, and a common interest of breathless intensity breaks down the barriers which fortune is slowly building, and binds the hap-hazard crowd in the bonds of brotherhood. Questions are preferred and answered and opinions discussed, with a consideration which shows how the dread peril in sight has levelled, for a time, the poor conventions which the absence (or unconsciousness) of a common interest sets up between man and his brother. The roughest of the bystanders are strangely tolerant of the incoherent and inconsequentially expressed terror of the women, who, after all, only give utterance to sentiments and fears that are stirring every man's heart. The schools have been dismissed for the day, and poorly-clad lads stand with chattering teeth and blanched faces, looking wistfully from the men in oil-skins to the water and back again, greedily listening to the scraps of bellowed conversation, and disregarding the occasional sharp order to get away home out of the wet.

Disaster has already accrued and stripped away the last remnant of ill-maintained dignity from the professors of sea-craft, who now eagerly listen to and discuss the statements of keener-eyed (albeit amateur) townsmen. A freemasonry of solicitude has been set up by the sight of a poor little "foreigner" (as she is called), a slight schooner or sloop—hardly visible, such a speck she looks in the driving spray—beating up for the harbour in a manner fateful and hopeless. Every man's soul is in his tongue as he watches the brief, ineffectual struggle, and short, pregnant exclamations of hope, of admiration for pluck, of encouragement (strangely touching these latter in their utter fatuity), come fitfully from the crowd, now careless of shelter, and clinging to the iron railings in the full force of the drenching blast. The pilots and sea-farers wear quiet, set faces · they know the little craft is past help. As she staggers on—now and then visible, but for the most part hidden under the frothy blurred turmoil—towards the great heaving range on the bar, she is seen suddenly to fall off and, in one swift awful moment, turn over in the folds of a great overwhelming mound. At the sight there comes to the plainest and meanest of the poor faces looking on, a sudden beauty which is that of the angels—the beauty of human sympathy, and the women, forgetting for the moment their own extremity, wipe their eyes with their shawls, and,—God help them!—take into their infinite solicitude the griefs of others.

Slowly the day wanes, but steadfastly the watchers keep their post, and as new-comers, pausing to recover breath and beating the wet off their feet, ask in awed tones, "How many now?" they tell the grim death-count. A brig was seen about noon, away to the nor'ard, and is pretty sartin to have "foondard." A hapless tug, disabled by a huge sea, was seen to drive on to the Herd, roll over and break up. The stern timbers and mizen-mast of a collier are pointed out, standing mistily up from the blurred mass of the Black Middens. *She* got inside the bar, but, caught by a tremendous sea, was hurried on to the rocks, pinned there, and instantly broken across the back. Wreckage is now surging up into the river, and venturesome steam-tugs are out beyond the "Narrows" trying to salvage it. The tide is slowly retreating, snarling wrathfully as it goes, beating the sand up into the superjacent water, and wreaking smaller damage on the shores of the river; but the gale grows worse, and as the black night settles swiftly and untimely over the harbour, the pilots say there will be worse work next tide, by far. Crowds now line the banks, and peer out into the infinite darkness, hoping against hope that no storm-beaten craft may try to make the harbour before sunrise. The wind is so furious that the few straggling street-lamps on the banks may not be lighted, and naught but the white shaft from the lighthouse, with the countless circling specks of sea-foam chasing through it, is visible, save it be the upturned faces of watchers catching a pale reflection therefrom

Down on the far-off beach gangs of men grope and stumble over rocks and sand ridges, seeking with lanthorns for corpses which old experience tells them they may surely expect. In some inexplicable way the pilots, skippers, and fishermen gain tidings of what is doing out in that fearsome, and to all others unseen, waste, and presently in hoarse tones, at once startling and oppressive from the intensity of suppressed emotion, make known that a "sail" has been glimpsed, and that she is in straitest peril. Landsmen strain their eyes in an attempt to follow the sheath of outstretched arms and pointed fingers, but they see nothing Nor can they gain much from the preoccupied experts who now, with strange lines in their eager faces and unwonted fire in their eyes, hold each other by the elbow, and swiftly point out and compare in short ejaculated sentences their several opinions of the poor, fated stranger's chances. More eager, more intent, become the faces of these men, and on the slightest change of expression the hearts and hopes of the bystanders hang;—at length, after one supreme rigid moment, there bursts forth in troubled tones—

"She's gyen, by God! she's gyen!"

And every soul there knows that the devoted ship is past succour.

She may sweep on to the Middens, or broach-to on the rocks under Oswin's ruin, or be lost amid the endless chain of breakers racing in upon the "Herd"; but though the catastrophe has not yet come, she is doomed beyond all possibility of doubt. There is something eerie, something to chill the heart in the knowledge that out there, in that raging strife, that soundless war of elements, the work of death is busy, under a cloud of darkness which other men's eyes are known to pierce. Soon the ultimate fate of the lost craft is quietly announced, though possibly not before the excited interest is diverted to a newer tragedy, or even to a number of them. For it was a frightful characteristic of this highway of death that its storms brought shipwrecks in groups,—a single disaster being so unusual that, after a "heavy night," men invariably asked how many ships had "got on." All through the deafening war of the night there come, in sickening iteration, fresh tidings of disaster; a blue light, or a rocket, sometimes helping the onlookers to share for a few startled moments the keen and absorbing interest which the night's work possessed for those who could unravel the scanty elements of intelligence. But not often this, for there was rarely time for rocket or blue light, the peril was so sudden,—the transition from the outer waters of the North Sea to the boiling fury of the Tyne estuary so sharp and startling to those not intimately acquainted with the dangers of the coast, that almost as soon as peril was recognised it had become unavoidable.

Down on the "Sand End," near the Narrows, is a curious, busy, striving crowd, from which, in strange contrast with the solemn sense of danger and peril oppressing all other groups, the jarring discord of a wrangling disputation arises. There are brawny pilots in great sea-boots, oil-skins, and sou'westers; huge fishermen in thick jerseys and woolcaps; riverside hands and steamboat-men in heavy pilot coats and moleskins; gaunt keelmen and giant ship-carpenters,—all shouting, gesticulating, and, at times, even threatening each other with upraised arm; expostulating, or denouncing in fierce earnestness something that is said to be "not fai-or." Strong-faced, herculean men, most of them, but not stronger in a certain dauntlessness of visage than other quieter and slighter-framed individuals whose dress denotes the ordinary non-seafaring townsman, possibly young doctor, or under-viewer of a colliery, or manager of an anchor works. The clamour is fitful but unending, its burly tones mingled with the voices of anxious, tearful women, clinging to or pulling at the arms of the unnoticing, contentious men. A few hand-lanthorns cast a flickering light upon the scene, and a dull, ruddy glow from the rude cresset standing by the doors of the lifeboat-house fitfully tints the rolling masses of vapour blowing in from the offing, the wind now and then carrying a whirling column of red sparks away over the top of the Look-out House

These are volunteers for death, and the deep-voiced struggle is for the precious right to a place in the forlorn hope. Shields is the birthplace of the life-boat, and this fierce wrangle for a place in the very ark of God is one of the most precious heritages of her sons. Men who were scarce strong enough to ship one of the big heavy oars, won by strenuous fight a seat in the devoted bark, and only when in the crux of a struggle with unimaginable billows, showed by lack of strength—never by want of courage—that it had been better they'd not been there. And there was reason, all-sufficient for the beseeching plaint of the wives who begged their men to mind their bairns and not go,—for no mere danger, however appalling, ever deterred a Shields life-boat crew from putting off to the rescue, and lives were too often lost on board the very craft which sped on its mission of help and mercy. Men were drowned or killed at their oars, thrown out of their places as they struggled through some frantic confusion of waters, and sometimes the whole crew was overwhelmed by the upsetting of the boat, and drowned in sight of the people on shore, whom they had just shaken loose from.

But in the terrible jaws of the Tyne, the greater peril of a cast-away ship lay in the fact that she could not be reached by the life-boat when in the sharpest stress of danger. The shoals of the Herd and the ridge of the Middens were accessible only in certain states of the tide, hence men chafed and fretted as they saw lives lost while the life-boat floated uselessly at the foot of the slips When, however, some battered craft passed through the iron portals of the estuary, and came to grief on a point that might by some lucky chance be reached, then with a rush the boat was crowded by a struggling mass of men, beating off frantic assailants, and angrily bidding their women and bairns to "be quiet"—palpitating with a great fear that the south-side boat[1] might be first—towed as far as the venturesome tug

[1] An equally devoted band was carrying on the same scene on the south side of the river

dared, and then cast loose in the face of a sea that would appal the soul of any man not born within the sight and common experience of it.

Through the day and through the night these men await their chance, and when it comes, hang by hours on the skirts of death, trying to get 'longside the shivering wreck and picking up now and then the man or two who have not already been swept off by the rushing mounds of live water which follow each other so swiftly over the broken hull. The roar of rude jubilation that rises when the drenched and battered boat brings in a few saved men is loud enough to stand out above the noise of the wind—there is cheering, gesticulation, and rough clapping on the back, and shaking hands, and exuberant welcome for the rescued waifs, as they are hurried off to warmth and hospitality. Sometimes she comes back with the dead or dying aboard,—the strained pathos of the night is terrible. Bodies are carried to the dead-house, bearded men break into a wail as the not yet cold form of a father, brother, or son is leant over and recognised as it lies back on the wet sand. Women on their knees weeping over a lifeless boy—"maa poor poor bairn"—swiftly recall to the on-lookers' mind the rude picture on the "Good Design" banner. *Messis ab Altis!* the Angels of Death might say, *Messis ab Altis!*—but these are only the first-fruits.

In the earliest dawn the forms of four, of six, of twelve, or maybe more stranded vessels slowly break through the darkness,—some mere hulks with the sea running clean over them, and every sign of life gone,—others going to pieces but with yet a man or two lashed to the mizen, unrecognisable as living or dead, but nevertheless the object of toiling and unremitting effort on the part of the life-boats. The shore is strewn with wreckage, and the desolation in the hopeless grey daybreak is unspeakable. Children, whose parents have not been at home all night because of the peril of some dear one, come down to the beach in the early morning, cold and trembling, whimpering with hunger and fear, and gaze curiously at the salt-coated salvage men. The search for the dead is commencing in earnest, and for the whole day, desolation is busied with the homes of the poor. Less unhappy they, however, who so soon and so surely learn the bitter worst; others there are whose dead never come to them, and whose heart-sickening sorrow out-lingers the brief interval of public sympathy.

In a day or two the waters of the harbour wear an aspect of tranquil beauty that bears no trace of what has passed; ships are

SHIELDS HARBOUR.

being tranquilly towed to sea, a mild breeze filling their unfurled sails; the fishing fleet is already departing and spreading like a flock of gulls; the rocks of the Black Middens stand out of a glassy expanse of faint blue, and cockle-shell row-boats carry freight of country-folk to see the shattered quarters of the hapless brig which lies wedged between the topmost rocks of the reef, and to listen, open-mouthed, to the scullerman who points to the place from which the poor sailor was seen to dangle head down, while his life was slowly battered out as he swung against the mast. The wreckage has been sold by auction, and is being carted away, a few poor wretches have been sent to prison for picking up an unconsidered trifle or two of flotsam; the town is busily making up for lost time and—a few children, who last week played lustily and noisily in the Low Street, have found sudden gravity in the sodden atmosphere of the Poor-house.

But to this community death comes in other forms as terrible and nearly as familiar, bringing in its dark wake a heroism that, in steadfast disregard of awful consequence and in profound self-devotion, is unspeakably beautiful. Of the dire sounds that may break upon the human ear none is more awful than that of a colliery explosion, and when the dread cry—too well known on the Tyne banks in those days—went up that the "pit had fired," a moving scene of agony broke among this same great class of the poor. Not recklessly and ignorantly, and therefore unconsciously, did intrepid men stand up for the rich privilege of going upon rescue duty but, in the full knowledge of experts, with the assured conviction that the chances of a safe return were outweighed beyond expression by the prospect of death in its most dreadful form; knowing, too, what the death of the bread-winner implied in such days for those left behind. They, the poorly paid, the overworked, the scouted workers—the "rabble" of England—pressed in upon the noble-hearted viewer and manager, and with difficulty were held back while the workings were being cleansed of the poison that would have involved instant death.

Down in the workings the highest forms of bravery and self-sacrifice were the constant elements of a pit accident, whether manifested in the touching prayer of the wifeless or childless man that his mate would no longer help him along the fire-stricken byway, but think of his bairns and hasten for life's and their sake while there was yet time; or in the dogged refusal of the father, with the yearning of his soul for his loved ones above there in God's daylight forcing the tears to his eyes, to lay down the insensible body of some pit laddie he was bearing to the shaft, and so make his escape from the raging Hell around him Sons of these men, in years to come, simply and unostentatiously showed the stuff that was woven into the very being of this people, by some act of devotion as noble as it was unnoticed (and comparison can go no further) The engineman, steadfast at his lever down in the engine-room of the slowly settling screw-collier, wistfully facing in dark loneliness the creeping water steadily rising upon him, facing unflinchingly the knowledge that his devotedness was affording his fellows on deck the chance of an escape which he could not hope to share. Men speak of the forlorn hope of the field, but what is that to such a grim, lonely act of immolation as this? These, the precious, priceless lessons of self-abnegation taught by the poor, contemned, abused, and almost hated "lower class," found no poet to sing, no impassioned orator to vaunt, no statesman to laud, among a people which yet vaunted its military exploits with an iteration rendering them well-nigh contemptible, and which thought it needful to "reward" its heroes of the sword with a vulgar lavishness that raises in the breasts of the thoughtful a sense of resentment and disgust.

All round the horizon that encircled the Shields poor lay untimely death and chronic destitution. The fateful sea which beat on the harbour rocks or lapped its green-grown wharves, was at once the inevitable source of livelihood, as it was the assiduous agent of poverty and misery. Children growing up close by it and learning to read its mystic moods and understand its prophetic voice foresaw a cruel, coarse life, and thereto a sudden, violent end. Men living in daily touch with the mighty and more tragic phenomena of nature, and hardened in the school of privation, lost all sense—perhaps never gained any—of the petty distinctions that man and man set up for worship, hence nowhere could be found a more fearless, unquailing set of people than those of the lower streets and quays of North Shields. They would argue with any man and fight him afterwards. Horse-play and practical joking of the roughest sort had to be endured by all who came among them, and the rudest banter quietly put up with. Young apprentices found they must face for a series of years a course of brutal treatment imposed by, not cruel but, hard-fibred, unthinking youths and men, who (sharing—in a vulgar way though—the faith in punitive measures held by the great

AN UNRULY PEOPLE.

ones of the earth) regarded it as a necessary regimen for effecting the "hardening" of a boy and for developing his manhood.

Of this "hardening," assuredly there was enough! Cabin-boys and powder-monkeys—mere children—told their comrades unvarnished tales of low and coarse morality, and coarser and crueller ill-treatment; the little chimney-sweep could sear the souls of his casual acquaintance with stories of outrage which, though almost unbelievable, were nevertheless true, and known to be true by people who deprecated any interference with the "*interests* of employers."

Neither example nor precept were wasted on any such as these, and the haughty frowning contempt of those above was met by a noisy, assertive disregard, in which there was no jot of deference.

Such were the lads—the unruly sons of an unruly people—"the very rudest boys in all England," as some titled unknown once called them—whom it was the new-found privilege of Thomas Haswell to encounter, and—if he might—tame and teach.

CHAPTER VI.

A BEGINNING.

"Seek him that maketh the seven stars and Orion."

On the 6th of May, 1839, some twenty-one years after leaving the "Jubilee" as one whose education was to be advanced no further, the erewhile finished scholar of ten winters entered upon his duties as master, taking up his abode in the little plain-featured house attached to the school.

Looking round, he found things had not greatly improved in the interval. Inside, they were indeed worse, for the scholars had dwindled in number to some forty, and their condition in all respects was disheartening; outside, a public opinion hostile to any considerable improvement in the mental daily bread of the poor urchins. The "system" in vogue was dull, monotonous, and stereotyped, lacking every element of vitality; nothing in it to stir the imagination of the brightest of lads, nothing to open their eyes or to touch and win their hearts; nor, indeed, was it deemed good there should be. And so, the wearisome copying out of platitudes upon slates, the listless reading of dull monitions from repellent lesson-books, the aimless iteration of the four simple rules of arithmetic went on as of old.

The boys attended school only "when it suited their parents," and in this matter parents were in the last degree wayward, for the scholar was often wanted to assist the family bread-winners, and in any case was handy for carrying his father's dinner to the docks, or to the pit, or for helping in his boat, minding the baby, or working the mangle, and for all such purposes the lad was kept from school without leave or notice. It was only when he suited himself, and took unlicensed holiday—a thing he gloried in, and was envied for by less adventurous comrades as "playing the neck"—that the parental indignation was aroused, and the poor cuffed and buffeted ragamuffin towed up to the dread portals of the House of Chastisement and bundled right into the clutches of retribution.

Unpunctual and disorderly when they came, the boys did their utmost to avoid coming at all, and perhaps that fact as much as any other proves how cruelly antagonistic to all the instincts and sentiments of childhood were the prevailing methods of teaching. As in the great outer world, so in the microcosm of school-life there reigned a stern intolerance of amusement, relaxation, fancy, and imagination. 'Twas an age of undiluted statistics and naked facts; Gradgrind was in his zenith, political economics of the aridist type were forced into the discussion and solution of every question; the doctrine of demand and supply had come as a new gospel to men, and "proved" all its adherents claimed: an atmosphere of "useful knowledge," like some deadly after-damp, was choking the beneficent inspiration that renews the human imagination in every generation, was stifling all the generous impulses of childhood, and driving them to find development in what was called mischief, for which there was ever ready the sovereign remedy—punishment. It always in the end came to *that*.

Such schools were taught on what was called the *monitorial* system—that is to say, the "classes" were taken chiefly by monitors, the monitors being instructed by the master (provided always that he had sufficient interest in them and zeal for his work). But these were, after all, only the older boys, and in common with the whole of the scholars they left school at an early age, few remaining after their twelfth year—the majority at eleven, and many even at ten.

School buildings were little better than ugly barns, badly lighted, and, of course, wholly unventilated. People had scarcely decided whether cleanliness was not ungodly; whether a bath might not in its nature be something sinful, but as to ventilation, it was very obviously a craze—perhaps a dangerous one—hence the windows of the stuffy schoolrooms were never opened and the air growing fouller and more asphyxiating as the long day slowly spent itself, rendered the sprightliest youngster drowsy and dense in spite of himself Narrow benches or forms, too high to allow his feet to touch the ground, gave him "pins and needles" in his legs, as the villainously ill-contrived "desks" twisted his back and gave him a stitch in his side. To say that his lesson-books were printed as badly as they were written is to say that they could not have been worse—paper and type unsuited for the eyes of children were yet much too good for the dismal rubbish set forth by their means. Written by persons devoid of capacity for (to say nothing of experience of) teaching, many were couched in a tone of ponderous priggishness and turgid self-satisfaction wholly detestable to any healthy mind.

But no allowance was made for any of these deadly influences. If the boy were drowsy from poisoned air, or restless because of his tingling feet, or irritable from headache, or if he caught infection from the dullard whose book he was straining eyes and wits to extract some gleam of meaning from—the result was unvarying and inevitable: he expiated the sins and shortcomings of all such oppressors in his own proper physical person. The one great agent of elevation, the great lever for raising boyhood, the lever of the very first and only order, was the cane; and upon the backs of generations of unlucky urchins folly and ignorance were allowed—with this instrument—to cut the record of blundering arrogance. It is not difficult to perceive how seriously the sense of justice must have been distorted and deformed in the minds of children by the consciousness of wrong deduction and dogged persistence in error on the part of those to whom they were expected to look up. No boy in his heart harbours any resentment for deserved punishment, and he will forgive almost anything save unjust treatment, hence, when it is remembered that an element of very gross injustice ran through the whole system of teaching in the earlier half of the century, it is difficult to resist a conviction that enormous moral harm was perpetrated.

In their poor homes the opportunity for study was practically *nil.* The family "lived" in a single room, and in this, more often than not, the long protracted toil of the day extended far beyond the bedtime of the children The father, even if an artisan, could not possibly maintain a family on the scanty wages of the time save by taking work home with him, and, if a decent man, he rarely failed to endeavour to increase his earnings in that way. He might perhaps be a tailor or shoemaker, and if so his "hours" more than ran round the clock. Carpenter, pitman, tinsmith, labourer, let him be what he may, there is always work at home in the evening, and for this he requires all the artificial light that can be afforded. The mother takes in washing, or mangles, or sews, or she has some little business—as selling fruit, vegetables, fish, wilhcks (periwinkles)—and her stock must be prepared and arranged over-night, wherefore the single tallow dip cannot be approached by the student, nor can he long be sure of being allowed to spoil his eyes by striving to master his spelling by firelight. For on one side or the other, either father or mother, there is rooted objection to the sacrifice of time this new thing called "eddicashin" involves, and the boy is fiercely ordered "to get oot o' the hoose an' maa way"—or pettishly told to stop wasting his time and to get some work into his hands. It is never thought possible he can by any chance need play; that it is a physical necessity for him if he is to develop into a well-balanced man has not yet broken in upon the minds of the superior classes, who know everything, and particularly what is right and proper for the poor. And the poor have derived some ill-defined notion—possibly from a copy-book heading, perhaps from a local preacher, or from one of the dismal moral story-books of the time—that the Devil lies specially in ambush for idle hands, and hands, of course, are always idle, however young and unformed, unless they are toiling at work of some kind The boy doubtless puzzles now and then over the problems presented to him in this curiously inconsistent world of his—he is no young Newton or Stephenson; he does not *want* to sit by fire or by candle to pore over the crabbed characters that are hateful to him; but he knows that unless he can knock some of their sense into his head ere the morrow he will be flogged as surely as that morrow comes, and with as much sincere application as though he had all the chances and opportunities a student could need.

Nobody of his class precisely likes this "eddicashin," then. His father perhaps hates it, and denounces it,—nay, goes so far as with threatening fist to interdict it. Then the mother, liking it no more than he, but fearing and respecting as fearing it, will shield the boy and help him to keep it out of father's way. Or maybe the father, a thoughtful man, sees that with this thing—this l'arnin'—lies the future, and sees too that though it has gone hopelessly past for him, it will afford his lad a better chance than he himself has had of making a decent living. In this case he will take the boy's hand in his own and lead him up to the school, where he will try to have the work set afoot on lines he can comprehend, and which will accommodate certain unspoken designs he has upon the leisure of the youth. Get it quickly over, that is the desideratum demanded alike by boy, parent, and master, spiritual or otherwise. Dose him and drench him as quick as may be with what he has to *take in* to be a scholar, and then get him off to some useful work where the Devil can have no legitimate right to meddle with him. L'arnin' was given, and taken, very much like tar-water, because of a belief that, being nasty, it may be good and do good. So of teaching and l'arnin' there was as much, or little, as might be, but of *edu*cation absolutely none.

To the new master, with a passion for his work lying warm at his heart, there was no enigma to solve in all this The apparent contradiction between the apathy—if not something stronger—manifested by these boys and his own life-long yearning for the light of culture and knowledge, was reconciled the moment he confronted the problem, and a resolution of the difficulty as quickly grasped Filled with a tender sympathy for children of every grade, his heart was touched at the sight of these dull, weary faces—dulled too often, alas, by hunger and cold, and he swiftly recognised that his first work must be to kindle in those young minds some new interest, curiosity, wonder—what you will—to rouse the intelligence that had been as it were so deliberately darkened and deadened. Deep down in the heart of every child, whether rich or poor, there lay, as in a mine, precious ore, and he knew that his work as a winner was to get at, bring to the surface and purify, the metal, while e'iminating the baser elements with which it was in varying quantity associated,—a work surely never to be achieved by mere crushing and stamping. Educationalists are to-day still engaged in learned disquisition on the wisdom or unwisdom of equal culture of the physical, intellectual and æsthetic faculties, though it is doubtful whether the case of the children of the very poor has come into the purview of the discussion; but the absolute necessity for such method of training for *all* classes had intuitively been grasped, fifty years ago, by the new teacher, and he straightway set about laying down as perfect a combination of the three as it was then possible to contrive.

"In the very first year," he says, "I introduced vocal music."

Music—of a kind—is now a quite common, and indeed, in Board Schools, a compulsory subject, but away back in 1839 "John Hullah had not yet been appointed by Government to teach music to the million," and it is altogether impossible now to realise what a craze this innovation was held to be. The thoughtful old Quakers were in this matter as hopelessly in the dark as their darker neighbours, and only now are finding their way to the light. It was a tremendous step, yet an instant and extraordinary success. But here was no mere matter of learning "by ear," that is by rote, to drawl a few children's songs or psalm tunes. The scheme was genuine, thorough and systematic. Such of the boys as possessed any natural capacity for music were taught to *read at sight* from both the Staff notation and from a *Sol-fa* system which was held by the master—an expert in all three—to be superior in most respects to the *Tonic Sol-fa*, and to that used by Hullah.

First was prepared a colossal music-board, an affair of some twelve or fourteen feet in length, and perhaps two in depth. On its surface the master himself painted four *staves* in white lines on a black ground, of such dimensions as to be readily visible from a distance equal to half the length of the school. On music days this great-manuscript—a reminiscence of the bandsman's slip—was mounted upon two easels and placed athwart the school-room, facing the parallel rows of desks, the lesson for the day chalked upon it with a celerity remarkable in itself, having regard to the beautiful character of the writing, the marshalled pupils, all standing, then being examined, one after the other, as to the characteristics of the piece of music, before beginning to sing.

What key?—E flat. How many flats? What are the flat notes? How do you know the key is E flat? What is the relative minor? State the notes forming the common chord. Common or triple time? How do you know it is $\frac{3}{4}$ and not $\frac{6}{8}$ time? *Sol-fa* the first two bars (the master writing under the notes the syllables as given by the boy—if right, or if wrong, asking the next boy). So proceed the preliminaries; then, sounding an A tuning-fork, a boy is asked how he'd proceed to get the key-note. A C fork is then produced, sounded, and the same question propounded. Striking the fork sharply and resting its foot on the board the note C swells out on the ear, and the class is asked to "take" it. Beautifully in pitch the note rings out from the whole body. "Now give the key-note, E flat." Not quite so unanimously comes the correct pitch, for there are always present a few beginners, and they have not noted that the interval is minor, an omission they are immediately made conscious of by an indignant stare from their surer fellows. "Now sing the common chord of E flat," which done, the key is firmly fixed in the minds of the boys.

"How do you count this time?" "Down, right, up, sir," answers the boy, suiting his action to the formula, raising his right hand—bringing it down with an audible slap upon the extended palm of the other—moving it horizontally to his left and finally raising it to the first position as he says, "one, two, three."

"Now beat four silent bars and go off"

In a moment fifty, seventy, sometimes a hundred, pairs of hands are going rigidly through the triangular evolution, making a sounding crack at the initial beat of each division, and at the opening of the fifth bar there comes forth from the strong vocal chords of the united group of learners a burst of sure melody.

The "intervals" are steadily worked at from seconds to tenths, keys, relatives, rests, times—broken and syncopated (old Corelli and scraps of crabbed melody from old ecclesiastical composers being much used for this latter drill)—all systematically dealt with Two-part and three-part pieces written out on the board are analysed, dissected, *sol-fa'd* and sung: rounds and catches of prodigious intricacy worked out—the lovely Elizabethan madrigals and later glees and part-songs being mere child's play—finally the ready-hand of the master chalks an original melody, adds "seconds" to it, and then, striking his fork, leaves the boys to attack and go through a piece of music that they have neither heard nor seen before.

The unerring precision with which such reading was usually accomplished was regarded by visitors who came to look on as a marvel. When opportunity presented itself the dominie, offering a piece of chalk, would ask the visitor—and in later years, when the school had passed under inspection, the official—to write a test phrase or melody with which to put the class to proof, but it was rarely the gentleman accepted what was rather an ordeal for him than for them—the sharp-set, well-drilled young scamps being sufficiently "up" to recognise a 'prentice hand at composition, and cruel enough to show it

The mysteries of the clef were to these youths no mystery, for they were schooled in the uses and meaning and necessity for not only *treble* and *bass* but also the *alto* and *tenor* clefs. The theory of music and harmony were taught to such as evinced any special faculty for the divine art, and the esoterics of the figured bass opened up and expounded to those of them who cared to explore the subject.

What a new emotion all this made for the poor youngsters! 'Twas like a newly-found sense; the avidity with which the music class assembled—the bright exultation beaming out of young eyes as the voices swept triumphantly along the steeps of some broken range of intervals—the deep, intent concentration bestowed upon the more abstruse portions of the lesson, all assured the master—who needed no assurance, however—that he was saving, not wasting, time, and afforded adequate proof of the high popularity, with the boys, of this "useless subject." John Hullah's admirable adaptation of *Wilhelm's Method of Teaching Singing* appeared a few years later, and was much used in the elementary classes, though his system of *sol-fa* was carefully excluded from use.[1]

On the bare white-washed walls of the school hung neither map nor chart. At one end of the room, on the chimney breast, was painted in large letters of yellow on a black ground—doubtless by the quondam journeyman-painter himself—a double alphabet of flourished capitals and soberer small characters. At the opposite end, in flourishes and scrolls, a list of donors (and the amount of their donations), headed by his Grace the Duke of Northumberland,—and these constituted all the mural aids to learning possessed by the institution. Big maps might be purchased with money, but no money was to be had for such purpose. Nor were the donors sure that money might be wisely bestowed to that end.

The teacher, however, felt that he must somehow solve this question of affording his lads the benefit of another new subject taught on practical lines, and so, with characteristic originality, diligently cast about for a means. With the great music-board, perhaps, unconsciously stirring him, he hit upon the one practical plan, and here again his skill as a painter helped him. "I next projected on the walls of the school—in oils—the two terrestrial hemispheres, and coloured and varnished them; the diameter of each was *eight feet*, and they were much admired, teachers coming from long distances to see them."

---

[1] The *Musical Times* first appeared about this time, and the Maister was always enthusiastic in speaking of the benefits conferred upon the people, in this excellent publication, by worthy Vincent Novello.

These great hemispherical charts of the world—unusual in size even now, reaching as they did almost from ceiling to floor, and difficult to project in such a position—were painted direct on the walls (the master paying Tom Suttie, one of the lads, sixpence per night for holding the candle) and, until in the course of years they scaled off, afforded to successive hundreds of pupils a more vivid grasp of the broad features of the earth's surface and their inter-relation than could by any other means have been possible, and they further made the subject of geography a favourite one with the scholars. Hundreds of ship captains must yet have these great maps stowed away in the recesses of their memories, and recognise, when they chance to think of them, how their own memory-impression of the great oceans first took form and grew out of their silent ever-presence. For years the Jubilee lads were recognised, and feared, by Shields skippers, as tartars at geographical cross-examination.

From these big charts the boys were taught systematically to copy the various continents, islands, and other land divisions, and, what is equally important, though not universally recognised as such, the oceans and seas themselves as entities apart from the land. The correct projection of meridians and parallels (which in few projections are "parallel") was fully explained, for of course no skeleton maps had yet appeared, and the student commenced with a blank sheet of paper before him,—after all the only method of mapping possessing any genuine value.

But though the smaller details of geography—perhaps rather topography—necessitated the use of plane surface maps, the master had a rooted objection to their use for the larger purposes of earth-study, and held that the indispensable instrument, particularly for beginners, was the globe. When the chaotic condition of the majority of atlases in regard to the "projection" of their different maps is considered, this truth is instantly recognised, and the effect, upon the minds of children, of the hopeless inconsistency between the outlines of the same country as they appear in different maps of the same atlas, appreciated. With an absurdity quite inexplicable that beautiful though most conventional of projections—the Mercator[1]—is used as a frontispiece to most children's atlases of to day, and it would be

[1] That delightful writer on subjects of this class, the late R. A. Proctor, F R A S, suggests that the principal use of Mercator's projection now is to "*demonstrate*" how greedily Russia has absorbed territory as compared with other less rapacious States. Mercator might, in our day, have devised it for that very purpose.

difficult to find an ordinary school geography with even a half-page of explanation of its uses and properties, or a word of warning against its illusory presentation of proportional areas.

The globe, then, being the only legitimate basis for the study of geography, our dominie set his heart on obtaining one, but the globe was a costly instrument, and, again, not "necessary" for the education of poor children. As no funds could be obtained from the governors of the school, the only alternative was to buy one with his own money. And shortly after painting the great planispheres he was lucky enough to come across a pair, celestial and terrestrial, twelve inches in diameter, in good condition and complete in respect to accessories "These," he says, ' I purchased myself, and afterwards found them of great service in the geography classes,"—for of course, though his own property, they were at once transferred to the service of his boys. But the celestial member of the pair was now available, and the possession was too precious a one to be left unused,—"it suggested the introduction of astronomy, the elements of which afterwards became one of the most prized of all the subjects taught in the school."

The purest, most elevating, and ennobling of the sciences, into the study of which there need intrude no jot of that impertinent question, so detestable to Faraday—"What *use* can you make of or out of it," astronomy, was carefully taught to those poor children of the poor fifty years ago, not as an "aid to navigation," but as a subject of such intrinsic excellence and beauty as to be indispensable in the work of raising and dignifying the thoughts and aspirations of young minds. "Yes, I suppose," said a Birmingham man to the author when talking of this matter, "yes, I suppose astronomy would be useful to people in a seaport town." He perhaps gave unwitting expression to the sentiments of the vast majority of his fellow-citizens, for in Birmingham, the very *Mecca* of popular educationalists, where, in its noble Midland Institute, with its thousands of students, its numerous suites of class-rooms and laboratories, the boys and girls of the people may learn almost aught from Greek to the euphonium; where modern science holds proper terms with the classics (meeting on terms of equality and not as a poor relation), where ethics, æsthetics, philosophy and mechanics are all presented in their most attractive garb and their pursuit encouraged by accomplished teachers and abundant apparatus—in this temple of modern learning there was, up to the year 1891, no small niche for that science which the ancients honoured as the greatest of all; the science which is set in the heavens themselves and whose glories are spread before the eyes of every sentient creature. Astronomy found no place in the Midland Institute until 1891, when a small class of about twelve students made the beginnings of an experiment which should have been attempted in the day-schools. It is true Birmingham is no seaport, but she might nevertheless find something even "useful" in a moderate attention to that sublime study which is at once nature's system of pure mechanics and the source and fountain of all that is highest in mathematics.

In the offices of a great manufacturing concern a discussion one day arose among a group of mechanical draughtsmen as to whether the sun does or does not rise due east and set due west every day in the year. One or two held that its position at rising and setting varies day by day, but a large majority was positive that it does not, or, at any rate, by so inappreciable an amount that it could not be observed. Others said it appeared probable that there must be *some* variation, but no one of them had any notion that it is enormous—that it varies day by day, and that its amount depends upon the latitude of the place of the observer, and finally, that the phenomenon is known as the sun's *amplitude*, and, as such, made daily use of in navigation.

Such ignorance would be impossible were geography taught from the globe, for in dealing with the most elementary of the problems which the merest handling of that neglected instrument forces upon the attention and solves, the laws ruling the sun's position at rising, culmination, and setting, as it were, evolve themselves. The significance of the incident lies in the fact that it occurred among men whose daily avocation treats of mechanical laws, and whose very formulæ are the derivatives of astronomical observation and theory. The widespread ignorance, or rather anti-knowledge, of astronomy, is perhaps the most striking feature of that general ignorance of science for which the unrestrained hand of the *classic* and metaphysician is responsible. Let but a comet appear, Jupiter and Venus culminate, a meteor shower be predicted, or an eclipse of favourable presentation accrue, and the flood of newspaper "science" that follows is something to marvel at. A recent outburst about Mars furnishes an instance which is perhaps rather melancholy than contemptible, for it indicates that while nature has given to most men the great *sehnsücht* for natural knowledge, viciously one-sided systems of learning have pushed aside contemptuously the best elements for developing that devout trustfulness which, early manifested in the child, may be nurtured and increased to the last days of the longest life. It is curious a man should be ashamed to avow his inability to construe a sentence in Greek or Latin and yet laughingly admit that he cannot explain why solar and mean time differ—if even he know that they do differ—or by how much. Yet could he but fully realise what his pastors and masters have deprived him of, he would probably be more angry than amused.

Howbeit, in 1840 the boys of the Jubilee were being grounded in a system of geography and the elements of astronomy, which, while taking in its sure course all the vital and fertile elements of both, was yet accomplished in an amount of time incredibly small, though, obviously enough, such time-economy was due precisely to that quality of dealing with fundamental essentials which, once grasped, are never forgotten. The globe, with its extraordinarily facile methods, taught at once, and to the eye as to the imagination or intellect, the antipodal relations of the various land and water surfaces, the relative surface curvature of different land masses, the *rationale* of seasonal changes and the sun's spiral path between the tropics; the phenomena of sunrise, noon, and sunset, and their variation according to latitude, of twilight and dawn in different parts of the world, the whole subject of local time, so puzzling to sea-going passengers, and so inadequately explained by many who think they comprehend it; the subject of dialling too, regarded by many as an abstruse mathematical one, was, as it were, incidentally unfolded in using the globe. the whole of these—with, of course, many others obviously needing no reference—so bound up or interfused that in grasping this or that fact another came within reach and in getting some difficult relation well into the eye, some new one floated into the range of observation. Considered in respect to the amount of mind development and relief afforded by a "use of the globes," the time occupied week by week was, indeed, astonishingly little. The manifest defects of maps, of whatever projection, was elucidated by a comparison of the spherical with any plane surface to which its delineation might be transferred—a matter of importance not generally recognised. The trustfulness of the child-mind is unbounded until discovery is made that it has been misplaced, when, like some sensitive plant, it shrinks from contact with the offending element, and this being true of the intellectual as of the moral nature, it is not difficult to realise how much instinctive uncertainty, not to say distrust, arises in the minds of students when the inconsistencies suggested in the best maps are encountered, unless they are carefully shown to be results of conventional treatment, and, hence, *not* inconsistencies. The degree is said to equal $69\frac{1}{4}$ English miles, but if, inquisitively desiring to prove this, the boy tries the scale of miles absurdly affixed to most maps, he finds not only that the degree rarely measures $69\frac{1}{4}$ miles, but that its value *varies* with the position in the map from which it is taken. Parallels of latitude are seen to be nowhere parallel, the great circle called the equator is a straight line, but the two circles lying on either side of it, called the tropics, bend their backs to each other In the "Mercator" every attempt to verify geographical factors is foiled and the world is discovered to be without poles. Maps, in fact, are instruments of so highly conventional a character that, if the beginner must be taught from them, the earth's surface should at first be shown on *circular* charts bearing neither meridians nor parallels.

With the globe all convention of the sort disappears and the teacher goes along his path free from apprehension of falling into traps and springes, the puzzling Mercator and the obvious orthographic projections are seen to be, not only useful but necessary forms of presentment and, in showing this, half their uses have already been taught.

But all this was ancillary, as it were, to geography or earth-study. The subject of astronomy covered a close and thorough investigation of such of the features of the solar system as could be accomplished without the aid of mathematics. The phenomena of solar and lunar eclipses, of the moon's phases, the equation of time, the tides and their relation to the moon's motion,—these and a host of like subjects were carefully studied in class, the problems being invariably worked with the globes at hand, each boy having in his turn to demonstrate his full grasp of the matter under consideration before it was passed There were no books in the school treating of such subjects, hence all diagrams had to be extemporised on the spot (the most certain and permanent of all methods of teaching), and a rigid drill with chalk and blackboard developed a valuable facility of explanation. Some few years later a second-hand copy of that admirable old work, Thomas Keith's *Use of the Globes,* came into the hands of the master and, being at once transferred to the service of the school, gave extension to the operations of the astronomical class. A knowledge of the star groups and the changes in their seasonal apparition was obtained by the best of all means—viz., a careful and systematic study of the celestial globe as a preliminary, and a comparison star by star with the display in the heavens.

On a clear winter night, long after school hours, when the steadfast eyes of the firmament looked in upon a dark world, the globe was carried out into the school-yard, placed upon a table, and there —surrounded by a small band of lads—the master stood with a hand lanthorn, ready to impress the young minds with that overpowering and soul-stirring sense of the profound truthfulness of nature which can only come of a devout study of her wondrous face. Some of the lads, in woollen comforters, are bare-footed, and stand with blue, watery noses, looking silently on at the preparations. The globe is "rectified" as speedily as thought, and generally by the youngest astronomer present—for they all know *that* operation as they know the alphabet—who is then desired to say what constellations *may* be seen at this hour and season—*Orion* and *Canis* perhaps in the south, *Taurus* and *Cetus* in the west. "Find *Omicron Ceti*, then." The butt of a pencil is placed over the figure of the star on the globe, the point stretching skyward, and all eyes follow its direction out to the winking *Mira* down in the southwest. A month or so later the quest may be for *Spica Virginalis*, when again the pencil points to the brilliant gem scintillating through the lower regions of the atmosphere near the horizon. Less conspicuous and unnamed beauties of the group are followed through until the lad has their relative positions fixed in his mind; and as he and his comrades, with tingling fingers thrust into trousers' pockets, trot home, they now and then glance up at the group as a new acquaintance not readily to be lost in the flux of years.

The rising, culmination and setting of the principal stars and star groups are steadily worked at, the right ascension and declination at given times, the sun's place from season to season, zenith distances, amplitudes, azimuths, and so forth, until the art of navigation has been approached and largely acquired as a mere incidental outcome of these astronomical inquiries. And, as *Monsieur Jourdain* found he'd been talking prose for forty years without knowing it, these lads in chatting with skippers and mates discover that they have unconsciously acquired some considerable knowledge of the art of navigating a ship. The regular study of navigation was indeed so skilfully approached that it became a privilege and a delight to be admitted to the class. Many of the boys took up the subject as a recreation, and doubtless, living in a seaport town, found it a "useful" one.

Necessarily the treatment of many of the problems in astronomy involved the use of geometrical construction, hence it became apparent that with the introduction of the "globes" practical geometry must be made available for the scholars, but here again lack of funds was a stumbling-block of more than ordinary difficulty— for a time, indeed, proving insurmountable. There was not a "case of instruments" in the school, and any levy upon its resources for such purpose as obtaining one was not to be dreamed of; indeed the master recognised clearly enough that any suggestion of the kind would not only involve a prompt and peremptory refusal, but possibly a sharp *taboo* of the subject itself. Yet his heart was set upon giving his boys instruction in geometrical drawing and, casting about for some way out of the *impasse*, he at length hit upon the idea of making the compasses of wood. With the aid of a carpenter he extemporised a few sets having legs some twelve inches long, and these, so contrived as to hold a piece of chalk in a clip, and with well-fitted point pins, enabled the classes to work effectually on blackboards. For a quarter of a century or more the Jubilee boys handled these honestly made tools and, with the added help of straight-edges and carpenter-made T squares, acquired a full, practical grasp of geometrical drawing.

Freehand drawing, introduced at about the same time as music, was at first, and for a long period, practised on small blackboards with chalk, afterwards on the rough, unframed slates with which all but the better-circumstanced boys were furnished. So indispensable was chalk, and used in such quantity, that at intervals three or four boys were despatched, with wheel-barrows, to the docks, where from some collier in ballast a generous freight of the useful material, wet and green grown, was at once turned over to the well-known Jubilee lads by the skipper as he banteringly threw at them some such question as " A harr'n' 'n' a harf for three ha'pence, hoo mony for 'liv'n p'nce?" unbounded derision on the part of the boys being the response. Great affairs were these chalk quests, and largely prized the privilege of forming one of the party; for the booty consisted not only of the lumps of writing stuff, but often included ship-biscuit, a bit of pitch, some tarry twine, at times even a bit of sugar-cane, a cocoa-nut, some locusts, or a daub of tamarinds—for if an *East Indiaman* lay off shore or near the dock walls, it would go hard but these young explorers would wheedle out of the officer in charge (generally an old Jubilee lad himself) some school-boy treasure.

The chalk, wheeled back in triumph, was deposited in the yard, carefully sorted and selected, then baked in the school oven, among the boys' dinners, whence it came in beautiful, firm condition. Pieces of specially fine grain were neatly trimmed into suitable form for fitting the clips of the wooden compasses and others laid in places to which the master's hand would instinctively wander in search, while giving one of his lessons.

For a long time slate pencil of a quality suitable for use was difficult to obtain, being either too friable to cohere, or more commonly so hard as to scratch the slate · and, moreover, it cost money. Like the chalk then, it was mainly treasure-trove, the boys searching among the rocks at Tynemouth on Saturdays or other holidays for a substance they called Scotch cam, which, when good, made an excellent writing material. Greatly envied was he who, out of the manifold stores of his trouser's pocket—among the chalk, cobbler's wax, twine, cock-spurs, nails, top prods, leed fardins, *et hoc*, produced a finely grained piece of "cam." It was almost the standard of boy-currency, and could be swopped for nearly anything.

A bare, gaunt place was the school—sixty feet by twenty, and perhaps thirteen or fourteen high—the ceilings and walls whitewashed, with a stone-coloured dado of oil paint running round at a height of about five feet. Wisdom in high places had decreed that though a higher wisdom had said, "Let there be light," light should only be had by paying for it, hence the dwellings of Englishmen of that day suffered from a kind of cataract, most of the windows being what was, with unconscious irony, called "blind"; in other words, bricked up to avoid window-tax. The founders of the Jubilee had, however, provided for ample lighting, and the walls were pierced with a sufficient number of large, broad windows. The floor was of free-stone flags, and these, between the parallel lines of desks or writing benches, were worn into deep channelled furrows—like giant corduroy—by the two hundred odd pairs of feet (mostly bare and coloured, in winter, like red cabbage) which now daily chafed them. For the forty had soon increased five-fold, and the unwonted sight of patient mothers waiting, anxious faced, at the gates of the school-yard—poor, pinched Peris—on Mondays for the doubtful chance of securing an admission card for one or two of their boys, was becoming a painful experience of the kindly committee. Gaunt and bare as it might be, the school was now a place of undefined but undoubted comforts, the windows—now finding a function hitherto unconsidered—being opened whenever possible for ventilation, so renewing the rapidly vitiated air and removing more than half the dulness which had in the past been ignorantly attributed to the scholar. A huge coal fire at each end of the room, the special care of the monitors, not only gave warmth and comfort, but was pressed into service for object lessons in mine ventilation. The channelled stone floor was swept each evening by squads of boys chosen in rotation, and to this end moist sea sand was freely scattered over its whole surface, before sweeping began, to prevent the dust from rising. Like the chalk, the sand had to be fetched, and at intervals a gang of happy lads went off to the beach to wheel a few barrow-loads up to the school-yard. So, too, the firewood, given in plenty by graving dock owners or block and mast makers; it came, pleasant with the scent of pine-resin and oakum, in the form of adze chips; to go for "sticks" (as Shields called firewood) was a great privilege. Coal was supplied gratuitously, in unstinted quantity, by a generous, untiring benefactor of the school and of the Shields poor—Hugh Taylor, Esq., of Chipchase Castle—for years one of the most bountiful patrons of the schools of Tyneside. Order, decency, and cleanliness insensibly developed as brighter methods of teaching gave moral health to the minds of the rough sea urchins; and the injunction on the card of admission, that the scholar should come "with face washed and hair combed," was being literally obeyed, though, at first, both combing and washing were of an elementary sort.

There was not a class-room in the building, nor was there an assistant master (though among the two hundred scholars were children beginning to learn the alphabet, and boys acting as head monitors), yet the atmosphere of busy silence and hushed diligence was remarkable. At all times of the year, save in the depth of winter or when the weather would not admit of it, the classes were "taken" in the school-yard, and then the buzz of oral study was pleasant indeed to the ears of all who had a heart open to human sympathy. In this or that class, erect, alert, and vigilant, but with a singular, benevolent sweetness of expression, was always to be seen the bare-headed dominie, devoting his inexhaustible patience to the slower units of his toiling world. Toiling—yes—those who carry the burden of elementary teaching even now, when all the accumulating effects of fifty years of popular education help to leaven the heavy inertia of ignorance, know what toilsome labour it is for the young to scramble up the lower steeps of that mighty *Sisyphean* mount called knowledge; but this is as nothing to the difficulties that lay in the path of the poor children of the early "forties"—children, as they were, of generations of illiteracy, coming into a heritage of absolute darkness, where there was no scattered light.

It was necessary to begin again and again at the very beginning with each child, and there can be no doubt that the acquirement of a familiarity with the letters of the alphabet required much more time and patience and toil on the part of teacher and taught than is now needed.

Teaching was indeed in its experimental stages, and some funny essays resulted. For the very groundlings—and they came as young as mothers could secure admission for them to this newly discovered *crèche*—there was, and had been for years, in the school a queer apparatus, a sort of alphabet mill, which ground out the letters one by one, and thus deprived the wondering, round-eyed, little ones—as in semicircle they stood before it, hands clasped behind the back—of any help which a remembrance of the ordinary sequence of the characters might afford. This strange engine formed a principal function of the master's desk—a huge, wooden, hollow, cube-shaped erection, like a hut, some four feet high and perhaps as wide. Inside, on an axis, suspended against the face fronting the school, was a great disc or wheel, the whole height of the desk; bearing on a circle drawn just within its periphery the alphabet in capitals, upon an inner circle the same in "small" characters, and on yet another (the innermost) a series of arithmetical figures. Three apertures in the front of the desk, one above another, and each closed by a slide, enabled the teacher to expose to the class the letters or figures of any of the series, one by one— but only one by one. A winch handle on the axle afforded the means for rotating the disc and bringing to the open eye of the machine any of the characters—and, in any order chosen to bewilder the class. Sometimes a boy was put inside the mill, and there in the dark, left to reel out knowledge in which for the time he could be no sharer. It is not easy to fully grasp all that the inventor of this wondersome apparatus had in his mind, but, beside the fact that primers were not available in sufficient number for the children of such schools and that complete alphabets printed on cards have the defect of producing a merely consecutive knowledge of the characters —afterwards to be broken off, there is no question that the sense of wonder, expectation, and speculation were stirred in the minds of the young folk by the vagaries of this creaking and rumbling educational toy; and that, therefore, their attention was to a considerable extent sustained while engaged in the most wearisome of all school tasks.

The elements of spelling and the beginnings of arithmetic came from this wheel to successive hundreds of children; for though, often enough, a quite disconcerting series of letters, as B W Q I O K, etc., showed themselves for a moment at the little window, or an errant line of numerals, as 2 0 7 1 9 3, yet at tranquiller times B was followed by O, and O by Y, or R by A and T; or 2 was succeeded by 3, and the onlooker asked to add them, and thus a sort of memory-spelling and mental arithmetic was initiated.

It was, however, but mere children, little more than infants, who worked at this wheel-of-fortune. Spelling was a serious matter for every scholar, of whatever grade, up to the time of leaving, just as it is for every thoughtful teacher. The appalling disproportion between the time required to acquire this artificial trick and that needed for subjects of infinitely more value is the despair of all sensible educationalists. Its perverse violation of all the elements of sound and sense, its hopeless inconsistencies and contradictions, its paramount defects and weaknesses, are perhaps not so exasperating as its destructive consumption of precious time. Let any intelligent man take the trouble to put one of his younger and, as yet, untaught children through a course of elementary English spelling, and he will quickly realise what an amount of *negative* work must be done upon the child's ear before it begins by the merest mimicry to get a grasp of the unnatural results, and this will be all the more obvious the more musically gifted the child is. It will, indeed, be found that most men who vaunt their spelling, and say they acquired it without effort—or, as they commonly express it, "naturally"—are strikingly deficient in musical ear; in other words, the musically gifted must work harder than others to learn to spell "well." Of course its advocates—and there are even such—claim that it furnishes a valuable mental discipline, a memory drill; but having regard to the shortness of the time that children have for schooling, and the vast range of elevating subjects.

it would be well they should learn something of, it is nothing less than scandalous that progress should be hindered by mere artificial difficulties. Remembering that reading and writing are but tools with which the 'prentice student is to cut his path up the steeps of knowledge, it is somewhat ludicrous to contend that the mere grinding of these implements should occupy the greater portion of every one of his working days.

There was however no help for it, and the heavy drill at the spelling books was kept steadily going, its monotony relieved however by a searching course of training in definition—a matter regarded by the master as of infinitely greater importance and consequence; and, naturally, the difficulties of spelling were found to be thus made easier. It was not, however, a mere case of testing the learner as to the direct meaning of the words he chanced to be spelling, but a systematic course of training in the art of verbally defining shades of difference, and of giving the best and tersest expression of the meaning. It is difficult to make people who were educated in the early half of the century see the whole absurdity of the position which makes a man feel thoroughly ashamed of being unable to spell a word of which, nevertheless, he admits without hesitation, he cannot satisfactorily state the meaning. Yet, having regard to the real use and object of language, what could be more preposterous? When, a few years ago, the *Spelling Bee* was spreading dismay and humiliation among rash competitors, the master was wont to remark that the consternation would have been greater and the distribution of laurels very different had the candidates been asked to state in adequate terms the meaning of the words given as tests of spelling, and it would be found not a little entertaining to try the effect—upon, say, a School Board, or a Committee of the House of Commons—of securing the doors and submitting the members to an examination in the meaning, not of the remote and inaccessible terrors selected by the only happy man at a *Bee*—him with the dictionary—but of the simpler words in every-day use.

Writing on sand had long passed away, and slates had become common. Copperplate texts printed on narrow strips of stiff cardboard were handed out to groups of boys, who carefully transcribed from them sententious philosophy. It was too early as yet for the copy-book with its moral headlines, because of the heavy duty on paper—as wicked an impost as that on salt or sunlight, and defended as tenaciously. Most of the slates were without frames, and by fracture and friction became rounded almost like a painter's pallet; others had the frame neatly secured at the corners by copper or tin strips, but whether framed or not they formed the ready field on which evolutions in writing, ciphering, drawing, mapping, algebra, poetry, and composition were performed, quickly cleared again for action by a rub from the jacket sleeve. There was not a sponge in the school, hence careful mothers sought to minimise the effects of continuous friction by providing cylindrical calico coverings—called "sleeves"—for their sons' arms, tied at the wrist and elbow, and giving them a comic baggy appearance.

Derivation was worked at as honestly as definition, and exercises set in the substitution of so-called synonymous words. Letter-writing to persons in various relations, and therefore involving different modes of style, was practised weekly, great attention being given to the smaller matters of correctly placing and stating the date, address, and signature.

From the earliest days the master had perceived the inestimable advantages to be derived from the systematic use of the newspaper as a source of fluent idiomatic every-day English, differing in every respect from the turgid heavy inflexibility of style in which the school-books of the day were written—hence the "higher" boys (*i.e.* the more advanced) had regular exercise in reading out a "leader" or special "article," its subject being afterwards discussed, explained, and criticised. The foundation of a taste for literature was at all times a passion with the dominie. The subtle music of good prose was to his mind more delicate and delightful than even that of poetry, hence the English Classics were introduced as soon as they could be obtained, and the boys became familiar with the "Spectator," Rasselas, Waverley, Robinson Crusoe, The Vicar of Wakefield, The Pilgrim's Progress, Don Quixote, Uncle Toby, Humboldt, Mungo Park, the inestimable voyages and travels of Pinkerton, and all the Arctic exploration books—as part of their daily school work. Shakespeare, Milton, Goldsmith, Cowper, Wordsworth, and, as a source of fine English, the Bible were read aloud and paraphrased. In after years, when an old man, it was the master's delight to suggest and superintend a course of reading for his older pupils, and a more generous or catholic survey of the realms of literature it would be impossible to have suggested.

Not a few of the books referred to were his own, generally second-hand copies, purchased with infinite consideration and hesitating discrimination at a book-stall in Newcastle or other large town, instantly to be transferred to the service of the school where they became tattered and threadbare. But the best of his work could never have been done had not the generous forethought of a group of intelligent men set afoot in the early days that beneficent and beautiful agency, the Mechanics' Institute. If, as some essayist has remarked, "the soil of a seaport town is the most uncongenial for the tree of knowledge," then to those who tended and nurtured the frail plant through the dark winter of social aversion and popular indifference, the later generations of Shields youth owe a debt which they can never adequately discharge

It was at the very outset of the Birkbeck movement that old Shields took of the fountain. The year 1823 saw the formation of the "London Mechanics'," and in 1825 the "Shields Scientific and Mechanics' Institution" was founded by a few of the wiser gentlemen of the town. About one hundred members joined, but the movement was premature, the stress of opposition too great; the scheme declined and, in 1828, fell; the books going into the hands (as has already been mentioned) of an excellent man and friend of the Shields poor, Matthew Robson, who held them safely until the winter of 1831, when a meeting was held at the Commercial Hotel— the Rev. William Mark, afternoon lecturer at Christ Church, in the chair—to consider the possibility of re-starting the institution. Under the title of "The Tradesmen and Mechanics' Institution," it was born again, and up to the time of the Free Library movement was known simply as "The Mechanics'."

In a long upstairs room on "the Banks," with a broad bay window overlooking the harbour and affording a wide view of the sea, was the Library, and at night it was a truly cosy place, with its snug fire, warm light, its broad green baize-covered table and group of silent readers. Here tradesmen, mechanics and professional men met on common ground, all interests for the time being merged, all accidental and secular distinctions lost in the immensity of their veneration for genius and their love of science and literature. It was a wonderful time, that, for the middle-class Englishman, when the new world of letters burst upon him, and books were loved with all the intensity of a new passion In these latter days, with all the treasures of literature thrust upon us in cheap editions, when no man, of whatever station, need lack almost any book he desires to possess, and when the real difficulty is the *embarras de richesses*, —we can form no adequate idea of the deep regard and passion for reading that possessed the folk who were first benefited by the Birkbeck libraries.

At times lectures were given by the local *alumni*, some of them, however, to extremely "select" audiences, as may be gathered from the titles—William Bramwell on Chemistry; Dr. Johnson, a "curse" (as some waggish youth worded it) of six lectures on the Indefinite Article, William Greenwell on the Philosophy of Dr. Watts, and so forth. On the same floor as the Library was the room of the Natural History Society, whose curator, one Hill, lived on the floor below, and dealt in hot coffee and penny pies, and over whose wares discussion arose, often enough towards midnight, among the young leaders of the Institute who had formed themselves into a discussion class for the due investigation of the many great questions which then moved Englishmen, and of others that have stirred mankind since the beginning of time. "Here," says one of the group,[1] writing fifty years afterwards, "here, after deciding forms of government, characters of kings, greatest amount of happiness principle, the origin of misery and sin, and so forth, it was pleasant to descend to the platters and platitudes of Hill, who was a Unitarian and a philosopher in his way."

For years the Institute grew and waxed stronger in the comfortable old room, its books, selected at all times with the rarest literary insight, accumulating at an increasing rate and forcing the question of greater accommodation upon the band of honorary workers who carried all its cares and responsibilities upon their willing shoulders; but no funds were available for acquiring enlarged and permanent premises, and the work had to be carried on as it best might in the now overcrowded rooms.

The Jubilee master had taken a large part in the revival of the Library and for a few years after acted as secretary, an office which the increasing pressure of his other duties presently compelled him to relinquish, though he remained on the committee, and in that capacity eventually took on an even greater amount of exacting labour for the pleasure and benefit of the members. His close association as secretary with the inner working of the Institute, and

[1] Mr. James S. Edington, who for two generations has poured the treasures of a rare literary nature into the lap of the Institute, and constituted an educational *Providence* for Shields youth.

his subsequent life's friendship with the generous group of young townsmen who continued to give it their unremitting help, afforded him the privilege of securing for·his school-boys access to the growing pile of literary wealth, and enabled him to give a breadth and variety to the school work which in that day of dear books must otherwise have been wholly impossible.

His faith in the intrinsic value of music as a beautifier of life was always with him, and in a record of the progress of "the Mechanics'" about 1845 is the following passage.—"Mr. Haswell first suggested the delightful addition of music to the rather dreary business meetings, which the chairman, Mr. Tinley, once characterised with his accustomed felicity as the annual *yawn* of the Institution." The idea was at once seized upon, and its realisation eventually proved the means of securing the new building so urgently needed for the expansion of the beneficent agency.

Suggesting the delightful addition of music, of course, involved the entire labour of providing it, and a series of winter concerts, then commenced, was continued for some twenty years by the master, who drew round him the scanty amateur "talent" available, and raised a school of music in so doing.

About the same time a movement was commenced in some of the larger towns to provide twopenny concerts for the working classes. In Shields a series was initiated by "the gentry" of the town, the value of whose assistance may be appreciated from the following notes made by the Jubilee master :—

"Several respectable gentlemen called upon me and persuaded me, with another musician in the town, to join them in promoting a series of concerts for artisans and their families. The other man was John Lamb, a violinist who had spent twenty years in the orchestras of the London theatres, and ultimately marrying a ballet-girl, brought her down to the North and commenced a dancing-school. There was already a small orchestra, numbering perhaps eight or ten, in the town, and Lamb was desired to meet them once a week and make what he could of them, while I was coolly requested to get together as many vocalists and glee-singers as I could find, and drill them for the weekly concerts. Happening to go into the band-room one evening as practice was about to begin, and seeing the double-bass lying on its side, I took it up and joined in, the result being the extortion of a half-promise to play the instrument at the performances I was thus committed for four or five nights in the week for this scheme alone, having to attend rehearsals, coach the choristers, prepare the programmes, and revise the printer's proofs For a little while the respectable gentlemen forming the committee attended, then gradually fell away, and at length I was left with Lamb and another—John Pollack, who looked after the twopences—to carry forward this benefit scheme of the 'gentry.' We got to the end of the season at last, and, fortunately for us, the final concert was a bumper, yielding us indeed sufficient funds to pay off the few debts standing against the enterprise for rent, hire of piano, etc, which otherwise we three, who had given our services gratuitously for a whole season, would have had to pay out of our pockets, every one of the gentlemen on the committee having repudiated all responsibility and declined to contribute a farthing towards the expenses."

The Philharmonic Society, which had come earlier to grief, was now revived for a time, and gave a series of dress concerts in the George Tavern Of this the indefatigable master was a director, librarian, and one of the orchestra.

But the Society did not hold together for long, and decay arose from the same cause as in the case of the twopenny concerts; the patrons, who did none of the work, first fell away, and "some of the old members died; others left the town, some grew indifferent; the grand old Oxley was now too old, Jamson, although a professional musician, seemed to hate music, and did all he could to thwart the efforts of the Society, and at last succeeded in poisoning the mind of John Tinley against some of the new members. So with enemies in the camp, a grave depression of trade, and the defection of many supporters, it was deemed useless to contend longer with adverse fate. A meeting was held, the music divided, the piano sold to pay the debts, and thus ended an institution which had afforded pleasure and delight of the purest kind to hundreds of people for a number of years, and which might have gone on doing so but for the solemn fact that there are men so constituted as to be happy only when doing harm to others."

A share of the music thus divided fell to the Librarian, who at once devoted it to the use of "The Mechanics'." With the double failure of the "Philharmonic," and the collapse of the workmen's twopenny concerts fresh in his mind, he recognised that in future efforts for the cultivation of musical taste he must rely upon himself and accept no proffered help from respectable committees, patrons, or gentry As a first step the amateurs must be got together and weeded out, and what a task this was can never be realised by those who do not remember the state of music in the provinces half a century ago The spirit of the "late Mr. Harris" was still abroad, inspiring the

English people with his own poor opinion of music dissociated from poetry. There could be no *lieder ohne worte* for *his* disciples, and they were the multitude. The musically obvious was your only code, and the commonplace in melody, with the sparsest possible harmonisation, the correct thing. Generations suckled on an unvarying pap of *tonic* and *dominant*, could not tolerate the intrusion of parts intermediate to the "tune" and its bass; and hence, though Belinda's early-century sonnets, twittering with trills, shakes, and *appoggiature*, and scarcely touched by the thin, feeble spinet accompaniment, had passed away, Music was still the poor relation of Verse, and was being severely kept in her place. The vamping orchestration of the purely Italian school of operatic writers undoubtedly secured in England the early acceptance of their works, as indubitably the wondrous tone-poem running through the "accompaniment" to Gounod's masterpiece would have shut out *Faust* for a score of years.

'Twas a time when those who had no ear for music rather plumed themselves upon the fact. Amateurs were consequential in direct proportion to their inability to "read at sight," and in reply to the common question, "Do you sing (or play) from the notes?" would unhesitatingly reply, "Oh, dear no, do you?" How strangely the following letter from Woolhouse to his friend reads now:—

"The value of the theory of the musical scale," says Woolhouse, writing in 1846, "is well appreciated by those who understand it. To tuners it is invaluable, in violin playing I find such knowledge of great practical use. These things are generally disparaged by persons who, not having the knowledge, *think* they can do as well without it. Those who sing by the ear, as well as those who play by the ear, have a certain amount of distaste for reading from the notes. They seem to forget that a knowledge of the notes is not designed to enable them to execute better, but is for the purpose of giving them a greater command over the resources of music."

It was from this class, and from his pupils,—for he had now begun to teach the piano, flute, 'cello, and singing,—and from the sparsely distributed amateurs who *could* read, that the master had to select his material wherewith to introduce the "delightful addition of music" to the Mechanics' Institute; and some curious artists presented themselves. There was old H——, who played the clarionet in one of the churches He had lost three fingers from one of his hands—perhaps had chopped them off, being a butcher to trade—but never allowed their absence to concern him when playing his canary-coloured instrument. If a note before him required a finger he had not, how could he help it? He had a half-comic, half-pathetic knack of shuffling the hand up and down the keys and holes in an attempt to avoid blanks, which he managed to do fairly well when there was time, as in church with the long-drawn psalm-tunes, but in the concert-room or at rehearsal the unlooked-for effects produced by his substituted intervals were startlingly disconcerting. There was "Fiddler R——," so-called by everybody in Shields, not because he fiddled, but because he sold fiddle-strings, Jews' harps, resin, tin whistles, accordions, harmonicons, and horrible mouth-organs for children. Old, bent, hook-nosed, and bearded like Father Time, this strange being played a plaintive, almost forgotten, kind of bag-pipes—the very mildest of all its fierce race, and known as the Northumbrian small-pipes. For some strange reason, known only to Heaven and himself, he invariably selected as his *pièce de résistance* (on the rare occasions when he was allotted a solo) "Il Segreto" from *Lucrezia Borgia*. Seated on a low stool in the forefront of the platform, crooning over his instrument as though conferring with it, his hair hanging over his face, he would play in an almost inaudible bleat (lost to the audience in the hum of general conversation) some forgotten Border melody, and then, without any interval, glide into the "secret," the transition being invariably received by the noisiest of the youths in the room, with a dead and ominous silence—the silence of anticipation; for they were on the look-out for the *finale*, which ever produced shrieks of laughter and imitations of cock-crowing On the pipes, and as played by him, it was truly a droll passage. The old man was

always deeply gratified at this burst of interest, and bowed like a mandarin as he left the platform.

There was, too, an excruciating cornet who was never for a moment right in the concerted pieces, but who breathed his whole soul into *Il balen* as a solo, giving it a rendering (called by the local critic in a burst of inspiration a "rendition") all his own. The well-known melody, transfigured by a strange inversion of the length of the notes, was sometimes lost in the intensity of his *chiaroscuro;* yet he was enormously popular with the audience, though dreaded and detested by his fellows in the orchestra He never respected "time" in his life, though *there* he can scarcely be said to be peculiar, for doubtless no cornetist ever did. His flourishes and *cadenze* were conceived in the loftiest spirit, but often, from very pathos, broke into a voiceless gurgle, which moved many of the audience to tears, and the band almost to acts of personal violence.

A dreadful young lady pianist there also was, ever bent upon having a solo, whose inexhaustible *repertoire* rendered her inevitable when a programme had to be drawn. She had a weakness—which many of her admirers could not detect, but which was perfectly appalling to musicians—for improving upon the composer and extemporising her bass, always of a severely *tonic-dominant* character, with chords to suit. It was something to watch for the effect upon professionals of their first introduction to this terrible young person's style when, in the language of "the fancy," she "put in her left." There were vain tenors—vainer even than the cornetists; ambitious *soprani*, and worse, young ladies who aspired to vocal duets; violinists who never got their fiddles in tune, flautists who were always out of tune, baritones who tried to be bassos by tucking their chins deep into the folds of their breast scarves, altos who strained at a *falsetto* till the varicose lines on their faces frightened the ladies,—all these were clamorous for the honour of a place in the programme, not as chorus-singers or orchestral units, but as soloists; and all their waywardness, vanity, and mutual jealousy the patient dominie—his musical soul harrowed by their terrible efforts—had to appease, conciliate, and gently push back into native obscurity. Here and there were occasional instrumentalists and vocalists—modest people—who could play and sing, but hardly knew it; these he brought forward, and with the aid of his school-boys, who sang the old madrigals with finish and precision, secured for the institution he loved a steadily increasing host of supporters.

In local phrase "Mr. Haswell l'arned music" (which he did, all his life, but that was not what was meant), and the people who came to be "l'arned" grew so in number that he had pupils before breakfast, in the dinner interval, and during the evening up to late hours in the night; times dictated not always by his having a vacant interval, but by the necessities and occupations of the pupils. The young butcher who breathed—he could not honestly be said to play —the flute, could only come after ten, and his efforts to "away with melancholy," which he knew as *dolsey-content-o*, gave him premature wrinkles. The prim, middle-aged shop-walker, supposed by churchgoers to have designs upon Miss So-and-so, really burned at the bosom to overcome the mechanical difficulties of the "Krakoviak" with both hands at once—a labour of love left after many days, like other noble aspirations, in the limbo of the unachieved. Anxious *maters*, with winter parties in one eye and economy in the other, brought pairs of daughters to learn a duet or two, and bargained for a reduction on taking a quantity, the curate perhaps was ambitious of singing "The Wolf," and dropped in at mid-day once a week, for a quarter, to acquire the correct style of baying the moon with hideous howl, two mild little men, inoffensive shoemakers, for quite six months strove to assure their home circle, jointly and in musical terms, that "All's Well." A strange circumstance it was that so many of these neophytes should burn for distinction in a single song, but this doubtless arose from the custom then prevalent at social and festive gatherings of insisting that each and every individual, without exception, should "sing a song or give a sentiment." Men were known by their song, and sang it year in and year out till the pathos of the thing in old age became one of the most touching of human experiences.

It was a strange metamorphosis that overcame the aspirants to musical honours when they found their way to the quiet parlour of the Jubilee teacher, and stood humbly at the little square piano. All Shields came,—the hot-tempered ship insurance secretary perhaps had a *penchant* for the eight-keyed flute; the lawyer sought solace on the broad bosom of the 'cello, his clerk jostling him as *he* goes in to have an hour's torturing spell on the "cornopean." Young sparks of shipbrokers wish to play a set of Julien's waltzes on the piano, or to acquire the knack of vamping an accompaniment to some comic songs. Ladies come in groups and tunefully tell each other that "Red leaves are falling on the ground, the wynd no more is still—tha wheat," and so forth. All classes in the town rub shoulders as they go through the Jubilee gates, and all implicitly believe the teacher in all he says, save one thing only, and that he has marvellously often to state at the close of a first lesson. "I am bound to tell you that I cannot recommend your proceeding with the study of music, for you are devoid of musical ear, and that cannot be remedied by any amount of study or practice."

But the advice was rarely heeded, and so the hopeless task endured from season to season. Many good friends were made in this musical intercourse, and only one man ever took advantage of the schoolmaster. He was a well-to-do shipowner—somewhat deaf, dull intellectually, and hopelessly unmusical—who determined to learn the flute, and stated as much to the master, from whom he received the usual warning. Somewhat indignantly persisting, he was taken in hand and drilled for six months, when he himself perceived the futility of further perseverance. Ceasing to come for his lessons, he was after a while asked for payment of the two quarters' fees due, —"I came to you to teach me the flute," replied he. "You failed to teach me, therefore I decline to pay you a penny." And he kept his word.

A weighty business was the selection or recommendation of a pianoforte for some cautious couple, whose daughter being old enough to l'arn music, was made use of as an outward symbol or sign (to neighbours) of slow but sure growth in worldly gear. "A good second-hand one" is the parental idea, forcibly urged on the grounds of certain knowledge as to a bargain to be had, but furtively and feverishly resisted by the perturbed girl, who looks to the master for help. Many visits are made, and pros and cons carried home for long-drawn discussion. Perhaps the bargain is a whole note or more "down"; it needs tuning, several wires are broken, two or three keys are stiff in the joints, and altogether, as the girl eagerly urges, the price asked for it, together with the cost of repairs, is not much under that of the fine rosewood with amber-coloured silk, which also carries with it a stool and shilling instruction book.

Never was assembled such a broken-kneed set of pianos as those the master had to face when first he announced his assumption of the profession of "tuner"—an art he had taught himself, long before, on his own piano. His tools were made by a friendly harmonious blacksmith who shoed horses, repaired farmers' gear, and sang occasionally at the concerts—his boys shining in the music class at the school. A heart-breaking job, truly, this tuning of old-world pianos, involving hours of uncertain toil, bleeding fingers, and greatly begrudged pay; for none of the older generations could "for maa part see enything tha matter witha pee-anna," and wondered why the instrument they had bought should so soon need "mending!" Sometimes he was sent for and asked to mend the leg, or foot, or pedal, or put on a caster which had been snapped off—the office of tuner covering all repairs in the minds of those early children of harmony. He was called upon variously to tune a lady's harp, string a guitar, put a reed into a clarionet, and once, by a solemn, taciturn, fat man who had bought a set of musical glasses cheap at a sale, to arrange them for him in diatonic sequence —though he did not call it that. There was little or no printed music in Shields at that early day, and he sometimes earned a little by writing out—in a beautiful hand—a copy of some precious borrowed "piece," or "*morceau*," or song,—but not often, for the slender remuneration for teaching covered the laborious preparation of all the necessary manuscript music for the pupils, and not seldom, long after the household had gone to rest, the sound of his rapid quill broke the stillness of the sma' hours.

But when some night the last pupil left early, or perhaps had not come at all, and there was no concert, benefit, rehearsal, or other call to heed, he sat at his piano with rapt face and poured his soul into some glorious bit of Handel, or Mozart, or Beethoven, or in the firelight took deep calm from his 'cello, and was repaid for all the unrest of his toilsome life. Children were now coming to him, and these were born and nurtured in music, their *wiegenlieder* the strains of the Immortals.

Woolhouse and he kept up a brisk correspondence, and each urged the other to maintain an active practical interest in the divine art.

"You have not yet told us," writes Woolhouse, August 1841, "when you are coming up to London, that it may be properly inserted in the Court Circular. You will be able to have some good musical treats at the concerts at Drury Lane . . . besides our own concerts at home. I have now got a first-rate violoncello which will be the very thing for you. When does your vacation commence? Cannot you give your boys a long time of it? How goes your bass? Do you want any fiddle-strings? You had better stick (fiddle-stick) to the right sort. I am sorry to trouble you, as the pin said to the periwinkle, but you must write."

His friend was continually sending him parcels of 'cello strings, pretending, with a delicacy all his own, that the quality could not be equalled, and so relieving his old chum of a somewhat expensive consequence of their joint hobby. Again, August 1841:—

"I send you a first and a fourth of the most approved sizes. You must not spoil your bass by indulging it with thick first strings. When you pet them so they are very apt to scream and cry, and sometimes kick.— Yours truly, "Scratch Gut."

This is addressed "Thomas Haswell, Esq., F#, G♭, Rasping Lodge."

Writing again in January 1842, under signature "Fiddlestick," Woolhouse describes certain inquiries he has made at the National Schools as to Hullah's publications, and says that having looked through them, he recommends Wilhelm's method as best

"I was glad to see that the Shields gents had the good sense to appreciate the value of your excellent services and to afford you decisive evidence of it. This you have much reason to be proud of, as it is a rare occurrence in such a place as Shields. With such ability I expect to find the school converted into a singing paradise when I come over in the summer. We meet every week for Haydn's quartets, and wish you were here to join us. I hope you pull away at Corelli."

September 1843:—

"Why do you not come up now? we should be overjoyed to see you both. I have plenty of instruments and music—Haydn, Mozart, and Beethoven quartets, etc. Why do you not take up the violin? I have made much progress, and now find no difficulty in reading any quartet at sight. I now play the tenor at a quartet party in the city—much better than Lamb's—and wish you could only drop in."

January 1846.—

"Well, my lad! I am glad to hear that you are coming on, and that your concert has come off se weel. I wish I was only among you to stir you up a wee bit. Howsomedever, I mun be content and take my chance of catching you at it the first time we come down to Shields. You request me to recommend you a quartet to polish off. I think Mozart No. 3 in B flat would do for a general audience [alas!], at least it is a favourite with our party. I think you will find the slow movement perhaps require more rehearsing than the others, as the time is much divided and the different parts require very nice taking up. The last movement is easy, and very lively and effective, and, like hot water and sugar, should be taken with spirit, not forgetting playfulness. . . . Whenever I determine upon coming to Shields I shall send over my quartets to you some time beforehand, and we must make a decided attack on Haydn, Mozart, and Beethoven. The last, Beethoven, is the musical genius of the age. He is a perfect giant, and leaves them all behind for delicious melodies and accompaniments and marvellous combinations. *But your audience will hardly be prepared for him yet.* You would oblige me by enclosing a programme of your concerts as they appear. That's a good lad! Good luck ta ye!!

"FIDDLE-DE-DEE"

The "determined attack" was sometimes a protracted one—on a famous occasion, in holiday time, the enthusiasts kept it up for twelve hours! The reference to Beethoven was a sly poke at the master's devotion to Handel, to whom he looked up as the Jupiter of the musical Olympus.

December 1846:—

"You say when I come over we can have a quartet now at any time. If you have a party that meets for the practice of such music—which of all other is most interesting to performers—I will have great pleasure in sending you a selection of the best quartets of Haydn, Mozart, and Beethoven, which I can well do without for a year or two. I have got an excellent flute duet for you by Kulau, and will send it first opportunity, also Beethoven's trio in E flat for violin, tenor and bass."

Such was the genial astronomer's way of making a present; these works were far beyond the means of the dominie, but his friend would never consent to the return of the copies so "lent."

January 1848 —

"Mendelssohn published five quartets which I have had some time, but I have only played two of them. There is also a quintet for two violins, two tenors and bass, which is very beautiful. I expect to have a good quartet at my house on Wednesday, and intend playing Beethoven exclusively. He leaves them all in the shade."

May 13th, 1848.—

"I am glad to hear that Mrs Haswell and the little ones are well. It is well for you that George Handel's three notes are *diatonic* This is not often the case among the smaller fry, and it is more than I can boast of at home. I had a music meeting y'day evening, when we played a trio by Bruni, a quartet by Mozart, No 3, a quartet by Mozart in C, and a quartet by Beethoven in E flat, and I led them on a valuable violin newly purchased Let me know when you are coming to London and I will arrange a series of evenings on which you can play violoncello I will, if possible, have them two or three evenings in the week, so as to give you a variety of authors"

The three diatonic notes of George Handel were the wailings of a year-old son, whose musical beginnings were obviously receiving professional scrutiny from his father. As touching this youth's advent, an old letter shows the kind of regard in which the schoolmaster was held among his town-fellows The letter is from the family doctor, and runs:—

"*January 11th*, 1849.

"MY DEAR MR. HASWELL,—In going over my accounts for last year I find you are indebted to me for a small attendance, etc, on your child. This is a receipt in full for the year. Though I am not a subscriber to the Jubilee School, I hope you will allow me in this way to express my high opinion of your services in the town I only wish they were better paid for —I am, my dear Mr. H , sincerely yours,

"J R· OWEN."

Some time in 1850 or 1851 the post of organist at Christ Church fell vacant. Every Sunday since he took the mastership of the Jubilee it had been his duty to marshal the boys—such of them, that is, as belonged to the Establishment—in the school and march them thence to morning service, and there keep a watchful eye upon their every furtive movement. It was perhaps the ugliest church in England,[1]—an opinion deprecated by the folks of the town only to the extent of a pleading expostulation that it was "not so bad as St. Hilda over-the-water,"—an uncomely enough sister one had to admit. Inside, it was as dull, depressing, and dismal as any of the churches of that day, and nothing stronger could be said. A plain whitewashed structure with heavy lurching galleries supported on thick squat stone columns which ran up to the spring of the ugly flat arches. The long windows with rounded tops were obscured with a wash or pigment once white but long turned to a dirty yellow, which gave a murky tinge to the brightest sunlight. On the ground-floor were pens. —they could not be called pews—for the poor;—down the centre of the main aisle, conspicuously exposed to all present and securely isolated, ranged short benches in which sat the school-boys, the paupers, the lame, the halt, the blind, and, separately, the workhouse children—in short, all objects of charity. For the rest, as rigorously preserved as game coverts, were the square wells over the high sides of which occupants glared at the hapless visitor who in nervous bewilderment sought a place in the House of God. The wood-work, "grained" in horrible imitation of oak, emitted a fungoid odour of dry rot. The flagged floor—worn and cracked, with corners broken off, and forming crannies in and out of which mice chased during service—was damp and chill and mouldy. The mural seraphim

---

[1] As to exterior, Gibson, in his *History of Tynemouth*, says, " It is a nondescript structure, the style of which, agreeable to modern barbarism, has been as far as possible removed from the ecclesiastical, and in the shape of which there is not one of the distinctive features of a church."

shaded in dust were draped in decayed cobwebs, and the clammy prayer-books, shut up in the stagnant air from Sunday to Sunday, overrun with wood-lice.

Up in the tower gallery—beyond the great arch which, as it were, took it into the church—loomed the King of Instruments, with a serrated crown of gilt carved wood on the centre bunch of dummy pipes, and on either side a reclining angel (of the figure-head, "carver and gilder" type) blowing into a golden trumpet. Along the front of the organ ran the singing-pew, and at opposite ends of the instrument, equally out of sight, were the posts of organist and "blower."

In front of the communion-rails rose from the centre of the aisle the treble-decked pulpit with hand-railed and carpeted staircase, a threatening sounding-board impending over the whole. On the right was the roomy churchwardens' pew, with four white wands standing erect at the four corners,—and, across the way, the sexton's (he was not called a verger *then*) bench with his silver-knobbed black staff up-reared over it.

Peering from the tower door, his foot in the loop of a rope which he holds by one of his hands, is the sexton's son (sometimes at afternoon service, his wife) slowly tolling the closing call to worship, and looking anxiously for the signal of release—*he* never attends service—from his father, who presently with fat deliberation rises, takes his staff in his right hand, nods his head to the "tolling" son, holds up a monitory finger to the organ gallery, and then waddles away to head-off the parson and clerk and conduct them to their respective posts. Here they come To the middle-deck slowly mounts the minister; into the lower slowly subsides his man, both being latched in with deliberate care by their attendant, who then betakes himself to his bench, and setting up his silver-headed staff, settles into his seat. The bell stops,—*exit* the ringer *vice* the organist, who now ushers in the service with his extemporised voluntary.

"Wh-en th' wicked ma-an," sings the parson, a thin column of white vapour rising from his open mouth to the extinguisher above him, and watched greedily by the boys, who begin to be restless the instant service commences.

"*Ow Lo-ard, ow-pen thau aw la-a-ip-s.*" Surely the response is the strangest jumble of discordant sounds that could rise from human throats The *versicles* were of course not chanted, and every man read off, if he could, what was before him in his own time and in his own way. Every pitch of intonation, every style of accent, every rate of articulation was mingled in unmusical confusion, quite unnoticed, however, by all but the singers, whom it provoked to ill-concealed mirth. The like with the psalms of the day, wherein "the people" seemed to be inspired with a passion for getting through the alternate verse falling to them at the quickest possible rate,—the result, an unseemly, shameful gabble. No listener could unravel a single syllable of what was uttered, but he *could* come in at the *Gloria* with responsive certainty and conviction; and the swell in the volume of tone as the latter half of this was reached showed only too clearly what a vast proportion of the congregation it was that could not read. It is curious to consider what these oft-repeated formulæ meant for the poor unlettered folk who uttered them Sunday by Sunday. The Master was indefatigable in his efforts to check the growth of mechanical and unconsidered utterance in the school, yet he found even among his best lads the strangest misconceptions as to what a response, often uttered but never thought about, really involved or implied. The Lord's Prayer among Shields boys began "Our Father chirton Heaven,"— Chirton being the name of one of the town's suburbs (where glorious Ralph Gardner had lived), and the association of sounds was not unnatural. With those then who never in their lives acquired the art of reading what distortions must not many of the most familiar and beautiful sentiments and passages have undergone!—a matter never regarded in the hasty impatience of mid-century days.[1]

If the verbal responses were discordant those that were sung were not less so. A certain invincible and deadly syncopation, heard yet where congregations sing, transformed even the best known of the beautiful old psalm-tunes—and many were indeed beautiful—into a wail of the utterest untunefulness, dreadful, nay intolerable, to the sensitive ear of a musician. The organist as a rule found relief in the full power of the great organ, and cared only to be in at the end of each verse with his congregation. Each separate verse was read out by the minister and then sung, a survival of needed custom when none of the people could read, and not wholly unnecessary yet, and the strange alternation between the sound of the solitary voice and the overpowering dissonance of the many-mouthed was startling.

[1] Richard A Proctor, a precociously intelligent boy, somewhere declares that he invariably gave a certain passage in the Creed as "Suffered under Punch's Spider," with absolute sincerity!

Old musicians will have no difficulty in recognising an old favourite in this disguise—

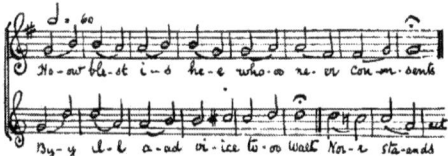

Custom dulls the ear as it shuts the eyes to much that is startling, but the awful medley of sounds that went up from such a congregation never lost its surprises for the well-trained Jubilee lads, who perhaps rarely tried the patience and forbearance of the dominie so much as by their unconcealed enjoyment of this unspeakable din. The choir and organ, upstairs, were hardly audible to those who sat downstairs, but the effect of their being a full note in advance of the congregation, throughout each verse, was only too evident.

And as to the congregation, a complete independence of action was maintained. Men who had the ear to do it droned the melody an octave lower, sometimes two octaves lower! as a *bass;* others fell off here and there into a note or two of the true *bass* and then relapsed; others again, more ambitious, soared upwards in a tenor of glaring inaccuracy; while, most trying of all, some of the females, with a precision and persistency perfectly deadly, sang a steady third below the melody and secretly exulted in having "taken" the *alto*. But these were musical people. Others, making no pretences whatever but intent on the words, sang melody of their own, which rose and fell like the wintry wind at a casement; and not a few portly old owners and skippers read out the verse in steady monotone, differing widely from each other though in pitch. The *inertia* of the whole body was enormous, and the pace could neither be equalised nor urged, though at times the exasperated organist irritably pressed down his chords, *staccato*, in a fruitless attempt to jog the laggards, and thus put the last touch to the dreadful war of sounds.

Old Oxley's beautiful voice, and the voices of his trained choir, had long been lost to the church, doubtless through one of the many feuds that at intervals broke like flame from among the embers of contention and antagonism which ever smouldered on amid the "parties" in the congregation—the music party, the no-music party; the anthem party, the no-anthem party; the paid choir, and the free choir party; the Puseyites (dread epithet!), and the anti-Puseyites. Whatever the one proposed—it might be an excursion in a steamer to Marsden Rock for the choir-boys, a concert for the Soup Kitchen, a trip to Durham Cathedral, the introduction of a new anthem—it mattered not; the other side put up its shoulders and resisted bitterly. The poor parson was a perpetual subject of this guerilla warfare. Did he mildly suggest that the choir, not being paid, merited an outing, or that the *Gloria* should be sung, not said; should he shorten his sermon by ten minutes or lengthen it by five, *intone* the Versicles or stop the Voluntary—an excited mob poured out of the church doors after service, and, like an army of black ants, ran on, stopped, gathered in little groups, waving their arms like mandibles, and after mutual threatenings dispersed in all directions, to fight the battle again in the bosom of their families over the Sunday "joint." These mean squabbles had no great significance for the master, though at times a grave shade passed over his face as his young children clung to his hand and asked him what was the matter with Mr. Blank, whom they had just parted with after listening to his thundering, ponderous, and ungrammatical denunciation of something he disliked; but for the poor organist it was another matter. Like some rock on the Black Middens, the froth and fury of these disputations surged and broke mainly around and upon him. Sometimes the parson and he were jointly denounced, sometimes one or other of them; sometimes, again, they were at high tension as between themselves, and so the strife waxed and waned and changed, but never subsided into anything like peace.

It happened then that, in 1851, one of the customary differences broke out 'twixt the curate and organist, which, however, developed into more than usual bitterness, and the genial old vicar was called in to mediate. Finding it impossible to reconcile the parties, he was reluctantly compelled to ask the unyielding man of harmony to retire, which he straightway did. Proceeding from the scene of hostilities (the church vestry) to the close adjacent Jubilee School, the vicar explained the position at some length to the master, and ended by asking if he would oblige him personally by officiating as organist on the ensuing Sunday. Assenting, the master was at once offered the post of permanent organist and choirmaster, and, with the thought of his increasing family in his mind, he accepted, —so passing from the complex confusion of noises on the floor to the gallery dedicated to music.

So, too, he gave up the very last remaining moments of leisure. He now worked literally day and night. There was the school day by day, music pupils before breakfast, in the dinner interval, immediately after school, and at all hours, up to midnight. Often a meal, just sat down to, had to be left for the drudgery of musical tuition, or, sometimes, the "lesson" was given to more familiar pupils while he partook of it. There were three services each Sunday, at each of which he must attend, and between, or after them, choir practice; concerts and entertainments in which he never failed to take a part if he did not organise and conduct them, "benefits" for this broken-down townsman or that impecunious *artiste;* colliery explosion funds, seamen's widows and orphans' aid movements, men of science to meet, too; new subjects to work up for the school, and the apparatus for them to design, and perhaps make; a young family to train,—truly a busy life, and, but for the joy of *doing*, a poorly requited one.

The best of the school-singers were at once entered for the church choir, and such adult amateur vocalists as cared to join, invited to take part in the practices which had been initiated at the moment of his appointment. Old Oxley's books, handled by the dominie so many years ago, were reverently re-opened, and the fine old anthems of Clarke, Ebdon, Purcell, and others of the English school again rang out upon the darkness of the night, to the delight of a mob of street listeners. The Handelian choruses and the gems of the "Creation" once more began to be whistled in the streets of the town by shopboys, or hummed over the counter by their masters. Soon the excellent drill on practice-nights became recognised by amateurs all round as a gratuitous school of music, which opened up possibilities of reading at sight the works then regarded as the ultimate goal of a vocalist's ambition, and men attended with a devotion and enthusiasm which for years yielded to Shields her best concert material. The interest of the general public ebbed and flowed from influences that sometimes were occult and sometimes not. A popular parson with a genial manner and a "nice" voice would attend the rehearsals, and presently the ladies of the congregation joined the choir in perfect *bouquets*, speedily followed by the young bucks about town, who crowded up to the school on practice-nights and became care-marked with anxiety to overcome the thick-set difficulties of the *Sol-fa*. At such revivals the choir, glacier-like, slowly extended down the tower gallery, displacing many old landmarks in its progress, and became the centre of gossip for female Shields. After a while, the parson being replaced by some ascetic brother who loved not music in his soul, but rather hated it, the front line slowly and steadily retreated, till at length only the men and boys—the real nucleus of the choir—remained

Sorely harassed by contending parties are master and choir The musical parson some Sunday evening introduces an anthem; some whisper of the possibility of such a thing has oozed out during the week, and the congregation muster in large numbers, and, psalter in hand, await the announcement of the psalm. Quietly he states that the anthem is taken from etc., etc., and reseats himself. A flush of anger runs over a moiety of the expectant faces, and over the rest an expression of gratified, not to say exulting, surprise. When the music commences half the congregation refuse to rise, and sit obstinately through " the performance," as they angrily call it when, after service, they foregather The tower and south galleries had their exit in a staircase that lay just under the singing-pew, over the front of which, just before the descent commenced, each communicant filing out in turn, cast a glance at the organist busied with his closing voluntary On such occasions of musical hazard as this, the choir-boys gazed with special delight on the slowly approaching and disappearing faces, and marked the different shades of frown, scowl, scorn, disapproval, or what not, with all the glee of irresponsible youth Outside, the organist found contending groups waiting to expostulate, reason with, thank, or threaten him, as he walked over to the Jubilee, and for a week or two a quickened current of heated contention ran through the slow veins of the town, gradually spending itself, and subsiding until some new innovation rekindled the flames.

Minor complaints came in endless succession. "A lady" writes to ask whether the boys could not sing the *Te Deum* a little more slowly. "A gentleman" whispers over the front of the singing-pew that a friend of his asks "whatever the choir drawl the chants at such a snail's pace for," Miss Blank thinks the new psalm-tune very unsuitable for a place of worship; three maiden sisters, of great weight in polite circles, detest the Gregorian chants, and tell the master so; two churchwardens wonder, audibly, in the porch, "What the deuce they want singing a thing like *that*," referring to the new *Kyrie*, a perfectly deaf shipowner thinks the voluntary is not devotional enough, a ship-broker considers they are "infernally slow"; members of the congregation wait to ask the organist "why we cannot have prettier responses, such as they use in some churches three counties away. Whose are they? Oh, I haven't the least idea, but they're *so* pretty, and I felt sure you'd know them. Can you hum the treble? Oh, *dear* no, but they're really *so* pretty, and ours, you know, are so *dismally* dull."

There are amateurs composers too, and generally among the "gentry." These bring dreadful things, and ask that they may be sung on an early Sunday. The parson is sometimes utterly unmusical, and does not know it. For a while he insists on conducting the practices, and continues until he has driven all the men out of the choir; to remain out until he tires. A particularly harassing sort of man this, who frets the soul of a musician beyond expression "Naow, b'ys! I want you to sing 'Farrant,' b'ys. Come, follow me—

Dow | dow : ry | mee ‖ Sol | fa : mee | ry : ry | dow."

Thus, in the untunefulest of voices, he gives out the sorry strain, and the wearied youngsters, who could put him to instant shame in reading at sight, purposely sing the melancholy thing as badly as they can, and then nudge each other in mockery of his gratified approval.

As troubled, truly, as the restless waters of the North Sea is the current of parochial affairs, and as uncertain. The master quietly takes the criticisms at their proper value, and steadily does his best with the sordid troubles that set in round the organ-loft; a flash of humorous incident sometimes lighting up the dark atmosphere of squabbling complaint.

On a certain Sunday morning, towards the end of the sermon, when his colleague at the bellows' end of the instrument, Blind John, was reminding the slumbering ones by certain creaking preparations always made in due course, that 'twas time to rouse, the faded "ugly" on the bonnet of the pinched, sad-coloured female pew-opener was seen at the top of the staircase, the face under it expressing anxiety to confer, *sotto voce*, with the organist.

"What is it, Mrs. ———?"

"Oh *plee*-se, Mr. Hass-w'll" (with a dozen sibilants), "the vicar says, will ya play tha *Ten Vargin's Solo*, sir?"

"The what?"

"The Ten Vargin's Solo, sir."

"The Ten Virgin's Solo?—nonsense! I don't understand."

" Yiss, sir!—he says, will ya play it?"

"There is some mistake—better go back and ask again."

Five minutes later the "early-English" hood of the bonnet, and under it the upper half of the pew-opener's face, wearing a reassured look, reappears at the front of the gallery, she beckons to the organist, who leans over and puts his ear down, to hear her say, "The Ten *Varses* Solo—the vicar sez; the Ten Varses Solo, sir"

"The—ten—verses—solo—woman! I cannot imagine what you mean—you'd better send W—— to ask the vicar what it is he wishes me to do."

The mortified face is withdrawn, and after a few minutes the bonnet is seen inclining over the back of the sexton's bench, down by the pulpit. Slowly that official pulls himself together, walks over to the clerk in his dock and speaks him in the ear. The clerk, turning round, arrests the placid flow of the vicar's homily, nods as he receives some message, passes it on to the sexton, who, drawing his silver-topped staff from its resting-place, slowly rolls up the aisle and presently projects his red face over the singing-pew front, and—wheezing with exertion—says, deliberately, "Mr. Keelson's *did*—died last night—vicar says—will ya play—tha—*Did* March in Sarl?"

And to the *manes* of the deceased shipowner is offered the strains of the immortal *Dead March in Saul*, played as a voluntary.

If the dead chance to be a very rich, or very popular, man, he may be lulled in his last sleep by a performance at evening service of that highly descriptive, morbid, and therefore popular anthem—a sort of parochial "Battle of Prague"—"Vital Spark," and on such occasion—perhaps only then—the voice of opposition is stilled. Not the most obstinate of anti-Puseyites or non-anthemites dares to suggest—wishes to suggest, a breath of objection to the due performance of this most respectable *requiem*. The church is crowded, and every person in it on his feet as, in mechanical indifference to the meaning of the words, the basses steadily call upon men to "Hark" at the moment the trebles and altos, in thirds, are telling what

" *The* wh-is-per-*the*-whis-per angels say."

Rien n'est sacré pour—un chantre. The choir-men are sad dogs and have no taste for the sermon—a matter of perpetual friction between the vicar, or the curate, and them. Like the bell-ringers, they seek escape from church at the earliest possible moment after the text has been given out—and generally find it too; returning furtively on tip-toe as Blind John at the bellows begins to work up his wind pressure. Persistent in the face of all difficulties presented by time, space, and weather, in attending rehearsals and services, they will not be induced to sit out the homily. Sad, incorrigible dogs! The old vicar, who now comes but occasionally to preach, cannot away with this, and sometimes, when the enormity of it rises upon him with more than usual oppression, he quits his surplice with a celerity that shocks the clerk and sexton, and hurries round to the west door, in an attempt to cut off the retreat of the hardy sinners, so that he may publicly admonish them. But he never succeeds And the organist—who with Blind John of the bellows tapping his way down the organ-gallery stairs, is generally the last to leave the porch—usually finds him impatiently beating an unsaintly tattoo with his foot, as with gentle indignation he denounces (to himself) the unseemliness of the proceeding,—for he is alone, and now waiting to walk homeward with the Jubilee teacher.

Sometimes the organist and his blind colleague find the vicar in a little group of comet-*tee* and other shipping men who have been arrested at the church door by the receipt of news—brought by a broker's clerk—of the loss of some "bottom" away in some distant part of the world. "Is she insured?" "How much is she covered?" "How much in the 'Illegible'?" "How much in the 'E-*quit*-able'?" "Is she a total loss?" "Ay." "A bad job, sur, a bad job," and so runs the current of question and comment

"How about the hands?" quietly asks the vicar. "The hands? oh, they're all gone, poor cheps" "Poor cheps!" "Aye, poor cheps,—it's a gudd loss for Mr. Bent though," etc., etc

Sometimes the discussion concerns the badness of trade and the lowness of *frights* (freights). Much gloomy shaking of heads is going on, and portentous hints as to what is amiss. "Are they then so very bad?" cheerily asks the vicar. "Yes, sur, they are, they are. What we want, you see, is a gudd war—a gudd war, sur."

As a chorus of approval rises the vicar's face falls, and he hurries off with his arm in the schoolmaster's, glancing presently at him with a queer expression of mingled deprecation and amused sympathy. Silence for a while, and then the master, "What do you make of that? Men, in the act of leaving the very sanctuary, wishing for 'a good war,' to mend their worldly gear Are we ever to get right in this matter?"

A BEGINNING.

The other, slowly pouting his lips, in very dubious tones hopes we may, who knows? in all times there have been such inconsistencies, such wishes, such hopes,—perhaps they don't realise all their desires imply,—what does he think?

He thinks that if 'tis to be done at all, 'twill have to be done with the newer generation; that one must begin at the beginning—the very beginning.

THE ALPHABET MILL.

CHAPTER VII.

LIGHTEN OUR DARKNESS.

"To know the Divine Laws and harmonies of this Universe must always be the highest glory of a man, and not to know them the greatest disgrace for a man."— CARLYLE.

EARLY in 1848 Woolhouse—calling attention to an advertisement in the *Times*, running thus :—" A mastership in the English Department of the Greenwich Hospital School is vacant. The salary is £125, to increase to £200. Evidence of superior skill in the management of a large school is indispensable. Candidates must apply by letter to the Secretary of the Admiralty "—wrote :—

"Now, I do not see why this should not suit you, as you are well qualified, and could produce abundant testimonials. I dare say you are aware I am personally known to the mathematical master, who is an intimate friend of Mr. Leitch, and it is more than probable that on seeing a favourable testimonial from Mr. L. and myself he might be induced to recommend you himself. No time should be lost. I was glad to receive your former letter, which proved you to be in genuine Christmas humour, developing the *true sense and importance* of what some moping persons would call nonsense."

Apparently the Jubilee master hesitated, and sought fuller particulars as to the requirements and qualifications, for a second letter came strongly urging him to apply, and enclosing a testimonial addressed to the Secretary of the Admiralty:—

"SIR,—Mr. Thomas Haswell, who is a candidate for the vacant mastership in the English Department of the Greenwich Hospital School, I have had the pleasure of knowing most intimately for upwards of twenty years. He has for many years been master to the Royal Jubilee School at North Shields, and I have often had occasion to admire the skill and tact displayed by him in his profession, and the modest exultation evinced by him on certain valuable improvements introduced by him for the benefit of his pupils. He possesses perseverance in an eminent degree, and has always shown considerable interest in the general principles of education, and the various systems adopted in public institutions, with the view of advancing his own school. In short, from a thorough knowledge of his attainments, character, and habits I can confidently recommend him as in every respect eminently qualified for the appointment he seeks."

"Let your testimonials," says this wise counsellor, "be select and *not* numerous, if you send many they will not be read. In these matters *brevity* is a great advantage."

The testimonials sent up for approval are pronounced to be "very judicious and of the most satisfactory kind, and sufficiently numerous as well as good," but the unavoidable delay in making application it is feared are much against the (in other respects) excellent prospects of success. The master, in fact, was less than half-hearted in the matter, his natural diffidence causing him to shrink from a serious effort to capture such a scholastic prize; Woolhouse, on the other hand, had set his heart upon bringing his old friend into closer touch with himself, so that they might better resume the musical studies and speculations in which they had indulged as boys; and to that end took every possible step likely to secure a prosperous issue, writing to and interviewing his many friends at the Admiralty and elsewhere, with whom his extraordinary powers had secured him interest.

But the master remained in his native town, and gave himself finally and irrevocably to the Jubilee; toiling strenuously on at the work which, lying among the children of the poor, was nearest his heart. He was now rapidly broadening and deepening the stream of culture which steadily flowed through the crowded classes of his school, and pressing into the service of the boys everything likely to incite their best efforts and give them a permanent bent for self-instruction. It was now, too, that he became generally known to his friends, to the rapidly increasing number of men who had been taught by him, and generally throughout the town and district simply as the "Maister." Brown sailors came rolling up to the half-door of the school, and beckoning in a shame-faced way, rather than entering, asked if "the Maister" was in; or a dark-eyed, smart-looking captain, knocking sharply at the house door after dark, would make the same inquiry. Soldiers at the barracks heard their comrades speak of him in the same relation; and doubtless many of the folk in and about Shields knew him by no other name.

Bright, smart-witted monitors now rapidly came to the front and gave devoted service to their slower school-mates, but they were taken away at so early an age that they as rapidly ceased to be available. The quick sympathy between these capable lads and their chief was the fru t of an intimate and searching investigation on his part into their several particular qualities, and a remarkable intuitive perception of their best points The monitors were the particular care of the Maister in respect to their home or after-school work, but in school hours it was his fixed principle to devote his own attention mainly to the younger pupils and especially to the duller of them. "Any one can teach a bright, capable boy," he was wont to say, "any one can teach a boy what he has a special aptitude for; any one can teach the scholar who by long attendance at school has become familiar with the operation—acquired the momentum, so to speak—of being taught." But the true function of the teacher lies in developing the dormant faculties of the beginner and directing them into the most suitable course, or in selecting the means by which the torpid wits of the mentally deficient can best be exercised. This sounds like a mere truism, yet it involves the direct contrary of the whole system of "paying by results," which is still the fundamental principle upon which popular education is based. Just as certain boys have a special aptitude for a given study, others are peculiarly inept, and lads who are simply incapable of any considerable acquirements in, say, history, grammar, literature, etc, may be found to possess a very strong faculty for science. An infinite patience with those poorer creatures whose deficiencies were general rarely failed to develop some quality worth uncovering; and one effect, at any rate, of sympathy and encouragement was to produce a struggle for progress if 'twere only to gratify an anxiety to please the Maister. At one time a poor half-witted boy, who was the despair of the monitors, became first in the school at freehand drawing, and he wrote so beautiful a hand that at the annual examinations it invariably drew universal admiration from the visitors. When the Maister detected some sprightly youth teasing poor R—— by making fun of his spelling, he would, in the face of the class, ask the two boys to write out a sentence, and then hold up for inspection the result—a test which rarely failed to bring to the face of the tormentor a flush of shame and to that of his butt a smile of pride.

The wonderful variety of the subjects taught in the school prevented that deadening, enervating *repetition*—veritably *damnable* iteration—which defeats its very object, and afforded ample time for all that was dealt with. A chapter from Parry's *Arctic Voyages*, as a reading lesson, might suggest, for instance, questions as to the compass, the magnetic needle or the *aurora borealis*; a compass being at hand, its properties were thereupon examined, and the history of its "variation," and the curious phenomena of deviation and dip carefully explained.

"As time went on," says the Maister, "I introduced new scientific subjects as soon as I could obtain the necessary apparatus. In my teens I had the pleasure and advantage of becoming acquainted with an old schoolmaster named Thomas Haigh, who was, and had been all his life, lame; somehow he had acquired a large knowledge of the sciences, and was never so happy as when imparting their wonders to young men like myself. From this clever and kind old gentleman I learned how to make for myself a set of magnetic bars, and to magnetise them by frictional induction. Very powerful they were, and of endless use and value in enabling me to study, and experiment upon, the mysterious subject of magnetism; one which afterwards proved highly interesting to the boys." Later, another set was forged by the Tubal Cain of the church choir (who made the tuning-forks) and magnetised by the Maister while explaining the process to his lads, thus affording them the advantage of seeing the results brought about. For years these magnets were used to illustrate lessons in the simpler phenomena of magnetism, showing Faraday's "lines of force" on a sheet of paper strewn with filings, and classifying substances as magnetic or otherwise.

At long intervals a "barrel" electric machine was for a short while borrowed, and then the magic-working properties of electricity were carefully worked at. But nothing permanent could be effected with borrowed apparatus, hence in dry, frosty weather, glass tubes, carefully varnished inside and dried at the fire, were vigorously rubbed with a bit of silk or a cat's skin, and a Leyden jar slowly charged, pith-balls attracted or repelled, electroscope films made to diverge or fall together, and the phenomena of induction experimentally followed. As much practical instruction as could be wrought out of such extemporised appliances—and it is more than is generally imagined—was diligently acquired, but the Maister all the while was wistfully looking about for a second-hand electric machine that would come within the narrow limits of his personal means, when, one night, he was suddenly overpowered by the apparition of a fine new plate machine, with quite a shining retinue of accessories. Oh, the delirium of that evening when, placed upon the sitting-room table, surrounded by a group of wondering monitors, chafed, if not *caressed* with a warmed silk handkerchief, and generally petted and fondled, the noble visitant responded to the first questioning turn of the handle, in an amazing flood of dazzling sparks, and otherwise proved his title to be treated and respected as "a magnificent fellow."

"After having the machine on loan for some time I one day met its owner, and told him how much I was obliged to him for his kindness, what a large amount of information I had by its means been able to impart to the scholars, and promised to return it to him in a day or two, when, to my surprise and delight, he replied, 'I am indeed very glad to hear that you have made such good use of the machine, but do not send it to me; keep it, you are heartily welcome to it, for it will do more good in your hands than mine, as I know you will continue to interest and instruct your scholars in the wonderful mysteries of electricity.'"

The Maister could hardly believe his ears when he was told that he was to have and to hold the magnificent instrument as a present from the maker, a brilliant young townsman, whose scientific attainments and foresight were only equalled by his modesty. The nephew of the worthy old Matthew Robson who released the precious volumes of the young "Mechanics'" from the broker's man, Mr. James Robson, constructed the machine and handed it over to his old friend to aid him in the work of inspiring the boys of the town with that love of natural science which possessed both so strongly.

"Frictional electricity," as it was then called, at once became a serious subject at the Jubilee, and a field-day was appointed for a special display of the powers of the newly-acquired wonder. How fondly one looks back to those old expedients for stirring the souls of the young, and oppressing the sentiments of the old with suggestions of the uncanny! The startled head of hair, the mysterious chime of bells, the "thunder-house" from which the wooden window—enormously disproportionate in size to the gable in which it is placed—is violently projected by the discharge of the battery of Leyden jars, the dancing pith-balls and paper figures, the wonders of the glass-stool on which a venturesome youth stands, finds his hair emulating the quills on the fretful porcupine, and has sparks drawn from his nose-end, the lighting of a gas jet through the pointed finger, the beauty of the "brush" discharge, the marvels of induction, the busy preparation for a lesson with its tinfoil, pitch, resin, gutta-percha, sealing-wax, *aurum musivum*, its sulphurous crackling and sparkling, and general atmosphere of magic!

Shortly after the acquisition of the electric machine, a Ruhmkorf coil and galvanic battery came to hand as a gift from a once "poor Irish lad," now the superintendent of a foreign telegraph station. "This he presented to me in gratitude for what, he said, I had done for him while he was under me, at school." The wider subject of "Voltaic" (the old terms come naturally to the pen) electricity is thus experimentally entered upon, the principles of the galvanometer, the telegraph instrument, the decomposition of chemical compounds, and the earlier steps in electro-depositing being steadily worked through.

Natural phenomena, such as the *aurora borealis* or the more frequent thunder-storm, were invariably seized upon—as they occurred—for emphasising and driving home the wider significance of these, as they may be termed, laboratory experiments. Against nothing was the Maister more on the alert than that besetting vice of scientific smattering—the taking the mere name of a phenomenon for an explanation of its nature. In those (scientific) early days, much as now, a wordy formula sufficed to allay, among the unscientific, all curiosity as to the true significance of any natural wonder, and that necropolis of scientific interest, the "scientific corner" of the newspaper, was ever burdened with complacent explanation of all the mysteries. "Sound strikes up" was a great favourite; the precipitation of moisture on the inside walls and windows of a house when a thaw sharply succeeds a long frost, was due to "damp striking out"; glass "sweated"; the air was "heavy" when the glass was low; "attraction" was the solvent of most electrical problems. Eclipses were "foretold" just as the coming weather was "prophesied," and lightning, the "electric fluid," as it was correct to say, was "attracted" by steel to the exclusion of chimneys, church steeples, and ships' masts. If a fishing coble, off at sea, came to grief in a thunder-storm, "the unfortunate occurrence, it is conjectured, arose through the electric fluid being attracted by the anchor." Such paragraphs afforded perennial amusement to the Maister, who generally kept a few "cuttings" of the kind in store for the science classes. The (newspaper) manners and customs of lightning were special favourites alike with him and the boys, and the zest with which he'd read out such a bit of pretentious absurdity as the following was shared by every youngster present:—

"Last night, the house No. 60 Wellington Street, belonging to Mr. Smith, block and mast maker, of 3 Walker Place, and at present occupied by two females in the employ of Mr. William Scott, the well-known hatter and glover of Tyne Street, was struck by lightning. Mrs. Jones and her niece had retired for the night, but had not gone to bed, when the destructive element struck the chimney, and passing down into the room below destroyed the plaster, removed the wall-paper in two places, and burnt the wood-work of the door. The electric fluid then proceeded"—(looking up at the boys with a smile at the word *then*, and resuming)—"*then* proceeded down the chimney into the front room, smashing the fire-place, dislodging a toasting-fork, and destroying some of the ornaments. Fortunately no one received any injury."

The fact that lightning does not "then" proceed—as though it were a policeman on the track of a burglar—but that its course is the sequence of a polarised condition of the matter through which it passes, set up before the actual discharge takes place, is carefully explained. Like the early lesson-books, many of the scientific text-books were most defective, being written by amateur book-scientists, and many of the profound misconceptions which are yet repeated in works on popular science, and linger on to-day in newspaper "leaders," can be traced back to them. They were dull, pretentious, heavy with interspersed moral reflections, and utterly devoid of system. Many of the difficulties presented to beginners were wantonly artificial. Long after the chemical equivalents had been shown to bear a ratio to each other capable of being expressed in simple whole numbers, the older school clung to the tables in which oxygen was given as 100, and consequently most of the other elements in long rows of figures arranged round a decimal point, requiring useless expenditure of time to memorise. To the expostulation of more sensible teachers who pointed out that such numbers concealed relations between the elements which it was invaluable, nay indispensable, that the student should recognise, the wrong-headed retort, heard even nowadays in other connection, was made that the *effort* of committing such numbers to memory was a valuable mental training in itself. The fact that the student wished to learn *Chemistry*, and would have ample scope for mental drill in the process, weighed as nothing with these obstinate oppressors of the young. A craze against making things "too easy!" a mere form of the old esoteric selfishness, animated many of the educationalists of the day, and caused them to lay waste the precious seed-time of generations of children. When one thinks of the boundless realms of knowledge, of the vast infinitude of things man would like to know, and do well to attempt to know, and reflects too on the little that can be accomplished with the fullest opportunity, one can partly realise the inexcusable wickedness of creating artificial difficulties, and of setting up mere adventitious barriers

Chemistry had now long been one of the most prized subjects taught in the school, but the re-agents were costly and the apparatus more so. The simpler properties of the metals and their salts, the action of acids and alkalies on vegetable matter, litmus, tincture of violets, red cabbage, turmeric, etc; the wonderful changes of colour, and the curious transmutations of form in precipitation, could all be shown in flasks and test tubes. Oxygen it was possible to make in which to burn steel wire, and to deflagrate charcoal or phosphorus. Hydrogen, contained in a bell glass under which sound could be quenched; nitrogen, the negation of all active properties, and hence intensely unpopular with the boys; the solution of metals in acids, and crystallisation of the resultant salts; carbonic acid gas; chlorine, coal gas, made first in a small iron retort thrust into the school fire, then collected in a bullock's bladder and burned at a jet therefrom,— all these could be grappled and firmly handled. But the chemistry of weight and measure, the quantitative, the vital chemistry, there was no apparatus for, except when, occasionally, some chemical friend of the Maister's volunteered to give the boys a lecture, with experiments; or when the poor, half-starved, shabby, peripatetic philosopher made one of his visits—erratic and unlooked-for as a comet. This class has ere now probably quite died out, but in mid-century it was one of the enduring surprises and joys of school life.

Fitfully he came, raising his greasy hat long ere he reached the half-door, and glancing with preternaturally bright eye round the premises to gain some preliminary notion of the reception to be encountered. Pale lantern jaws, grizzled hair, a shabby frock-coat distressed at all the wearing-parts, and scant trousers strained desperately between braces and straps, there is yet an air of gentility about him which none of these can keep down. Nay, a certain intellectual aspect there is in the head and features which invests the faded figure with a strange halo of pathos. His manners are a queer blend of aristocratic *hauteur* and winning propitiation

'Twixt him and the Maister ensues unheard conference, and if the issue be favourable, he walks quickly away with stately step and smiling face, to reappear at a later hour in the day with trestles, a board, a green baize cloth, and sundry boxes covered with shabby oil-skin. Before dispersing for the dinner interval, the scholars have breathlessly listened to an expected announcement from the Maister to the effect that "Professor" Dicks will give a lecture—with experiments—on chemistry, at 4 o'clock, and that such of the boys as wish to attend must bring with them a penny for admission. Poor lads!—for so many of them such a sum was as unattainable as the North Pole. Later generations can never know how much one of the heavy pence of that day meant to school-boys. The lecture was generally a ruinous investment for the Maister, for when the Professor was ready to begin, and the lucky lads who had paid for admission were assembled and the doors shut, there was always a group of wistful-faced little ones outside—many of them the particular pride of their class—whose appealing looks were too much for the dominie, and the issue in general was, "Well, well, get in then, be quick now, and don't disturb the lecturer,"—the pence for such being rigorously pressed upon the poor philosopher, though, in fairness it must be said, against his strenuous protests.

And what marvels these poor early demonstrators unfolded! How like magicians in their dexterous manipulation of apparatus of every bewildering variety, and in the dead precision with which they effected all they undertook Chemistry, optics, natural history, astronomy, seemed to open their inmost secrets to them at bidding, and—unlike the mere conjurer (who occasionally came)—they carefully and minutely explained their tricks, pressing the boys into active service and making them go through the experiments, to the unbounded delight of their schoolmates.

Some came with a Drummond-light magic-lantern, and then the teeming life of a drop of pond water, the struggles of a live flea, the eye of a bee, the polity of an old cheese, the decomposition of water, the formation of crystals, and a hundred other wonders would be displayed in the deepest silence, and disappear amid rapturous applause. Astronomical slides followed, showing the solar system hard at work, or the moon gliding steadily through her phases, or Jupiter's satellites revolving several times a minute, a few comic subjects being thrown in at the end to relieve the mind from the tension produced by the awesome spectacle on which it had been so steadfastly bent. Often these men had apparatus to sell, as microscopes formed out of a glass bubble filled with water, "cheap at a penny," or small kaleidoscopes, pseudoscopes, horse-shoe magnets, etc., though it was but few they sold, the price of admission having exhausted the funds of most of the boys. At times the financial outcome of an arduous hour and a half's work was so miserable that the poor fellow would utterly break down, and, sinking back on a bench, draw his shabby coat-sleeve across his red-rimmed eyes, when the Maister, encouraging and expostulating with him, would ask him to come over to the house and have a meal.

Not all who came to pick up scant pence were philosophers. The half-door revealed a strange motley of human beings who made for the amusement of our easily-pleased fathers. There came conjurers of all nations and colours, men who frightened the smaller boys and maintained a severe moral ascendency over the whole audience. Indian jugglers, with fearsome scimitars, who charmed toothless snakes out of baskets by squeaking on a pipe, and did marvels with eggs and top-hats. Men with performing dogs—saddest of sights, and one the Maister was ever loth to even tacitly tolerate. Needy Frenchmen there came, who persisted in being allowed to recite *Molière* on the chance of taking up a collection—forlornest of hopes, surely! Punch and Judy, ever welcome to young and old. The poor Italian man-orchestra, with drum on his back, bells on his head, cymbals on his elbows, bagpipe, triangle, and what not, wandered into the school-yard and flashed a *vendetta* out of his dark eyes on being requested to go. Girls on long stilts appeared at the high windows, to the music of drum and bagpipes, and rattled tin boxes for money

From most of these some element of reflection and study was drawn, and a generous recognition of good in all things slowly fostered.

"Soon after (receiving the Ruhmkorf) I saw a second-hand air-pump, an instrument I had long wanted, in a Newcastle optician's shop. There was not much apparatus with it, but it had a large plate, and I bought it at once."

The pump was a good one and in good condition, with a well-fitting receiver, and a pair of *Magdeburg* hemispheres some two inches or more in diameter. Lessons in pneumatics now became experimentally available, and the properties of gases in respect to their tenuity and its effect on sound, demonstrated. The receiver, filled with hydrogen, illustrated the curious attenuation undergone by sound as rarefication proceeds, or, when "exhausted" as far as the construction of the valves would permit, its practical extinction. The impressive picture was drawn of a silent world, a world in which not the loudest roar of thunder, cataract, or earthquake could be heard, but for that invisible mantle, the atmosphere, in which it is wrapped. Thence to the density of the air, its rarefication as the earth's surface is receded from, the Torricellian vacuum, the modification of the boiling point, the reason potatoes cannot be effectively boiled on Chimborazo, the velocity of falling bodies and how affected by the atmosphere (the famous guinea and feather apparatus could never be shown, the cost of the apparatus being far beyond the Maister's resources), the water-hammer, the bursting of a bladder of air by hanging it before a fire, refraction and its effect upon the apparent rising and setting of the sun and other luminaries, twilight and its varying duration, the velocity of sound in air, in water, in wood, in metals; thence again to the refraction of light. The prism was brought over from the Maister's parlour and conveyed into a lumber-room (used for storing coals, fire-wood, etc.) which could be entirely darkened, and a small bar of sunlight like molten gold admitted through a hole in the shutter, split up by the prism into the glorious sheaf of colour called the *spectrum*. Soap-bubbles, filled with coal-gas or hydrogen, were blown to illustrate the levity of gases lighter than air, and then a divergence made to the amazing world of colour that evolved itself as the film grew thinner Pneumatics naturally led to acoustics, which had long been reached by the approaches furnished in music, and thus the marvellous correlation of—not only all the sciences—but all subjects of human contemplation was insensibly revealed.

The Maister had, indeed, a passion for the study of all the more recondite phenomena of sound, and his delicate ear enabled him to recognise them and hint at their explanation long before Helmholtz and others had experimentally solved much of their mystery. As a boy, he had wandered round the old churchyard, stumbling over the green mounds, pausing here, hurrying there, and noting the weird and wailing storm of harmonics surging up out of the clang of the church bells. He knew under what buttress or wing to shelter to get this or that effect,—knew where the shriek of high overtone was most fiend-like, or where the warring dissonances subsided into a broken sob. It was a world of fearsome sounds that opened on the ear of any whom he induced to go with him to "take a taste of my harmonics," and, to most who went, an entirely new sensation. *Tartini's* (or resultant) tones he knew, and could produce for musicians who, hearing them all their lives, had never perceived them. The theory of "harmonics" led him to seek the society of any of the more eminent organ-builders who happened to come to the North, and long discussions ensued on the arrangement of the old *cornet* and *sesquialtera* mixture-stops, though few of the "practical" men cared greatly for the subject, being content with the old methods and old (mistaken) theories. The phenomena of interference, beats, etc., he had discussed in the early days with Woolhouse, who combined high mathematical powers with a profound knowledge of the theory of music; and he never left off testing and observing and noting combinations from every possible source. In the old church, certain pews would begin to buzz, a pane in the window shiver, or one of the gas globes rattle, at the sound of some deep note on the diapason. These must be found and tried and tested, and the several "stops" capable of producing like effects discovered. The "tone" of everything that sounded was known to him—the ring of tumbler glasses, the hum of the caulking hammers down at the docks; strange musical notes detected in the crackling of the winter fire or the throb of its flickering "low", in a boy's toys, such as the Jew's harp, the squeaker, and the "roarer"—a curious, very ancient and world-wide source of sound, consisting of a thin piece of wood, some ten to twenty inches long by two or three wide, with deeply notched edges, and swung round in a circle at the end of a long string. Now and then there would spring up a rage for these "roarers," and when school was dismissed as many as a hundred boys would rush off homeward, in different directions, making the air burdensome to the ear with throbbing and booming sound-waves. The Maister gravely examined and expounded the properties of the "roarer,"—showing the lads that to get the best results, the length and thickness of the string should bear a certain ratio to the weight and surface of the wooden blade—and in the process discovered a very good means of demonstrating the limits at which the ear is able to combine vibrations into a musical tone. the "syren" was of course out of his reach. Tuning-forks and their many curious and interesting phenomena he had always studied. The "wolf" in his 'cello was the subject of searching experimentation. Chladni's sand figures—the ripples produced on the surface of water (blackened with ink), or mercury by setting the vessel containing it into vibration—the compound vibrations of the monochord,—all these the boys were made familiar with. The strange charm of the Æolian harp was a revelation to many of the visitors to the school, for he had a specially good one which was placed in one of the windows of the house whenever there was sufficient aerial impulse to bring out the lovely harmonics—the murmuring sweetness of its lower tones as an autumn zephyr stirred the strings, as delicious as the rushing mystery of its combinations and the metallic crash of its higher overtones, when a nor'-easter swept fiercely over the strings.

His lessons on acoustics were indeed instinct with suggestion and observation. The physical basis of the scale was shown by endless alterations in the divisions of the monochord and the places of its nodes. The laws governing the vibration of strings, plates, rods, and of air in tubes, found a ready exponent in the old bandsman, whose skill with the various wind and stringed instruments gave precision to his demonstrations—the trumpet, trombone, 'cello, flute, clarionet, harmonicon, and even the musical glasses (carefully conveyed, these latter, from the parlour to the school-room and back again) being pressed into service and deftly used to illustrate or elucidate a point. The infinite complexity of the vibrations coming from an orchestra, and the marvellous analytical power of the human ear in resolving rather than merging or combining them,—the profound emotion stirred in the human soul by deep notes and their wondrous effect in the works of the great symphonists were lovingly expatiated upon. A certain readiness in seizing familiar natural phenomena to explain theory was one of the open secrets of his success as a teacher, but it was the fruit of ceaseless observation and thought, and perhaps in some measure of the invention that comes of necessity. The well-known sudden increase in the pitch of a sound that is rapidly carried towards and past the ear, and for an example of which most writers on physics select the scream of the locomotive's whistle as an express rushes through a station, was brought into every-day experience by the acute observation that every buzzing fly or bee or wasp that swirls past one's head in the heat of a summer day, or lumbering cockchafer in the autumn twilight, affords a better instance, and one that gives a means of appreciating the velocity with which the insect is flying.

This aptness at illustration fascinated the boys, secured for the Maister their steadfast attention, and kindled in them something of his own fire. Jack might, in the fulness of animal spirits, be a mischievous but was never a dull boy; his work was so varied and shaded in the happy *contrast* of his studies that each subject formed a relaxation from its predecessor.

But the precious import of recreation and physical exercise was from the first recognised and acted upon by the Maister—yet the sports of the lads were turned to intellectual service without abating a jot of their fun. Land surveying had long since been introduced as a means of securing exercise and fresh country air for the boys, without too seriously encroaching upon the few hours devoted to the whole course of their education. On some fine autumnal afternoon, when the corn had been saved, and while the bleaching stubble was yet unturned, the whole school was taken out "for a walk" into the country, where, by arrangement with some farmer, a field was surveyed with staff and chain by the older scholars—the younger looking on with eager interest and resisting the charms of leap-frog as long as the absorbing evolutions involved in marking out a *trapezium* yielded any intelligible grounds for speculation. These half-days in the country were the particular delight alike of Maister and boys, for though every object of natural interest and beauty was lightly touched upon, 'twas never so done as to mar in the slightest degree the holiday-like character of the occasion. When the field operations were finished, the notes duly entered in the surveying-book for future reduction in school, the chain neatly folded, the "arrows" strapped together, and the poles stacked, the boys had free charter to play as they liked, and then there went up from two hundred shrill treble voices a mighty shout—the peace-offering of youthful happiness, surely as grateful to the good God as any smoking incense!

Clustering round the Maister wherever he went, like ants at a piece of honey, a group of boys held out to him, it might be, a curious leaf, a metallic tinted fungus, an amorphous oak gall, a ladybird; or perhaps they lay in wait for the surprise he was sure to have in store. With a small pocket-magnifier the structure of some common insect, or the loveliness of some simple field flower was shown to those of the lads who evinced a taste for such investigations —the smallest boy in the group always being allowed the first peep. The early beginnings of botany were allowed to develop as the superb coloration of a bramble leaf, or the delicate beauty of the radiating laminæ of a mushroom were exhibited. It was a deep-seated sympathy with the lowly that caused the Maister to select his subjects from the commonest of field flowers, and to point out the hidden loveliness that lies in the very weeds of the hedge—a piece of lush green moss, fresh from the decaying roots of an overthrown oak was to him so unspeakably beautiful that he rarely broke silence as he passed it round, with the microscope, among the striving crowd of heads. Not a nest was touched, no bird's egg disturbed, nor insect wittingly hurt, on these expeditions, and even the wanton plucking of dog-rose or honeysuckle or daisy was deprecated by the teacher, as hurtful to a child's better nature. The destruction of any object of beauty, nay, even an idle cut with a stick at the rank hemlock was distasteful to him, and so, gradually, the boys grew instinctively to shrink from what annoyed the Maister —with what ultimate good to themselves it is hard to measure.

At regular intervals during the summer the school—which now never numbered fewer than two hundred and twenty or more boys— was marched down to "the sands" at Tynemouth, there to bathe in the sea, to swim or be taught to swim, to scramble on the green rocks and gather bladder wrack for putting into the fire at home to startle mother and sisters; to touch with their toes the beaded tentacles of the sea-anemone, or to watch angry cancer scurry off into the deep recesses of his temporary aquarium, down among the fairy colours. What an intoxicating frolic the whole thing was! Two hundred boys divesting themselves, at the word of command, of their outer hull, neatly piling their clothes at four hundred feet, and then, after a great shout, four hundred naked legs rushing across the burning yellow sand into the curling waves, and dancing and kicking about blinding showers of spray. What still-born attempts to swim in water too utterly shallow—what portentous puckering of mouths and blowing out of cheeks as the immature attempts are made! What shivering regard, for a few minutes, of the luckier ones disporting themselves in the blue water out beyond the breakers, where the Maister too was diving and leaping like a dolphin! What racing on the beach! What mad revelling in the sensation of a free sun bath (a luxury that went out with the Greeks, the hygienic value of which does not appear to have floated into the ken of the healing profession)! What shouting for and at each other! What a confusing resumption of clothing as tattered shirts and ventilated breeches are held up to the light for identification, with all the glorious unconsciousness of boyhood!

The lads are gathered on one of the reed-grown sand dunes, and a part-song or madrigal lustily trolled. Ships in the offing are classified to the finest distinction of rig, build, and nationality; a Cullercoats coble displays her lovely lines as she comes out—broad of wing—from behind the Bear's Back. If she be within hail, the Maister, who is a keen hand in a sailing-boat, will ask what the fishermen will take for giving some of the lads a turn as far as the target out at sea. "Nowt, sur!" They know the Maister too well to make any charge, and off goes a cargo of broad grins. It may perchance be impossible for the coble to approach the target to-day, for there is gun practice from the castle-yard, and the round shot is seen, at intervals, to flirt the water up into the air like the spouting of a whale. Then some of the monitors and older lads stand and wait for the flash of the gun noting the time of the splash near the target and of the sound of the explosion. The Maister, observing this, approaches, and taking off his watch gives it to the oldest boy, so that he may work out the relative average velocity of the projectile and of sound. By walking towards the Castle, in a line roughly parallel to the course of the shot, the sound is found to reach the ear more and more quickly, whilst by proceeding towards Cullercoats—away from the Castle—the flash of spray is seen before the sound is heard, by an increasingly longer interval. Careful notes of distances, times, etc, are taken home for subsequent reduction.

Racing, leap-frog, "bait the bear," tug-of-war, and other games go on vigorously until the signal is given for home-going, when instantly the ranks are formed and the march back is begun. Droll it is, on such occasions, to note the deportment of some young fellow—once school-mate, now suddenly, it seems, turned man—when the ranks file past, grinning a half-friendly, half-derisive, recognition of him as one who has passed hopelessly out of good times like these.

For the boys were absolutely happy with the Maister, and loved him with all the devotion of which boy nature at its best is capable. He joined in their sports, provided them with better athletic appliances than were elsewhere to be found in his day, and, above all, let them play as boys love to play, in their own way. And that they revelled in the gymnastics provided for them in the great mast, its ropes, and the "high bar," off which they darted into space like birds from a precipice, every wonder-struck visitor had no difficulty in perceiving. The sons of sailors for the most part, these boys were half-trained for going aloft while yet at the Jubilee. Scrambling to the mast-head and standing thereon was a test that divided the playground into an envied aristocracy and a crowd of aspirants thereto. The swing—called the "hykle"—was put to trapeze-like purpose, which resulted in cuts and contusions that sent the victims to the "Mistress" for lint and plaster and sympathy. Climbing up the inclined ladder like monkeys, and performing feats with legs as well as arms, pale, weak boys seemed to undergo a complete metamorphosis after being some three or four months at the Jubilee, and but for the insufficient food with which so many of them had to be content, would have become strong, hardy men Quoits, "shinny" (a better kind of hockey), "stand-all," a spartan game in which forfeit involved the placing of the back of the hand against a wall and having a hard ball thrown at the palm; tops, *the* game of games, fascinating all boys, from the smallest to the biggest, in the playground. What tops they were, too! The common cast-iron "prod" (peg) found in the new purchase was, like an old tooth, instantly drawn, thrown away, and replaced by a prodigiously long one formed out of a carefully filed wrought-iron nail, or better still (if the blacksmith could be bribed to part with it), a bit of steel. Such a top—of hardwood—was a prize which gave the owner recognised ascendency over his fellows; the concentric grooves cut in the upper surface were proudly coloured with cheap but gaudy pigments. Great top-champions owned and carried perilously in the trousers' pocket three, four, or half-a-dozen tops all with inordinately long, pointed pegs. When scientifically spun these long-legged spinners hopped like peas on a hot shovel, and were known as "dickey-dancers." It was the privilege of the possessor of a good dickey-dancer to walk up to the chalk ring, within which perhaps twenty or more tops might be spinning, and after busily winding on the hard whip-cord and placing the smooth brass button at the end between his fingers, purse up his lips and look intently for a victim; and, as the humbler competitors looked uneasily at him, with one sharp swing of the arm above his head to launch his weapon. If the swoop be successful the foredoomed top is split from head to peg, while the victorious one hops with vindictive crepitations all over the ring. Marbles, too, are in great vogue, from simple "dabby" to the involved "boorie"; and "clayeys" and "stoneys" and "tars" and "alleys" and "bullickers" change hands as rapidly as scrip on 'change. "Leed fardens"—by which the unelect are to understand lead farthings—came up and died out at intervals of a few years. There was great virtue in the possession of a bag of good leed fardens, for they would fetch almost anything a boy possessed. Those who could make them controlled the finance of the playground.

A pair of moulds formed of dried chalk and having the farden, bearing some fanciful device and the name or initials of the maker, rudely cut on the inner faces,—a ladle of melted lead, and there you were. Cockspurs have probably passed quite out of school-boy

ken, but they were greatly affected in the days when pocket-money was so desperately scarce and *bought* toys so few. These cockspurs were little glazed earthenware things used by potters to keep the bottom of the "saggar," in which articles are placed for baking, from "setting" on the kiln floor, and they were found in comparative abundance among the rubbish thrown out of potteries. A good set of cockspurs, containing all the sizes, was worth a bag of "stoneys," or perhaps a double score of leed fardens.

There was as yet no cricket, and no football; but a kind of tennis was played against the school wall involving the occasional destruction of a window-pane, and with it the peace of mind—for a time—of the urchins responsible. For a pane cost ninepence to replace, and ninepence was a tremendous sum for even a dozen boys, selected at random, to pay.

But if they loved their games, the lads equally loved their studies, and many a time the dominie in his later days told how they were wont to come to him and beg that he would withhold a half-holiday that they might instead have a lesson on, it might be, astronomy, electricity, or chemistry Surely this is the very triumph of the master's art. It is not the mere successful teaching of given subjects which marks out the true teacher (indeed, seeing for how short a period the children of work-people and labourers could be spared, their actual acquirements at school could not be other than slender), but the inspiration of a love for and devotion to the subjects of study and the resulting unquenchable resolution to *afterwards* pursue them, and judged by this standard, few men of his day attained a higher ideal than the Jubilee master. Writing of him, one is forced by the mere effect of contrast to think of Charles Lamb's delightful, though curiously wrong-headed essay on *Old and New Schoolmasters* With a waywardness all his own, Elia demonstrates that it is not in nature for a dominie to be really loved—even liked, by his scholars; that, in fact, their mutual relations preclude the possibility One is loth to admit this, recognising what a terrible slur it is upon the teachers whom he knew; probably, however, he was merely theorising; throwing off in his beautiful prose a mere whimsical speculation having no basis in experience, nor needing any. But surely he was strangely wrong, else, undoubtedly, the affectionate regard that Thomas Haswell inspired in his boys was phenomenal, for beloved he was by them, as all who knew old Shields, knew well

Besides the gymnastics of the playground there was a systematic code of physical drill indoors. Each morning and afternoon, for ten minutes or more, the whole assembly was called to its feet, and faced towards the desk, where stood, on a stool, one of the monitors. In dead silence the mass of boys steadily followed the evolutions of this youth, who forty or fifty successive times thrust out his arms at full length in front of him, then as many times upwards above his head, again towards his feet, and so on, the Maister watchfully scanning the plain of heads to see that no one shirked the task. Winter and summer there was systematic marching and countermarching in the playground to the tune of drums and fifes. Here, in the ampler space, standing at open order, a course of exercises for "expanding the chest" was gone through; the extended arms being brought in front till the palms touched, and then carried horizontally behind until the backs of the hands came in contact;—the open palms, thrust above the head to the utmost length of arm, brought, knees rigid the while, in a sweep to the toes. This doubtless is all familiar and commonplace now, but in mid-century it was very new indeed, and most dubiously regarded by many who posed as authorities on popular education.

For a year or two, perhaps, a smart drill-sergeant from the garrison at Tynemouth, or the frigate lying in Peggy's Hole, might be open for an engagement at the school, and *then* the drill was no joke. The spirit of the martinet inspired every spasmodic jerk of his active physiognomy, and his sharp snap of command was like the crack of a whip. The punctilious self-importance of these gentlemen was greatly enjoyed by the Maister, as, after handing over the reins of authority to the spare little official, he quietly looked on with a smile Fencing was occasionally taught by these old sergeants, and even cutlass drill, but the Maister never very cordially welcomed these.

As the holidays approached—and they were invariably held in autumn, so that the serious work of the harvest might be helped on by every hand, young or old (and if work in the field was not always to be had, gleaning at all events was a necessity which touched all too closely a vast number of the poor in Shields)—preparations for the annual examination became visible in the work of the school Elaborate specimens of writing, long drawn-out sums in division, neatly balanced formulæ and equations in algebra, sums in tare and tret, and so forth, were prepared on the best writing-paper procurable, generally the unused pages of an old ledger or log-book given by a patron of the school; maps of remote and unfamiliar portions of the earth's surface, drawn on white cartridge and coloured, charts of some particular Arctic expedition with the "course" plotted out, geometrical drawings shaded with indian-ink—all these accumulated steadily against the coming of the great day. The drill in mental arithmetic is rendered more stringent, and all the remoter, and therefore uncertain regions of syntax, history, and what not, are swept over again and again

All this in deference, not to the opinions or views of the Maister, but, to the established custom of holding an annual exhibition, so to speak, of the accomplishments and acquirements of the scholars. Originated, unquestionably, rather as a means of propitiating or impressing the public than of benefiting the children, the ceremony was now little else than an open competition among the latter, and, as such, distinctly distasteful to the head of the school. He had a rooted objection to the whole system of competitive examination *in education* (where the benefit of the taught should be the sole object in view), and always held that the results of such competitions were not only wholly misleading but mischievous; that the most deserving boy rarely won; that elements came into the arena which were never allowed for; that the object of true education—the inspiration of a love of knowledge for its own sake—was lost in the lower and meaner passion for supremacy which is over-developed in most natures. For these and like reasons he declined to sanction prize-giving, and only reluctantly yielded to the representations of the committee when they desired to have special mention made of the boys who were thought to have done best. Such boys, he said, rarely worked anything like so assiduously as many of their comrades, and had more than ample compensation in their greater natural abilities—in a word, he believed that, in the eyes of a greater than human wisdom capable of measuring the strength of will and of wit in these striving units of humanity, there is little to choose between them, though probably some of the lowliest would be recognised as deserving most.

On the great examination day the sweeping squad have quite early cleansed the floor, others have gone off with wheelbarrows to the saw-mills and fetched a great heap of fresh sawdust, which is soon scattered thickly over the floor. The maps, diagrams, drawings, "problems," and specimens of writing are being tacked up against the dado; the wooden compasses equipped with new "chalks"; the great music-board mounted on the easels. Faces are chafed with soap and towel with somewhat more than usual rigour, the hair combed a thought more carefully, here and there a few white collars show over the well-brushed jacket, and the proportion of bare feet is a little, though not much, reduced. A few decent, anxious-looking mothers are at the iron gates. The placid-faced committee sedately cross over from the master's house to the school-room, and are received with a storm of shrill cheering; patrons, subscribers, and visitors follow, and the work of examination is set about, a psalm-tune first being sung in the freshest crispness of boy-treble. There are *viva voce* tests in all subjects, and the "gentlemen" become involved in labyrinthian difficulties, and are relieved to get out again. A skipper asks a few questions on the "compass," and is disposed of by the smallest youth that can be found. Reading, spelling, singing, the working of sums mentally, and a few other tests are applied, a display of gymnastic drill is gone through, then the company file slowly round the walls and peer as wisely as they may at the hieroglyphics there displayed, and after expressing surprise and admiration return to the great desk, where one or two of the most capable boys are brought before them,—lustily cheered by their comrades as they blushingly approach the chief visitors, especially when some tiny mite of a fellow hardly big enough to be breeched is called forward for examination in Bible history by one of the benign Quaker ladies in scuttle bonnet, and wins her smiling approbation Then is sung some tricky three-part catch, which compels the sedate Quakers to smile, in a sheepish way, at each other.

> "Sir! pray be so good,
> Have you seen a boy
> Running like a hare
> Towards the wood?

> "There, there he goes, hark, hark away,
> He bursts across the open heath.
> They little think that he can hide
> 'Neath a tuft of grass."

And after it, the anthem of the occasion—

> "When I'm at school my father
> Is working on the farm,
> The harvest he must gather,
> And shield the fold from harm.
> My brother is at sea,
> My sister is from home,
> She must at service be
> Till Christmas-tide doth come."

The lines are set to a pretty air, greatly favoured by the boys.

The honorary secretary next steps forward, and in a voice filled with all the best elements for getting at a boy's heart, makes his little annual announcement. He says the committee are proud to see how well they have done, and how favourably they have impressed the gentlemen who have left their business to visit them. (Cheers.) They are getting as good an education as any rich man's son, and are benefiting by it (Cheers.) They are fortunate in having so many good friends. (Loud cheers) Mr. —— has just announced that he will continue to supply sticks (fire-wood) for nothing. (Shrieks) He has also offered to give a new set of ropes for the mast. (Prolonged tumult.) Mr. —— has promised the *whole school* an excursion by steamboat, in the holidays, to—— (Remainder of sentence lost in terrific din.) Their good old friend, whose kind face is smiling on them to-day, Mr. Hugh Taylor, has just undertaken to supply the school during next year, as heretofore, with coals for nothing, and—yes—wait—wait—and—now wait—will give the Christmas dinner as usual (The sustained piercing scream which follows this causes the laughing visitors to stop their ears until the Maister restores silence.) The holidays will continue for six weeks, the school resuming—— (Unrestrained deafening applause.) He hopes they will never forget how much they owe to that kind and generous friend who every day is with them, and whose whole heart lies in their welfare—he means the M——. (No more can be heard, this time the cheering cannot be stayed, and must exhaust itself) Then, silently, the boys are put through their desk drill, the "Grace" is solemnly said, and after a decent pause the signal to march off is given, and the drum and fifes begin to play, but to no purpose Twelve score throats give voice to all the pent-up joy that the last and culminating item in a day of successive delights has filled to overflow, and the committee and visitors are glad to turn once more, with ringing ears and somewhat dizzied heads, into the school-house parlour, to receive the reports and yearly statement of accounts

After the business is disposed of the Maister is called in and informed, with many compliments, that the committee recognise that his remuneration is much less than it ought to be—than they like it to be—but that, as he knows, the funds are not in a condition to admit of their doing more for him. They however ask him to accept a bonus of *ten pounds* as a mark of their esteem and of their recognition of his zeal and attention to his duties.

In a few minutes the school is left silent and void, the big iron gates are shut, and the youngsters are off to the harvesting, the gleaning, the helping of father in his boat, or mother at the mangle. For the long holidays are but a time of harder labour than usual for most of the Jubilee scholars. Many go off to the herring fishing, some to potato weeding, bird-scaring, or other temporary occupation lasting far into the night, as errand-boy in a shop.

The occasional holiday gave a better opportunity by far for indulgence in any of the enterprises to which boys devote such leisure as they may get. At "Fair" time, twice a year, the school was dismissed at noon on two or three successive Fridays, with the distinct object of enabling the scholars to take part in that somewhat frowzy carnival; and what a rush was made down the banks and stairs to the open space looking on the river, and known as the New Quay. Here the confusion, noise, dirt, and smell, the crowding, shouting, and bustling made a boy's paradise. There were shows, all front and no inside, with drum and panpipe, clown, and lady in dirty fleshings; booths all inside and no front, into which boys never got; peep-shows which it had been better boys could never have seen, roundabouts, shuggy-shews, and sky-fliers creaking, grinding, and turning successive cargoes of youth sick; shooting-galleries, cheap-jacks, galvanic-battery men with hideous range of bottles containing tape-worms *et hoc*, and exhibiting horrid sections of the human body, painted in crude colour on strips of oil-cloth. Ballad-roarers, evil-faced and filthy in person, howling, in twos or threes, indecent doggerel for the edification of groups of grown rowdies, sham cripples, hoarse blackguards with cocoa-nuts for shying at; stalls for candy, ginger-bread, barley-sugar, spice nuts, taffy and claggum, toy vendors, oyster women and apple-women, black-pudding and periwinkle stalls, and stalls for sheep's trotters, mince, shrimps, cockles, hyuldoos, and spice soles, profile artists; quack-doctors with store of dried weeds, a wax-work of unusually diabolical horror, or a small menagerie with overpowering stench, booths where men—and even women—grinned for "baccy,' or dipped in treacle for rolls; greasy-poles; crowds of sailors, keel-men, pitmen, countrymen, country lasses, girls without hat or shawl, foreigners, organ and hurdy-gurdy men, blind fiddlers, beggars, poison-dens called "Museums of Health and Anatomy," and other nameless "attractions." It was almost invariably cold and bleak at fair-time, and not unfrequently snow lay on the ground, soon to be trodden into a deep soaking mire. There was no gas, but flaring naphtha lamps made up for that. Noise, ribaldry, foul language, and coarse indecency were omnipresent, and yet it was not thought well to keep children away from such a pandemonium, or, better, to clear the thing away. With an unconsciousness that says much for human nature, the young folks seemed to pass through the morally-poisoned atmosphere without contamination, and, intent upon the gaudy pleasures that most attracted them, seemed to have no eyes for the sores that lay so thick around. For them there was but one drawback—a besetting one, though—to wit, lack of pence. There was no money wherewith to buy anything, for the ha'penny or rarer penny with which the owner had come there, holding it so tight in his hand that it was hot to the touch when the blue-nosed round-about man took it, had gone for an exciting ride or two on one of the rampant pie-balds that held a short course round the ring. So the ginger-bread piles, the nuts, crackers, etc, could only be gazed at until the angry vendor cleared off, like flies, his hungry-looking *entourage*. The shows could only be seen through a crack in the side door or a rent in the canvas, and this involved certain corporal possibilities of great unpleasantness.

When a half-holiday came to the boys unexpectedly, and there was no fair or "hoppin'" to assist at, an afternoon on the "timmers"—floating rafts from the timber-ships—or a scramble among the rocks at Tynemouth, perhaps a cutting-out expedition 'gainst the sleeping scullerman, and the carrying away of his boat, would be indulged in. Or may be, a blackberrying raid on the fields at Whitley, the hunting of a hedge-hog, a stolen visit to the Monk's Stone, with an endeavour to decipher the inscription, which every Shields lad "knew" to run as follows, but of which no trace existed:—

> A horrid dede
> To kill a man for a pigg's bede.

Perhaps a group might go to catch tadpoles or "asks" (newts) in the Spital Dene, or to explore Jingling Geordy's Hole—a burrow near the old Abbey, invested (traditionally) with more alluring witchery than the cave of Ali Baba or of Aladdin. What searching there was for the "passage" that never existed! What tales of unhallowed (and ungrammatical) utterances, and sounds and incomprehensible manifestations never heard or experienced!

Some got a trip "over the bar" in a steam-tug, and came back late at night tired, and perhaps sick—but in any case with pockets distended with ship-biscuit. Others found amusement in teasing the men unloading the little French apple sloop until they were bought off by the gift of a wool nightcap-full of fruit. There might be a performance by a military band on Tynemouth Green, in which event a dozen or two boys went down and competed for the honour of holding the soldiers' music. There was no band-stand then, and bandsmen would presently — while playing — become fascinated by the sight of his boy squinting down the page, reading the music upside down, following with absorbed interest the progress of the player and turning the page at the right moment.

If a soldier's funeral got wind, a dead set was made at the Maister for leave to attend, and the *cortège* was followed from the Castle to the burial-ground and back again with the greatest enthusiasm and enjoyment.

On certain joyous forenoons in the spring, the "Good Design," or the "Loyal Standard," or some other seamen's mutual benefit association, attended morning service at the old church, and afterwards, in procession, threaded the streets of the town with the ultimate object of reaching the "Marquis of Granby," on the Banks, where the annual dinner was held.

Quite early in the morning sundry outward manifestations suggested a public holiday; the Royal Standard was flapping above the battlements on the tower of Christ's Church; the bells rang out at intervals in "peals" of increasing complication, not to say unsteadiness, and by nine o'clock groups of women and children took up a position near the gates of the churchyard to wait there for the chance of securing a good place among the graves and tombstones when the sexton should throw the iron portals open. The low churchyard wall, with its broad, flat stone coping, was already a romping place for adventurous youths who dodged the single constable in a perpetual game at "tig."

Opposite the church gates, and embraced by the outstretched arms of one of the venerable churchyard ash-trees, hung out over the roadway the newly-decked signboard of the "Queen's Head"—symbol of the loving association of Church and State. Again, across the road, this time diagonally, the cosy bar of "The Old Hundred" showed its rows of bright pewters, its oak kegs, and fresh store of churchwardens (pipe-clay variety), and round the open door, outside, loitered certain early celebrants—Dusty Bob and his compeers—whose fitful and precarious employment held a certain melancholy relation to every dear brother and dear sister in the town.

The Jubilee, with the sexton's cottage closely nestling under its eaves, the old church, the "Queen's Head," and "The Old Hundred,"—one church, one school, and two public-houses—formed the four corners of the cross-roads at the intersection of which the great iron gates of the churchyard stood, and in this highly ecclesiastical locality a crowd of gossips foregathered to see the procession. But the Jubilee lads were *in*, and not *out*, side the school walls, wearing this morning an aspect of preternatural gravity quite portentous, every mother's son straining his ears to catch—amid the jangling clangour of the church bells—the sound of a certain distant, but unmistakable dull throb which shall bring release. At length it is faintly suspected, then positively heard. The Maister takes up a volume of music and his hat, and going towards the door, raises a warning finger as he says, "Now, mind boys! two o'clock *certain*" Alas! 'tis one of the days that unmake Jubilee boys, and wreck their best resolutions, some few will forget the compact and literally "come to grief" next morning. The hoarse braying of brass instruments is now faintly heard, and the steady dead thump of the big drum comes nearer and nearer. The Maister has crossed over to the tower gallery with a few choir-boys, who will get into trouble by singing as badly as possible because of enforced absence from the fun outside

With a great cheer the school-pack clears the gates and rushes into the medley, crowding upon the churchyard wall, or clambering upon the iron-spiked pallisading of the vaults, or swarming up into the boughs of the old ash-trees that droop across the Tynemouth Road. Here comes the procession,—the road is filled from side to side with successive rows of overgrown lads, men, and girls, arm in arm, and marching in time to the strains of the band (which the crash of the bells is now rendering awful), shouting their recognition of some comrade on the steps of the "Queen's Head," or mounted on the graveyard wall. Young nurse-girls frantically rush in and out of the crowd, carrying babies into endless danger. Romping urchins thread the moving mass, like shuttles, in some incomprehensible game, but keep warily out of range of the threatening boots of the bearers of the first banner—a glorious, capricious thing of silk, borne on a cross-bar stretched between the gilt tops of two poles, the lower ends of which are held in leathern sockets slung round the shoulders of a pair of sailors, too preoccupied even to chew, and whose motions, governed entirely by Boreas in his rudest mood, are of a rather tottering and uncertain kind Guy-ropes are run from the tops of the poles to other sailors, and the ship's company of not fewer than six A.B.'s, have more ado in navigating the exasperating craft than they would a man-o'-war. The device on the banner is simple and friendly—two large hands, with frilled cuffs, in a tight grasp of amity. The artist has had some doubtful trouble with the proper placing of the thumbs, but they are both abundantly present. There is much dodging and dipping of heads on the part of the crowd to catch a view of the emblem of brotherhood, though it is known to them as well as the standard on the flag-staff of the church. After a few lesser one-man banners have passed the band is glimpsed, the projecting trombones in the front rank swaggering from side to side, and the keyed ophicleides swaying proudly in the fullest enjoyment of the *basso obligato*, which, with quite a small modicum of popular tune, makes up the marching pieces of the time.

Close in the rear of the indefatigable drums follow the ranks of the "Good Design," rolling along in all the good-natured abandon of seamen, making no pretence, nor thinking any necessary, of keeping in step or marching to the music; out of form, out of time, out of line, they struggle along, taking a chew, smoking a broken long clay, or stepping nonchalantly aside to greet a chum in the crowd, and returning to the ranks with lumbering run Another banner coming along is in difficulties; several times the poles bend to the verge of breaking, and the guy-ropes get involved; the silk is twisted round the cross-bar and hanging down in folds which belly out in the wind Tars from the procession lend a hand to "get hur reet agyen," and after much ado the folds are unravelled and the "subject" displayed to the crowd. A familiar enough scene!—known to every person in that swaying mob. A dead mariner lying on his back, in jersey of blue and white bands, on the Lowlights Shore, a kneeling woman, with her apron held up to her eyes, weeping over him, a child standing by. Waves curl behind them, in the distance, with geometrical and impossible symmetry. No sailor ever seen (off the stage) ever wore such a jersey, the art is crude, but the picture tells a tremendous truth, and the banner is the popular one of the procession, without which the ceremonial of the day would be regarded as a hollow fraud

The band files through the iron gates into the churchyard. The crowd trample upon the grassy mounds and clamber over the table-shaped tombs in an endeavour to catch a sight of the sailors entering the south door under the old sun-dial The flags and banners are laid across the graves, the band instruments lie scattered here and there in charge of "the triangle," and boys skip madly round them. The bell-ringers come down from the bell-loft and go off to "The Old Hundred," whither the bandsmen, headed by the chartered libertine of the occasion—the sexton—have already "adjourned." The rumble of the organ is heard by men sitting gossiping and smoking on the churchyard wall, whilst the parson, as he slowly works his way through the service, hears the shrill noise of the boyish riot outside, borne in through the great door as it fitfully opens and shuts to the wind. The dead sailor and the weeping woman lie restless on the graves of old Shields, while children flit over, about, and around them like May-flies, or vault across the "stocks" that moulder away in the sun by the tower door.

In due time the jovial sexton shuffles to his feet, and warning the "professional" men, who with loud guffaw have rewarded his jokes, that 'tis time to be on the move, waddles off to the vestry to receive his dearly-beloved brother; the bell-ringers climb the winding stair, the bandsmen pick up their trumpets after cuffing "the triangle," who, in the fulness of his position, has allowed some of the boys to try a blow, and presently the sailors slowly emerge from the porch, blinking at the sunlight, and looking cramped and just a touch depressed For they have been listening to a homily of peculiarly home-touching character, dealing with the uncertainty of life, and the likelihood of some among them being "missing" on the next annual meeting day The bells have gone off in a salvo of clashing dissonance; the wayward banners have again been reared and the guy-ropes manned, the drum has given three warning whacks on the damp sheep-skin, which yields a tone as dead as anything in the grave on which it erewhile lay up-ended,—off goes the band, and after it surely the most draggle-tailed procession the world ever saw The "Good Design" slowly toils through the narrow streets of the town, and comes finally to anchor before the dinner which closes the day's ceremony,—meanwhile back to the Jubilee, for the afternoon, come the scholars, somewhat unsettled and demoralised by the sudden and all-too-short frolic among the graves of the old churchyard.

. . . . . .

To the school came the sons of all the tribes. The Irish Catholic, the Wesleyan, the Primitive Methodist, the Jew, the Scotch Presbyterian, the Baptist, the Independent, the "Salemite," the "New Connexion" boy, the boy from "Little Bethel," and the poor unclassified little chap, whose mother on being asked by the benign "committee gentlemen," "What place of worship?" glances deprecatingly at the faces of her interlocutors and begins, hesitatingly—

"Well, sir—if ya please——"

"He must attend *some* place of worship on Sunday, you know."

THE "GOOD DESIGN" BANNER.

"Yis, sir" (making nervous play round her lips with the edge of her apron).

"Will you see to it?"

"Oh yis, sir."

"What place would his father prefer?"

"Well, sir,—he's not—partic'lar, sir."

"Church of England, then?" (encouragingly).

"Oh yis, if you *pleese*, sir" (much relieved).

And so the small unit is taken to the broad bosom of the Establishment.

"They will be required on the Lord's Day regularly to attend the place of worship which such parent or friend shall appoint,"—such, the charter of religious liberty under which, in 1811, the institution was launched; and, with the most scrupulous honour not the slightest attempt was ever made to influence the parent or friend in his choice, those placid-faced Quakers, for all the calm and repose of their countenances, being sharply on the alert to secure the absolute discretion of every father, mother, or guardian. But when no choice could be made or suggested, then the crumb was picked up by mother church.

Absolute equality in the eyes of the governors, committee, and master was found by every sect and every split. The "religious difficulty" had not as yet been invented. Every day at the opening of the school the morning hymn, "Awake, my soul, and with the sun," rang out to the massive strains of Luther's great chorale, and then "the chapter" was read; and the little black-eyed Jew sang as lustily as his mates, and took no harm. *Per contra*, no cowardly attempt to insult his parent or his parent's creed was, under the specious pretext of "explanation," ever dreamt of, nor would it have been permitted.

When Lazarus Marks appeared at the half-door, bearing on his back the crate of window-glass and putty which, together with a certain vitreous polish on the cuffs and sleeves of his coat, betokened his vocation of glazier;—lighted up his black beady eyes with a certain diamond-like sparkle (his way of smiling), and, with the courtesy of his race, awaited an invitation to come in; the Maister invariably left the task that occupied him, and looking down at the little son of Judah, whose hot hand—now that two hundred pairs of boy's eyes were gazing curiously at him—was more tightly grasping his father's, quietly asked his name, his age, whether he'd brothers and sisters, how many, and how old; so gauging the boy's capacity as he restored composure and inspired confidence. Then placing his hand, in a certain indescribably protective way upon the lad's shoulder, he tells the father to an accompanying sympathetic and acquiescing rising of black eyebrows and scintillation of Jewish eyes, that his faith will in no manner of way be assailed through his boy; that certain prayers are said and psalms sung each morning and evening; that the boy need take no part in these, nay, that he need not enter school until after they are finished, or may leave in the evening before they are commenced; that he can do so without in the slightest degree prejudicing himself or even rendering himself unpopular with his fellow-scholars. Does he wish to avail himself of these conditions?

"Surely not" (with amused scintillation).

"There are prayers to Christ!"

"Surely, sare" (with a thousand sparkles).

"You do not object, then?"

"No, sare, they will do 'eem no ha'm."

' On Sundays he will go to ——?"

"The Synagogue, sare—oh, surely" (this reverently and solemnly).

The like with the Widow Bridget, whose propitiating smiles are amplified in the grin of her bare-legged and hatless Mike, who in some strange way has become popular with the whole school the moment he is seen,—" Shure he will go to the Hooly Chapel on Sundays, but if his 'anner will let him say his prayers now wid the rest, he will have the blissin' av his mother, shure!"

For years to come there was no school in the Poor-house, hence by arrangement with the Jubilee authorities, involving some small contribution to the funds, the pauper children were educated at the Jubilee School. Many of them had been scholars in freer days ere some tragedy on the Black Middens had taken away the breadwinner, and drifted the helpless little one into the stagnant back-water of an English workhouse; on the other hand, again, some of the uncaged scholars had only been emancipated from the coarse dominion of Bumble by the re-marriage of a widowed mother, —hence a fluctuating and uncertain flotsam passed and repassed the narrow shoal that lay between the seafaring poor and the bars of the Union.

No delicate shades of social caste, therefore, embarrassed the intercourse of the Jubilee lads and their Workhouse comrades; their relations were free, frank, and unfeignedly fraternal and equal. In one respect, indeed, the pauper boys formed a sort of aristocracy—there were no holes or tatters in the shameful garb with which their guardians (as by the wildest freak of perversity the local Poor Law authorities were misnamed) unnecessarily chose to distinguish them from their fellows. They wore coverings, too, on head and feet, and could count upon regular—if unvarying—food.

Not so the rest. Almost without exception poor—extremely poor—ill-clad and ill-fed, there were vastly more feet than boots and heads than hats. Artisans in the fifties rarely wore a black coat, even on Sunday. Corduroy or moleskin trousers and jacket, with bone buttons, or, in summer, cotton ducks and a calico coat were universal. And these, when done with by the father, the mother cut down for the sons. The best of the well-to-do lads wore clogs, a sort of wooden sabot with leather uppers and tipped at the toe with a strip of brass, but the majority went bare-foot.

They came from long distances, too, walking bare-footed through mud or snow—and often wet to the skin—from far-off villages, and bearing with them in—oh! such tiny parcels, what they called—how pathetically mis-called one hardly has the heart to think of—their dinner. A huge fireplace at each end of the school-room was heaped with fuel in the winter-time (great-hearted Hugh Taylor made *that* possible) and a large oven kept hot for the warming-up of the poor scraps. Herein were baked potatoes—some bringing three, some four or even five, and cutting in the skin a device or initial, or other distinguishing mark, so that at dinner-time they might be identified,—cans of coffee or of milk-and-water were heated,—red-herrings, bacon, and (very rarely) a meat pie, all warmed up together and emitting vapours which commingled in a heterogeneous stench that haunted the room for an hour or more. Somehow there was always a potato or two missing, for they sometimes burst in baking, or got bruised, or in some way lost, and tearful little children came and knocked at the school-house door to tell the "Mistress" that they could not find their "dinner." Sometimes three or four brothers would come for a series of days, and—making no pretence of having anything to eat—sit quietly out in the play-yard, too hungry to join in any game. The "Mistress" would find on inquiry that the mother was down with fever, or had just died, or father couldn't get work, or had just been crippled in some accident. Some of the poor creatures were ashamed to show what they had in the tiny parcel, and would avoid the comfortable blazing fire and shrink into a corner to eat the poor morsel alone and unobserved—and 'twas terribly soon eaten—a few bits of bread and, perhaps, dripping—generally not At times there was not even bread—not a potato, and the child would hide that too.

The pathos of such things is very keen, and the school-father of the lads could scarcely bear to speak of them. Many a time his bright little wife made a hot mess of savoury something for the hungry ones and asked him to divide it, but the pleasure of seeing them eat it was, for him, too terribly allied to pain, and he silently moved away.

It was such real suffering he saw round him, and so hopelessly vast and invincible. On all hands lay evidences of that most dread of all the inscrutable mysteries with which Providence perplexes the thinker, the physical deterioration of children brought about by insufficiency of food, and the relentless exaction of suffering therefor by Nature. What a nightmare 'tis to look back upon and shudder at! There were sore faces, sore ears, sore eyes, faces tied up for face-ache, carbuncles, boils, and abscesses; the children's hands were covered with warts, their feet and hands cracked and bleeding with chilblains, rickety children, deformed children, children disfigured with small-pox, or other unseemly scars,—and, as the good Doctor Owen would sadly tell the Maister as they looked across the moving plain of heads, it all flowed from a chronic condition of semi-starvation.

Only a few of the boys knew what it was to have a good meal, but every boy knew only too well what it was to have more than a full share of suffering. Little chaps came with swollen eyes and heads swathed in flannel, to beg the Maister to give them something to take away a dreadful pain " here " (pointing to the region above the ear). There was, then, a frightful prevalence of what was called ear-ache. Epilepsy was common, and the school was therefore never free from the poor child who " took fits." Children came to school emaciated from fever, or bearing the still burning scars of small-pox. Abscess on the brain, and that dreadful affliction called by the mothers of the day " water in the head," tortured for long periods before they manifested their real nature, and made poor children unfit for even the lightest work in the school. To all those stricken ones an invincible patience and mute, because unspeakable, sympathy was extended by the Maister. His wife assuaged such pain as a wide experience in domestic medicine enabled her to, and her kitchen during school-hours was half surgery. Kind-hearted medical friends who came for the Maister's music lent him a hand in dealing with such of the "cases" as lay within the scope of ordinary treatment. For toothache, which in the winter tortured its scores, was there not "Mr. Hudson," a boy-hearted philosopher, the friend of every oppressed man, child, or dumb creature who had the good fortune to come across him The friend of the Maister, enthusiastic lover of art, of music, of literature, and, above all, of humanity, this "benevolent druggist," as Harriet Martineau called him, gave free charter to every Jubilee lad to come across the river to his surgery, when tortured by the "hell o' a' diseases," and have the tooth out *free.*

Poor wee chaps, how they loved and dreaded him as he looked at the raging fang, calling it a "nasty beast," and, concealing the horrid forceps in his great generous hand, told them to "sing out" if he hurt them! How they loved and dreaded him no more, when, after the "nasty beast" was out, he held it up and objurgated it, then crammed a comforting plug of cotton-wool, steeped in some aromatic essence, into the vacant socket, and told them to rest a while till they "got up the steam again !" then asked them to sing one of the Jubilee pieces, applauded it with a mighty "By Jove !" and a clap on the back, saying that it was worth twenty teeth and a penny for the ferry into the bargain,—pushing, as he said so, a "cart-wheel" into the patient's hand, and telling him to get off to school again and keep his mouth shut while on the river lest he should catch another toothache.

Amid the pathos of so much child suffering and wretchedness the Maister took the only course likely to prevent a sensitive mind from yielding to a sense of hopelessness—that of resolutely attacking the vulnerable points, and of turning neither to right nor left in the work of doing all that 'twas possible to do. So, in spite of the short time for which he had them under his charge, he unceasingly bent his efforts to the upwaking of the dormant intelligence of the soft-witted—the "daft," or "silly," or "fond," as they were called; repeating the lesson with inexhaustible patience—blending the tones of authority with those of winning encouragement; firing the boys' eyes for a short moment, as they trustfully gazed upon him, with the light of his own. Now he has standing before him one or two scholars grievously afflicted with stammering, and is slowly "counting time" for them as they painfully repeat the difficult elements of utterance, and smile, after partial success or failure, at the words of encouragement. The poor little hunchback has a gentle course of drill superintended by the Maister himself, and devoted to the development—as much as may be—of the crushed chest; and after a time he takes his place fearlessly among the others at drill-time and feels that he has conquered something even worse than his deformity—namely, his exaggerated sense of shrinking shamefacedness. Now and then the school has a boy whose speech is rendered unintelligible by the misshapen form of the roof of his mouth. Even with him, as with the stammerer, marvellous improvement is effected by the searching investigation that is directed to the sources and elements of the difficulty and by the subsequent carefully thought-out exercises, and their patient—infinitely patient repetition.

And for many of these stricken ones his heart went out until they so grew into his life that when, as not unseldom happened, some fever or accident carried the poor broken frame eternally out of sight, even the thoughtless school-boys were hushed for a few days when they saw how the Maister quickly passed the seat where the little absent one erewhile raised his wan face and smiled as his friend came near him.

There was hardly a deformity or an infirmity that had not its subject in this busy microcosm, yet, in some way, he turned to sweetness the very elements that among thoughtless children—and alas! many not children—provoke mockery. The little fellow hopping about on crutches was always made room for at marbles, or what not; his shot was ever allowed to have done an execution which he himself doubted. When the left-handed writer—whose right hand was deformed or paralysed—showed his slate and won particular praise, the cheers were always heartiest, and pride in the fellow-scholar grew into regard, and regard into affection.

And so, year in, year out, the work went on. In summer the hum of classes in the playground made pleasant music for sympathetic visitors. Summer deepened into autumn, when for a few harvest weeks there was dead silence throughout. Autumn lapsed into winter, and the shortening days gradually curtailed the afternoon's work, though as long as the Maister's eye could pierce the deepening gloom as it rapidly settled over the further benches, the work was kept up. There was neither gas, nor lamps, nor candles, hence as the darkness grew, the red light of the fires threw changing shadows on the ceiling and the walls; and the silent rows of boys looked almost like ghosts.

Sometimes on a drear afternoon in late November the darkness settled down prematurely. The vane on the old church when last looked at was swirling wildly, the dripping rain-drops blowing out from the eaves almost horizontally before the wild blast that has been working up wrathfully since morning. The roar in the chimney and the whistle through the key-holes and crannies rise now and again to a shriek, and the storm-cloud blackens every hour. It is, as yet, not nearly the time for dispersal, but the boys must bend over the desks with faces close to their slates to see their work.

With a strange look on his face the Maister takes his place at his desk and slowly reaches out for the bell with which he is accustomed to summon attention. Glancing up, for a moment, at the thundering windows as a heavier squall strikes them and carries past a hurtling burden of seaweed, foam and sand, and then looking down with grave face at the long lines of heads (now almost invisible) busied with no thought of peril, and full of the heedless things of youth— he pauses again.

For he knows that Death is busy this afternoon with some of their homes, and that—certain as Death itself—at roll-call next morning Dixon, or Boyce, or little Thomson will be returned absent, and that some small shrill voice will utter the quite familiar explanation—

"Pleese, sir, his father's droondid."

Somewhat more solemnly, then, than usual, or possibly only apparently so because of oppressive forebodings, the bell is rung.

"Attention! Slates—away!"

Then, in the darkness, amid the wild noise of the storm outside, comes from the Maister in deep tones, followed by the higher response of the lads, the evening prayer—

"Lighten our—

Lighten our darkness, we beseech Thee, O Lord, and by Thy great mercy, defend us from the perils and dangers of this night, for the love of Thy dear Son, our Saviour, Jesus Christ. Amen."

CHAPTER VIII.

ENTER, THE POLITICIAN.

"To have promoted the artistic cultivation of any natural talent is matter for honest pride in the highest."—GOETHE.

ROM all climes and latitudes now came to the school, borne by stout, bearded and tanned mariners—not at once recognised as "old boys"—curiosities, specimens, natural wonders, etc., all grist for the educational mill —and round the erewhile bare walls of the schoolroom hung the beginnings of a steadily growing museum. There was a dried pelican with membraneous pouch, a sword-fish with broken weapon, a small porpoise or a dog-whale, curiously spread bats from the tropics, a porcupine, a harpoon from a whaler, a pair of walrus tusks, a few Indian spears, a boomerang, snow-shoes from Greenland, bows and arrows with savage decoration of teeth, an armadillo, a turtle, strange "instruments of percussion," a nose flute, huge lizards, hairy tarantulæ in "spirits," a trap-door spider with tunnel and trap-door, butterflies and beetles, a bursting-ripe cottonpod, unheard-of nuts from Brazil or the Gold Coast, sponges and corals, a piece of drift-wood pierced by a sword-fish, or riddled with the labyrinthean borings of the *Teredo navalis*, barnacles, minerals, dried fruits, a few locusts, splendid bamboos, a sugar-cane, Japanese knick-knacks, chop-sticks, a human skull dredged from the Tyne, fossils from the coal measures,—these and a hundred other things—everything in fact that could be got hold of, and which 'twas thought the Maister would be glad to possess, were brought to the "aad skyull," and tendered to its chief—not unfrequently to his unfeigned em-

barrassment, as when a live monkey came to hand and delighted the boys with his shrieking protests against coercion, or fishermen from Cullercoats lugged into the room a struggling devil-fish that they'd caught over-night, and thought "the Maistor 'd like ta see."

More discriminating, though not sincerer, friends contributed small presents of apparatus, books, or other things likely to help; and in this way many objects of great interest and utility were acquired and added to the educational stock. A precious fragment of an aerolite was thus obtained, and later, a piece of one of the early submarine telegraph cables.

But the apparatus was bought—mainly by the Maister himself with his own pence—or made out of such odds and ends as could be cheaply purchased; and in this latter case the boys were brought into the sphere of manufacture, and encouraged to improvise implements of study from the rudimentary materials lying around them In no manner of circumstance could the school funds be appropriated to such projects, and indeed no notion of the kind was likely to suggest itself to anybody.

Some of the closer benefactors of the school were professional men whose interest had first been awakened by meeting the Maister at some quaint quartet or chamber-music party (where one finds the best kind of human being in a relation more sweetly intimate than is afforded by any other pursuit).

"Harry Young had a snug little room, upstairs in his inn, where he allowed us to meet for practice as often as we wished; he had also a long room in which we sometimes gave a private concert to our friends Our leader, William Partis, a quiet, unobtrusive little man, who seldom spoke, but always to the purpose, whose head, face, and thoughtful expression suggested old Socrates, was a good amateur, and liked by all who knew him. Our second violin, Deenham, was an assistant school teacher, of asthmatic and consumptive appearance, rather crabbed and sarcastic with strangers, yet, to those with whom he associated, a pleasant and intelligent companion. Our 'cello—William Bewick—was in the office of the magistrates' clerk, played fairly well, and was excellent company. He used to declare that when he left the Grammar School at which he was educated, 'twas child's play to him to translate a sentence from a newspaper into Latin or Greek— an assertion invariably and immediately qualified by an avowal that 'at the same time' he could not do a rule-of-three sum to save his life, or point out England on a map. All this had to be taken *cum grano*, for though his most intimate friends never quite knew by how much his statements should be discounted, they felt it must be considerable. He had run through a fairish fortune, and was, at the time I speak of, living with his wife and family in poor circumstances

"We frequently had the company of two medical men, Doctors Owen and Meggott, both great friends of mine, the first a rapidly rising man, the other a retired physician—neither of them players, though both exceedingly fond of good music. They thoroughly enjoyed their pipes listening to us One evening, while enjoying a friendly chat on passing events, Deenham remarked that he 'supposed we would commence to play when 'twas time to leave off' As this was said in his usual caustic style the conversation came to an abrupt and dead stop.

"'What have you before you, Partis?' asked Bewick.

"'No 20, and a pretty thing it looks I don't think we have played it before, it is called "Fox pass,"' replied Socrates, wearing his most ancient look.

"We turned to No. 20, and found it named '*Faux pas !*'

"Dr. Owen, who was sitting near Partis, took a glance at the book, and then I saw him quietly touch Meggott with his elbow Both medicos raised their eyebrows, stared at each other, and Owen turned round to me I gave him a look which he at once understood to mean 'no remarks.' The piece was indeed a pretty one, and we often played it afterwards, but it was invariably referred to as 'No 20'—no one there would have dreamt of hurting the feelings of our sensitive old leader. Discussing one evening the necessity for a musician having an absolutely correct ear, it was agreed that nothing could be worse than singing or playing out of time or tune. After a short silence, Socrates, who had not spoken, said he thought there was something worse even than that, namely, when a man sang or played out of time or tune *and did not know it*"

No joke, indeed, to these was it for a man to play out of time or tune, whether he knew it or not! For music with them was a sacred thing,—no mere matter of enjoyment, of pleasure, of prettiness. They were of those—the small number—endowed by nature with a capacity for comprehending—or rather communing—with music in her highest, most exalted form. To that inner Arcanum, where music speaks in her own lovely voice, unaided by poetry or other adventitious ally, where the soul is stirred unutterably by beauty abstract and indefinable, only a few have the magic passport, and of these many are the lowliest of men To them no trick of sentiment, no appeal to things lying within the range of merely human experience or imagination speaks when the transcendent voice of Harmony—surely something of very Heaven itself—is heard To them music is a higher Freemasonry which in eclectic precision is infallible, whose password can never be betrayed, a language which can never, by outsiders, be learned or understood, but whose boundless power and refinement of expression are, by the elect, instantly perceived and comprehended. And in those early days, when the musical classic was fain to commune with himself, since most ears were closed to him, the joy of meeting a kindred spirit was such as to compensate for any labour or sacrifice.

The Maister one day went with his friend Woolhouse to visit the eminent north-country "viewer," scientist, and man of parts, John Buddle, for the particular purpose of discussing some obscure and knotty problem in natural science at that time attracting the attention of the mathematician. The preliminary chat glanced for a moment on the subject of classical music, when instantly the thoughtful face of the great pitman took fire; a few short interrogations revealed the mighty truth that there was present the material for a quartet, "and," laughingly says Woolhouse, recounting the incident years afterwards, " no single word of science was thereafter uttered; Buddle brought out his choice fiddles, his music, banished the outer world, and for the rest of the day we gave ourselves wholly to the worship of the beautiful."

There were scattered, here and there throughout the district, amateurs of unusual excellence to whom the glories of the quartet had not yet appeared. Their knowledge of Mozart, of Haydn, of Beethoven, was that only which came of having heard, perhaps taken part in, one of the great masses, oratorios, possibly overtures and symphonies, but they knew nothing of that closer communion, that intimate esoteric fellowship with the great ones of the art, enjoyed by those who are privileged to share in the rites of the Inner House of Music, which assuredly are not for the outer world of listeners.

And it was something to note the rapt look on the face of one of these men when for the first time he paused at the end of a movement in one of the immortal Beethoven set, and tried to give expression to the unspeakable emotion bearing in upon his soul. From thence he is for ever a devotee, and must at intervals find relief for his pent-up feelings. Hence, from long distances, the busiest men made opportunity to come to a quartet party, and were glad to be received and thought worthy to take a part with any fellow-being, whatever his position in life, provided he was able to "take" the "lead," or "second," or "tenor."

Among these north-country worshippers the sacred flame was fed by the restless enthusiasm of Woolhouse, who now, as a sedative for the exciting brain toil involved in his mathematical and astronomical work, was editing the classical chamber works of the great masters; writing the Maister at frequent intervals glowing encomiums upon this or that "delightful" movement in some quartet or quintet, " of which I have sent you a copy by this week's steam-packet "

To Vine Cottage, the leafy retreat of Harriet Martineau's "benevolent druggist" (he who drew school-boy teeth *gratis*), the Maister would carry the precious parcel and lay it out for eager perusal by the band of devotees who there at intervals foregathered. Thither came all who in any capacity might enter the Inner Temple of Harmony The Rev T——, Unitarian preacher, ripe scholar, and divinest of fiddlers, the speechless, timid colliery lad, gawky and awkward when addressed, who became transfigured as he carried the *Amati* into a corner of the room and there poured forth a torrent of impassioned impromptu; the prattling, loquacious, little, bow-legged tailor, whose flood of lisping gossip never ceased save when music spake, the tall, brown-clad, snuff-taking, and punctilious viola, nicknamed by the chattering tailor, because of his spareness of frame, "the illuthtriouth Boneth"—repaid in the sobriquet "Holy Motheth" (a favourite exclamation of the little man's), Socrates, of the *faux pas*, the leader of the opera or theatre orchestra at Newcastle, a "medico" or two; the local poet and perhaps one or more newspaper editors;—men of extreme views and opposed opinions on almost every topic of human interest, drawn from ranks of life separated by wide chasms, yet hushed at once when the voices of the great ones were uplifted

In summer the music-stands were sometimes pitched on the little daisy-sprent lawn, and while yet the fiddles were being tenderly uncased and the busy hubbub of political or art disputation ran on, a sudden stillness came as there rose on the air, say, the strains of the first of the Mendelssohn *Lieder ohne Worte*, then new, though no whit fresher than to-day, and rapt faces gazed up at the open windows festooned in biier and pear-tree leafage, whence came the wondrous sheaf of interweaving harmonies culminating in the beautiful phrase (and its tender echo), at the seventh bar.

Laughingly rising from the piano, at which he has carelessly sat astride the music stool, pausing for a moment to look with intense expression at the *Ecce Homo* hanging at the stairs-head, the preacher issues from the bramble-covered porch and, catching up a fiddle, asks what is to be played first, forgetting to wait for a reply as he coaxes from it a stream of lovely phrases.

"What shall we take first, eh?" he repeats; "the new Beethoven?" (of which he observes the 'cello furtively and uneasily taking a foretaste)

The Maister, who has been standing aside with Medicus comparing opinions as to the beauty of the coloration of a bit of lichen on an old apple-tree, draws near and suggests beginning with Corelli, whereat the parson makes a grimace and hums a burlesque recitative in the Handelian manner. It is the sole matter on which these two greatly differ; the Maister's profound veneration for Handel makes him—the other thinks—undervalue the work of later composers; and sometimes playful banter runs for a moment into earnest argument. But not often, for in general the incorrigible preacher, with a mock assumption of deference and conviction, begins, as 'twere unconsciously, to sing in exaggerated style, Handel's air from *Judas Maccabæus*—

> "*HOW—va-a-ain*
> *IS—ma-a-an*
> *WHO—bo-o-oasts*
> *IN—fi-i-ight:*
> *WHO—bo-o-o-oasts in fight,*
> *WHO—bo-o-o-oasts in fight,*
> *WHO—bo-o-o-o-o-o-o-o*-OASTS IN FIGHT"

And then, seeing that he has annoyed his friend, is instantly sorry for it.

Soon, however, all thought and feeling is bent upon the evolution of some great wordless poem, and a deep content rests on the souls of all present.

From the quartet on the lawn the party is beckoned by the genial host to the sitting-room, where the latest book of Dickens or Thackeray, or the new poem by Tennyson, or some late outburst of Carlyle's, lies open for dissection a "little bit" by some artist is produced for criticism, or, joy of joys, a new fiddle—say rather a newly-acquired old fiddle—awaits judgment. Like a group of mothers looking at a baby, the *cognoscenti* crowd round the interesting stranger, and with the keenest interest, speaking all together, discuss the varnish, the purfling, the *f* holes, the "beautiful" belly, the "lovely" back, the scroll, the neck,—everything, in a word, save the tone (which is a matter altogether apart) at such length that the tea and girdle-cakes are declared to be cold and a peremptory call to table is issued

Here the conversation runs on the characteristics of the great composers, the beauties of "that last *larghetto*" or "*Adagio ma non troppo*" The Maister tells of some lad whom he has noted to have a special love and aptitude for music, but who is so poor that he cannot, do what he may, acquire a fiddle, which it is his passion to learn to play. A collection is thereupon taken up by the local Greatheart (Hudson), and the requisite number of shillings at once produced to buy for Billy Malone the particular instrument which he has greedily looked in upon, for weeks past, at the music shop.

The "long-blessed Peace" has at last been broken in upon and the accursed spirit of War is abroad, working evil among men. No shooting down of John Babbington Stodarts now, though, no chasing into their homes and dragging off, amid the screams and shrieks of wives, unwilling hands. Demos is looking after himself, somewhat, and it cannot be done; but there is shame and horror and sorrow enough to glut the most "warlike" appetite. Not even from such gatherings as this can the brutal subject be entirely shut out, and for a while the talk runs in jangling discord on the debauchery of the Crimean expedition. On such a topic there can be no harmony of sentiment, and when the chattering little tailor opines that, "after all, war ithn't thuch an unmitigated evil, for it furnitheth employment to the quarrelthome among uth, and, above all, keepth down the populathion" (the little man was steadily adding to the said "populathion" at a rate perfectly disconcerting to his friends), there is a general move towards the fiddles to drive off the cloud that has, for a few moments, darkened the peaceful atmosphere of the "cottage."

At these re-unions there was one subject which rarely failed to come up for discussion, namely, the possibility of "raising the standard of public taste" by the introduction of purely classical items into the programmes of the concerts and entertainments given from time to time in aid of the fund for securing adequate buildings for the excellent Mechanics' Institute. The possible effects of a quartet—or a movement from a quartet—upon the audience, were debated as gravely and seriously as those of a new drug upon a hospital patient by a group of pathologists. It was not, so much, the "rabble" at the back of the room about which doubt was entertained, as the well-dressed groups in the front seats, who—all unconscious (as audiences ever are) of the keen though good-natured criticism bestowed upon them by performers—furnished, in bored expression or open manifestation of restlessness, an unequivocal indication of incapacity for entering into the sense of any music worthy of admiration.

It was, on all hands, agreed to be "safest" to play down to your audience, and that if any of the higher elements of music were to be introduced it must be *experimentally*, and on the smallest possible scale. The wealthy coal-owner only spoke the honest sentiments of his class when—in response to a request that he would allow his name to be put down among the guarantors of a series of high-class orchestral concerts in Newcastle—he replied, "Ye-es—that is, if you won't play any of those d——d symphonies."

The first experiment, made upon a crowded audience in the new rooms of the library, was unequivocal in result. After twenty bars of one of the brightest of the Haydn string quartets had been played, the audience as a whole settled down with unfeigned satisfaction to —general conversation *à haute voix*. Poor Socrates, who led, was so disconcerted, that after tremblingly persevering half-way through the movement he suddenly gave up and retreated from the platform, leaving the essay at raising the standard of musical taste still-born. Noticing presently that the players had retired, the auditory—always kindly—recognised that it was time to applaud, and thereupon applauded with touching sincerity.

To the "cottage" came painters, *litterateurs*, politicians, fugitives, refugees, stars of the local theatrical world, and, without exception, all who could, with any degree of serious intent, handle a fiddle bow. Among those who met there, and at the "Jubilee," were most of the far-seeing men, who for years had strenuously carried on the work of education and culture at the Mechanics' Institute, and their pride and exultation in the accomplishment of the object to which they had so long and so wistfully looked forward—the housing of the Institute in buildings worthy of it—was a goodly thing to see. "I hope," says Woolhouse, writing October 1857, "the Mechanics' Building will be worthy of the Borough, but fear that public spirit may not be large enough. It should be adapted to the importance that Shields may be expected hereafter to assume—say fifty years hence!"

The opening of the new Institute in August 1858 was celebrated in a ceremony presided over by the fiery Roebuck and joined in by most of the "leading people" of the town. *Most*, because, though the battle of "eddicashin" had, it is true, been won, there still lingered here and there a few groups of the defeated, sulking and scowling at the victors. For this opening day there was mighty preparation in the musical way, and a giant programme was arranged, and cheerfully faced by an enormous audience. Over the musical arrangements of this, as of most other ceremonials of the kind, the Maister presided, and brought together the band of vocalists and instrumentalists.

His children were now springing up, and by him—as early as they could speak—being led with infinite pains over the rocky path of musical theory and practice. Holding up his left hand with the fingers separated so as to form a "staff," and touching the intervals with the other, he taught them to read simple melodies at sight before they could properly articulate words. When, afterwards, they could handle a small "kit," or piccolo, or "reach an octave" on the piano, they were drilled in Spartan fashion over the fugues and thick-set syncopations of Corelli and Handel before passing to the calmer plains of Mozart and Haydn. Woolhouse, writing at intervals, gives him the latest "notions" on teaching the violin, and sends him the newest "schools," saying, however, "you may as well read Spohr as to position of the left hand, etc. . . . but exercises written by yourself are sure to be good."

He, indeed, wrote the whole of the "exercises" for his pupils, and yet found time for composition of a different kind. Some beautiful church music written by him shortly after becoming organist at Christ Church, and at intervals, later, is still heard in some of the churches of Tyneside. "Tynemouth Abbey," a pure, graceful melody, composed to some pretty lines by a town-fellow, Mr. John Stobbs, is known throughout the North-country. The Hungarian exiles, visiting the North, had their cause advocated in some stirring verses written by his close and life-long friend, Mr. James S. Edington, and these he set to music for a concert given in aid of the refugees.

And for years it was customary for these two, the Maister and the Hon. Secretary of the "Mechanics'," to contribute some original element of interest to the programmes of the concerts devoted to the advancement of the cause which lay so warm at the hearts of both —the cause of the humble toiler's mental elevation.

"With reference to 'Love Lore' and other compositions of your father, nothing about them was more remarkable than the rapidity of their production. After the concert had been arranged, generally on the near approach of the date, it would be suggested 'how nice if, instead of the old favourites, we could have something fresh, having, if possible, special reference to the occasion,'—and your father at once promised if I would have the verses ready by next morning he would be up to time with the music, and you know how admirably he kept his word."

So, modestly, the contributor of the verses, who was equally reliable in fulfilling his part of the compact. For the opening celebration of the new Institute these two respectively wrote and composed the Inaugural Hymn, the music being singularly suggestive of the delightful aria in Gounod's *Redemption*, "Lovely Appear" (written years after), in sentiment and construction.

The series of concerts now initiated was continued over a number of years, and the literary treasures slowly accumulating on the shelves of the library were mainly acquired by means of funds raised in this pleasant way—the sweet influence of Music lighting the path of her sister, Literature.

The volunteer movement, too, was beginning to stir the young manhood of England, Tennyson's anonymous "Form, form, riflemen, form," ringing in the ears of the nation, as soon, therefore, as the local rifle corps had been enrolled, the Maister was at work drilling, musically, their new and raw drum and fife band, and presently the streets of the town resounded with the shrill flourishes and trills of "The Nightingale" and "The Girl I left behind me." The band practices, held in the schoolroom, drew crowds of listeners, for the old passion for military band work was firing the Maister and impelling him to arrange the stirring old quicksteps he had known in his boy-days with such enthusiasm that they came to the new generation with all the freshness of novelty. Up at the workhouse, too, he was gratuitously teaching a smaller band of drums and fifes, which, notwithstanding Bumble, was allowed for a few hours a week to brighten the lives of the pauper boys. The Jubilee lads had, for years, gone through their marching drill to the roll and dirl of drum and fife, a set of instruments having been begged of the wealthier supporters of the institution.

The work at the school was now at its best, the ordinary elements of teaching firmly and securely in hand, while from the subtly contrived contrasts presented in the wide range of subjects, a surprising amount of work was effectively got through without any sense of weariness or pressure. The prime importance and significance of this was always dwelt upon with extreme earnestness by the Maister, who never could be induced to regard his function as that of a mere funnel. The development of character, the elimination or checking of the elements of savagery born in every child, the inculcation of right-doing for its own sake, and not for what he called the "kicks-and-halfpence doctrine of rewards and punishments," were to his mind the absolute, the essential, core of a schoolmaster's duty, and to these ends he bent his whole energy.

In the little school-yard garden there were, before its subsequent absorption into the playground, a few fruit bushes on which, in summer, the currants hung close within the reach of the boys as they played in the dinner-hour; and he told visitors that there was not a boy in the school who would put out his hand to touch a berry Yet every lad was conscious that no flogging would fall to the lot of any unhappy wight who might perchance be over-tempted The high dignity of truthfulness, the sacredness of trust — in a word, the sense of honour was so patiently and persistently inculcated among these sons of the "rabble" that any lapse of the kind would have been recognised as carrying a weightier punishment in shame and disgrace than any boy would care to face, to say nothing of the involved pain and disappointment for the Maister.

They were no saints these Shields lads—the infractions of duty and rule were numerous enough, and the punishment therefor swift and certain, yet it was a proud thing to see the instant response made when, hushing with raised finger the whole assembly, the Maister announced in distinct and fateful terms that complaint had been made to him (say) that some of the windows of the Catholic School had been broken by stones thrown by Jubilee lads, and then proceeded to ask "Which of you boys are concerned?" Up went the arms of the alarmed culprits, doomed inexorably, as they knew, to be ordered out for a sharp caning.

But, indeed, a sense of honour and implicit trust was imbibed by the boys from the first moment of entering the school, developing a regard for truth and honesty which was truly remarkable, and a source of pride to the Maister throughout his school career. There was no jot of trouble as to these; the toughest difficulty lay in eradicating or tempering certain unruly qualities developed more or less in all boys, but assuredly in larger than usual measure in the children of this untamed, striving, fighting tract of no-man's-land —Tyneside. A propensity to destructiveness, to stone-throwing, to enforcing arguments with sticks and stones, a noisy assertiveness, and a mocking contempt for strangers were inherited straight from the veins of men who had fought the French, the preventive men, the press-gang, and the "doggors" from up or across the river. The commoner failings of youth, the carelessness, indifference to waste and thoughtless cruelty, were of course as pronounced among the boys of Shields as those of other places.

Such qualities, obviously, could never be modified or restrained by mere punishment, which itself, in careless indiscrimination, is often enough nothing better than licensed violence. Yet in the quaintest way the old faith in the rod and only the rod was manifested by even the parents of the scholars, themselves but older children in the knowledge of better things. A quite common occurrence was the appearance, at the half-door, of a panting, heated, shrill-voiced mother, buffeting and pulling at her flushed and tousled son, and crying out in the agitation of exasperation, "Mister Hass-will, sur! if you please give him a *gudd* hiding, sur, a *gudd* hiding; hide him *well*, he's a *bad* boy." Or sometimes 'twas a man whose anger paled his face, and who requested that his lad might be flogged, soundly flogged, because of——

Ah! so often because of so little; so often because of shortcomings or failings, or misapprehensions on the part of the father himself; because of impatient or ignorant unrecognition of elements deep planted in the nature of the boy, and no more subject to his control than the circulation of his blood.

Always deprecating severity and urging the better plan of trying every other means first, the dominie carefully investigated the cause of the parent's anger, patiently recognising that he was but arbitrating between two semi-blind, wrathful children, and finally sending away the elder of the twain with a new sense of self-distrust and a quickened spirit of reliance and dependence on the strong mind to whose charge the small bundle of waywardness left behind might securely be entrusted. The discipline of the school was at all times remarkable and the absence of noise so striking, that visitors sometimes doubted, when approaching the building, whether the school was in session— indeed, for a long course of years it was noted for its perfect orderliness.

The mischievous destructiveness of the boys was gradually quelled by the creation of an interest in every object of utility and a higher sense of the value of all that human toil, so to speak, consecrates; and this interest grew out of an increasing familiarity with the processes by which the raw materials furnished by nature are painfully won or manipulated. For waste of any kind the Maister always expressed a perfect horror, and whether it chanced to be the sight of a bit of bread lying in the playground, a reckless charge of coal on the fire, or a broken window-pane, he under no circumstances failed to impress upon the lads, standing around, the intrinsic wickedness involved, and the indignation and pain it caused him. A quiet lesson, afterwards, on the boundless significance to mankind of the coal-fields, a sketch of the geological story of the coal-measures and an impressive picture of the cost in human life of coal-winning, a graphic description of the condition of human habitations before the introduction of glass, the wonderful history of its manipulation and improvement, or yet again, a flash of reminiscence from his own boy-days, when, in the dreadful "dear years," the horrid, putty-like mass called bread was drawn out by children into glutinous strings, always followed, and so instinct with life and sympathy was it, so utterly free from the Sandford and Merton style of "discourse" that, unquestionably, the whole object and meaning and spirit of the essay sank into the very mental fabric of his hearers. No bit of paper was ever wasted. The wrappers, in which came the parcels of school books, were neatly folded and put into the place specially appointed therefor. No string was cut if a knot could be untied, and in any case the boys saw the Maister neatly coil the piece, however small, into a hank and place it where it could be found. The drill in such matters was incessant and the vigilance unsleeping, the Maister holding that such little cares must be turned into habits before they could be of any true service in after-life,—the enormous, unmeasured significance of habit indeed was ever a subject of careful stress. The commonplace motto, "a place for everything, and everything in its place," was the key to much of the excellent order and quietude of the school, and, for all its commonplace, the Maister never tired of telling the boys that in its fullest observance directly lay very much of the issue of their coming struggle in life. The smaller virtues of personal orderliness, neatness of habit, respect for property, etc., were treated as co-equal in import to all the R's, whether three or three hundred. No man cared less for money for its own sake than he, yet he incessantly warned his pupils against its waste, and the hypocrisy of excusing such waste on the pretence of having a contempt for its possession. "It is less than honest," he would say, "to neglect an orderly care of one's money, however little or much it may be." Half the moral sentiments as ordinarily used are mere canting inversions of truth, and he was ever diligent in hunting out any piece of pretence or sham which took shelter under a high-sounding phrase.

"Fagging" and "bullying," though by some thought necessary to the education of a gentleman, was not deemed a fit thing for the Jubilee, but was rigorously suppressed. The mockery of deformity or personal peculiarity was shown up as the rankest meanness and—what perhaps boyhood most shrinks from—cowardice.

With an instinctive, almost painful, tenderness for, and hatred of cruelty to, animals, he was perhaps most severe with the boy-savage who, in all-ignorant indifference to pain in others, should be caught ill-using a cat, robbing a bird's nest, torturing a frog, or perpetrating any of the numberless outrages on the animal world which so many quite gratuitously regard as "natural." For "sport" involving the misery of the dumb creation he had a profound abhorrence, and would barely tolerate a discussion of the subject among his friends, some of whom, knowing how strongly he felt on the matter, would slyly introduce it His devotion to science was but the outcome of a profound, awe-full recognition of the bewildering variety, unity, interdependence, and relationship in the Universe as it presents itself to human sentience, and that men should deliberately and designedly, and for mere selfish pleasure, seek to increase the appalling total of suffering which, at best, is inevitable in the world, was to him a perplexing, a saddening, and a humiliating reflection. He did his utmost, however, to grapple with this vice at its source, and it was a beautiful thing to see his grave face, touched with sympathy and sadness as he discanted upon the lot of the humbler creatures of the Universe, turned towards the upraised countenances of his young disciples, and expressing wistful solicitude for their assent

The boys saw the Maister surrounded by animal pets, to which, busy man though he was, he always found time to show kindness. On a warm day the tortoise was carried out into the sun and a bit of fresh dandelion leafage or lettuce laid before him for which he might stretch out his scaly neck. The pigeons flocked round him when he walked bareheaded into the playground, and settled on his shoulders or on the tip of his fingers. He never failed in winter to scatter food for hungry birds before he sat down to a meal, and there was year by year a red-breast at the window-sill. The sparrows came safely among the feet of the playing boys, and birds "built" under the Jubilee eaves in the perfectest security. With a sense of the sacred preciousness of time, which made it impossible for him to waste a single waking moment, he yet encouraged every boy under him to cultivate a "hobby," assuring him that it would prove to be an investment which in old age would shower down a boundless return of interest, and, that one of the many delightful ways of storing up a fund of inexhaustible pleasure, which could be drawn upon when the infirmities of the closing years of life thrust unsought leisure upon one, was to study, sympathetically, the great teeming world of dumb fellow-creatures.

But there must be no imprisoning of birds in cages; no confinement and exposure of gold-fish in glass bowls (this he denounced as specially cruel). "Be on your guard, lads," he would say, "be always on your guard against gratifying a mere whim at the cost of some poor creature's misery, and then pretending that your action springs from a regard for, or interest in, animal nature." Some of the most hateful forms of cruelty to helpless "pets" are the work of kind but unthinking people who would not deliberately inflict pain, yet who, by the very disingenuousness of the arguments they use in defending themselves against an imputation of unkindness, show that they are not wholly unconscious of wrong-doing.

There were then no societies for the protection, from cruelty, of animals—none, indeed, for the protection of children, but in his little world the dominie was an ever-active agent of mercy, and therefore regarded by many who did not know him well as "an eccentric." The drovers who followed the cattle into town from Newcastle market knew him as the "aad man" who would come out of the schoolhouse and reason and expostulate with them, and send them away sheepishly grinning at each other, yet ashamed and abashed at his honest denunciation of the customary acts of brutality which—all our Christianity notwithstanding—then disgraced and yet disgrace our English high-roads,—and somehow there gradually came a relaxation of the rigour while the Jubilee was in sight. Carters and waggoners knew the Maister, and were not unwilling to suspend the habitual flagellation of their poor brutes when they saw him, for in his sternest denunciation there was a ring of such sound good-nature and manliness that the fellows rarely answered back. There was always a trough in summer-time, replenished many times in the day with fresh spring water, for stray dogs, and on market-days a look-out was kept for foot-worn and exhausted sheep and lambs lying in the roadway, to whom the boys were always enjoined to carry a " drink."

However much such "sentimentalism," as it was (and is yet) sneeringly termed, might be laughed at by those in whose nature a larger share of the lower brute remained uneliminated, there was a sneaking kind of deference to it—half shame and half love for the man—which never failed to quell cruelty or indifference to pain in animals while the Maister was present—as, for example, on an excursion down the coast in a steamboat, while lying off a little fishing village, some of the party of lawyers, shipbrokers, and others who had put down lines, were looking on at the struggles of a fish, from the gills of which the hook had just been torn, " Knock it on the head—quick—knock it on the head," cried one of the group, "*here's the Maister coming*" The fishermen down on the coast, the donkey boys, the butchers, all grew to recognise that while he was near there must be a truce.

And so the work of the school, of the choir, and of the Mechanics' Institute went on as the Maister grew older in years and in the affections of his town-fellows. He became a sort of court of final appeal for the wrangling and disputatious. Old skippers filled with weather lore, based partly on observation, but mainly on tradition and superstition, came up to ask him to decide whether or no foul times might be expected when the "moon lay on her back;"—whether the "glass" (barometer) had not much less influence on the weather now than in the old days when they were boys?—to ask if he'd show them the track of the *Fox*, or some of the later Arctic exploration ships, what he made of this or that phenomenon "that aw saw with me own eyes, Mr. Hass-will."

Now and then a boy would run into the school and up to the Maister, saying in shrill tones, "Please, sir, there are men in the yard swinging on the mast." These would be found, on inquiry, to be old boys who instinctively seized upon the ropes, from which years ago they had swung in amazing gyrations but now hung helplessly in fumbling confusion, redfaced and hatless. Letters from old boys, or the parents of old boys, came to hand telling of some old kindness, long forgotten, of the Maister. Among a number found after the old man died, two follow here; the first, from a poor Irish woman, bears no note or endorsement giving any clue to the "boy you allude to," save the pencilled word "Michael" in the Maister's hand:—

"GALWAY, *Decbr.* 12*th*, '53.

"SIR,—Your information is so correct that i feel obliged to you hopeing that i may be ever duty bound to pray for your eternal welfare and happiness. Kind Sir the Boy you allude to is my son, he went away from home some 2 or 3 months sinse and i did not know what part of the world he faced to, he did, for he had no home ever sinse his father's death and i assure you he once had a good home. Kind Sir he talks about wishing to be at home but i assure you that there is a poor prospect for him at present for a youngster of his sort and even of the ablest of men. Therefore, Sir, i would much sooner leave him under your own mercy in hopes he will benefit by it here after, he is young and when at home he promised to be a smart willing Boy smart and cunning and i hope he will prove it so as to satisfy you and all whomb controls him. Therefore i give up to your in Chanc until whatever time you think fit to do what ever you please for him i would not like him to stick to the sea on no account.

"I have no more to say at present but i feel so happy in mind that he fell in with a gentleman and father to him i hope —I am obet servant,
"BRIDGET GIBBONS."

"Please Direct as usual in care of
Mr. Nichls. Killian, High St., Galway, for me."

The other is from one of the lads—a young soldier—writing on his twenty-first birthday from the scene of the Indian Mutiny.—

"CAMP, NEAR DEESA, 12*th July* 1858.

"DEAR SIR,—I now sit down after a long silence, to write to you and I must own that I am very ungrateful in not having acquainted you before I left North Shields, as you always acted as a kind friend towards me; I often tried to take a pen in my hand to write to you, but I could not find courage enough to do so. I suppose you have quite forgotten me by this time, if you recollect the little boy under your charge when his mother died, of the name of 'William McEntee.' I was in Mr. Young's employ as an Apprentice for a sailor, but I am happy to inform you that I am at present in good health, hoping that you and your family are well also I shall now give you a little history of my life since I left you. I left North Shields in December 1851, working my way on board of a Coal Brig to London, as it was too much expense for me to pay my passage there I then proceeded to Portsmouth, where my brothers in H M's 95th Regiment were then quartered. After a few months' visit I took a licking to soldiering on account of having two brothers in the Service, and I took and enlisted for my brothers' regiment, and joined the band, and took to learn an instrument, the "Clarinett," which I am at present master off. My other two brothers are splendid musicians, one of which (John) is now at Kneller Hall Music School training for a bandmaster there, the other (Bernard) is band sergeant, that is the young man from whom you used to receive letters. The regiment stopped in England for a short period, until the Crimean War broke out, then embarked in April 1854 on board the steamship *Himalaya* with one thousand men of all ranks—as fine a body of men as ever stood on the battlefield—for the Crimea. I went through the whole campaign, also my brothers, without ever being touched —thanks be to God for all his mercies towards us all. After enduring the hardships of that horrid campaigne, and Peace proclaimed, the regiment were then ordered home, only for a short time to stay. You may think what hardships I endured all that time. After leaving the Crimea the regiment landed at Portsmouth, and a happy day it was for me to place my foot on English ground. We next went to Aldershott camp, where we were received by her Majesty the Queen, and our colors were much admired by her, seeing how bravely the regiment had fought under them. We then left Aldershott camp and went to Dublin, and after twelve months' hard garrison duty the regiment embarked from Kingston Harbour for the Cape of Good Hope, on Friday, the 26th June 1857, and sailed on board the transport ship *Beechworth* on Sunday, the 28th June. We had a long and tedious voyage to the Cape, which was accomplished by Sunday, the 6th of September, but on our arrival there news came on board that we were to proceed from there to the East Indies, where some mutineers had mutinized. We arrived in Bombay on the 1st November, and had to proceed from there and march up the country after those mutineers. The regiment is at present marching continually without even a boot or a shoe to their feet, but I am happy to say that I have had good luck for once. The band has been left behind here in a place named Deesa (on account of the band being broke up at the Crimea, and so many young boys in it now not able to march any further), where all is quiet. Our regiment has had their share of fighting this last four years, so I think. It is rumoured out here now that there is talks at home of the regiment going home after that peace is proclaimed, on account of losing so many men at the Crimea, and so many being lost here. During the space of four months the regiment has lost nineteen men through sickness. This is a desperate Warm Country indeed, you are not sure of your life a moment. A person may go out here in the heat of the day and get sunstruck and die after a few hours' sickness. I have now attained the age of twenty-one years this day, and I have had very good health since I have been in the country, and I like the service very well so far, as I have better times being in the band than a private soldier. I am sorry to inform you that my sister Mary died just previous to my departure from North Shields. My brothers are all very well and in a good way of getting on in the service. My brother Bernard wishes to be remembered to you. I can assure you that I have gone through a great deal since I left you, more than I can think of to tell you now. I hope that you shall forgive me for my ungratefulness. I suppose you thought that I was dead, but thanks be to God I am alive and in good health. I should be very thankful to you if, when you receive this, you would be so kind as to answer it. I have nothing more particular to say at present, so must conclude — I remain, yours truly,

"WILLIAM MCENTEE.

"Direct your letter to 'No. 2767, William McEntee, Band, H M.'s 95th Regiment, Deesa, India, or elsewhere'"

Not so lucky as this young William were all the boys who had run away to sea, and failed to run away from it. Letters came to hand brown, limp, worn at the corners, and bearing strange post-marks, written by a surgeon or nurse in a hospital, saying that a man who had died in the fever ward had begged, as one of the last favours they could do him, that a message might be sent to the "Maister" in far-away Shields, giving the poor lost one's last word of thanks. Sometimes a stranger came to the school whose accent and address sufficed, without his assurance, to make it clear he'd never been a Jubilee scholar, to convey to the dominie some keepsake or token from a ship-mate who had been buried at sea.

'Twas some time in the sixties when "Elfin," in his weekly article written for the *Newcastle Chronicle*, related that a fleet of Tyne colliers one unusually severe season, when winter had set in with exceptional rigour early in the fall of the year, found themselves prematurely ice-bound in the Baltic under such circumstances as to make it evident that there could be no release until the advent of the ensuing spring. On Christmas Day a number of the captains, some eight or more, crossed the ice to dine together on one of the vessels. Over their pipes and grog, having abundant leisure, they naturally fell to recounting the exploits of earlier days, and in this way made the curious discovery that each and every man in the company had been a Jubilee lad under Thomas Haswell. The "Maister" was never reminded of this incident without expressing deep satisfaction.

He had now found his full expansion, and settled down to the life which it had always been his ambition—if such a word can fitly be used—to live. There was now no stint of good books on all subjects, and these were read with extraordinary quickness and a

W. S. B. WOOLHOUSE, F R.A.S.

marvellous faculty for seizing the essentials and storing them securely in a capacious memory, where they were ever afterwards readily accessible. Woolhouse, writing to him on all subjects of intellectual interest, and occasionally on the particular beauties of the Beethoven quartets which he was then editing, urges him, continually, to come to London and hear some of the latest music.

"The packet-fares are now (September 1857) low—very low,—and you should avail yourself of the benefit. We shall both, indeed all of us, be delighted with your society once more My quartet keeps on regularly, and we meet on Mondays. I need not say we finish off the evening with the usual hilarity. You may be surprised to hear that I am editing a new edition of Beethoven's quartets, which are wonderful masterpieces, far beyond anything else of the kind I have corrected hundreds of wrong notes in the latest and best of the editions. I am pleased at your action of putting your son to the violin, and if you can come up you can manage to get a suitable instrument for him in London. I have myself a small instrument, and if it will do it is quite at your service I have also a volume of organ music expressly intended for you. . . . We are getting up an orchestral society, to be conducted by Mr. Rea. . . . My eldest son has been some time at the violin, and the youngest (Eddy) is a good violoncello player; so that if you will only favour us with a visit we can give you a little concerted practice."

And so on, a series of slyly contrived temptations arranged *crescendo*, and ending in a final assault that must have shaken his old comrade's resolution to the core—

"When you come up I can also show you a model of the orbit of the expected comet, which conveys all information relative to it in a few minutes."

Again (October 1857)—

"I enclose you a prospectus of the forthcoming Beethoven quartets. Nothing like them ! !! ('not a worrid !')"

The parenthesis is a reference to the life-long controversy as to the kingship of the divine art.

(May, '59.) "The first six quartets of my edition of Beethoven are published, and in a few weeks I hope to have copies, when I will forward you one of each. I am also editing the score, which will be interesting to you.'

With this letter he sends some violin duets for "your little son" and also a set of 'cello strings—

"When you want any more just say how you find these It is possible you may find them thin, as I suppose you scarcely ever tune up to a genuine concert pitch Country pianofortes are usually half a tone to a whole tone flat When you come to the Handel Festival you must bring Mrs Haswell and your little fiddler with you and see about getting him an instrument to suit him. You must also have a fork filed to a proper pitch"

"I have (says he, February, 1860) lately been at work on the mathematical theory of 'Harmonic Combinations,' and will before long publish something on the subject which will be of great practical use to musicians."

The outcome of these investigations was a fine work on "Musical Intervals and Temperament"—perhaps the best text-book extant. In the preface to the second edition appeared the following kindly reference to the old chum who with him had so often discussed the "chord of the fourth."

"The author has only further to observe that the publication of the first edition of this essay, which has been some time out of print, was originally prompted by the suggestions of an old and highly esteemed friend, Mr. Thomas Haswell of North Shields, who always took great interest in musical disquisitions, and was a diligent inquirer into every thing appertaining to them."

Mathematics, music, and science run a course throughout the correspondence of the two friends—united in the funniest way:—

"The best violin that Mr Buddle had was a *Straduarius* which Mr. Atkinson played upon when you and I called. It might be worth £200. . . . I send you a paper on submarine cables. Mr. Airy, the Astronomer Royal, has written me a very flattering letter respecting it. I enclose some first strings for your violinist."

Writing again, September 1860, he says—

"About a fortnight ago I bought a violin at the sale of stock of Manestel, who has retired from business. It is a copy of Joseph Guarnerius, whose instruments are now in the highest repute (and of which I have an original). Since having it home I have played a good deal upon it and quite approve of the tone, which is in every respect first-rate. It is also a fine model and a convenient stop (exactly the same as my original one), and for your son such an instrument will greatly contribute to his improvement. My son Wesley has left by this morning's train for the North, and I have sent the violin by him, with a capital bow by Henry, the best French bow-maker now living. It is a fine bow and will just suit him. . . . I have also sent you a copy of the new edition of the first six of Beethoven's quartets, which have just come over from Germany. You will find them to be all finer than Haydn's—which are not to be sneezed at. I have to request your son's acceptance of the fiddle, etc., and your acceptance of the quartets, which I may play with you some day."

In November 1860—

"I was right glad of your testimonial, although in amount it was so very far short of your services and merits. It evinced the right sort of feeling though not in exuberance. Dr. Dodds' address was perfect truth, and a sensitive and polished satire on the little-mindedness of society in general . . The quartets Nos 7, 8, and 9 are engraved and I am now examining them. They are much finer than the first six, which are again finer than anything else of the kind."

The "testimonial" in question was a portrait in oils of the Maister, painted by one of his artist friends, Mr. James Shotton, and a "purse of gold," subscribed by a group of townsmen who, however, little recognised how much such things tried the patient soul of their friend. He dreaded the ceremony, and would assuredly have declined to accept the offering but for the pain he knew it would inflict on his good friends. Yet the testimonial system was one he cordially detested, and the embarrassment he suffered from this remained with him for years.

The heavy demands upon his time for gratuitous services it was now—in the face of the burden of a large family, at its most expensive stage—necessary to resist. More teaching must be taken up in the intervals of school toil. A squabble among the contending parties at the old church drove him in 1865 to give up his position as organist, and with it the small salary for which he had been content to take so much on his shoulders over a long series of years

"What is this I hear," writes Woolhouse at the time, "about your being no longer coupled with the old church organ? I do not know any particulars, but am under an impression that anything productive of the slightest agitation must be to your permanent benefit in the end. In fact, you have for many years with quiet and unobtrusive submission, if not with contentment, fagged away in your various avocations with unflagging zeal, but with too little means. Your salary for the school ought to render you practically independent of other occupations except in the way of amusement, and what is now taking place may be the means of bringing attention to bear on the fact . . . It would afford me infinite pleasure if I could aid you in any movement arising out of the church organ affair"

17

The "small salary" would never have worked any change in the Maister's devotion to his duties, but a state of tension had arisen—mainly out of political considerations—which made it impossible for him to retain his position with self-respect; he therefore retired from the old organ gallery, whither thirty years before he had gone in the dark hours before dawn to steal a few chords.

There were now younger men in the town into whose hands the work of carrying on the gratuitous entertainment and edification of the townspeople might safely be left. The condition of the finances of the school was beginning to oppress the committee and others concerned in its welfare, and the Maister naturally felt that he must consecrate even more of his energy and zeal to his peculiar life-work. In the same year, therefore, he announced his intention of retiring from the musical direction of the entertainments given in that institution, to which he had devoted so many years of thought and toil, and from which he had drawn such beneficent store of knowledge for his school-boys. In the "Report of the Committee for the year 1865," the announcement is thus made —

"Your Committee have again to record the success of the winter course of lectures and reading, with music, which, to crowded audiences, have afforded high gratification, adding to the public enjoyment and your own income in a manner as instructive as delightful In this department of your service your Committee have to deplore the retirement—they will not say loss—of another old ally, Mr. Thomas Haswell, who from its infancy has been the Orpheus of the Institution, and was the first to soften its hard lineaments with the smile of 'Music, heavenly maid' He for years, with rare ability and generosity, gave his valuable services on all public occasions, and like a Spartan father, one by one led his children to sound allegiance at the same altar, until he supplied you with an orchestra from his own family; with a sincere acknowledgment of their gratitude to him for his delightful labour of love continued through so many years, on behalf of their successors, they would express a hope that he may be represented for many years at your concerts"

The embarrassed condition of the school funds arose out of the wholly changed state of public sentiment in regard to education. There was now no real contest as to the value of, nay, the necessity for, the education of the "lower" classes, indeed the working population was making politicians feel that the question of a National system of elementary education must shortly be seriously taken up.

It is doubtful whether a better course of training for the class it dealt with could have been devised than that which, for so many years, had been running its healing and vivifying course at the "Jubilee," yet for the greater portion of the period it was given absolutely free of charge. When it was no longer possible to do this a total payment of a penny per week secured all the advantages of the Institution for each child attending it, the expenses being met by subscriptions which the Maister *himself had to collect*. Benevolent ladies and gentlemen, who remembered the old battle for and against popular darkness, continued to manifest a kindly interest in the school they had helped to found—members of the Society of Friends taking by far the larger share in the work of management, administration, and the harder task of beating up new subscribers—and by these the Institution was carried on long after the interest of a new generation of people had grown lukewarm As time lapsed old subscribers died, and were not replaced, hence, when at length the great EDUCATION ACT of 1870, the real charter of emancipation of the English *people* had been passed, some of the survivors declined to continue their contributions on the ground—reasonable enough—that they could not pay both rates and voluntary subscriptions It then began to be realised that the distasteful necessity of placing the school under Government inspection in order to secure a Government grant must be faced, if the total collapse of the fine old school was to be averted—a cruel matter for the men who had so successfully controlled a wholly beneficent and effective scheme of education through several generations, and that they strove long and manfully against the fate that was staring them in the face is evident from their Fifty-Sixth Annual Report, made in 1867. Clearly they were not yet prepared to yield.

"During the past year nothing very remarkable has occurred affecting the interests of this, the oldest school in the borough, but your Committee can look back with pleasure to the manner in which its affairs have progressed during that period. The school is always full, and from this it would appear the parents set as much value as ever on the efforts of Mr. Haswell, the master, to give their children a good useful education, and it must be very cheering to one who himself received his early tuition there, and as master has spent more than twenty-eight years of his life as a teacher of the rising generation in this building, to find that those who were his pupils many years ago desire to acknowledge their obligations to him, and show their appreciation of his efforts on their own behalf by sending their children to him to be educated. More than 3,300 lads have received the whole or part of their education in this school during the time Mr. Haswell has been master, and who can tell the amount of good which they have received from the instruction given—the habits of order, cleanliness, and regularity inculcated, and the kindly manner in which their comfort has been looked after Truly, many of those filling responsible positions in society owe much to Mr. Haswell. There are at present about 220 boys on the books, 96 have been admitted, and about the same number have left during the year. Your Committee have once more to thank the president, Hugh Taylor, Esq of Chipchase, for his many thoughtful kindnesses—for the coals to which must be attributed the warmth and comfort of the school, for the excellent dinner in Christmas week which the lads so thoroughly enjoyed, and which was quite as great a treat to those who came to see their happy faces on the occasion as it was to the boys who partook of it; and finally, for the fact that the debt on the building is at last cleared off .. In conclusion, your Committee would urge on their successors in office the propriety of endeavouring to increase the number of annual subscribers One by one the old friends of the institution are removed by death; this year they have to record the decease of one of its oldest supporters, Joseph Straker, Esq., who died on the 13th October, at the age of eighty-three."

The Christmas dinner referred to in the Report was an affair of unlimited roast and boiled beef, mashed potatoes, gravy in buckets, enormous plum puddings which melted away like snow on the roof of a baker's oven; oranges, apples, and other fruit *ad lib*. The ladies and gentlemen who came to assist the "Mistress" forgot their duties as they saw, amazed, the celerity with which each young stevedore stowed cargo out of sight, and lost their faith for a time in the old truism that you cannot put more into a pint pot than a pint. In these later days there was not such pathos in the sight of children eating unstinted food as in the earlier time (though there were always some who had not food enough); but, indeed, the general condition of the boys was better to a degree hardly credible to any save close observers like the Master.

He was now busied with speculations as to how the impending change might affect the broad scheme of tuition so long and so successfully carried on by him. His concern was not for himself but for his *protégés*, and for the honour of education, of learning itself. Presently he heard that application was about to be made to Government to take the school under inspection, and that he —the old man of sixty-three, the schoolmaster of over thirty years, the successful educator of some thousands of boys—must submit himself for examination as to his fitness to conduct a school

With all his patient philosophy he was deeply mortified at this slur, though he said little about it. He had a way, when tried by the small meannesses of life, of walking bare-headed out into the night and gazing silently up at the stars—so fixedly that he appeared to have gained some new sense of their unthinkable parallax and to have lost himself for a time in the profoundness of the stellar depths—returning after a while with an expression of mingled sweetness and dignity. And his wife and children knew that presently he would tell them, in tones of the tranquillest placidity, of something that had moved him momentarily to anger, indignation, or resentment,—now all gone.

The old teacher enjoyed the respect and regard of all the cultured classes in the town, but there was a residuum of savagery left here and there among the "respectable," which sometimes broke out in unexpected ways. 'Twas the time of the ten-pound householder franchise, and the talk about the "rabble" and the "lower classes" (the classes without votes) had not yet retreated from the open and taken shelter indoors, but was preached resolutely from platform and hustings. The Maister, to whom was entrusted the education of thousands of the youth of the town, was driven at almost every recurring revision season to vindicate his title to a voice in the representation of his native place in Parliament; his right being assailed on various grounds, but generally on the question as to whether the school-house in which he lived was to be regarded as attached to the post of teacher, or whether he was to be considered as, in fact, paying rent for it.

On one such occasion his name was struck out of the voting lists, and when walking homeward towards the school he was accosted by a corpulent *bourgeois* of the old anti-eddicashin class, a rich, dull-headed maker of ship's cordage, who, in heavy blue surtout and weighty seals, slept the sermon through, Sunday after Sunday, all the year round, in the old church.

Hailing the Maister at half a cable's length (the old Shields manner of opening a conversation), he cried out—

"Well, sur? Well, well? How now, how now?" (meaning how had he fared at the revision)

The Maister told him.

"Quite right, sur! quite right, ya kno'! What bizznis 's a man like you t' have a vote?"

"What business have *I* with a vote?"

262   NO "STAKE" IN THE COUNTRY.

"Ay! what right's a man like you t' have a vote? *You've* no right to a vote, sur! *you've no stake in the country*, ya kno', sur! 't *carn't* matter to *you*, ya kno', what happ'ns t' th' country."

"Not matter to me, man!—why?"

"Yo've nothin' t' lose, ya kno'."

"Nothing to lose! Why, man, have I not my family? worth more to me than all you possess, a thousand times over."

"Fam'ly! yo'r fam'ly, sur! What's yo'r fam'ly, aw like t' kno'? Yo'r fam'ly's nothin'—nothin', sur; y've *no-o* bizznis with a vote, sur; *none*. Gud day, sur, gud day. Y've nothin' t' give y'r fam'ly— nothin', sur. Y'r fam'ly!"

And as the vacant dullard rolled on his way, talking with his back towards his collocutor and reasoning heavily, in short ejaculations, on the waywardness of a world that would give a poor man like that a word to say on his government, the Maister glanced down at his boy with an expression full of eager interest to see how the unintentionally coarse lesson had gone home. The teacher—the "Maister," was not fit to vote. So said the law; so said the semi-illiterate respectability which paid a rent providing a sure margin over ten pounds per annum. So said, in effect, all the speeches, however eloquent or otherwise, poured out against any disturbance of the ever-blessed *status quo*.

All, however, to be presently unsaid with the calmest and coolest assurance.

THE OLD "MECHANICS'."

CHAPTER IX.

"BREAKING UP."

"Hitherto education, both elementary and advanced, has rested on what may truly be said to be a mediæval basis, and this is evidenced by the fact that our only schools are termed Grammar Schools—where books, and not things, have been made the object of study."—SIR HENRY ROSCOE.

WHEN in 1839 Thomas Haswell was appointed to the mastership of the Jubilee School the salary was £60 a year, "house, coals, and gas" being thrown in. A charge of one penny per week or per fortnight was at that time made, but so few could pay anything at all that the amount realised was extremely small. During the second year of his tenure the number of scholars nearly doubled. In 1844 the managers voted him a gratuity of £5, a like amount being contributed by the Guardians of the poor. At the annual meeting in 1856 the salary was raised to £70 and a gratuity of £10 added. There was yet a large proportion of children unable to pay the weekly penny, for the amount collected in the year as "pence" was equal only to little more than half what it should have been had each scholar paid the fee; nevertheless, it was recognised by the management that a growing number of the boys in attendance belonged to a class able to afford quite twice the weekly charge, hence in 1864 it was decided to raise the payment from a penny to twopence. There were then two hundred and fifteen boys on the books, and the teacher's salary was increased to £80, with the usual

£10 gratuity. The attendance was not at all prejudiced by the doubling of the fee, but still the proportion of children who did not pay was considerable, being in fact three-tenths of the whole number.

From this time it became impossible, because of the strained financial condition of the institution, to give the Maister's services further recognition in the way of increased remuneration, a matter that never ceased to trouble the kindly committee, and when at length in 1870 the nation rose to a sense of its responsibilities in regard to the culture of its children, and in the GREAT EDUCATION ACT of that year opened a new era for its toiling millions, it became manifest that, so far from being possible to add to the stipend of the old Jubilee chief, it must be decreased, nay, that the school itself must be closed unless some outside financial help could be obtained. The list of subscribers was dwindling at an alarming rate, and though the town was vastly richer than in the day when a few of the more generous friends of the poor took upon themselves the whole burden and responsibility of carrying on the beneficent work of the institution, not a single new subscriber could be found to add his name to the list. So far the school had not cost the town a single penny; there was not a single paid assistant or monitor within its walls, and the whole duty of educating over two hundred boys was regarded as recompensed by a total payment to the Maister of an annual sum of fourscore pounds and ten.

Just at this *crux* one of H.M. Inspectors of Schools visited the Jubilee, with the object of obtaining the consent of the managers to Government inspection, a course he very strongly advocated, urging the committee to induce the master to submit himself for examination at Durham.

"The president, Mr. Hugh Taylor, and the honorary secretary, Mr John Foster Spence, joined in the representations of the Government official, and pressed the matter strongly from the point of view that if the school were examined yearly by the Education Department grants would be earned which would enable the managers to pay their respected master a salary more in accordance with his valued and life-long services."[1]

Undoubtedly, the interest of the Maister lay as near the hearts of these gentlemen as that of the fine old school; but the proposal touched an old wound which the old man found had not healed

[1] Letter from the Mayor of Tynemouth, J. F. Spence, Esq., March 1893.

over. After his retirement, and when the matter had passed away beyond the interest and memory of others concerned, he unburdened himself in the following statement —

"Not long after I had settled down to my work at the Jubilee School I received a kind letter from my friend Woolhouse in London, telling me that he had heard that the Government were about to give schoolmasters an opportunity of submitting themselves for examination in certain subjects with the view of obtaining 'certificates of proficiency,' which would give them a status in the country. He added that he was glad of this, as from what he knew of me he was quite confident of my passing any examination I might be subjected to; but that, of course, anything he could do for me in special mathematics he would gladly undertake in a course of weekly letters and *viva voce* lessons during holiday times, when I should see him in London.

"This was a grand offer, and I wrote to say how much I was obliged to him, and that I should commence at once.

"Strange to say, not more than a day or two afterwards Dr. Dodd called to give me the same information, strongly urging my taking the matter up, and adding that if I needed any help in Greek he would gladly give it. I told him of Woolhouse's offer, which delighted him. On leaving he stepped back to the door to say, 'Remember, no pay; 'tis one dominie helping another,—not another word; good day!'

"I confess to a feeling of something like pride when, on the ensuing committee day, I informed my managers of the kind offers that had been made to me. But to my surprise, nay, amazement, one of the committee, an active worker in the interest of the school, after a dead silence said he 'hoped the committee would have nothing to do with Government interference in the Jubilee. The school was their own, paid for, with a sum to the good in the bank; the numbers on the books rapidly increasing, and the institution, generally, rising in the estimation of the public; their master was giving every satisfaction; there was not the least necessity for any such interference.'

"So prejudiced, indeed, was he against 'Government meddling,' as he called it, that, growing quite heated, he threw his pen down on the table, lay back in his chair, and said that 'if the committee should permit any Government official to have part or parcel in the management, he would leave it altogether and for ever'

"In vain did I explain that my obtaining a certificate of proficiency as a schoolmaster could in no way give the Government any right to interfere in the work or conduct of the school, reason he would not, nothing but his own way would he have; so, for peace's sake, I had to give up this opportunity of bettering myself. There I made a grand mistake. I should have gone on in spite of the opposition of this or any man, and would have done so had my knowledge of the world been greater.

"It must have been some thirty years later that reports began to be heard to the effect that the committee were getting into debt; that the bank account was largely overdrawn, and that in consequence of subscribers dying or leaving the town the committee were seriously contemplating the possibility of having to place the school under Government inspection in order to obtain Government assistance And, at length, I was called before the committee and informed that this course was now unavoidable, that 'there was no help for it,' and that I must be prepared to submit myself for examination. Among the others at the table sat the gentleman who thirty years before had personally interposed between me and a certificate. Looking him in the face, and stretching out my hand towards him, I said, 'Mr P——, you will remember that it was you, and you alone, who so many years ago prevented my taking a certificate of proficiency, and who therefore now compel me to undergo the indignity of an examination which, on account of my age alone, and apart from my experience, I should have been spared.' Quietly smiling, he replied, 'Yes, but I have changed my mind since then.'

"I had to travel, early on a damp, cold, foggy December morning to Durham, where there was no place but a public-house to wait in until the college opened We were received by a fussy official, and after seeing H.M. Inspector, commenced our week's work. I remember the last paper was on music—one for which two hours were allotted, but not needing as many minutes."

After the lapse of about a week the hon. secretary received a letter from the College saying that Thomas Haswell had passed, and that a certificate would be sent in a day or two. In a day or two it came—a piece of parchment certifying that the Maister was competent to conduct the school in which he had already, unaided, trained from four to five thousand boys for the battle of life.

In the midst of the worry and turmoil arising out of this change the old passion for finding new subjects of interest for the lads crops up.

"I have to go (December 1871) to the city of Durham on this stupid examination affair on Tuesday first, and will be there until Friday. After I return we will have some talk about the cheap telescope. The enclosed diagram from H—— will show you how the matter stands at present. The three brass balls we have will not do, the short bits of tubing being nearly as large in diameter as the balls"

This referred to a fine two-plate electric machine he was having constructed. Again, "The examination went off well. Expect to secure the great globe in a few days." The "great globe" was a magnificent specimen, some three feet in diameter, which the Maister presently "secured" for the school from one of the Ship Insurance Associations, where it had stood, unused, for many years in the secretary's office. This noble instrument was the delight of the Maister, who grew enthusiastic as, slowly rotating it, he showed how it impressed the mind with some dim sense of the awful *massiveness* —so to speak—of the phenomenon of the earth's diürnal movement. He declared that it was worth an hour's lecture to merely see it turn. Alas! when, some seven or eight years later, the school had passed under the control of the School Board, the "great globe" was pushed out of sight, and presently subjected to such rough neglect that its surface markings became wholly obliterated.

"I wish you would call at some of the philosophical instrument makers and bring me a small balloon similar to that I once had. You might, at the same time, make some inquiries as to pneumatic apparatus."

Her Majesty's inspectors now came and went, and having regard to the profound modification that was stealthily creeping into the general scheme of education, there was wonderfully little friction Beyond a remorselessly pursued *narrowing down* of the subjects taught in the school much of the work was spoken well of by the official examiners. On the subject of music they at first admitted that the teaching was beyond their capacity to criticise; and, in general terms, they were complaisant, even complimentary, as to both methods and results. But in one matter there was unceasing difficulty between boys and inspectors—to wit, the irreconcilable dialects of both.

In no part of England, of equal area, is to be found such an extraordinary variety of dialect as in the Tyne watershed, and though certain common elements run through the whole, marking the group out from the surrounding or outer dialects, yet the distinctions and contrasts in the folk-talk of Tyneside towns and villages, lying within a mile or two of each other, are in most respects radical, or, at all events, so sharp and clean cut that not only can the denizen of this or that place be instantly "located," but in much that he says he is incomprehensible to any but his own set. This strange, intricate jumble of heterogeneous elements tells unmistakably of fitful strife, of sudden attack, of isolation engendered by feuds, and, later, of local antagonisms and jealousies. The unrestful, stormy, fierce history of this no-man's-land may be read in the sudden transitions in the elements of speech encountered by walking a few miles in any direction. But the sharpest of these transitions are, perhaps, found in that short stretch of river margin which lies between Newcastle and Shields. The latter, indeed, is in respect to dialect marked off from her fellow communities of the Tyne to an extent which is remarkable, or which would be so if the story of her relations with them had not been what it was. The famous Northumbrian "bur," so striking a characteristic of the Newcastle man's speech, and which spreads over so large a portion of Northumbria, is not only utterly absent from the Shieldsman's accent, but he can rarely acquire or even imitate it. There is scarcely a prominent peculiarity in the dialect of Newcastle or of the larger towns of the district which he shares. On the other hand, his own is marked with curious features which belong to it alone. There are indeed not fewer than two—perhaps there may be as many as three—variants existing side by side in North Shields which are not elsewhere to be found.

Apart, too, from dialectic peculiarity, there exists a curious and quite characteristic singing intonation, which from a strange inflection and a certain indescribable inversion of cadence at once arrests the ear of every stranger. "How I admire your *recitative*," said a gentleman once to a Shields lady in a London drawing-room, and the epithet is not altogether inapt, though the "recitative," owing to its utter lack of tonal relationship, could never be scored for musical accompaniment. This "sing-song" mode of speech of the Shieldsman must not be confounded with the "slow speech and soft voice" of the Northumbrian, as noted by Mr. Walter Besant. The voice is not soft, and the speech, of all things, not "slow." Shrill volubility would better define the manner of speech of the native of Shields, indeed, it would put the very smartest shorthand expert on his mettle to report the amazing burst of sustained utterance that pours from the throat of a skipper on the Fish Quay when giving his orders as to the proper making fast of his coble, or to take down the animated "conversation" carried on (not in antiphonic question and answer but in unison) across a quarter of a mile of river between a captain in the passing steam-ferry and his mate "aboard" at the buoys. The speed of utterance is quite startling, and the rise and fall in vocal pitch so curiously in excess of anything of the kind heard elsewhere that the performance might readily be mistaken for some outlandish folk-song.

This peculiarity in cadence, inflection, accent, and forms of expression lay so deep in the very fabric of the Shieldsman, that he could as soon put off his skin as give up any of them; and this fact the Maister had long grasped. Certain almost invincible forms of speech, involving a breach of grammar, he rooted up while the boy was at school. A common locution among the poor of the town was—and probably may yet be—"am is" for "I am." Almost any amount of labour was worthily spent in eradicating errors such as that, but to attempt to alter inflections and intonations which grew out of deep hereditary influences, of inseparable surroundings, even out of the structural form of the vocal organs themselves, appeared to him not only a wanton waste of time but a wrong. For, as a musician, he recognised that there are elements of beauty in all dialects, and that these could not be lost to the language without distinct detriment thereto, and he was utterly impatient of any attempt to level down to one uniform plane all diversities of folk speech. While, therefore, his boys read of "home" in the school, he willingly heard them speak of "hyem" in the play-yard. "None" in lesson times became "nyen" in play-hours. Hook, book, took, assumed the forms hyuk, byuk, tyuk; a pasche (or paste) egg was to the school-boy a pyest-egg. The *oo* sound in who and whom was never attained—indeed it is almost unheard among Shields folk of whatever class, "hoh" and "hohm" being invariable. On the other hand, the aspirate was never by any chance misplaced, the w'ich, w'en, w'at and w'ite, of Mid and Southern England being rendered almost hwich, hwen, hwat, and hwite.

Against all this Inspectors and visitors pitched themselves head-long, to the bewilderment of the children. The remarkably broad *a*—broader than the circumflexed French *ê* in *fête*—is a constant in the river dialects, and is undoubtedly unpleasant to Southern ears, in such words as paper, day, pay, fable, but not a whit less so than the Southern alternatives, pyper, dye, pye, and fyble to Northerners.

Hence when at examination the boys were put to *viva voce* reading test, something like this might occur:—

Child (red-faced, uneasy, and nervous, reading). Before coming to sk-ooo-l, ar——

Examiner. I—I.

Child. Eye—eye must wesh——

Ex. Worsh—worsh, boy.

Child. Wosh me han's 'n' faice——

Ex. Hends' end fyce, boy—say it again.
Child Han's arnd faice; coam me——
Ex. Cowm—cowm—cowm.
Child. Cow—cow—coam me hair; trim me fing-er nay-ls——
Ex (impatiently). *Fin*-ger niles. Say *fin*-ger.
Child. *Fing*-er——

By this time the child is hopelessly confused: the sounds he tries to imitate convey no sense to him. The other, too, is irritated and suspends the reading to ask the class to name, say, the parts of the body as he touches them. They follow his motions, responding one by one—

"Hid, body, 'r'ms, legs, feet, toze, han's, fing-ers, noase, eears, brew," etc.

Not altogether satisfactory, perhaps, but possibly as much so as the corrective alternatives—

"Hedd, bordy, orms, legs, feet, tows, hends, fingers, nowse, yaws, brar-ow," etc.

The singing inflection of the more advanced scholars is a puzzle to the college man, who impatiently struggles against it as he causes the paragraph, which he has given them to read from the newspaper, to be repeated again and again. Aside stands the Maister looking on with a grieved heart at the ridiculous business, foreseeing already how seriously such finicking must limit the opportunity for attending to better things

Education, now spelled with the biggest of E's, had fallen into the hands of the politicians, and every man of them, from the Minister on the front bench, and the leader of the Opposition, down to the lowest candidate for a seat on the School Board, was loudly proclaiming to an astounded nation his "views" on the subject. Amazing schemes and codes were formulated by men who knew less of the *art* of teaching than of almost anything else. The old blunder of blunders, that of regarding education as a mere matter of administering like physic, of pouring *into* the learner as much of a something (not clearly defined) as he could hold while at school, was now elevated to the rank of a first principle, and on that principle successive codes were expressly formulated.

Amid all the noisy jabber and babble of "education" the only man left wholly out of count was the schoolmaster himself. It appeared to none of the contending parties that they might do well to hear what that class had to say in whose hands up to then the whole duty of educating the masses had rested, or if it did they contemptuously pushed the notion aside. The old friends of national education, the men who had spent the leisure of their lives in nurturing the tender plant when it was precariously struggling against the chills of popular indifference and dislike, looked on amazed at the crude suggestions and experiments of the novices to whom the exigencies of party politics had entrusted the control of the "department." Others marvelled at the blindness of those who, as a first step towards elevating the children of the people, set about humiliating, if not degrading, the very class to whom these children must look up if their "education" was in any degree to fructify. But not much was said, though the phenomenon seems to have prompted an intelligent Chinaman[1] to speak out. Referring with some indignation and much contempt to the wretched scheme of wholesale bribery (as he termed it) which Mr. Robert Lowe very evidently regarded as indispensable for inducing the elementary school-teachers of England to do their duty, this "heathen" said—

"In England you look down upon the Schoolmaster. *We* honour him. You place him under inferior men; you make his social position such that it is almost impossible for him to be self-respecting. How can your children respect him whom you do not? How can they value the light of his example when they see you despise it, as you degrade him?"

If now, in somewhat better times, these strictures seem exaggerated, it may be profitable to consider awhile the spectacle described in the following sketch taken from an English daily newspaper[2] of the seventies :—

"THE BIBLE AND THE SCHOOLMASTERS.—A remarkable scene was witnessed at the meeting of the Birmingham School Board yesterday, when a number of candidates were examined in public as to the manner in which they would teach the Bible in Board Schools The regulation bearing upon the point is—' In every school under the control and management of the Board the Bible shall be read and taught daily, but due care shall be taken that all the provisions of the Elementary Education Act in sections 7 and 14 be strictly observed both in letter and spirit, and that no attempt be made to attach children with, or to detach them from, any particular denomination.' The Rev. Canon O'Sullivan, Roman Catholic Vicar-General, subjected the first candidate, Mr. Ball, to a *very severe*

---

[1] Mr. Quong Tart.   [2] *The Birmingham Daily Post.*

cross-examination. Questioning the teacher as to the manner in which he would introduce the Bible to the children, Mr Ball admitted that he would tell them that it was a Divine book, and written by inspiration. 'Inspiration' he was asked to define, and said every one had it to some degree in his or her conscience. The Rev. Canon inquired if Mr Ball would teach that every word was the Word of God, and was met by a reply that the translators might err. Mr. Dawson's suggestion that the translators were not inspired was thankfully accepted by the hard-pressed candidate, who *next fell into* Mr. Joseph Chamberlain's hands, and was questioned as to what doctrines he would teach from the Bible. Mr. Hopkins and other members of the Church party interposed to protect the hesitating and perplexed candidate, who was obliged, however, to admit that he believed in the doctrine of the Trinity, and would teach it to the children under his charge. Mr Chamberlain was quite satisfied with the answer, and inquired whether he would teach the doctrine of the Atonement. Mr. Dawson Which of them? there are twenty-five doctrines of the Atonement. The *victim of the Education Act* escaped without an answer in the din of the controversy, and was next catechised on the doctrine of Everlasting Punishment. This, he thought, was clearly taught in the Bible. In spite of Canon O'Sullivan's attempt to *involve him in a controversy* as to whether the word 'everlasting' was to be taken literally or not, Mr. Dawson said it was an open question in the Church of England. Did Mr. Ball not think it would be better if the Board had settled these questions for him? Canon O'Sullivan It can. (A laugh.) The Rev. Canon warned Mr. Ball that *if elected he would be closely watched* as to the manner in which he conducted religious teaching. Mr. Chamberlain regarded the candidate as intellectually highly qualified to fill a situation under the Board, but he would not vote for him because he would teach the doctrine of the Trinity. Another candidate said he would touch on the doctrine 'as lightly as possible,' but would teach the plain meaning of any passage that came in the ordinary course. If he could not understand the plain meaning he would consult the great Divinities of the Church of England. (Much laughter.) A third candidate was very off-hand in his answers, but said he would confine his teaching to doctrines 'universally received,' whereat there was much merriment. The same teacher told Mr. Joseph Chamberlain (a 'Unitarian') that he would teach the doctrine of the Trinity 'It was a point which was controverted, but only by a small minority.' (Laughter.)"

In such sort, to the tune of "much merriment" and "great laughter," with threats and warnings of "close watching," Birmingham gave an early object-lesson to her Board School children, and their parents, on the matter of respecting their teachers. The spirit animating the group of gentlemen responsible for this edifying scene is not wholly unrelated to that which inspired the patrons of the cock-race and of the bull-ring in the early eighteens.

And the "scene" is typical, too, of the treatment which throughout England was being meted out to a patient, helpless class of men and women by the bureaucracy into whose hands they had found themselves suddenly transferred Officialism of the most preposterous type was at work, making and unmaking "codes" and "regulations" with harassing frequency, and teachers found themselves charged with the task of making returns which absorbed the best of their energy as it disposed of most of their leisure. The "Department," insatiable for statistics, bewildered itself with the mass of worthless matter it was accumulating, and yet cried for more. A hard, nay, harsh administration of the powers of the Act worried school managers, while school children and their teachers were kept in a condition of unrest and irritation, wholly antagonistic to the interests of education, by the unsympathetic attitude of many of the inspectors, who, drawn exclusively from a class wholly out of touch with the people, were not seldom out of sympathy with, if not entirely opposed to, popular education itself. The irritation and insults were borne by the more thoughtful of the teachers with mute resignation, but the woeful narrowing down of the general scope of education, which was becoming inevitable, excited angry protest. Only certain "subjects" earned "a grant," hence it "did not pay" to teach any others. The ridiculously inadequate three "R's" were elevated into a scholastic Trinity, outside of which there must be no devotion.

The "Jubilee," soon after passing under inspection, began to earn good grants, and the managers lost no time in raising the remuneration of the Maister, but it quickly became obvious that the institution could not be continued on quasi-independent lines, hence it was, in 1880, turned over to the Tynemouth School Board.

Pecuniarily, this was an advantageous change for the Maister, his salary being at once considerably increased, but it is doubtful if his whole heart was ever after in the work. Not that he shirked duty or cooled in his enthusiasm for education; but he had no faith in the new ways, nay, he knew them to be retrogressive Up to the time of the transfer the only assistance he had received was that rendered by monitors, who were but older lads who had made better than average progress. Assistant masters were now introduced, who gave cordial and recognised help, but they too had no whole heart for the methods of teaching now desiderated. The Government grant, as the Maister had foreseen, brought in its train Government red-tape and circumlocution, and so, what with rigid codes, repeatedly reversed and inverted, and stereotyped regulations, the fresh, breezy, invigorating, and flexible scheme which for a period of more than two generations had successfully equipped many thousands of boys for the battle of life, was shackled and stifled; to be replaced by the procrustean methods which, ignoring all individuality, all human nature, it might almost be said, in the scholar, are yet the ideal of the "official" educationalist. Perhaps the fiercer struggle of modern times needs newer, more sharp-cut, hence narrower lines:—mayhap not—but however that may be, the work and the system were, for all essential purposes, at an end.

On one point only could the Maister speak favourably of the change, namely, the enormous improvement in the arrangement and equipment of the newer Government schools. The Old Jubilee was taken in hand immediately on its absorption by the School Board—the old-fashioned desks and the alphabet mill being removed and replaced by school fittings of modern design. "We got back into school," he writes in December 1881, "on Monday. The improvements are very great. The two class-rooms have dual desks of clean pitch-pine well varnished, each one accommodating two boys."

In his seventy-third year the Maister took up the new system of teaching, and in a half-sad, half-amused spirit watched and commented upon its developments. He had little or no trouble with the examiners, the average "results" being pronounced good; but there was now, at intervals utterly too short considering the real objects of schooling, a chronic state or condition of "preparation for examination" which broke in upon, and destroyed, all continuity in the essential work.

"I have not seen the book you speak of, but have intended, for some time past, to read it; and shall now have time to do so as the exam. is over, and I have a rest for some time to come. I do not, however, allow the matter to give me any anxiety for it is long since I found that it is hopeless to try to satisfy the conditions imposed upon and by the inspectors. Yet, for some time previous to their visits, the whole of the school—teachers and boys—are in an excited and worried state, not at all favourable to progress or comfort."

Music, after being, for a time, absolutely *taboo* in Board Schools, was suddenly made a compulsory—a penalty, subject. Hence the Maister had to rekindle the fire he had seen officially extinguished.

"I gave a music lesson (1883) to my first class on Monday afternoon. Having written on the old music-board Moore's 'Oft in the Stilly Night' as a duet, they sang it at sight, 'seconds' as well, to my great delight."

April 1883:—

"We are all at about the same pitch as usual. The annual exam. in May is drawing near, and the sooner it comes the better. It is long since I gave up bestowing any anxiety on the matter, it not being of the slightest use."

A few days before the examination he was seized by a sudden indisposition, which,

"After about an hour, left a severe pain or pains in my knees and up to the haunches, and from which I could get no relief—sitting was impossible, walking worse, lying on the sofa no better. At noon it left me, when I went to bed and had a good sleep. Of course I did not go into school that day, but the next I did for an hour, and had to come out. You may ask, 'Why go in at all?' Well, the exam. was due in a few days. However, after Saturday and Sunday's rest I was all right again and have been so since. Something new in the Code this year—the school was divided into three groups, with the following tests :—

"1st division.—Sing the scale up and down, Common chord, ditto, with *part* of common chord, as g, e, or c in the stave to the e below; then sing one song together.

"2nd division.—Common chord in any way, part up and part down; then a few bars of something written on the spot by H.M.I. Some intervals to be sung after hearing them twice.

"3rd division —Sing a piece written on the board by H.M I., modulating into G by an f sharp, going back to C, then modulating into F by a b flat, back again into C by b natural. Sing a piece in parts, duet or trio.

"He recognised that I did not use the *Tonic* sol-fa, and asked if I thought Government would 'recognise' the method! I said I supposed the Government would recognise any method that taught the boys to read music correctly"

Three months later (August 1883) came the report:—

"The report has come. It is of the usual unmeaning character—praising here and condemning there. One might gather from it that the school was 'advancing backwards,' yet the grant is increased by nearly one-half. Of the music it only says, ' It is recommended that the music be for the future taught either by letters or syllables (*c, e,* or *do, re*)' The *do, re* we know, but what about 'the *c, e*' ? Bah!"

How the old quartetists would have enjoyed this piece of musical profundity!

. . . . . .

With a passion for the marvels of science and the wonders of Nature, which waxed rather than waned with growing age, and a settled faith, founded upon a wide and watchful experience, in their peculiar value as stimulating elements in the training of the young, the narrowing down of the subjects taught in elementary schools, and the deadening method of going over the residual subjects with wearying iteration, evoked the deep-felt protests of the old teacher, who predicted with solemn confidence that the work must all be started anew in a period not far distant, though meanwhile, he urged, the generation in the hands of the "Department" was being injured and wronged. Instead of a broad road being made to light, a few deeply-cut ruts were marked out, and all progress was to be made in these. "They are writing on sand again," he said, "and with no jot of excuse."

How true all this was may be realised by noting the extraordinary spread, during recent years, of science and technical teaching in our board schools throughout the country; but precious years were lost in grasping truths that had long lain open and patent to the most careless observer—unseen only because of the indifference and contempt of the people of "culchaw" to whose control the earlier educational arrangements of the new, *genuinely* national schools had been confided.

Birmingham was early to the fore with a remarkably sound scheme for affording to its thousands of School Board children some foretaste of that scientific knowledge which her many magnificent institutions are so nobly qualified afterwards to supplement The difficulties in the way of those who advocated the practical teaching of science in elementary schools are obvious enough. The masters and assistants, overwhelmed with statistical work, and wearied with the ever-pressing necessity for securing a high number of "passes," had no opportunity, no leisure, in which to acquire even a moderate degree of familiarity with the elements of the several sciences necessary to be taught; the dexterity in handling apparatus and in successfully performing experiments could only be acquired by long practice and loving interest in the work, while the taste for science was in most cases absent, having been withered up by neglect in early days. Again, the cost of a sufficiently complete equipment of apparatus in each school was a consideration of the first magnitude in those early days of public impatience with School Board rates

The Birmingham Board solved these difficulties by engaging as "scientific demonstrator" a man of high scientific attainments—an educational enthusiast; and, with a sagacity rare in public bodies, left it very much to himself to formulate a scheme which should best accomplish the project in view. Mr. W. Jerome Harrison, F.G.S., was speedily at work, and with results altogether remarkable. At the outset there were no fewer than twenty-eight schools to be dealt with, and the problem which faced this gentleman was to get through the series in a time sufficiently short to avoid too long an interval between the successive lessons. A carefully arranged set of apparatus for demonstrations in chemistry, electricity, and physics was contrived to fit securely into a spring hand-cart, whence it might be swiftly lifted and as quickly replaced. The cart was trundled from school to school, four being visited each day, and the whole number thus covered in little more than a week. At each respective school, on the appointed day and hour, all was in readiness —a table set out, the blackboard mounted on its easel, the class assembled, and, in a very few moments after the arrival of his cart, Mr. Harrison was at work among his eager and intent young pupils. When the lesson, which lasted about three-quarters of an hour, was over, the apparatus was whisked away, and the school left free to resume at once its ordinary course, with an extraordinarily small amount of disarrangement and interruption.

It would be difficult to imagine a more fruitful essay than this of the Birmingham Board. The boys, mainly sons of artisans—boys who themselves were to become artisans—set to think, to ponder, to deduce results, to speculate (profitably) on possibilities, and—most difficult and precious of acquirements—to intelligently observe. Mr. Harrison invariably made his pupils work out the reasoning, the *rationale* of the lesson he was engaged upon. In the best and highest sense of the word he was *educing* intellectual processes. It was *education* truly so called, and though the scheme and its methods have since been expanded and amplified, the early fruits of this noble experiment were in all respects beautiful and beneficent.

For forty years the Maister had been struggling on in the arid wilderness of popular indifference or aversion to physical education, with no sympathising financial Board to help him. When, in 1882, he first heard of Mr. Harrison's operations, his heart was stirred with a warm exultation.

"What a glorious account of Mr. Harrison's mission among the Board School lads, with his 'kist of magic'! What noble-minded men you have about you! I am lost in wonder when I try to think what I should have done had these things been possible when I began—my only apparatus being my magnetic bars! The promoters of this grand movement must not be too sanguine of success, for strange as it may appear, I hardly know of a scientific schoolmaster in the local Association. They are well up in all Government requirements, grammatic niceties, percentages of 'passes,' etc., excellent algebraists, but there is an almost total absence of scientific taste. In coming home from the last school excursion we had in view for a long time a double rainbow. Said one of the dominies—

"' I never saw the second bow so clear.'

"' Ah !' replied the other, 'that is the *reflection* of the first.'

"' Of course it is,' responded the first.

"Again, in discussing the question of the time for the summer holiday—breaking-up time—one said the middle of June was best because the sun was about *crossing the line*, and as soon as he did the 'weather became insufferably hot!'

"But this will all get better in time."

This abiding hope, nay conviction, that most of the absurdities of the educational 'systems' would in time be eliminated, enabled the old man to look on with amusement at much of the nonsense talked and written in the name of science.

"I still [November 1883] go over for an hour or so to the Club, and have the pleasure of hearing the most abstruse matters not only discussed, but finally settled and done for I expect to hear some eye-openers this week anent the November meteors."

Speaking of the audience at a lecture on "Science-teaching in Board Schools," especially addressed to teachers, and illustrated by experiments, he says—

"It was a cold, bleak, foggy night with rain, and my cough had been rather bad all day. I knew it was rather a risky thing to go, however, go I did, and was highly pleased. The lecturer spoke for the first half-hour on the advantages of science-teaching in schools, of what was being done in Birmingham by Mr. Harrison, and also in Liverpool, and then opened a series of experiments, almost the most perfect I ever saw. The audience seemed to regard the display very much as a conjurer's, stamping with the feet and otherwise applauding when anything went very quick or happened suddenly: such, for example, as the radiometer spinning round apparently on nothing, or a mass of filings seizing upon a magnet."

The worry inseparable from Departmental control was not as yet able to break down the hardy nature that for over forty years had cheerfully faced the trials and sorrows which, in such a period, come to every man. A singular philosophic calm had settled on the old man's mind, and enabled him to find in his daily work and nightly studies a beautiful compensation for coming age. He had, up to this time, scarcely been absent from his duties for a single day on account of illness, and was as yet peremptory in declining the suggestion of his family that 'twas time he should take rest. On his seventy-fourth birthday he wrote—

"Of my health I am thankful to say nothing could be more satisfactory I eat, sleep, and go about quite as well as I ever did at any time of life No pains, no indigestion, no rheumatism, no lowness of spirits—nothing to complain of. Of course, I am not without some of Nature's warnings that I am at an advanced age—such as loss of teeth (which, thanks to McLeod's skill, is scarcely any loss at all). Sight, also (which on a dark night out of doors is very feeble) Hearing (what people say) is becoming more difficult, but musically speaking, as good as ever Sometimes I feel rather stiff, but that soon goes off, so on the whole I am, as most people say, 'a wonderful old chap.' And now I am done with myself. What a charming writer Darwin is! so careful that no objection to his theories or opinions shall be left unnoted; so courteous to other writers. I am half-way through the volume already and greatly delighted with it. The chapters on Disintegration and Denudation are truly startling; I had read some extracts from this work in the newspapers, but what one gets from newspapers on such subjects is generally worthless. The name of Darwin will become more and more famous when all the host of his detractors shall have 'sunk into utter magnificence.'[1] The eclipse was seen here in perfection, there not being a single cloud, and the air unusually calm and clear The passage of the shadow was intensely interesting."

His veneration for Darwin—the man as well as the philosopher—was deep and broad, and the study of his writings a profound delight, not mainly for their luminous beauty of expression and lofty philosophic calm, but because of the exquisite spirit of simple and manly modesty revealed in every line he wrote. He often laughingly remarked, when the storm of scarce articulate rage and abuse was surging round the recently-published *Origin*, that the solitary exponent of the truly Christian spirit was the great Darwin himself.

"Since I wrote you," he says May 1882, "that grand old man Darwin has become mute for ever, so far as touches anything more we can have from him, but he will continue to be heard and listened to more than he ever was during his useful life. I have been delighted to read in the London journals fine leading articles on the greatness and amiability of the man."

The keen, active intellect was as alert as ever, and the Maister spent most of his leisure in the systematic study of the latest scientific work. The early fostered *sehnsucht* for knowledge had long ere this developed into habit, hence nothing like rusting was possible for the energetic old student and teacher A healthy interest in all human affairs remained with him, and a serenity of thought which enabled him to enter into the amusement of the young with all the zest of a boy. He was greatly interested in watching the development of his grandchildren, and regularly corresponded with them on such terms as to draw from them letters filled with the spirit of boyhood, and wholly devoid of self-consciousness.

As Woolhouse wrote, *apropos* of the illness of some mutual friend, "I suppose I am something like yourself, we have so much to do that we have no time to be ill"—a piece of homely philosophy containing more truth for the old than is generally appreciated. He had at any rate no time to *think* he was ill. His old chum came down to Shields at the end of 1882 to see him—

"and of course brought his fiddle with him. We had one or two duets,

[1] The literally quoted peroration of a famous Shields shipowner's political speech

but, poor fellow, his tone is now very thin and feeble. In some of the *piano* passages it was so *very* piano that no sound (that we could hear) left the fiddle, which tickled S—— so much that I feared she must laugh outright. However, we spent a very pleasant evening: he was full of his jokes, and we went over some of our doings of fifty years ago. He is a fine old fellow! I had some wonderful descriptions of the properties of the *hyperbola*, and of a problem he has been propounding which he said he believed no one would be able to solve,—and you know he is no egotist. My health is truly excellent and my voice strong again, which enables me to give the music lessons as usual.

"We have received this morning your two letters giving an account of your visit to *Tel-el-Kebir*, and a sickening account it is; indeed, it could be nothing else. And, truly, it is as sickening and disheartening to read in our daily papers of the fêteing and feasting of the troops who have returned; of the processions, reviews, and entertainments; the honours, titles, and pensions to be given to the General and the Admiral, and others of lower rank, while scarce a word is said about the poor creatures whose dead bodies you saw half buried. Who can tell what they had to suffer before death came—long after all hope had been dead? But the whole thing is a huge, a monstrous wrong!"

War, like "sport," was a sore subject with the Maister, who never shirked the duty he felt to be his, of denouncing both. A wide spirit of tenderness to all created beings was the spring from which a sympathy—always manly—welled over for small as for great things.

"I am delighted the two lads have got into the Grammar School. They must have worked hard and close to have mastered the subjects necessary to ensure a pass at the examination. Many of them, in my opinion, are not worth the time spent over them. I do not wonder at your pitying the two as they entered the great place. It is all very well for those who succeed, but what about the poor sensitive beings who have to go home after failure?"

His "sterling constitution" was yet the constant theme of grateful reference.

"My health is really extraordinary"—"I am perfectly in tune, concert-pitch, myself"—"I have resolved to be in bed before ten every night"—"I could not wish to be better than I am. Sometimes in bed on Saturday night by half-past nine, and occupy the same position round the clock, sleeping all the time. An exile from home, splendour dazzles in vain."

A calm equable mind, a serene conscience, and the most systematic moderation in food, both as to time, quality and quantity, contributed to maintain a naturally fine constitution in wonderful equilibrium; but Nature's warnings were, as he said, beginning to make themselves heard, though he never regarded them as anything of the kind. A sharp attack of sickness came and as suddenly went in the Midsummer of 1882.

"At last I have so far recovered as to sit up and write you a line or two. All pain and nausea is entirely gone, and they have left me exceedingly weak and feeble. One wonders what can have gone wrong so suddenly and severely as to cause such an amount of anguish. However, my sterling stomach has regained its natural and wonderful powers The doctor says my heart beats like a timepiece, my lungs are perfect So you see I have much to be grateful for."

But a shadow was now coming over the life of the dominie, though as yet it was as indefinable as the *penumbra* of an eclipse. The bright helpmate who had kept his home cheerful with music and light was falling into a sickness which was destined not long thence to take her from him.

"Your mother's foot is better," he writes May 1883, "but she has rheumatic pains in her arms which come on with a change of wind Grandmother used often to say to me, 'Tam, there's going to be weather;' and she was generally right. However, when one hears 'The marvellous works behold amazed' resounding through the house, varied with 'All we like sheep,' '*Cujus animam*,' Morley's 'Now is the month of Maying,' down to 'Tynemouth Abbey,'—so long, I say, as we have these treats at intervals we think matters are not at their worst."

The sprightly temperament of his wife, which found a happy, natural outlet in spontaneous song, was as hard to break down as his own, but a malady, which was not rheumatism, was slowly making its way, and though it failed to dompt the spirit was surely sapping the physical strength, and much of the outdoor avocations of the old man were now devoted to the purpose of "restoring" the tone of his devoted partner's health. Little excursions planned with this view were all based upon a living faith in exercise and fresh air The "Maister" had never closed the window of his bedroom for a single night since first he had a house, and he always met the protestations of his friends who saw him in the school-yard bareheaded, in winter as in summer, with a smiling shake of the head.

'Last Saturday," he writes to one of his grandsons, "grandma, little Arthur, and I went in a steamer from the New Quay to the Haven, and got into one of Tom Fry's sculling-boats. Arthur would have the oars. There was a gentle swell, but no roughness nor wind, still, he could not manage at all. However, he persevered, and, strange to say, in twenty minutes or so managed to row fairly well. The sea was smooth and calm, with just a pleasant lifting swell; the sun, right over the Aquarium, was covered with thin clouds, which lessened the glare of his light and made the scene a delightful one. Almost all the boats were off; hundreds of people on the sands and on the banks; Punch performing near the two-gun battery,—we could hear his delightful screams softened by distance, which improved the quality of his piercing tones though it prevented our seeing his murderous attack on wife and constable. Well, Captain Pickle having command of the vessel, ran too far in-shore, almost touching the sand, and in turning the vessel round got her broadside on, when one of those little white-crested breakers suddenly rose, about *a foot* high, and gave the poor old lady sitting in the stern-sheets the benefit of a salt-water shower bath The suddenness of the shower produced a squall from the receiver of 'Admiralty Droits' that surpassed Mr. Punch's best efforts However, the life-boat was not sent off to our rescue, nor did the Life Brigade interfere, for in two or three seconds we were ten yards outside, and not a wave to be seen. The velvet dress was declared to be ruined, —a statement that may fairly be questioned. I wish Fred and you had been there to join the fun."

A month later—

"MY DEAR FRED,—We were glad to have your letter and to hear the result of your examination. You seem to have enjoyed the holidays, but mind don't plague the canal-men too much lest they get into a passion and shoot you in earnest. What, then, would become of your Latin, logic, Greek, and grammar? Never mind not getting a prize every time. If you apply yourself to your work and are able to earn your teacher's good opinion you need care for no other prize We are going on as usual at school, each class out for quarter of an hour morning and afternoon, when there is the usual scrambling for the ropes, plenty of noise, shouting, marble-playing, etc. We are all well except grandma, whose arms are rather touchy now and then, and it makes the old lady touchy too. Sometimes, however, we hear 'Drive the nail aright, boys,' in a loud voice, and we know she is all right again.

"The Board gave me a large proportion of the grant, so I, in all, got more than I ever before received, and came home from the office with a well-filled purse."

Poor old man, he was in his seventy-sixth year when this

relaxation of financial stress came to him. He was now, in circumstances, freer from anxiety than he had ever before been, and his first thought was to apply the surplus to an effort to restore the "old lady's" health.

A life's cherished desire to visit the native Isle of his mother, whence she took her three weeks' journey to meet the husband from whom the press-gang had separated her for three years, was now gratified. In the summer of 1884 he took his ailing wife to Douglas, writing thence on July 9th :—

"Do you notice the address? I had heard so much and read so much of the 'elasticity' and health-giving effects of Isle-of-Man air that I made up my mind to bring your mother here for a time. . . . The bracing quality of the air is marvellous; it is simply delicious to breathe, and is having an evidently beneficial effect on her health and appearance. . . . Next day we went to Castle Town, my mother's native place, and saw several names on the shop sign-boards, such as Taggart Curlet, etc., which I have heard her mention, but of course, as she left when a young woman—it must be nearly a hundred years ago—no one now could be alive who knew of her. We visited the castle and the other sights, and then walked through the streets of the old town, wondering in which of the houses she was born or had lived, but we could form no opinion whatever on either point, though I felt as if I could have given anything to know this. Douglas is the principal town now, and is a delightful place. I should like to live there the rest of my days. . . . I have another week's rest and then commence again."

[December 1884.] His 77th natal day:—

"Arrived before daylight this morning a wooden box containing two canisters of golden 'Honey Dew.' I only finished Henry's on Saturday last, so you see I am living in the clouds. I know you will be glad to learn that I am in perfect health, and although three-score years and seventeen am without ache or pain, and go about the school without any longing for evening."

In a trembling hand his wife has written across the foot of the page—"Thankful to say that papa never looked better than on his 77th birthday."

"She is now altogether in her bedroom," he writes a month or two later, "and gets up only for a short time in the evening. . . . As to her being able to read! That indeed is the only thing she can do. Three volumes are as nothing to her. I told her lately that in my opinion it did not matter greatly whether she read the third volume first, and she answered 'not a bit'; so you see there is some fun in her yet."

She was, however, rapidly sinking, and towards the end of March the old man began to realise that he was losing her

"There is little or no change in your poor mother's condition; if any, it is that she is becoming weaker and thinner, though still conscious, and, mercifully, free from acute pain. Her voice is fainter, still she is cheerful I suppose this state of things cannot last much longer, and I hope the end may come quietly and without pain."

It came a few days after, "quietly and without great pain," and the old man found himself strangely alone.

"I find the loss I have sustained more severe than at the time of her death. . . . The house once so full of life and vigour now cut down to two—and this for ever. I sometimes feel as if I cannot realise it; however, I must, I know, try to rise above it, and not forget that, bad as it is, things might be worse"

Speaking of the funeral.—

"I do not mean that hers was more so [expensive] than it ought to have been, or more than other people's in like circumstances; but I think *all* funerals are outrageously costly. I hope when my time comes—and it cannot long be delayed—you will remember that although such expense may be looked upon by people as a mark of affection, I do not think it so."

In the summer of 1885 the Maister's thoughts turned, as in the previous year, to the scenes and associations of early days, and a strong desire came upon him to make a journey, deferred through a lifetime, to Bamburgh, where he hoped, more earnestly than he realised, yet to find one or two of the friends he made when he sang "with John Stewart, bass, the Vicar joining in grandly," "The Red Cross Knight" in the vestry.

"The other day, Thursday, I took the train to Bamburgh, a place I had long wished to revisit, and where I hoped to meet friends whom I had not seen for fifty-six years—scarcely to be expected you may say. It was in the year 1829 that I was employed for some three or four months in that small village, and as it was the first time I'd been so far from home everything was strange to me; the country, the people, the fine old castle, the Cheviots in the distance, the Farne Islands only two or three miles away, all tended to make the place one of deep interest to me Then again, our master associated with us, and we had two apprentices to attend upon us; altogether we spent a very pleasant time. After finishing at Bamburgh we moved away to North Sunderland, then to Beadnel, Fles, and Lucker. At this Lucker I lodged with one of the apprentices, in a small cottage belonging to two old people who had an only daughter —a remarkably pleasant little girl just about fourteen years old. As we were there many weeks we became almost part of the family The old couple were Richard and Margaret Wallace, and their daughter was named Alice.

"During my first year in London, after leaving the North, I saw one day in a book shop in the Strand a neat Church Service consisting of a Bible and Prayer-Book in a leather case, and as I was about to go home for the winter, I bought it as a present for Alice Wallace, of Lucker, sent it to her, and received a letter thanking me for it That was the last time I had any communication with the family, for postage being high—sixpence, ninepence, and a shilling per letter—I did not like to put them to expense by writing.

"After a few years I became a schoolmaster, married, and duly had my portion of cares and troubles, so that Bamburghshire and its pleasant recollections gradually faded from my memory In 1838 Grace Darling's doings brought all vividly back to me, and I said I would one day go down and see my old friends, but the visit was put off from year to year until I did, this month of July 1885, carry out my long-projected pilgrimage.

"Leaving the train at Lucker, I went into the only inn to be found, and, feeling hungry, inquired if I could have some dinner.

"'Dennor!' said the girl at the door; 'no, neebody ivor wants any dennor heor but oorsel's.'

"'But surely you can give me something to eat?'

"'Yis, some biscuits an' cheese.'

"Soon I had some fine bread and butter, and a glass of ale.

"'Have you any very old people about here?'

"'Well, I've lived in this hoose for over twenty-eight years'

"'Ah! but you're not half old enough'

"'Well, my uncle, who is the schoolmaster, has lived here all his life, and he's about sixty, he's had the school for twenty year past.'

"'Where is the school?'

"'Why, that's it, other side of th' road'

"'Oh, will you, pray, tell him that a schoolmaster wishes very much to see him'

"'But he's at Belford, sir, for he's overseer as well, and has had to attend a meetin' of Guardians theor this mornin'. He had to let the school out at ten, but it begins at half-past one, so he will be heor about one. There he is!' said the lass, running out to tell him. A fine old man with a pleasant, intelligent face walked into the room, shook hands with me, and sat down. We soon got to work. He knew the Wallaces, and said they had been dead many years, that their daughter Alice had married a farmer and removed from the village long ago, and that only recently she had gone to the south of England, where she died, he had heard, only last year. 'But,' said he, pointing, 'there are two of her cousins going home from their field-work to dinner; we will go out and ask them.' Sure enough, the report was true. I cannot express how it affected me. However, so it was; there was nothing for it but to make my way to Bamburgh, some four miles away. As the day was fine, I walked. On reaching the village I was surprised to find it so little changed in fifty-six years.

"After enjoying a cool wash and an excellent tea at the Lord Crewe's Arms, I walked across to the house of Grace Darling's sister. It is now much used by visitors as a lodging-house. There were a few nobbishly dressed young people sauntering in the garden, and as my ringing at the door bell had brought no response, I asked a pair of them if there was anybody in the house; but after a supercilious stare they walked away without replying, evidently feeling that an unwarrantable liberty had been taken. However, the door was just then opened, and, asking to see Miss Darling, I was invited to go upstairs.

"She was standing in the middle of the room. I knew her at once, and holding out my hand, said, 'You don't know me!'

"She took my hand and said, slowly, 'No, sir, I do not know you.'

"'Now, carry your memory back fifty-six years, when you lodged with old Peggy Robson near the top of the village, and the church was painted by some men from the South.'

"Her face was all the while changing so as to be almost painful to look at, and presently she exclaimed, 'Mr. Haswell,' took my hand in both of hers, and sitting down on a sofa, poured out a torrent of questions without waiting for an answer. After a very pleasant chat, mostly about her sister Grace and her father, her eyes filling with tears as she spoke of Grace, I took my leave, promising to call again before leaving for home.

"I visited the fine old castle, sitting on the ramparts and looking down at the calm sea, the old church which I had painted, now 'restored,' and apparently 'high'; saw poor Grace's tomb—and very pretty it is—then got off to the hotel, very tired. While at breakfast next morning the landlord came in to say that a conveyance from the inn to Lucker would start in half-an-hour to meet the train for the South, did I wish to go? As all my acquaintances were either dead or removed, I made up my mind to return home, writing to Miss Darling explaining why I could not call upon her again. She died during the following year, and was buried beside her celebrated sister in the old churchyard."

A few explosive lines of indignation on the Crewe Charity and its maladministration close the account of this forlorn expedition.

The Maister was now nearing his eightieth year, and yet had no thought of giving up work. His loneliness, the stress of grief from the loss of wife and many friends, the every-day association with and commiseration for much poverty and hardship—for these were yet the lot of too many in Shields—were breaking in upon the magnificent constitution that a life of temperate moderation and healthy activity had conserved, but he would not recognise that "nature's warnings" were any other than those to be expected by every man who had passed middle-age In the bitterly cold December of 1885 he writes:—

"I went down to Richard Stephenson's shop to ask him to send a man to do some small jobs in the school, and as it was only a matter of five or six minutes I did not put on an overcoat. It however was sleeting and wet, and when I got back I was trembling with cold. So I told my assistant that I should not go into school again that day, had a fire lighted in my room, the sofa drawn in, wrapped myself up and quickly got into a state of warmth. At night, a basin of gruel with a glass of port wine in it, and off to bed at eight o'clock In the morning all right again, though rather feeble, so I remained in the house all day, and am now perfectly well. *It is strange how soon I am knocked up and how soon put right again.*"

Again, in March 1886—

"What a week we have had of snow! The school had to be closed for two days—some of the others did not open during the week. This never before happened in my time. . . . I was not once outside the gates for days, but made myself comfortable at the fireside with Herschel, Huxley, and other of that ilk, of whose company I never tire, and with whose work I am more and more delighted every time I contemplate it."

The first hint of retirement comes in a letter dated May 1886—

"I cannot foresee, nor is it necessary I should, how long I may be able to hold my place in the school, but it is evident that the time must come, and at no distant date, when a change will have to be made. This is only my own opinion, nothing has been said or even hinted so far. I am only looking ahead a bit"

But at length, on the 8th November, in deference to urgent appeals from his family, he made up his mind to give up the work of his life. He had indeed come to recognise that he could no longer continue to beat up against the narrow but swift current of innovation that was sweeping through educational channels.

"There is so much dissatisfaction with the authorities, whose whims seem to increase every year, that I find myself no longer able to contend with the work, and if I do not soon give it up for a rest, it will give me up. I find I can do no more, so I will send in my resignation in a day or two."

The resignation came before the Board on December 2nd, 1886, and having been read, the clerk was "directed to apply to the Education Department, under article 134 of the Code, for a form of application, with the view of obtaining a pension for Mr. Haswell, who seemed to fulfil all the conditions required by that Article." The Maister's desire was to be released at once, but he was asked to continue to officiate until the end of the year The resignation was then accepted, and thus, in his eightieth year, the old teacher handed up the control of the school to which he had gone as a scholar more than seventy years before, and over which he had presided as Maister for close on half a century.

"Among many incidents," says the *Shields Daily News* of December 7th, 1886, "that the public would gladly forget in the recent meeting of the Tynemouth School Board, a majority of them will single out and remember with melancholy interest the acceptance of the resignation of Mr Haswell, for so many years the unfailing friend of every poor boy struggling out of poverty and limited opportunities to manhood, character, and intelligence. It is with no ordinary pang of regret that the friends of education see such a faithful servant quit of his charge, when there seems such infinite need of experience and tact on the part of teachers, and especially that indwelling sympathy and comprehension of child life which brought so many a bronzed and broadened captain of industry, or merchant marine, after long years, back with boyish ardour to shake hands with the 'Maister.' In a time of great need, when a very little leaven of instruction was expected to leaven—oh! such a lump, the fortunate lads of the Jubilee School got, what lads often fail to get under Boards and Governors, such a thorough training as filled the few seeds of knowledge with climbing energy, and laid the foundation of that best inheritance, self-control and self-help Father Stark is reported to have said at the meeting 'that with regard to Mr. Haswell, he was proud to think that they had a master of whom the members of the Board could speak so highly.' Those who have a thorough knowledge of him, and know how faintly language can express the value or the merit of such service, have their pride sadly dashed by the reflection that the acknowledgment should be limited to words, even of encomium. For the man who for a lifetime has sown light and been the friend of youth, it is simple fairness that in his evening there should be light and troops of friends with deeds as well as words. The latter temper no blast and fill no aching void.'

On the 8th—his birthday—his old friends foregathered at the club, and among them the good and genial Uncle Toby, Editor of the *Newcastle Weekly Chronicle*, and creator of the famous Dicky Bird Society.

"It was my privilege," says Toby, "a few evenings ago to assist at an interesting celebration in North Shields. The members of a social club in that town met to commemorate the birthday of the father of the society—Mr Haswell, the venerable head of the Royal Jubilee Schools. That worthy and respected gentleman, now in his eightieth year, is about to retire into private life, after an uninterrupted service of nearly half a century. Under the old dispensation and the new the work he did in educating the children who came under his care gave the highest satisfaction to the managers. So long has he retained the mastership of the school that the original directors have all passed away, while the sons who succeeded them are now old men. When the school passed into the hands of the School Board Mr. Haswell's services were of course continued. Such, indeed, was the confidence he inspired that the Board, even at his advanced age, has been reluctant to part with him. Thousands of youngsters belonging to North Shields have been indebted for their education to Mr Haswell. There is probably not a colony of the British Empire—there is certainly not a quarter of the globe—where some of his scholars may not be found. Not a few of them have risen to positions of influence and responsibility. From time to time some of these scholars have returned to the old town, sought out the old schoolmaster in the old school-room, and imparted to him the information that they were captains of steamships, or managers of great concerns, or merchants of established reputation in distant parts of the world. Well, it was to celebrate the birthday of this industrious and estimable man that the gathering I have mentioned was held. The little speeches that were made, the recitations that were delivered, and the local and other songs that were sung, rendered the evening one long to be remembered. The pathetic and the humorous were so mixed together during the proceedings that most of the emotions of the human mind were called into play in the course of the evening"

Pathetic as the occasion undoubtedly was for the old Maister, he was able to detect the humour which underlies most human things.

"We had," he writes, "a large meeting, and spent a pleasant evening. 'Tynemouth Abbey' sung by six different Sims Reeveses (in six distinctive styles), a verse each, and the chorus not so cruelly murdered as I have heard it, was pronounced 'beautiful.' The 'Hungarian Exiles,' generally most inhumanly treated, met with great favour."

On the 23rd December 1886 the Jubilee School "broke up" for the Christmas holidays in circumstances set forth by the *Shields Daily Gazette* under the heading—

"A VENERABLE SCHOOLMASTER.—This afternoon, on the breaking-up of the Royal Jubilee Schools, Mr. Thomas Haswell, for forty-seven and a half years head-master, was presented with a valuable microscope by the scholars and teachers. The presentation took place in the boys' school in the presence of the scholars and a number of teachers.

"Alderman Spence, in making the presentation, said they were met that day to bid good-bye to their old master, who had so long conducted the school in such an admirable manner. When a man reached the age of seventy-nine years it was high time that he had a holiday, and when he had struggled on to the best of his ability—and with very great ability—for forty-seven and a half years to teach the young idea how to shoot, it was time he had some rest, as he could not expect, in the ordinary course of events, to live many years more. For his own part, if he lived as long, he would like to shake hands with Mr. Haswell on his hundredth birthday. He had come there to present, on their behalf, the beautiful microscope to Mr. Haswell, and he hoped that the instrument would prove to be a source of very great pleasure to him—as he was sure it must to any one who had tastes such as Mr. Haswell—in the examination of the beauties of nature. He was sure they were all very glad indeed to see their old friend enjoying such excellent health as he did at present, and they hoped he might live for many years to enjoy his well-merited retirement. He then presented the microscope to Mr Haswell amid hearty cheering.

"Mr. Haswell, in reply, said it was seventy years since his brother first brought him to the school as a scholar. At that time scarcely any one stayed at school after eleven or twelve years of age, and he remained there only for two or three years. When he became master, the school was managed under what was called the monitorial system, and it remained so for thirty-one years, during which period it never cost the town one penny It was supported entirely by subscriptions, and one of the principal movers in connection with it was the father of Alderman J. F Spence, who acted as secretary for several years after he (Mr. Haswell) came As the friends of education died off, their sons failed to follow their views, and the consequence was that in the year 1870 the school came under government inspection He had to go to Durham, where he got his certificate Afterwards he had a staff of teachers For the last six years the school had been under the management of the School Board. As one of the incidents of his life he might mention that he introduced vocal music into the school two years before Mr. Hullah commenced his classes in London. He wished to thank Mr. Spence, his brother, Mr. Procter, and other gentlemen who had always paid untiring attention to the schools He did not know how to sufficiently thank them for the present; there was nothing they could have thought of that would have pleased him so much. He was glad to be able to say that he had always had the good opinion of the many thousands of boys who, in his day, had passed through the school. It was a source of great gratification to him. In conclusion he again thanked them cordially, and assured them that in the hours of his retirement he would find great pleasure in using the microscope, as he had always taken a great interest in the wonderful works of nature.

"The Rev. H Vian-Williams, in moving a vote of thanks to Alderman Spence, expressed his best wishes to Mr. Haswell for continued life and happiness, and trusted his days might be long and bright, and that his future would be full of glow and blessing

"The interesting proceedings were brought to a conclusion by cheers from the boys.'

So ended the long, fruitful task at the "Jubilee", but though no longer the master, the old man remained yet "the Maister" to every one in the town.

"I wonder,"—wrote his friend Edington in the *Shields Daily News* of December 27th, 1886,—" I wonder whether, amid the anticipated happiness of a holiday, the lads of the Jubilee felt the peculiar pathos of their breaking-up on Thursday, the last lesson of their old master, the final utterance, in the old school, of the voice of authority, mellowed by the ripe service of forty-seven years, the friend of the playground, the guide and counsellor of study; a ruler who in his little government more than realised the wish of wisdom in directing the entertainment as well as the instruction and promotion of his charge? With all the improvements of Parliaments, Departments, and Boards they will not look upon his like again. The one old order that never gives place to the new is the touch of Nature that makes the whole world kin, nowhere so effective, so potent, as in the world of school, whether it proceeds from the blossoming of the rod or the fruitful sympathy of the master's love. The presentation of a valuable microscope was a very grateful and suggestive *finale* to such a long term of noble service. There are few records of public duty that will better bear microscopic investigation than that of a painstaking, conscientious teacher, who has had the disciplining and enlightenment of quite a crowd of children of adversity. To feed a multitude with the barley loaves and small fishes of a charitable endowment in the dark days when ever so little learning was thought a dangerous thing for the lower orders, and the poor teacher had to depend entirely on his own resources; no staff of teachers; no public interest shown in his work. The men whose forlorn boyhood found shelter, sympathy, and guidance in these dark days, in the Jubilee School under Mr. Haswell, may well rise up and call him blessed in his retirement. When they hung up their caps on the Jubilee pegs, they had the shortest possible time to pick up the crumbs of knowledge that were then thought sufficient for all who had to serve. It was of the utmost importance to them that the crumbs should be true bread, given with a relish and sustaining sympathy,— found after many days to have nourished an intelligent, honourable, and prosperous manhood When you multiply the possibilities of such years of culture among the thousands of boys who rapidly passed through the ranks of the Jubilee, the more powerful the lens under which you place them, the truer will be your estimate of the value of the services just brought to such an honourable close at the Jubilee School For those who remember the old days, it was impossible not to contrast with satisfaction the clear-eyed, smiling faces of the well-fed lads, comfortably clothed, who gave the parting cheers on Thursday, with the pinched and poorly clad orphans of the sea who in the early foundation filled the school. We may well congratulate our boys on the multiplication of the friends of education The State and the nation, departments, boards, and voluntary school federations clamouring for their suffrages, and eagerly competing for the honour of coaching them into the wonderland of knowledge. But let them never forget that with all their advantages they are still largely dependent on the personal character and tact of their teacher. He must be one whose labour of love can awaken 'the instinct in the human heart,' the master key of knowledge, reverence."

For more than forty years in the wilderness of popular indifference; from the days of the men who took children in "to bate", of him whose only qualification was that he was lame and therefore unfitted for earning a livelihood in any other way; through long decades of neglect and contempt down to the dawn of the School Board system, when Birmingham gentlemen baited the educator amid cries of laughter, the old Maister's career carried him to the Pisgah from which he might see the Promised Land for young England. Had he lived a year or two longer he might have witnessed *Free Education* made one of the charters of our country. He might have read how a French Minister of Education had requested all *Prefects* to send in the names of schoolmasters—to what end let Monsieur Bourgoise answer in his circular.[1] "You may have thought it out of order, perhaps, to propose a schoolmaster, notwithstanding any merit, while officers of the Education Department placed above them, and in constant communication with them, were not decorated I do not think that the consideration should have an absolute influence over your choice. A director of a Board School, even though without high university degrees, who has displayed constant devotion to his duty up to the end of his career, and whose life has been exemplary, has acquired a worthy record for the Legion of Honour."[2] He might have read an utterance which would have given him even higher gratification. Monsieur Pasteur, speaking on his seventieth birthday, December 1892, to the delegates of the foreign learned bodies deputed to do him honour, said·—"Their presence filled his heart with joy, for his belief in peace and science was invincible, and he looked forward with unshakable faith to their overcoming ignorance and war. The people of this world would end by understanding each other, and would form alliances, not to destroy, but to build up and to heal. The future was to those who were doing most for suffering humanity"

．　　．　　．　　．　　．　　．　　．

"Well, then," he writes, December 28th, 1886, "we move off for good and all *to-morrow*, and will sleep no more in the 'old house at home.' One can hardly realise it."

There was a pathos in this parting from the dear old home, which was all the more touching for the simple spirit of patient resignation with which he spoke of it. The house whither he took his newly-married wife, in which his children were born, and nurtured in music; the home so full of life and vigour and tunefulness, to which generations of townsfolk had come in their youth or manhood as pupils;

---

[1] August 1892.

[2] In the course of the summer of 1887 the School Board notified the veteran that the Education Department had been pleased to award him a pension of £30 a year, and that they also had returned his certificate raised to the first-class—the highest granted under any circumstances. It was found that, at the time of his retirement, he was the oldest schoolmaster in the kingdom in active service.

where his wife died, and his children one by one parted from him to go their several ways.

The old home was gone, and he had taken his last look through the west window, whither for fifty years he had day by day gone to watch the glory of the sunset.

THE MAISTER AND ASSISTANTS.

CHAPTER X.

VALE.

"*December 27th,* 1886.

Y DEAR HASWELL,—It was indeed a piece of news to hear that you have retired from the appointment as master of the Jubilee School which you have occupied so honourably for nearly half a century. It was also with much pleasure that I lately read the glowing account of you spoken at the Club, knowing so well that it could not possibly exceed your deserts. You say that on the 8th of December you completed your seventy-ninth year; well, on 6th May next I shall have closed my seventy-eighth, so we are a pair of fogies! When your dear wife 'Tilly' died I felt I had lost one of my best and kindest friends. What your feelings might be I judged by my own sad experience. . . . The 'rest' you so much require is from the monotony of school duties. You must now follow some favourite hobby; your mind will not stagnate any more than mine. I still enjoy quartet playing and have not given up mathematics. I also expect soon to bring out a new edition of my book on Musical Intervals. We join in sending you all the good wishes of the season; so, with a desire for the future to be a better correspondent to a very dear old friend, I remain, ever yours,

"W. S. B. WOOLHOUSE."

School duties had never been monotonous to the Maister, and the rest which began with his eightieth year was devoted to a vigorous pursuit of, not one, but a score of "hobbies." Stagnation could never come to one who always lived a full life, who found pleasure unspeakable in the opportunities now vouchsafed him of bending his whole mind to the contemplation of beauties and wonders from which his busiest avocations had never been able wholly to divorce him.

"You ask [February 1887] if I have found the rest I expected I can truly say I have. After breakfast an hour's reading, then out for an hour's walk—sometimes country way, sometimes to the river or to the sea, then home. After dinner, a pipe; then S—— wheels the sofa round to the fire and I enjoy a nap After tea, three hours' reading. If the evening be fine I go to the Club for a while I am greatly pleased with the microscope, and wish I could have had it twenty or thirty years ago, but then thirty years ago they were neither so good nor so cheap, indeed were quite beyond my reach. Both it and the brother telescope certainly elevate one in a way little else can "

What profound delight the microscope yielded can perhaps be appreciated only by those who have longed vainly through a lifetime for such a possession. Yet the lack of such aids to study was not all loss, for doubtless it helped to develop a power of observation and a capacity for finding in the every-day aspect of common things the profoundest subjects of contemplation, truly remarkable and in all ways valuable. Hobbies lay at hand everywhere, and the busied "rest" of the old man was a never-ending quest. Nor microscope nor telescope were needed for the sympathetic investigation of most of the phenomena and objects on which the studious old eyes were bent. A close, life-long observation of cloud masses yielded a subject of discourse startlingly fascinating to those who, never having more than carelessly heeded what was nevertheless ever open to their eyes, learned what an upper world of beauty they had been insensible to. At the tea-table, the "caustic of reflection" produced by the candle light in a tea cup, or the myriad protean effects of shade and shadow were noted with a quiet ecstasy. A lighted candle was an inexhaustible subject of delightful comment. Strange phenomena of interference and diffraction presented in the gas-lamps of the street, and unwonted freaks produced by irradiation on objects in a room lighted by a shaft of sunlight, were perceived for the first time by those who listened to the old man's talk.

The more obvious beauty of the Aurora, the thunder-storm, the meteoric shower, the sunset, or the snow-storm never failed to receive the watchful devotion of the Maister, but a storm of rain was no less pregnant with significance for him, and he would stand at the window gazing with the deepest absorption at the swirling sheets of water, noting the track of the rain-drops on the panes, and drawing the most unexpected deductions from all he saw. In schooldays he had shown the boys how beautifully Bradley's law of the aberration of light is illustrated in the changing angle at which raindrops course down the window panes of a train which stops and starts at stations not too far apart to allow of the speed being considerably varied in short spaces of time; and this is but one out of an endless variety of parallels he drew from the commonest phenomena. The advent of an eclipse or an occultation of a planet invariably found him in the busiest state of preparation, with a group of his old boys there to share the treat in store. Snow crystals, spiculæ of ice, hoar-frost, hailstones, were again and again examined, and their many exquisite attributes contrasted and compared. He knew the resultant pitch of the surf beating on the shore a mile away at Tynemouth, and had discovered in its variation a certain rather truer than ordinary weather (or storm) lore; hence, on frosty nights he'd go out on to the road and listen bare-headed to the "tone of the sea," noting the presence, or absence, of certain component sounds which betrayed to him coming changes. The booming of the guns of H.M.S. *Castor*, when signalling the Life Brigade to turn out to the aid of some craft in peril, had for him its recognised phases. The most unlooked-for things carried their quota of significance, and the presence of omnipotent Law was not only believed but recognised and known to invest and control and dignify everything manifested to the senses. There was no "bad," or "horrid," or "wretched" weather for such a man—such expressions, indeed, rendered him uneasy; all natural law, all manifestation of law was beautiful to him, and the privilege of being permitted to look on at the unending evolution of natural phenomena was one that yielded a deep and full content.

"Speaking of spring, although I feel an indescribable pleasure at the return of each of the four seasons, still, to see the swelling buds on every hedge, the bursting into life after the sleep—and apparent death—of winter, is a marvellous, an overpowering sight, and yet of the many millions who every year witness it, how many give it a passing thought? Situated and engaged as you are, no microscopical or other work can be so beneficial either to mind or body as your garden. Nor do I think there is, among all the many ways of employing leisure, one so charged with pleasure and benefit as the cultivation of that most beautiful section of nature With me it is different I have not strength for work, but, in my arm-chair, I can sit and admire

"At no time in my long life do I remember being so free from care and anxiety. I go and come and do just as I feel disposed, am in excellent health in every respect, though of course unable to walk far, or quickly."

Notwithstanding which—

"Out this August morning hunting *animalculæ* in a pond near the old pit in Hawkey's Lane. I fear I've not been very successful, but among my prizes are some strange-looking chaps though not numerous."

This animated, vigorous interest in the beauties of nature, of science, of art, and of literature, filled the closing days of the old man's life with a glorious light. He often spoke, with reverent gratitude, of his rich endowment of tastes, through which he was able to drink deep joy with almost every sense, such joy not being mere pleasure, but a lofty exaltation of soul. Whether 'twas a passage from Shakespeare, a phrase from one of the great symphonies, the expression of some great law in astronomy, the sight of a budding tree, or a view of the great placid sea lapping the rocks on the shore, all were profound delights to be paused and pondered over as sermons for all time. The sight of the firmament on a crisp, clear winter's night was to him so overpowering that he could never trust himself to speak of it until some minutes after he had drawn away his eyes from the wondrous pageant.

"I never felt the power of music more intensely than when we played old Corelli. Some of the chords never failed to bring the tears to my eyes, and in one or two cases, where the sub-dominant harmony is taken, it was, to me, almost more than I could bear, and as nearly painful as could be."

This mysterious kinship of deep pleasure and pain is perhaps more readily recognised by musicians than by any other class of men, though it is one with the storm of acute emotion that sweeps through the deeper recesses of human consciousness when a pregnant phrase from some great poet assumes a new meaning. He often said he wondered how vocalists could control their voices when taking part in some of the sublimer choruses of the great writers, and declared that when at the great triennial Handel festival, as one of the choir, he dared scarcely open his lips throughout the performance.

[May 1888.] "I enjoy the sight of flowers more and more the longer I live. . . . The ordinary garden flowers seem to me more marvellously beautiful every year. . . . The world of vegetation is indeed delightful to behold just now; your garden, I suppose, must be Eden itself. No trees of evil—no serpent—all good."

[July 1888.] "The School Board has commenced to pull down the old house, our old home. I wonder if the beautiful sycamore could be removed to your garden? It would be an interesting souvenir, for I planted it myself, though I don't remember the date, but I much doubt whether it could be successfully moved."

A souvenir, truly! Hundreds, nay thousands of boys had been taught to see and note the beauty displayed year by year in the swelling buds, the falling away of the silken bud cases, the exquisite folding of the new leaves, the venation, the colour changes in spring and summer; the splendour of the autumn tinting, and the wonder of the deciduous throwing-off. How often the lads left their play when they saw the Maister standing motionless, deep in study of the little world of wonders in that one remnant of the school garden, and stole up to hear what might fall from his lips.

"I am afraid," he writes a few days later, "it will be impossible to preserve the tree from destruction. It is now surrounded with bricks and lime, and must soon be killed."

A like fate, about the same time, overtook the great three-feet globe. It was left in the school-room exposed to damage while structural alterations to the buildings were being carried on, and was found by the late master—who went to look for it—half buried in brick dust, lime, and plaster. "I went down to the old school, and found the globe standing in one of the class-rooms. It has been rendered useless for geography, as the whole of the surface is defaced."

In the eyes of the old man this reckless destruction of a fine instrument was but typical of the reactionary change which had set in with the newer education; and it grieved him bitterly to note how little any one cared. His expostulations were undoubtedly unintelligible, even to those who listened to him with respect. "Was there not an abundance of beautiful maps, crammed full of data, and covered with topographical facts? No globe could possibly show them, whereas in the first page or two of any geography, or school atlas, might be found all the necessary information about the globe." He remembered how painfully he had struggled to save the needed shillings to acquire the apparatus that had been so fruitfully used among his boys, yet here was an instrument, the possibility of purchasing which would have been beyond the wildest dreams of his youth, thrown carelessly aside as a worthless toy.

"In such matters we are little better than Hottentots." Presently a quiet smile spread over his face as he remarked that he had, that morning, come across some of his friends smoking glass to look at the eclipse, "a lunar one!" he added softly, with a chuckle following like a note of admiration.

Much time was now spent in superintending courses of reading for such of the boys as sought his counsel, who, sitting at the side of his arm-chair, noted down the discriminating observations that each suggested book prompted. Assistant-masters and pupil-teachers, working for an examination, came in the evening to have some difficulty in physics or astronomy made clear, or to be coached in the mysteries of the theory of music. The course of reading was selected from a wide range of books, the "hundred best books" notion being scouted as the absurdest and most mischievous of "cranks," its limitations, as exemplified in the lists recommended by the "authorities" who were foolish enough to pen them, being pointed out to the student with the nearest approach to scorn that the Maister could command. His own bent in these latter days was for scientific reading, and his delight in such books as Darwin's then recently-published monograph on Earth Worms knew no bounds. Some of the lady writers on science were also affording him a new interest.

[December 1887.] "When I was a young man, your grandmother presented me with a copy of Mrs Marcet's *Conversations in Chemistry* in two volumes, which interested me immensely. This was the first lady's book on scientific subjects I ever read. Long after, I read Miss Somerville with pleasure and profit, and now you send me Miss A. Clerke's book on Astronomy. It is a wonderful book, full of wonderful corrections of long-standing errors. She must be a marvellous woman. I should like to see her and hear her speak."

A month later.—

"Miss Clerke continues to amaze and delight me. I think I told you I would like to see her and hear her speak . . . So old Sirius has a companion! It makes one look at the wonderful giant with increased interest. He is blazing away every evening in front of the house. I was not aware that Darwin had a son an astronomer,—am glad to hear it though. Proctor's new book will be a great treat." [1]

The lamentable death of Richard A. Proctor in America was a great and lasting grief to the old man, who had long followed the career of that extraordinary genius with the deepest admiration; and the sudden quenching of such a light touched him greatly.

[1] *Old and New Astronomy.*

"I was shocked to hear of the death of that truly great man—indeed, for several days I searched the newspapers for some contradiction of the report, for I could not bring my mind to believe in a loss to civilisation so great and—apparently—unmeaning as his untimely death. To me it is a perpetual charm to read his books, so free are they from vanity and 'bounce,'—but he is gone, and the world is the loser."

[December 1888.] "'Thomas Huxley' turned up here last Saturday, and since then has kept me busy as a certain personage is said to be when it blows hard. Same day I stumbled across Edington at the Free Library, and he immediately began to talk about 'The Music of the Waters' by Miss Laura A. Smith,—and with Edington anything about sailors puts all else out of court. And I had scarcely got home when the 'Chanties' arrived, so I have been sol-fa-ing sailors' songs, etc, and following Huxley through his three hypotheses,—certainly two very different subjects. Nevertheless, I have enjoyed both books immensely. The *Ice Age* I have of course read much about, but of the *cause* of it never a line. The title of Dr. Ball's lecture implied that Jupiter and Venus were, jointly, the cause. I must confess I cannot by any arrangement of the perturbations of the two planets—one *out*side the earth's orbit, the other *in*side—produce such a result; but doubtless Ball is right. If you chance to lay your hand on any printed matter relating to the matter, I should like to see it. Huxley is a rare man!—so too is Tyndall, Ball, and others, but none of greater magnitude than he whose light suddenly and unexpectedly set in America lately. I hope some one will give the world some account of his valuable life."

The concurrent study of Huxley's "three hypotheses" and the sailors' chanties fairly typifies the many-sided, well-balanced temperament of the man. He had no touch of pessimism in his nature, though no one ever contemplated more closely or sympathetically the suffering spread so widely over whole classes of men and throughout the animal creation. His sense of humour—a humour that could never be induced to wound—was perhaps the quality that first impressed those who came to know him, as it was also the one that his oldest friends invariably referred to. Woolhouse, in his own whimsical way, had often referred to the "importance of nonsense" which was his manner of expressing a conviction in the absolute necessity for systematic relaxation, but the Maister's humour always touched one's sensibilities in the very quick and left one laughing while wondering why one was not crying. He loved to stand by a group of lads playing on the roadway and presently be invited—as never failed—to join in the game. Whether 'twas to spin a top, or shoot an alley taw—knuckle down—he could delight the boys by doing as well as the best, while he made them roar at some droll comment on the game or the players. No boy could half so well as he fly a kite, or make so much out of a toy. His interest in young children and their ways was inexhaustible and altogether delightful, and a gentle spirit of playfulness broke out whenever he was among them.

Writing of a rather masterful infant grandson—his namesake, and seventh in the family—in whom he took much interest, and of whose mischievous doings he had been receiving some account, he says—

"As to that Dominant Seventh, Thomas Sydney, although a discord, he must be a sweet discord—a regular *dominant seventh* in the family, not to be dispensed with under any circumstances where good harmony is wanted. I should much have liked to look into the little man's face on the rising of the curtain" (at the Pantomime), "to have witnessed the effect of the wonders working for the first time inside the young *cranium*. The spectacle seems to have paralysed his very tongue; and no wonder, when we remember the startling effect produced on 'older heads.' W—— is pegging away among his music-murderers" (pupils).

The departure of another grandson for school in Germany at once by association causes the mind to flash back to the early days of the air-pump experiments.

"So you have left Fred in the town where the 'exhausted hemispheres' could not be separated by the united efforts of two strong cart horses—Magdeburg! Well, I suppose his poor little heart would swell up and fill when the moment came for saying 'good-bye.' It is no small matter for one so young to be left among strangers in a foreign land."

A year later,—

"In a short time Fred the Exile will have completed half his sentence. I hope his larynx will not be injured by having so many gutturals crammed down his *trachea* for two long years. You see I am dealing in scientific terms—explained at once when I tell you I am reading Morell Mackenzie's book on *Frederick the Noble*. Ball lectured in Newcastle lately on Jupiter and Venus as the cause of the Ice Age. Not one of the newspapers reported a line of it!"

[March 1888] "I am answering your last long letter. Did you see old Etna's smoke, and his chum Vesuvius? Were they having a quiet pipe over the old Emperor William's *quietus*? I see the papers say he is laid out, dressed as a general of the army! Is this done to please the old man's ghost? for when alive he was a true blood-and-iron worshipper."

Customs and observances like these, he said, were now only to be found among the crowned heads of Christian States and African savages.

[Aug. 1888] "See what I got from Woolhouse the other day —

"'My dear Haswell,—. . By-the-bye I have completed the new edition of my book on *Musical Intervals, Temperament, and the Elementary Principles of Music* It is now in the printer's hands, and I expect will be out before many weeks. I have scrawled you out a copy of the preface,[1] so that you may form some idea what it will be like. You will see that your conversations with me on musical matters, in our boyhood have been like bread cast upon the waters. Had it not been for those discussions I do not think the book would ever have been in existence, and sometimes it occurs to me that I have made a good thing of it. If that be really the case you will not, I hope, protest against the use of your valued name. Your highness should have been mentioned in the first edition, as originally intended, but this was forgotten until it was too late.—Yours very very truly,   'W. S. B WOOLHOUSE.'"

"I question much," writes the dominie, after getting the book, "whether there is another man in all England who could produce such a work, musical and mathematical."

But notwithstanding all the alert, animated, cheery interest in life's affairs, all the busy pursuit of hobbies, and the tranquil enjoyment of the humorous, the vigorous physique was now giving way, the old man quietly contemplating the process with all the complacency of an experimental chemist watching the slow settling down of a precipitate.

"I was awakened last Monday, about 7 A M, with a sharp spasm of pain in my left side, which compelled me to sit up and rest upon my elbow. Just where the pain was there was a sensation of cold as though a piece of ice were lying there. A cup of tea somewhat relieved the pain, but the ice remained all day, so, lest I might have it throughout the night, I sent for the doctor. After one or two doses out of a large spoon like a ladle (it must have been from the river Styx—the dose, not the ladle—so delightful was it), the pain fled in dismay, and the piece of ice with it, at any rate I have felt neither of them since Perhaps the happy facial expression during my performance with the ladle may have had some effect in putting them to rout. I once saw a poor fellow take a dose of 'laughing gas' at the old Mechanics' Institute, but I don't think my expression much resembled his."

The suffering, however, had been great, but with characteristic unselfishness he made light of it to avoid alarming his family The

---

[1] *Vide* page 256.

end was, however, foreshadowing itself in letters to follow. Old chums, too, were fast dropping away, all round.

"One of the 1826 band died yesterday, leaving only Robert Hill and myself. Did I tell you in my last of the death of my old playfellow George Frazer? He and I in the summer time used to have my father's boat and sails on Saturday afternoons to go where we liked, sometimes to sea, to the Haven, Jarrow Slake, or to cruise about the river; I captain, and he mate. We seldom had a crew, not needing one. He was six months older than the captain; both rated A.B.

"I hear you've been to Liverpool—

> 'Sally's gone to Liverpool,
> Sing, Sally, ho!'

I remember the 'chanty' being sung on the Tyne when timber-laden ships were discharging I myself—as the grammars say—am *in statu quo:* hearing and weakness of heart action in the same case But I may say with Whittier—

> 'Age brings me no despairing
> Of the world's future faring,
> In human nature still
> I find more good than ill'"

The portrait referred to later in connection with the memorial proceedings, was painted about this time, and an article in the local press runs thus:—

"'Portrait of Mr. Thomas Haswell in the eighty-first year of his age, forty-seven years master of the Royal Jubilee School, from 1839 to 1886.' Such is the inscription on the latest production of our clever and faithful limner, Mr. James Shotton, who has never done anything more acceptable to a wide circle. Even to those who do not know Mr. Haswell, that forty-seven years' masterly occupation of our wild garden of human culture, in the long-continued winter of educational apathy, will establish an immediate interest in his presentment as he lived and influenced so strongly the lives of others With all our dependence on Acts of Parliament and control of Departments and Boards, there is still sufficient sense and manliness left in us to recognise the preciousness of the strong hand, firm will, and clear insight of individual character, in the guide or governor of every little band of human hope, and in that final payment on results, heralded by the 'Well done, good and faithful servant,' we cherish the belief that many a poor dominie, who discharged his thankless duty for a crust and churlish thanks, in the days when the ark was abuilding, will have a rare balance at the fountain of honour But nobody can look at the face of the 'Maister,' as friends and pupils, synonymous, delighted to call him, without recognising that his work has been its own exceeding great reward; a labour of love, wrought with conscious enjoyment, the glow of life still shining through the burden of four score years To those who know the circumstances and the conditions of his long service, it will be a matter of wonder how he could get any glow out of it. For the salary we now give to pupil-teachers, he had to graft the wild olive plants of the neglected population on to the tree of knowledge, under every disadvantage, in the briefest period; passing the most of them in the wise standards of those times, practical usefulness to their generation, happiness and contentment in their lot of life Many and many a one (A1) of them came back in after years, with their diplomas of good citizenship, able seamen, to thank him for the schooling That was the silver streak in their grey dawn of life. He had given them sufficient possession of the three R's to ensure the three S's of success We all know that the charter of the Royal Jubilee School was the desire of the Royal George that every child in the kingdom should be able to read the Scriptures. Our Maister carried the foundation further. He taught them to sing the Psalms as well as read the lessons of the day; made them beneficiaries under the will of the Royal David as well as the Royal George, and softened the hard lines of their lives with the sense of melody and the solace of song, a contribution to the education of the people that was not confined to his school. Many a dreary winter has been enlivened by his efforts at concert and conversazione, many a local movement benefited by his zeal and genius, for his musical gifts are not unworthy of that high stamp. There are passages in his setting of some local themes that the greatest masters might be proud of; passages of thorough harmony that cling to the memory, a joy for ever I hope many of our citizens and old scholars of the Jubilee will give themselves the pleasure of looking on this admirable work of Mr. Shotton, a result of art and friendship of special value, and, looking into the familiar face once more, greet with well-deserved acknowledgment one who has done his best to help us onward and to cheer the way. From the records of the school they may learn that an aggregate of six thousand lads came under the moulding of the master, many of them most forlorn in the time of their greatest need. How their lives were brightened, heightened and mellowed by the touch of nature that made them all akin is known to hundreds of grateful admirers " [1]

The love of natural beauty is still warm [March 1889]—

" We are in arctic conditions again, the snow lying six to eight inches deep—in some places 'deeper and deeper still'. yet it is fine and sunny. This morning, my bedroom window, which faces the north, presented a sight of marvellous beauty. The lower sash consists of two large

---

[1] *Shields Daily News*, September 24th, 1888

squares of glass, one of which looked like ground glass, but on close examination proved to be covered with a fine arborescent coat, of infinite delicacy and minuteness—such indeed as I had never before seen, though often enough on a larger scale. But, strange to say, the other square exhibited what I never before saw or even read or heard of. There was no arborescence, no branching, but innumerable rigidly straight lines, some short, others longer—say from quarter to an inch and a half, all of them parallel and, long and short, crossed at right angles by other lines about one-third of their length. No language can describe the beauty and delicacy of the whole. The lines seemed straighter than straight—the cross lines more perpendicular than perpendicular. There had not been a breath of wind all night, and I suppose Mr. Jack Frost had been allowed, undisturbed, to play his beautiful pranks to his heart's content, the difference in the two squares could not have otherwise arisen. What does Sydney think of snow?"

"The fine weather" [March 1889] "brought an enormous number of people to Tynemouth on Good Friday and Easter. The warm sun, smooth sea, and no wind, made it very enjoyable, but I cannot take long walks. One hour on my legs is as much as I can manage, then I lie down on the sofa for a half-hour and get up like a giant refreshed. Be sure and take *rest;* continuous toil is not fit for man *or his ancestor.*"

[April 1889.] "I am really very well and enjoy my fireside and my books, but am exceedingly feeble and have to throw myself on the sofa for half-an-hour. This gives me a little strength, and I go on again as before. My heart is now becoming very weak, and the chambers of that wonderful force-pump must be getting thin! Presently they will become too feeble for their ceaseless work—when, some day, I shall be popping off without saying 'Good-bye,' just as my own father left us. But this is better than lying on a bed of sickness and pain perhaps for weeks, with people moping about asking 'How are you?' I have nearly finished Proctor's *Other Worlds*. It has delighted me, and I am a large gainer by its perusal. And now I am tired and must say 'God bless you all.'"

Now came the last of the long series of letters—which commenced in 1829—from his friend Woolhouse:—

"The 'Musical Intervals' has had a favourable reception, and is well spoken of, as you will see from the enclosed slip. I hope you are quite well. We have now become two old boys, and no mistake. It is a very long time since we *hurled our gairds with the new jinglers on*. I still go on with quartet playing, and shall be leading to-morrow night, when it is proposed to do No. 10, Beethoven, among others."

In April 1889 the Jubilee School, which had to all intents and purposes been re-built and refitted "in the most approved modern style," was re-opened, and the old Maister was invited to be present at the ceremonial. He was, however, unequal to the demand on his strength, and had to decline.

The physical weakness was now such that he could not venture to walk to any of his favourite haunts, but the invincible spirit of interest in his fellow-men broke through all infirmities. The love of fresh air and of human faces was paramount, and he probably derived a short term of lengthened life from seeking them daily, while the weather was such as to permit his doing so. But it was only on fine sunny days that the old Maister was now seen out of doors. In his bath-chair he made his lessening circuit among the beauties of nature and the society of old friends—full of kindly interest, in every human being he saw—

"I have been out this morning," he writes on Midsummer-day, "for an hour and a half, and very much enjoyed the ride. One of my scholars is the motive-power, and I steer myself without a compass. Being a wooden vessel there is no local magnetic attraction. My first voyage was to the School Board offices to see Lambton, and he kindly came down to speak to me."

This expedition was an endeavour to rescue the "great globe" from final destruction.

"During this beautiful weather I get out twice every day for an hour and a half each time, and thoroughly enjoy the ride. Around by Preston, the sea banks, a look from the bank top at the busy scene on the Fish Quay, Chirton, Hawkey's Lane, and all over the town, or to Tom Hudson's garden. Thanks to the salt water irrigation, the roads are as smooth and as hard as concrete, thus allowing gentlemen to take a daily drive in their 'carriage.' The 'chair' has been a great success."

Down among the captains, pilots, owners, steam-boatmen, and trawlers, near the lighthouse overlooking the river, or on the Library "flags," nothing was more welcome than the sight of the venerable white head leaning forward in the bath-chair, cracking a joke with a purple-faced Nor' Sea pilot, or teasing the old seamen as to their leaky and unseaworthy weather-lore which cannot stand the stress of five minutes' criticism.

"The wind's aal west, Mr. Hasss-w'll, but 'twill be mair westerly yit, sur! 'Twill, noo! Ya didn't see th' moon las' neet sailin' on hor back 's *aa* did."

"The moon on her *back!* Bah! nonsense; you know nothing about it".

"Well, but—noo—look here, Mr Hasss——"

"Is NO use, *J'orge*," urge the others, plunging their big hands deeper into the deep trousers pockets and fondling themselves for mere enjoyment of the discussion, "NO use, J'orge; he's too much for you"

Foot-sore wayfarers and tramps stop at a call from the old man in the "chair," and look surprised at hearing themselves gently spoken to. The onion vendors from the French sloop know the face of the Maister and pause to answer a question or two in their rude *patois*. Fisherwomen, staggering along under the heavy creel, stop to ask in shrill, healthy treble, how the old man is, and boys everywhere run up to catch a smile.

But infirmity comes on apace, and late in the autumn the chair makes its last voyage.

"Your visit to the seaside would help you to fight our dangerous climate during the winter and spring months. It is more than I expect to accomplish myself, for very little would finish me now; but that is just what may be looked for in my case, and I am not afraid of the end, come when it may"

It came not long after. The last letter was written, October 30th, 1889, after a period of partial heart-failure

"I am glad to be able to sit up and write you a line or two myself, for I know it will do you good to know that I am strong enough to do so. I have suffered a great deal lately, and have wished for God . . . who has the ordering of these things to bring me my end, for I am only giving labour and trouble to those about me. . . . I am far from well, though much better than I was. I suppose my end cannot be far off now, nor would I wish it to be, for I have had my full share of life and health. I have no fears for what comes after death.

"When you come over at the finish I know you will not permit any superstitious extravagance or expense. Have none but yourselves present—none but yourselves to consult. I hope the young ones are well,—and the little pet. You will then be the *father* of the flock, and will be willing to give your best advice for their welfare and good. I am now tired and must take a turn on the sofa for a sleep. God bless you all."

.   .   .   .

At length, early in the afternoon of Sunday, the 8th of December 1889, his eighty-second birthday, the patient soul of the Maister broke away During the last few hours of his life he rambled, in semi-consciousness, back to the busy scene of his beloved life-work, and that he was again among his "boys," there can be no doubt.

For in the lessening intervals that lay between periods of total unconsciousness the old passion rallied, and in whispered sentences, carrying all the old intent, diligent earnestness, the work of the school was urged on.

When, finally, the end was at hand, he was heard to repeat as his last mortal utterance the words that for near a half century had been, each evening, the closing formula of the day's work—"*Slates away, boys.*"

. . . .

Round his yet unclosed grave, whither he had been followed by a long procession spontaneously formed—among the many who had gathered to pay a last tribute of affection stood men, stricken in years, who had been among his earlier "boys"; others, not so old, but with the silvery touch of life's winter already on them; younger men, too, who had known him only as the "old" Maister, and, what would most have pleased him, some poor women and children.

. . . .

So ends the story of the Maister's life and work. To the profound question, "What have I done with life?" and the still deeper one, "What were the impulses moving me to do what I have done?" (a tremendous test that every man, when looking back across life's twilight, must perforce apply to himself)—the response not seldom must be, that though great things may have been accomplished, they were but incidental to a course directed in the main to self-aggrandisement, "self," maybe, including its common *alter ego*, one's family

But, as touching Thomas Haswell, the answer is that he did his life-work with whole heart, for its own sake and for what it enabled him to do for others.

With capacity and attainments which, applied solely or mainly to the business of "getting on in the world," must surely have won for him what is called a "position," he had other views as to their fitting use One of his earlier pupils, himself an accomplished teacher, wrote of him, "As an educationalist he stood prominent, and thousands, if only by their own success in life, can bear testimony to this" But it was something worthier, greater, higher than what is commonly termed success in life that he strove to secure for his lowly *protégés*. "Why did not some one teach me the stars?" cried out Carlyle, in that one pregnant phrase arraigning the educationalists of his day for deliberate and contemptuous neglect of one of the most precious longings of youth. But the Maister was by very nature incapable of this blunder. Success in life, by all means, but no exclusive or main devotion of life to "success!"

He taught his boys the stars, as he taught them all the fruitful wonders he had been able to wrest from scant opportunity, to sweeten and dignify their lives; knowing full well that the surest warranty for a truly noble life is to be found in the health of a well-ordered, well-trained mind, chastened by devout recognition of the tremendous possibilities of evil and wrong flowing from ignorance. He believed, and believed he *knew* Knowledge to be "the wing on which we fly to Heaven", but the shamefullest ignorance, he thought, was the ignorance of the "learned" as to the great universe, which offers to man a study at once the most dignifying and the most humbling. "He," said Dr. Johnson, "who enlarges his curiosity after the works of Nature demonstrably multiplies the inlets to his happiness." But the "happiness" of the student, the Maister held, is not the main end to be sought, nor curiosity the legitimate incentive. The study of Nature was, with him, an act of devotion, of worship. He believed it enlarged the sympathies, widened the avenues of universal pity for the hapless creatures who, after all, are our fellow-beings in the great mysterious scheme, sobered men's ambition, chastened their arrogance and vanity, and enabled all to see, with somewhat truer parallax, however little, the real universe by which we are surrounded.

So far, then, from holding any terms with the whining school which asks "is Life worth living?" he regarded life as infinitely too precious a thing to be wasted on the arid struggle for place or preferment. Tender, always, with children, compassionate with the poorest and most wretched of the destitute, amiable and trusty with friends, and courteous to everybody, he had no obeisance to make to mere rank or wealth, indeed, the sentiment of deference to either was one he very evidently could not comprehend, though he often expressed a sincere sentiment of pity for men who, in making themselves rich, had lost for ever the opportunity of drinking from the fresh, eternal springs of Knowledge.

A beautiful modesty was blended with a perfect manly dignity; and a chivalrous hatred of cruelty and wrong, which never shirked an issue however unpleasant, with a wide and tender sympathy for those who erred through ignorance or evil example. "Look at the shape of his skull—at his face," he would say, half in awe, half in pity, as some poor wrong-doer was brought up for punishment. "Try to get behind those eyes of his and peer out with his poor, distorted sense of vision,—should *we* do a whit better?"

On the hot, breathless race for wealth, in which the whole life of so many is lived, for which the high duty of bringing one's nature in touch with the great works of God is thrown aside, or at best relegated to the jaded and preoccupied intervals of so-called leisure, this man deliberately turned his back, and to the praise of culture gave his whole soul; as, in the devout investigation of the wholly wondrous mysteries of creation, he devoted himself to the true worship of its Almighty Architect.

"He instilled light, and music, and the elements of a well-ordered life" into the poor wastrels who were his special charge, and in giving to them all he had been able himself to acquire, thought he was doing his highest duty.

TYNEMOUTH ABBEY.

CHAPTER XI.

IN MEMORIAM.

HE story of the Maister's life is perhaps most fitly rounded-off by some account of the ways and means through which his fellow-townsmen sought to perpetuate his memory. At his death a general expression of affectionate regard and admiration spontaneously appeared in north-country newspapers, followed presently by suggestions from old scholars and others that the old man's example and influence should have some permanent recognition, helpful, if possible, to the cause of popular education.

"Our community is poorer to-day," says the *Shields Daily News*, "by the loss of an old and true friend, who in a long life did the people most excellent service, at a time of peculiar need, in the thorny path of toil, when the light was low, and the stress of circumstances most contrary to the acquisition of knowledge. It was a jubilee year for the lads of the low streets when Thomas Haswell took charge of the Jubilee School and devoted himself to instilling into them light and music, and the elements of a well-ordered life; something more than mere rudiments of knowledge, understanding of the discipline and duties of their existence. Independent of codes and official standards, he was a born trainer and moulder of youth, influencing the heart as well as the intellect of his pupils, and having his reward in troops of friends in all ranks of life who were proud to call him master, and come back after many days, anxious to do him honour. On his eighty-second birthday he threw off the infirmities of age and entered into rest, honoured and loved by all who knew him."

"The large company that yesterday surrounded the grave where the late Mr. Haswell was laid to his last rest, paying a final tribute to his worth, would by no means exhaust the number of the admirers of the deceased teacher. In north, south, east, and west, wherever the enterprise of English commerce can take the sons of Tyne, a sympathising thrill will be felt by one and another now bearing their part in the busy world, who are all the more fitted to do so by the instruction of the 'guide, philosopher, and friend' who now rests from his labours in Preston Cemetery. There was a touch of peculiar sadness given to the occasion as one looked upon the schoolfellows of bygone days, and called to remembrance many an incident of boyhood, when lessons were more a pleasure than a task under the wise direction of him whose life's lesson is now over; who, even in his death, teaches us the one more lesson that to us all there must come 'the inevitable close.' It was touching to see the grand old man, in the later months of his life, before his last illness, being wheeled about among familiar scenes, and seeming not unlike the 'ruin hoary' of which he sang so sweetly, as at eventide it falls into the shadows. He has left us richer by a number of tuneful lyrics, and, in one church in the borough at least, some of the hymns sung have an added beauty lent to them by the charming setting he gave them. Of him it may truly be said that he has left the world better than he found it, for the beneficial influence of his life's work will be felt over a wide circle in years to come. The ripe age at which he was gathered to his fathers takes the edge from the grief felt at his death, but all the same the company turned away from his grave with feelings that were strangely stirred And from many a point all over the globe, when tidings of Mr. Haswell's decease shall reach them, wanderers from the banks of our river will look back on days that are gone, and think of the cliffs 'where yon Abbey ruin stands hoary,' and of that God's acre at Preston where winter winds are now sighing among the trees, 'and the dead in silence sleep'

. . . .

"To the late Thomas Haswell we are vastly indebted for our present position in musical culture. For many years in North Shields it was scarcely possible to be jubilant in tune without the aid of the master of the Jubilee, whose well-earned leisure was given up ungrudgingly to classes, practice, and rehearsals, and the worrying diplomacy of getting up concerts, to which he contributed not only his acquired skill with instrument or conduct, and his original gift of composition, but devoted his accomplished family; and though we now stand in a crowd of instrumental and vocal proficients, the true ear turns back with infinite relish to the memories of the twopenny concerts in the old George Tavern days, and the Christmas entertainments of the Tradesmen and Mechanics' Institute. He is indeed a benefactor who not only weds our choice words to lovely airs, but also sets his generation to music in the business of life"

AN OLD PUPIL.

"Uncle Toby," of the *Newcastle Weekly Chronicle*, writes —

"A north-country worthy of the highest character has lately departed this life at North Shields. I allude to Mr Thomas Haswell, head-master for nearly fifty years of the Royal Jubilee Schools in that town. It was my good fortune to have the honour of Mr. Haswell's acquaintance. A more genuine, upright, amiable man than he was I never wish to meet; nor, indeed, ever shall meet. But Mr. Haswell was more than merely gentle and kind—he was a man of rare gifts as well. An accomplished musician, well versed in the sciences, and a skilful and successful teacher of the young, he has left a mark in North Shields that will not speedily be erased. An old pupil of his, Mr. John J. Sharp, bears witness to Mr. Haswell's many excellencies in a letter to the *Shields Daily News*.

"'SIR,—As an old pupil of the late Mr. Thomas Haswell, would you allow me to make the following communication to your paper concerning the said gentleman, by whose death our town has been deprived of one who has done almost more for its moral and intellectual well-being than any other person. Mr. Haswell served his apprenticeship as a house-painter, but his genius caused him to direct his powers elsewhere, and a school being opened in South Shields for the mental improvement of those who desired to become teachers, he availed himself of the opportunity, and in a very short time had completed the whole school curriculum. At the close of this course of instruction Mr Haswell was appointed master of a small school in South Shields; but a few weeks after his appointment an advertisement appeared for a head-master for the Royal Jubilee School, North Shields, and after pressure had been brought to bear upon him by his friends, he was induced to make application for the situation. Mr. Haswell was the chosen person, and during the service of nearly fifty years the committee never had cause to regret their choice. He was a born teacher, and, being unfettered by code regulations, he adapted his instruction to the needs of the day. He certainly taught the three R's, but he taught much more, for under him we learned both the sciences and the fine arts. His own attainments were of the broadest character, and consisted not of mere book work, but of practical application, and his immense learning he transmitted to his pupils. He was the possessor of such a stock of scientific apparatus as would have done credit to the laboratory of a professor, and there was no single piece but what he could effectively make use of in giving his instruction. Many is the enjoyable afternoon his pupils have spent when he brought into the school his electrical machines, and had a half-day of experiment and instruction in that important science, or when he brought out the terrestrial and celestial globes and telescope, and gave an exposition of the starry firmament. He saw a beauty in every object of nature, and he had a wonderful propensity for making others see and feel that beauty also. Many a time he could be seen surrounded by a crowd of boys, whose looks showed the keenest interest while he expounded the wonders and beauties of a beetle, a butterfly, or a flower. Indeed, with him as a teacher, the dull monotony of school work gave place to the keenest delights that can be got from learning. Nor did he neglect the physical education of those under his charge, for he not only encouraged the boys in their games, but he became as one of them, and joined in their athletic exercises. When the weather was fine he would occasionally take out the whole of the pupils for a walk, and after giving short lessons on the objects of interest on the way, the afternoon was spent in racing, bathing, or some other way by which the bodies were developed and the minds clarified. Indeed, his aim in dealing with children was to produce the *mens sana in corpore sano*, and he did not fail in that aim. As a musician Mr Haswell also held a high place, beginning as a choir-boy in Christ Church, then being organist in the same place, and afterwards a composer of no mean order. He will live in his songs as long as "Tynemouth Abbey" with its associations shall nod over the storm-vexed billow or the silent tide, and when that venerable pile shall fall his name will live in the "Life Brigade" as long as sailors shall roam o'er the deep. He was ever a friend of learning, and sought the companionship of those skilled in the same, with such effect that as a man of general knowledge he had few equals in our midst. In manner he was most kind and affable, and no one could come in contact with him without feeling the deepest respect for him, or without feeling honoured by having had the privilege of holding converse with such a man.

"'Trusting you will find space for the above, and thanking you in anticipation, I remain, yours respectfully, "'JOHN J. SHARP'

"'*December 9th*, 1889.'"

"It was he," wrote the same pupil some week or two after, "who created in me a love for those very sciences . . . The many experiments and observations made by him in my school-days stood me in good stead at my college and university examinations, and enabled me to obtain a first-class in more than one science. Indeed, in astronomy I relied entirely on the information I had got from him, and was enabled thereby to answer every question."

Another old scholar and "old boy of forty years ago" gives in the following letter the first public expression to a desire now becoming general among the Maister's old friends:—

"SIR,—Within the past few days death has taken from your midst a gentleman whose name for over half a century has been a household word among you. I allude to Mr. Thomas Haswell, who for the long period of forty-eight years was master of the Jubilee School. Hitherto Shields has done nothing to perpetuate the memory of any of her famous men, and the resting-places of your dead remain to this day without a public memorial to do honour to those who did honour to the town which gave them birth. Shall it remain always so? Here is a man, than whom none was more worthy, a man whose long life was devoted to every good purpose, and who possibly did more towards the educating of the masses than any teacher in the Northern Counties. In days gone by, before your borough existed, and while your aldermen, and the majority of the members of your common Council were yet unknown to the town, Thomas Haswell stood foremost in every good and charitable work And shall such a man as this remain unhonoured in death? Shall your children and children's children hide their heads in shame when a future generation asks them to point out the resting-place of one of the greatest and best men your town ever gave birth to?'

"As an educationalist Mr. Haswell stood prominent, and thousands, if only by their own success in life, can bear testimony to this

"Oh, sir, the pity of it! To think that a man of such sterling worth should have been permitted to toil and slave for a whole decade after he had passed the threescore years and ten meted out to man!

"In life, hard work and scanty pay was his recompense, then surely in death we can raise to his honoured memory such a memorial as will show to future generations the high estimation in which he was held by his old pupils and fellow-townsmen.

"Much of the little success I have achieved in life was owing to the excellent training I received at his hands, and no doubt many more in various parts of the world can bear the same testimony. I was honoured with his friendship till the last, and only those who knew him can speak of the value of the friendship of such a man

"Sir, I should propose that some of his old pupils still resident in Shields, together with a few of his many friends, should form themselves into a committee, and receive subscriptions for a public memorial to be raised in the Preston Cemetery. I would also suggest the placing of an appropriate tablet in Christ Church, and another in the school wherein he worked so successfully for so many years. I should like to hear from any old boys of forty years ago upon the subject, and shall be pleased when a committee is formed to forward a donation.—I remain, dear sir, faithfully yours, "AN OLD TOWNSMAN

"Flint House, Lowestoft."

The suggestion so thrown out was already taking form among a group of fellow-townsmen, who, convening a meeting of old scholars and friends of the Maister, elected a preliminary committee consisting of "two old personal friends, two former pupils, and two young friends and admirers," and at Vine Cottage, where for so many years the harmonies of the great masters had drawn together the musical worthies of the North—these six prepared the following circular —

"5 BEAUMONT STREET, NORTH SHIELDS

"SIR,—It is proposed to erect a suitable Memorial to the memory of the late Mr Thomas Haswell, who for forty-eight years was Head Master of the Royal Jubilee School in this town, and whose ability and influence during that period tended to raise the moral and intellectual welfare of the Borough to a much higher standpoint than it had previously attained.

"In furtherance of this object the Committee respectfully solicit subscriptions from all friends, old scholars, and admirers, which will be received at the offices of the *Shields Daily News*, the *Shields Daily Gazette*, or by the Honorary Treasurer, Mr. Thomas Hudson, Vine Cottage, North Shields, or by yours respectfully,

"JOHN BURNET, *Hon. Secretary.*"

They next considered a number of suggestions as to the form the memorial should take, and resolved to recommend that a portrait of the Maister be placed on the walls of the Free Library; that a memorial tablet be erected on the front of the Royal Jubilee School, and that, should there be a surplus, it be invested in the names of the Mayor and Corporation of the Borough, the interest or dividends to be annually given as a prize—to be called the "Thomas Haswell Memorial Prize"—to the best scholar in the Royal Jubilee School. "The desire is," they sensibly say, "to make the memorial widely representative and the number rather than the individual amount of the subscriptions the object of their efforts"

At a public meeting in the Town Hall, on January 16th, 1890, the preliminary committee stated that they had met with hearty encouragement, and that they had not the slightest doubt but that they would be able to carry the matter to a successful issue— "always keeping in mind the quiet, dignified, unostentatious character of the man" whose memory they all desired to see honoured.

At a second meeting, held April 18th, 1890, Alderman John Foster Spence, the life-long friend of the Maister, presiding, the committee announced that the subscriptions already received, together with the amount realised from a "Grand Concert and Dramatic Entertainment" held on the 12th March, enabled them to recommend to the subscribers the purchase of a portrait in oils, painted by Mr. James Shotton, for presentation to the Free Library, and the placing of a memorial tablet on the front of the Jubilee

School. The sanction of the School Board for the erection of the tablet had already been obtained, subject to approval of the inscription proposed to be placed upon it. As to this, the committee submitted one which, having been written by the oldest living personal friend of the late Mr. Haswell—Mr. W. S. B. Woolhouse, F.R.A.S.—they trusted would be favourably considered. The balance, it was suggested, should be invested in the names of the Mayor and Corporation or the School Board, by whom a medal should annually be given to the *dux* of the school.

The proposals of the committee were heartily endorsed and adopted by the assembled contributors

At a subsequent meeting, December 3rd, 1890, the Secretary announced that they were there that night with the medal and a draft of the deed,[1] which it was proposed should be executed by the committee and the School Board. The deed had been approved by the general committee of the School Board, and their sanction to the investment of the requisite sum of money had been obtained They had the sanction also of the Controller General of the Post Office Savings Bank Department, which was necessary. The deed having been read and the medal passed round, the following resolutions were carried unanimously:—

"That the committee be and are hereby authorised to invest in the Post Office Savings Bank, in the name of the Borough of Tynemouth School Board, the sum of £20, the interest thereon to be devoted annually to the provision of a memorial medal to be called 'the Thomas Haswell Memorial Medal' in the terms of the deed, and that the committee be empowered to execute such deed on behalf of the subscribers.

"That the portrait of the late Mr. Thomas Haswell be unveiled in the Free Library, North Shields, on Monday, the 8th instant, at 2.30 P.M., by his worship the Mayor of Tynemouth.

"That the first memorial medal be presented at the Royal Jubilee School by the Reverend Father Stark, the Chairman of the Borough of Tynemouth School Board, on the 8th instant, immediately after the unveiling of the portrait."

It had been intended that the tablet should be unveiled on the same day, but an accident in the course of its manufacture necessitated the making of a new one, and the postponement of that feature of the ceremonies.

"The subscribers to the memorial," says the *Shields Daily News*

---

[1] See Appendix B.

of December 6th, 1890, "will be glad to learn that the undertaking has resulted so successfully, and it is only fair to state that the success achieved is in a great measure due to the exertions of Mr. John Burnet, who as Honorary Secretary has spared neither time nor thought to bring the affair to the happy climax it has reached.'

The communication from the School Board to the committee intimating their acceptance of the Trust is as follows:—

"Tynemouth School Board,
Dec. 1st, 1890.

"Dear Sir,
"Thomas Haswell Memorial.

"I have pleasure in appending below a copy of the Resolution recommended by the general committee to be adopted at the Board Meeting on Friday first.

"That the Borough of Tynemouth School Board has the greatest pleasure in accepting the trusteeship of the *Thomas Haswell Memorial*, and thanks the committee and subscribers for the Memorial Medal to be presented annually to the best boy in the Jubilee School.—Yours faithfully, "(Signed) J. W. Lambton, Clerk.
"John E. H. Burnet, Esq, North Shields."

At the meeting of the School Board on the following Friday, the first business was a "discussion on the question of providing a series of concerts to be held in the whole of the schools in connection with the Board," the matter arising out of a letter from one of the head-masters, "stating that the concerts held in his school lately, *for the delectation of the children*, had been attended with a full measure of success." How full of the new spirit which the Maister had spent a lifetime in cherishing is that "delectation of the children"!

"A deputation from the Haswell Memorial Committee then waited upon the committee and placed various matters before them which were duly considered. It was agreed 'that the Board has the greatest pleasure in accepting the trusteeship of the Thomas Haswell Memorial, and thanks the committee and subscribers for the Memorial Medal to be presented to the best boy in the school.' The deed of gift was then read by the Secretary.

"Dr. Robson moved that the seal of the Board be affixed to the deed of gift. Mr. Lisle seconded the resolution, which was carried.

"A letter was then read from the Memorial Committee stating that the unveiling of the portrait would be performed by the Mayor in the Free Library on the afternoon of the 8th instant at two o'clock, and that immediately afterwards the Reverend Father Stark would present the first Memorial Medal to the *dux* of the Jubilee School. The members of the Board were also cordially invited to be present on the occasion.

"The Rev. David Tasker, speaking of the resignation of another old teacher, said that when the resignation of the late Mr. Thomas Haswell was placed before them, and he, along with other members of the Board were singing his praises, he remarked that the schoolmaster was worth more than twenty policemen. That remark appeared to have given offence to a useful and worthy section of the community. They had not reached the height of his argument. He was looking at the matter from a higher standpoint—viz., the *moral* standpoint, and he still contended that the man who occupied the position of a master or a teacher in a school and was brought in close contact with many children, exercised a large amount of influence over them, more so even, in some respects, than their ministers and clergy."

The memorial ceremonies took place on the day appointed, and the account which follows is taken from reports published in the *Shields Daily News* and *Shields Daily Gazette* of the following day, though the proceedings were referred to in the North Country press generally.

UNVEILING OF THE PORTRAIT

Yesterday afternoon the Mayor of Tynemouth (Alderman Whitehorn) unveiled, in the presence of a large gathering of the general public, in the Free Library, North Shields, a portrait of the late Mr Thomas Haswell, who for nearly fifty years fulfilled the duties of head-master of the Jubilee Schools. It will be remembered that in the spring of the present year, at a meeting of several of the old pupils of the deceased gentleman, it was decided to get up a memorial to perpetuate his memory. In addition to the portrait in the Free Library, it was decided to erect a memorial tablet in a conspicuous position outside the schools, and to invest a sum of money in the name of Tynemouth School Board for providing a memorial medal for presentation annually to the *dux* of the school. An indefatigable secretary (Mr. J. Burnet) and an energetic committee worked hard to bring the affair to a successful issue, and so far the results have been most gratifying. Among those present at the ceremony were Alderman J F. Spence, Messrs. Burnett, J. Park, Councillors Eskdale (Chairman of the Free Library Committee) and Marshall, Rev. S. Horton, G. H. Hogg, Thomas Atchinson, John Humble, Pearson Humble, J. W. Lambton (Clerk to the School Board), M. Detchon, W. Spence, Thomas Hudson, Superintendent Anderson, two sons of the old Maister, and many others.

Mr. Thomas Hudson briefly called upon

The Mayor, who said he was glad to accept in his official capacity the invitation of the committee to be present on that occasion to do honour to one of the worthies of the North of England. He was not so intimately acquainted with the late Mr. Haswell as many present had been, but in a few professional matters which brought them together he had ample opportunity for judging him, and he soon came to the conclusion that he was a noble type of man—(hear, hear)—and he felt sure they would all re-echo that sentiment. His longer experience justified that opinion more and more. (Applause) He presumed that most of them had seen the narrative of the life of the deceased gentleman, which appeared some time ago in the *Weekly Chronicle*, written by one of their worthies of the North, Mr. Richard Welford. Those who had an opportunity of reading that narrative would come to the conclusion that Mr. Haswell had been an extraordinary man. He was born in the beginning of the present century, when the facilities for education, which were now rampant, were not in existence. In point of fact Mr. Haswell had but two and a half years' schooling, and got so expert with regard to the three branches which were then supposed to make a man's education, viz. the three R's, that at an examination towards the latter part of his school career every one looked upon him with amazement. That was the commencement of his educational career, but he had ultimately to go to work, and as the eight hours movement was not then extant he would probably have to work twelve hours, which would leave him very little opportunity for improving himself mentally. But he was not to be done with regard to his education. Possessing more than ordinarily refined and elevated tastes, he naturally became associated with those who lived under more favoured circumstances than himself, and by that means was soon able to add to his stock of knowledge. He was from his early days an ardent student of the art of music, and made such rapid progress that he soon became leader of a military band in the district, and catered for the amusement of the people in both the harbour boroughs. His scholastic career commenced in the Jubilee Schools, and when he arrived at the age of thirty-two years the head mastership of that school fell vacant, and, with the assistance of his friends, he was appointed to the position, the duties of which he fulfilled for close upon fifty years. The school was exactly the same as it was when he was a pupil there. The education imparted was limited indeed, but during his career, by constant reading, etc , he was enabled to add many more branches to the code which then existed, and to the last he turned out efficient scholars, who could take their place in any society. Men proficient in navigation and other important subjects received tuition at his hands, and were now occupying some of the highest positions in life. (Applause.) As they were all aware, he became exceedingly proficient in music, and his popular setting to the well-known verses by a local writer, entitled "Tynemouth Abbey," would keep his memory ever green. During his management of the Jubilee School no fewer than between 5000 and 6000 pupils must have passed through his hands. At sixty-three years of age he was obliged to sit for a certificate of competency to carry on the school duties, the Education Act having come into force, and the Government having to make some contribution towards the school fees He should have been inclined to think that Mr. Haswell might have been the grandfather of the whole of the Education Department—(laughter)—but Mr. Haswell was not to be done. He would not relinquish his position without a struggle, so he sat for the certificate and succeeded in obtaining it, and for nearly twenty years after he continued —under the auspices of the Educational Department, and then under the Tynemouth School Board—to be master of that school. (Applause) When he arrived at a very old age, the Department, on his retirement, sanctioned the payment of a superannuation allowance of £30 per year, and that he considered was one of the best things the Educational Department ever did. (Applause) Unfortunately, their old friend did not live long to receive that grant, for in less than three years he departed this life. A good many of his scholars and friends thought it was only their duty to do something to preserve the memory of so distinguished and honoured a man, and the outcome had been that beautiful portrait of the deceased gentleman, whose features had been so truthfully delineated by one of their local artists He felt confident that many who visited the Free Library and gazed upon that picture would think of the history of Mr Haswell, and if they followed his example, the subscribers would feel themselves amply recompensed for any trouble they might have been put to in their efforts to perpetuate his memory. (Applause.) It afforded him pleasure to hand over the portrait, in the name of the subscribers, to the Free Library Committee and the ratepayers of the town. (Applause.)

Mr. Eskdale, on behalf of the Free Library Committee, tendered thanks, and expressed pleasure that the gift had been extended to the ratepayers. He then paid a high tribute to the memory of the late schoolmaster, and said that the committee were at present considering the advisability of erecting a new Free Library, and it was to him a pleasant reflection that the portrait of Mr. Haswell would be one of the first to take its place in the new building, which they were sure to get. (Applause.)

Alderman J. F. Spence moved that a vote of thanks be accorded to the Mayor for his services that day, and in doing so paid a becoming tribute to the memory of the late Mr. Haswell. For something like twenty-four years, he said, he had the pleasure of being honorary secretary of the Jubilee Schools, during which time he was brought into close contact with the deceased gentleman, and a more worthy man, a more persevering, capable, upright, and candid man he could not have wished to meet. (Applause.) As a schoolmaster he possessed much ability, and he always took a special interest in bringing his scholars forward. He not only imparted to them knowledge of the useful though common subjects, but taught them almost everything, from discipline to navigation. He was very much struck with one excellent quality which the deceased gentleman possessed, and that was his desire not only to turn out efficient scholars, but to keep them right morally. In this respect he thought many of the schoolmasters in their midst might emulate him with considerable advantage to themselves and the community at large. He always taught them to respect property, and his boys invariably acted upon his advice, seeming to recognise the value of it. (Hear, hear.) He was delighted that day to be able once more to look upon the countenance of his old friend. The likeness was an excellent one, and he trusted that it would be handed down to generations to come, for it was the portrait of a man who had indeed done good in his day and generation to his fellow-creatures. (Applause.)

The motion was carried with hearty applause.

The Mayor, in returning thanks, said it was his desire to promote the best interests of that borough, and he believed that nothing would conduce to the welfare of the inhabitants of that town to a greater extent than would the unveiling of the portrait that day. (Applause.)

After a vote of thanks to Mr. Burnet, the committee, and subscribers,

Mr. James Edington, in a few well-chosen remarks, paid a tribute to the late Mr. Haswell's memory, and said he thought that the portrait of the deceased gentleman could not possibly have been hung in a more fitting place, for it was in that hall that Mr. Haswell many years ago delighted the people of the town with music, in a manner which he could scarcely express. (Applause.)

The portrait, which is from the brush of Mr J Shotton, a well-known local artist, bears the following inscription :—"This memorial portrait of Thomas Haswell was placed here by his pupils, friends, and admirers, in recognition of his many social qualities and his long service in his native town in the cause of education. A D. 1890."

PRESENTING THE MEMORIAL MEDAL

At the conclusion of the ceremony of unveiling the portrait, the company proceeded to the Jubilee Schools, where the Reverend Father

AT THE JUBILEE SCHOOL.

Stark, Chairman of the School Board, presented the first memorial medal to the *dux* of the school.

The medal, of which the cuts below are a *fac-simile*, was designed by Mr. John Park, North Shields, and, as was to be expected, is of a most finished and chaste design. It represents on one side the house in which the late Mr. Haswell lived, the school in which he was for over forty-eight years the head-master, and the tower of the church in which he was for sixteen years the organist. The clock in the tower is telling the hour at which he died. Surrounding the design are the words, "Thomas Haswell Memorial Medal," and underneath, "Royal Jubilee School, North Shields." The reverse side bears the inscription surrounded by a beautiful wreath. The dies for striking the medal were made by Mr. William Marshall, of Chelsea, and are fine specimens of the die-sinker's art.

There was a large attendance of old pupils and friends. The Mayor was voted to the chair, and at the outset briefly called upon

Alderman J. F. Spence, who asked the Chairman of the School Board to receive on behalf of that authority the memorial medal, the dies, the deed of gift, etc.

The Rev. Father Stark said it afforded him the greatest possible pleasure to receive, on behalf of the School Board, that which had been handed to him by Alderman Spence, and to undertake the trust that had been placed in his hands. It was indeed rather a peculiar trust. It was not often that a School Board was called upon to carry out any work of that kind, but it had been a source of great satisfaction to every member of the Board to know that such confidence had been placed in them by the subscribers to the memorial. Those who had promoted that testimonial had not done so in the midst of their school-days, but after they had passed from school through the turmoils of life. Although they had

had many difficulties to overcome since the termination of their school-days, and had had to fight the battle of life, more or less bitterly, their minds had gone back to the day when they were under Mr. Haswell's tuition, and naturally enough they felt it their duty to perpetuate his memory in some way, and thus show their appreciation of his worth as a master and a gentleman. It was one of the most pleasing things in life to find that a master's efforts were appreciated by his pupils. (Hear, hear) Unfortunately, it was too often the case that boys were inclined to look upon their master as one who had been placed over them to give them a practical lesson in the sense of touch and feeling. (Laughter.) But that had not been the case with the boys under Mr Haswell's care He had commanded the affection and admiration of his former pupils by his own life and example, and by his model treatment of those placed under his charge. (Applause) The boy who was to receive that medal had not been selected by any individual or from any manner of personal choice. They knew that he had attained it in an honourable and fair examination, and he felt sure that all the boys present would be glad he had got it, because he had been proved to be the best boy in the school (Applause) But that medal, which was to be presented annually, would not be given merely for scholastic proficiency, but also for good conduct He thought the subscribers had done well to make that stipulation, for he believed that it would have been Mr Haswell's ardent wish that the medal should be presented to the boy whose conduct was considered the best, as well as for intellectual efficiency. (Applause) He then handed William Dowson, an intelligent little fellow, the medal amid loud cheering.

The recipient briefly returned thanks. "Mr. Chairman, ladies and gentlemen," he said, "I thank Mr. Stark for presenting me with this medal." (Cheers)

The boys then sang "Tynemouth Abbey," the music to which was composed by the late Mr. Haswell.

Mr. Thomas Atchinson moved that a cordial vote of thanks be passed to Father Stark for his services that day. Father Stark, he said, took a great interest in the education of young people, and the manner in which he had fulfilled the task allotted to him that day must have given every satisfaction. (Hear, hear) As an old Jubilee boy, he was glad to notice that the services of the late Mr. Haswell in the interests of education had been recognised in the way they had. It was certainly an excellent idea to have a portrait of the deceased gentleman placed in the Public Free Library, and to have a memorial tablet fixed on the outside of the school, but he for one considered the medal was the best of all The portrait would become obliterated by the ravages of time, while the tablet would eventually fall into decay and crumble into dust, but the memorial medal would last for ever, and thus perpetuate the memory of their late revered dominie until the end of time. He trusted that the boys present would do their best to gain the medal. Of course they could not all win it, but if they strove to obtain it, and came pretty near doing so, much good would be accomplished, and the efforts of the subscribers would not be vain. (Applause)

The motion was carried with acclamation.

Father Stark briefly responded.

Councillor Marshall moved a vote of thanks to Mr. Burnet and the Committee for their invaluable services in promoting the success of the memorial.

The motion was carried with applause.

Mr Burnet, in replying, said it had been a sincere pleasure to him to do what little he had to help to honour the memory of one to whom honour was justly due. He must ask to be allowed to take that opportunity of heartily thanking the members of the committee for the very kind assistance they had rendered him as their honorary secretary, which had made his humble duties so pleasant to himself He sincerely hoped that the boy, William Dowson, would long live to treasure his medal, and that there might always be in the future a noble ambition among the boys in that school to attain what he was sure would always be considered a coveted prize. He was sorry that they were not able that day to place the tablet on the front of the school, owing to an accident which happened to it in the course of its construction. A new one from the same design was being made, and would be fixed as soon as they received it. He again returned thanks on behalf of the committee and himself.

The proceedings, which were throughout most enthusiastic and interesting, were brought to a termination with a vote of thanks to the Mayor for presiding

On the following anniversary of the Maister's death, December 8th, 1891, the closing ceremony in connection with the memorial took place

UNVEILING OF THE TABLET.

The Memorial Tablet erected at the Jubilee Schools, North Shields, to perpetuate the memory of the late Mr. Thomas Haswell, was unveiled on Saturday afternoon. Mr. Thomas Hudson presided, and among the large number of ladies and gentlemen present were Mr. R. S. Donkin, M P. (the Member for the Borough), the Mayor and Mayoress (Ald. J. F. and Miss Spence), Rev. D. Tasker, Mr. J. Burnet (Hon. Sec. of the Committee), Mr. T. Atchinson, Mr. and Mrs. L. M. Johnson, Mr. A. Wood, Mr. J. E. Miller, Mr. M. Detchon, Mr L. H. Leslie, Mr. R. K. Fenwick, Mr. J. W. Lambton, Mr. John Moffat, Mr. J. Lisle, Mr. McKelvin, Mr. J. Park, Mr Geo. Horton, Mr Shotton, Mr. W. Haswell, and Mr. R. Bone.

The Chairman said he had been asked, as chairman of the Haswell Memorial Committee, to express the gratitude of the promoters of the Memorial to the subscribers for the liberality they had displayed and which had enabled them to perpetuate their revered friend's memory. The originators of the movement had, with the view of giving general satisfaction to the subscribers, adopted a three-fold plan—viz., first, the presentation to the Free Library of a portrait in oils, painted from life a few years ago, by a very old friend of the deceased gentleman, Mr James Shotton; second, the tablet unveiled that day; and lastly, the vesting of a fund with the Tynemouth School Board for the provision of a bronze medal to be presented annually to the *dux* of the late Mr. Haswell's school. The portrait of the veteran schoolmaster now adorned the walls of the reading-room of the Free Library, where for many years their departed friend took a leading part in directing the musical festivals and entertainments which were the means of raising a substantial sum towards the erection of the present building. Mr Haswell for upwards of forty years was one of the principal members of the old Mechanics' Institute, which was the father of the present institution. The tablet about to be unveiled was the beautiful design of Mr. John Park, the celebrated etcher, whose valuable services had been given gratuitously. The provision of a bronze medal annually had been secured by a sinking fund, and, they feared not, the medal would for generations yet to come be duly given to the *dux* of the late Maister's school. He was indeed a gentleman who had done great good in his day and generation; a man of unbounded benevolence, of active purity of purpose, wholly void of selfishness and vanity, filled with a courageous chivalry in denouncing cruelty and wrong. His penetrating pity extended to the humblest creature in God's creation, and his whole life was devoted to the welfare of mankind, both socially and politically. As a schoolmaster he was conspicuously successful, always inculcating into the minds of the boys under his charge the desirability of endeavouring to retain an unblemished character through life, as well as teaching them the subjects contained in the ordinary *curriculum* It was only fitting that they should do honour to one who had so devoted his life to the benefit of his fellow-men, and he was pleased indeed that their appreciation of his services had taken the form it had. (Applause.) His great love of music and well-stored studies in astronomy made him a charming companion. His singular simplicity of life, love of wife and family, deep devotion to duty and morality, enable us to say with solemn fervour—

> " Green be the sod above thee,
> Friend of our happy days.
> None knew thee but to love thee;
> Few named thee but to praise."

The Mayor supplemented the remarks of Mr Hudson, dilating upon

Mr. Haswell's great ability as a schoolmaster. The deceased gentleman, he said, had been responsible for the training of several thousands of boys, and the education he gave them was sufficient to fit them for almost any station in life. (Applause.) One thing he particularly instilled into the minds of those under his care was the taking care of other people's property. (Hear, hear.) He remembered one day visiting the school when Mr Haswell occupied the head mastership. The deceased gentleman called him into the playground adjoining the school, and, pointing to a couple of red-currant bushes laden with their luscious fruit, said in tones of intense satisfaction, "There's not a boy in the school who would not sooner cut off his hand than steal a single berry from one of those bushes." (Loud applause.) Mr Haswell was unquestionably an able master, and his scholars were always proud of him. (Applause.)

Mr. J. Burnet, the secretary, said "there are one or two items of interest with reference to the tablet to which the committee have desired me to refer. The tablet, as is well known, was designed by Mr. John Park, of this town, a member of the committee. It is made from a selected block of red Penrith stone, and has been executed by Mr. William Johnston, the sculptor, of this town, himself a former Jubilee scholar, who received his education under the late Mr. Haswell. He has carried out the design faithfully, and has given his labour in fixing the tablet as a tribute to the memory of his old master. The panel to the left is filled with a representation of seaweed, emblematical of the first line in the song, 'Tynemouth Abbey,' 'Where the sable seaweed 's growing, Tynemouth, on thy rocky shore,' to the words of which song the late Mr. Haswell composed the well-known music. The panel to the right is filled in with a laurel branch, a fitting tribute to his well-nigh half century of labour within these walls. Each of these panels is enclosed by the representation of a rope supported by pulleys at the corners, emblematical of another well-known song to which the late Mr. Haswell also set the music—namely, 'The Life Brigade,' which I need not remind those present has so often been sung, and I hope will long continue to be sung, at the annual meetings of the Tynemouth Volunteer Life Brigade, by our worthy Mayor, Alderman Spence. The centre is devoted to the inscription, written by one of the oldest living personal friends of the late Mr. Haswell—viz., Mr. Wesley S. B. Woolhouse, F.R.A.S. The quotation underneath was suggested by a member of the committee. The whole is framed in by three lines of polished tiles of harmonising colours. The committee have had embedded behind the tablet a bottle, which contains a copy of the *Shields Daily News* of Tuesday, the 9th December 1890, containing an account of the unveiling of the memorial portrait of the late Mr. Haswell in the Free Library by the late Mayor of the borough (Alderman Whitehorn), and the presentation of the first memorial medal by the Rev. Father Stark, the chairman of the Borough of Tynemouth

School Board, at the school here on the same day, together with a list of the subscribers to the memorial, and a programme of the concert and dramatic entertainment given in aid by the members of the North Shields Temperance Dramatic Society. I am also desired by the committee to express their thanks to the late Mayor (Alderman Whitehorn) for the kind manner in which he so readily consented to unveil the portrait, which occasion was, I believe, his first public appearance in his official capacity; also to the Rev Father Stark and the members of the School Board for the way in which they have met and accepted the views of the subscribers; and last, but by no means the least, their thanks to you, Mr. Mayor, for the generous aid and assistance you have rendered to them in a way which you have not permitted me to acknowledge more fully. They, however, cannot allow the opportunity to pass of asking you to accept their grateful thanks and to express the pleasure they feel that you are enabled to-day, in your person, and as the Mayor of the borough, to perform the concluding ceremony, and thereby to add one more tribute to the affection and regard which you for so many years and in so many ways showed to the welfare when he was living, and to the memory now that he is gone, of a man whose characteristics you so much admired" (Applause)

The company then left the schools and proceeded to the place where the tablet is placed, when the Mayor unveiled the memorial stone amid lusty cheers.

Mr. R. S. Donkin, M.P., briefly moved a vote of thanks to the Mayor for his services

This was carried by acclamation, and the Mayor having replied, the proceedings terminated.

Finally, as concluding the record of the Memorial proceedings, a few passages from a letter written by the honorary secretary of the movement may be quoted :—

"Personally I feel that what little I have been able to do has only been a duty I owe to the memory of your father, whom I knew during the last thirteen years of his life, and to whom I owed a deep debt of gratitude. When I first came to North Shields from my native place, Morpeth, a stranger, your father was amongst the first whose acquaintance I was privileged to make; and I will always remember with a thrill of pleasure the kindly interest he took in me, and the invaluable counsel and advice which he gave me as a young man leaving home for the first time, and separated from all the ties which bind one to *home*. It was during walks I had with him on Saturday afternoons and Sunday mornings (which I look back upon with feelings I am quite unable to express) that I was able to appreciate the wonderful grasp of his mind, the kindliness of his nature, and his marvellous faculty for illustration by the most convincing methods, and his ever-readiness to impart information. The smile of satisfaction that lit up his face when he found he was understood was something to remember. I must say that I am well pleased to think that I have been permitted to help in doing something to keep green the memory of so good a man, whose quiet, unostentatious dignity of character made him so beloved and respected by all with whom he came in contact."

APPENDIX A.

Jubilee School.

North Shields, Sept. 30, 1811.

At a General Meeting of Subscribers towards the Establishment of a School for the Instruction of the Children of the Poor of this Town, and its Vicinity, held pursuant to public Advertisement, from the Committee appointed to superintend the building of a School, in lieu of an Illumination on the 25th of October, 1809,

JOHN SCOTT, ESQ., IN THE CHAIR.

RESOLVED,—1. That as the school is now complete and ready to open; and this meeting being convinced of the facility and economy of the improved British system of education on the plan of Mr. Joseph Lancaster, concludes, that the same be adopted; and appoints Nicholas Joycey, who has been regularly instructed in this method of education, as master of the same.

2. That a president, three vice-presidents, and a committee of fifteen governors be annually chosen by ballot, for regulating the affairs of this institution; but that not more than ten of the committee of the former year shall be re-elected, any five of this committee of governors shall be competent to act; and the maintenance of the school shall be provided for by annual subscriptions and donations, under the direction of the said committee, consisting for the ensuing year of the following persons:—

JOHN SCOTT, ESQ., PRESIDENT.

STEPHEN WRIGHT, ESQ.—WILLIAM LINSKILL, ESQ.—AND ROBERT LAING, ESQ.,
VICE-PRESIDENTS.

COMMITTEE.

Alexander Bartleman	Thomas Wilkinson	Henry Taylor
Thomas Appleby	Joseph Taylor	Myles Foster
Robert Spence	William Richardson	William Taylor
William Wright, Esq.	William Cornforth	Thomas Fenwick
Thomas Curry	William Barnes	Joseph Procter

APPENDIX. 333

3. That Robert Spence, and Thomas Appleby, be requested to act as secretaries and auditors, and William Reed, Esq. as treasurer to the institution.

4 That the first annual meeting be held at the school, on the 25th of October, 1812, at which time the subscriptions for the ensuing year shall be considered as due; and, in the mean time, annual subscriptions and donations, however small, will be thankfully received, and applied to the benevolent purposes of the institution.

5 That annual subscribers of half a guinea, shall have the privilege of recommending one scholar, of one guinea, two, and so on in proportion. But, for the present, subscribers are desired to recommend only one scholar each; and to be attentive to the circumstances of the parents of the children they recommend, as it is not the intention of this institution to interfere with that useful class, the regular schoolmasters, by educating those children whose parents can afford to pay for the same.

6 That the committee shall attend at ten o'clock on Mondays, Wednesdays, and Fridays, during the first fortnight, and its first meeting be held on Monday next, the 7th of October, for the purpose of receiving the children recommended. These must be accompanied each by a parent, or friend, who shall be informed that the children must attend the school regularly at the hours appointed, viz. nine in the morning, and two in the afternoon, and be always sent clean and decent, with hair combed, and face and hands washed, and that they will be required on the Lord's day, regularly to attend the place of worship which such parent or friend shall appoint Also, that when any boy leaves the school, due notice of it must be given by the parent or friend to the sub-committee at the school, on the Monday morning previous to his being taken away, when the committee will present him with a Bible or Testament, at their option, provided his conduct has been satisfactory, and such as to merit approbation. To prevent mistakes, or groundless excuses, the above notices shall be printed on a card, and delivered to the parent or friend of each child on his admission. That afterwards, two members of the committee to be specially appointed at the intervening committee meeting, shall attend on the first Monday of every month, at the said hour, to receive such children as may be occasionally recommended.

7. That before the children proceed to learn in the morning, silence shall be observed, when a chapter in the Old or New Testament shall be solemnly, and audibly read by the master, or, at his discretion, by one of the elder boys: and the same practice shall be repeated at the close of business in the afternoon

8. That an annual subscription of one guinea, or upwards, shall constitute a governor, and the school shall be daily visited by one or more of a committee of six governors, taken in alphabetical rotation from the list of those who reside in or near North Shields; and a printed form of notice shall be prepared to be filled up by the master, and sent by the boys every Saturday to the visitors for the following week. This committee shall however be considered as an open committee of governors, whose presence in the school, as may best and most frequently suit their convenience, will be particularly desirable. To facilitate and as much as possible insure the daily visiting of the school, members of the weekly committee may visit by proxy, such proxy being a governor The visitors are requested to enter such remarks as may occur to them, on the management of the school, in a book to be provided for the purpose, which book shall always be laid before the committee at its regular meetings.

9. That the treasurer shall keep, or cause to be kept, an accurate account of receipts, and disbursements, and exhibit the same to the general annual meeting of subscribers, which accounts shall have been previously examined by two auditors, appointed by the former general meeting.

10. That an annual exhibition shall be held of the mode of instruction practised in the school, when an examination shall take place of the proficiency of the several classes, and prizes distributed to such of the children as shall have made the greatest improvement during the year, and whose constant attendance, and orderly conduct at school, may have entitled them thereto

11. That the committee make a report to the annual meeting of the number of scholars admitted and discharged during the preceding year, and of the present state of the school; which report, with a statement of the accounts, shall be published.

12. That all new rules and regulations, and all alterations and amendments of the present rules and regulations, shall be made at the general annual meeting, or some special meeting of the governors which may be called for the purpose by the annual committee, or any ten governors, on giving eight days previous notice by public advertisement of the business to be brought forward.

13. That strangers (unless introduced by some member of the committee) can only be admitted on Fridays, from eleven to twelve o'clock, but for a short time after the school is opened, it is particularly requested that strangers will postpone their visits to it, until the plan of education is somewhat matured.

N B. Strangers visiting the school, are not required to give any thing; but should any person incline, a box is provided to receive whatever they may choose to give, the sums contained in which shall be strictly applied to the purchase of rewards for the children, whose conduct renders them deserving of it.

14. That a copy of these resolutions be transmitted to His Grace the Duke of Northumberland, accompanied with a request from this meeting, that His Grace will accept the patronage of this institution.

15. *That the following Directions be observed by the Master.*

First The master shall attend with punctuality during the hours of from 9 to 12, and 2 till 5 o'clock, or an equal portion of time under any altered arrangement, which the committee may at any time judge expedient

Second The master shall enter, or cause to be entered, daily, in a book kept for that purpose, an account of the lessons performed by each class, also of the absentees from school, and from their respective places of worship on the Sundays; and shall keep a weekly account of the causes of such absence. That if the boy so appointed should from illness or other cause be unable to attend, his parents or friends be expected to inform the master, who shall in that case appoint a deputy

Third. That in order to this, he shall make out distinct lists of the children who are to attend each particular place of worship, that one boy out of each list be charged with the custody, as inspecting monitor of worship, who shall return it to the master every Monday morning, with the names of the absentees, and of such as may have behaved improperly in the time of public worship, accurately reported.

Fourth. That the master shall make a monthly report to the committee of the attendance of the scholars, and the business they have performed, adding an account of the boys who have passed from class to class, in consequence of proficiency, and of the rewards distributed during the month.

Fifth. That the committee do not desire to receive a similar account of punishments, in the ordinary course, but that the names of such boys as repeatedly give offence, be reported by the master to the committee, who, upon hearing the complaints alleged against them, will direct such punishment as they may think suitable to the offence, will cause a representation and remonstrance to be made to his parents or other friends, and in case of great delinquency, will expel him from the school.

Sixth. That whatever expences it may appear to the master desirable should be incurred for the use of the school, shall previously be laid before the committee, and receive their approbation and sanction.

17   *That the following Books be used in the School.*

Lancaster's Newly-Invented Spelling Book.	Miracles of Christ.
.... Dictionary do.	Parables do.
A Spelling Dictionary.	Discourses do.
Watts' Hymns.	Sermon on the Mount.
Scripture Instructor.	Testament.
History of Christ in the Words of the New Testament.	Bible.

And the committee are recommended to cause some of the elder boys to be instructed in the art of navigation before they leave school.

18. That the following card be delivered to the parent or friend of each child on his admission into the school.

Take Notice, That it is expected by the governors of the Jubilee School, that   be sent punctually to the school at nine o'clock in the morning, and at two in the afternoon, and that he always come clean and decent, with his hair combed, and his hands and face washed. Also, that he will be required to attend regularly the public worship of God on the Lord's Day, at   which place you have yourself chosen for this important purpose

                       (Signed)

                                                                    Two of the Committee.

It is further expected that you give due notice to the sub-committee at the school, on the Monday morning previous to taking him from the school.

             N.B. You are required to take care of this card.

19. That these resolutions be printed, and sent to the subscribers, who are desired to pay their subscriptions for the present year, to Robert Spence, or T Appleby, from whom they will receive cards of recommendation.

20 That the thanks of this meeting be given to the committee appointed on the 15th of January, 1810, and also to John Scott, Esq, Chairman of this meeting for his judicious conduct in the chair.

APPENDIX B.

DEED OF GIFT TO THE SCHOOL BOARD.

This Indenture, made the 6th day of December 1890, Between Thomas Hudson, Chemist; Michael Johnson Detchon, Accountant; John Park, Artist; George Edward Horton, Artist; John James Sharp, School Teacher, and John Edward Harrison Burnet, County Court Clerk, all of North Shields, in the County of Northumberland, hereinafter referred to as "the said Committee" of the one part and The School Board of the Borough of Tynemouth of the other part. Whereas several friends, admirers, and former pupils of Thomas Haswell, for many years School Master at the Royal Jubilee School, North Shields, aforesaid deceased (which school has been taken over by the said School Board), have recently subscribed various sums of money to form a fund for the purpose of establishing a Memorial to the said Thomas Haswell in recognition of his long services to the cause of education and of his sterling qualities as a man, and the said Committee have been authorised by the subscribers (*inter alia*) to deposit out of the said fund the sum of Twenty pounds in the Post Office Savings Bank at North Shields aforesaid in the name of the said School Board for the purposes hereinafter expressed, which said sum of Twenty pounds has been so deposited accordingly with the sanction and concurrence of the said School Board. Now, this Indenture Witnesseth, and it is hereby declared, and in particular, the said Committee doth hereby direct that the said sum of Twenty pounds so deposited as aforesaid shall be for ever held in trust for the following purposes—that is to say—

1. The said sum of Twenty pounds shall always remain invested in the name of the School Board, for the time being, of the Borough of Tynemouth, who shall for ever hereafter receive the interest accruing thereon, and shall with and out of the said interest once in every year provide a Bronze Medal, to be called "The Thomas Haswell Memorial Medal," which shall be stamped with the Dies which have been handed over by the said Committee, and are now in the possession of the said School Board.

2. The Medal shall be presented on the 8th day of December in each year, which is the anniversary both of the birth and death of the said Thomas Haswell (if the school be open on that day, and if not then, on the first school day after that date) by the Chairman or Vice-Chairman of the said School Board for the time being, as a prize for general proficiency in scholarship to the *dux* or boy who shall be declared by the certificate of the Master of the said School, approved by the said School Board, to stand highest for such on the 30th day of November immediately preceding the date of presentation, with an inscription engraved on the reverse side of the

APPENDIX. 337

Medal, setting forth the name of the boy, and that it is presented to him for general proficiency in scholarship for that year, and the date, "8th December," and the year. PROVIDED ALWAYS that the recipient of each Medal must have been at least for four consecutive years immediately preceding the 30th November of the year in which he qualifies for the same a pupil or scholar in the said school, and if the *dux* or boy who stands highest for general proficiency in scholarship shall at the said last mentioned date not have been that period in the said school, or shall on any previous occasion have been awarded the Medal, then the Medal shall be presented to the boy who stands next highest in general proficiency in scholarship who has been that period in the school, and who has not on any previous occasion been awarded the Medal PROVIDED ALSO that if at any time the interest of the said sum of Twenty pounds shall be more than sufficient to provide the said Medal and Case, then the surplus shall be expended by the said School Board in providing a prize to be given to the boy who stands next highest in general proficiency in scholarship to the recipient of the Medal in such manner as the School Board for the time being shall direct.

IN WITNESS whereof the said Committee have hereunto set their hands and seals, and the School Board of the Borough of Tynemouth have caused their common seal to be affixed the day and year first before written.

Signed, sealed, and delivered by the said THOMAS HUDSON, MICHAEL JOHNSON DETCHON, JOHN PARK, GEORGE EDWARD HORTON, JOHN JAMES SHARP, and JOHN EDWARD HARRISON BURNET, in the presence of	THOMAS HUDSON	O
	MICHAEL JOHNSON DETCHON	O
	JOHN PARK	O
	GEORGE EDWARD HORTON	O
	JOHN JAMES SHARP	O
	JOHN E. H. BURNET	O

JAMES T. REES,
11 Coburg Terrace,
North Shields,
Clerk to the Board of Trade.

The Common Seal of the School Board of the Borough of Tynemouth was hereunto affixed in the presence of
JOHN W LAMBTON,
13 Dockwray Square,
North Shields,
Clerk to the Borough of Tynemouth School Board.

Seal of the Borough of Tynemouth School Board

APPENDIX C.

BOROUGH OF TYNEMOUTH SCHOOL BOARD.

In the "Review of Proceedings of the Seventh Board, 1889-90-91, ordered to be printed January 2nd, 1892," is the following report of the Memorial Proceedings:—

"THOMAS HASWELL.

"An old and former head teacher of the Jubilee Board Schools passed away from this life on the 8th day of December, 1889, in the person of the late Mr. Thomas Haswell, who had resigned his position at the end of 1886. The Education Department granted him the maximum pension, which he had up to his death. An influential Committee was formed and funds raised to provide a memorial to his memory. A portrait in oil from the brush of Mr. J. Shotton, a well-known local artist of the town, was presented to the Free Library Committee and hung in the Library. It bears the following inscription :—'This memorial portrait of Thomas Haswell was placed here by his pupils, friends, and admirers, in recognition of his many social qualities, and his long service in his native town in the cause of Education, A.D. 1890.' The ceremony of unveiling the portrait was performed by the then Mayor, Ald. A. Whitehorn, on the first anniversary of his death."

"THOMAS HASWELL" MEDAL.

After the unveiling of the portrait, the company present proceeded to the Jubilee Schools, where the Rev. James Stark, the Chairman of the School Board, presented the first memorial medal to the dux of the school. The medal was provided by the Committee.

The presentation is reported as follows in the columns of the *Shields Daily News*, the editor of which has kindly granted the use of the blocks for the above:—

"The medal, of which the above is a fac-simile, was designed by Mr. John Park, North Shields, and, as was to be expected, is a most finished, chaste, and accurate design. It represents on one side the house in which Mr. Haswell lived, the school in which he was for forty-eight years the head-master, and the tower of the church in which he was for sixteen years the respected organist. The little clock in the tower is telling the hour at which he died. Surrounding the design are the words 'Thomas Haswell Memorial Medal,' and underneath 'Royal Jubilee School, North Shields.' The reverse side bears the inscription, surrounded by a beautiful wreath. The dies for striking the medal have been made by Mr. William Marshall, of Chelsea, and are considered to be splendid specimens of the die-sinker's art."

The dies for the medal, a deed of gift to the School Board, and a Post Office Savings Bank Book for a deposit of £20 were placed in the hands of the Chairman of the School Board.

The first medal was awarded to William Dowson, who received it amidst the loud cheering of the boys. The boys then sang "Tynemouth Abbey," the music of which was composed by the late Mr. Haswell.

MEMORIAL TABLET.

A few weeks ago the Committee finished its labours, when there was fixed on the outer wall of the school a Memorial Tablet, also designed by Mr. John Park. The tablet is of fine red sandstone, and bears the following inscription in gilt letters:—

TABLET PLACED, 1891,

IN MEMORY OF

THOMAS HASWELL,

Who was for forty-eight years the able, worthy, and esteemed Master of this School, and much honoured and respected.

"The occupation dearest to his heart
Was to encourage goodness."
"Learning grew
Beneath his care, a thriving, vigorous plant."

The second medal was presented by the Chairman of the Board on the 8th day of December, 1891, being the day fixed in the deed for such presentation. The recipient this time was John R. Darnall.

THE WALTER SCOTT PRESS, NEWCASTLE-ON-TYNE.

FIRST LIST OF SUBSCRIBERS.

A.

Adams, W E., 32 Holly Avenue, Newcastle
Aitchison, R , Cottage Hotel, Wooler, Northumberland
Allan, George, 9 Osborne Villas, Newcastle
Andrews, Hugh, Swarland Hall, Felton, Northumberland
Annand, Jas., 10 Tankerville Terrace, Newcastle
Armstrong, Miss Janet, Jarrow-on-Tyne

B

Barclay, Thos , J.P., 17 Bull Street, Birmingham
Baynes, Miss, South Preston Villa, North Shields
Bell, I. Lowthian, J.P., Uplands, Wimborne, Dorset
Bell, Mrs. Jno , Linskill Terrace, North Shields (2 copies)
Bell, Mrs. Sarah M , 21 Brighton Grove, Newcastle
Bennett, W E , Tivoli Villa, Westoe, South Shields
Birmingham Library, per Messrs. Cornish Bros., Birmingham
Black, Isaac, Tynemouth
Bone, Robt., 42 Stanley Street West, North Shields
Broad Lane Reading Room, Illogan, Cornwall
Browne, Jno L , 15 Thornhill Gardens, Sunderland
Brown, T. Forster, Guildhall Chambers, Cardiff
Brown, Mrs. Hy., Inglewood, Livingstone Road, Handsworth, Birmingham
Budge, Miss, Edmar Lodge, Plymouth
Bunce, J. Thackray, Edgbaston, Birmingham
Burnet, Jno., 5 Beaumont Street, North Shields
Burton, W. Spelman, 19 Claremont Road, Gateshead
Butler, Jos., 33 St. Andrew's Road, Stoke Newington, N.

C

Carr, Cuth. G., Low Hedgeley, Glanton, R S.O., Northumberland
Charlton, Geo , 41 Grainger Street, Newcastle
Christie, Charles W., Cardiff (2 copies)
Clark, S. Allan, 11 Whitehall Park, Highgate, N.
Clayden, P. W , Bouverie Street, London
Collins, Geo , 64 Saville Street, North Shields
Cornish Bros., New Street, Birmingham (4 copies)
Cowen, Joseph, Stella Hall, Blaydon-on-Tyne (2 copies)
Craske, Mrs., Beverley Road, Colchester
Crawford, Mrs. Thos , Northumberland Place, North Shields
Cresswell, Jno , Rothbury House, Heaton-on-Tyne
Cruddas, W D , J.P , Elswick Dene, Newcastle
Curry, H. S , Percy Gardens, Tynemouth (2 copies)

D.

Dale, David, J P., West Lodge, Darlington
Davison, R S , Dene House, Walbottle, Northumberland
Delaplaine, General, Madison, Wisconsin, U.S.A. (2 copies)
Delaplaine, Miss Annie, Gilbertstone, Kingston Vale, Putney, S W.
Delaplaine, Miss Blanch L , Madison, Wisconsin, U S.A.
Dendy, F. W., Eldon Road, Osborne Road, Newcastle

FIRST LIST OF SUBSCRIBERS.

Dickinson, Jno., Park House, Sunderland
Dickinson, W. B., 10 Sandhill, Newcastle
Dick, Mr., Royal Jubilee School, North Shields
Dodd, Mead & Co., 149 Fifth Avenue, New York, U.S.A.
Dowson, William, First Haswell Medallist, Royal Jubilee School, North Shields
Drummond, Chas., Tynemouth

E.

Edington, Jas. S., Squire's Walk, North Shields
Edington, Mrs. Mary, Squire's Walk, North Shields
Embleton, D., M.D., F.R.C.P., 19 Claremont Place, Newcastle
English, Thos., 99 Brinkburn Avenue, Gateshead
Everly, Adam, Philadelphia, U.S.A.

F.

Featherstonehaugh, Rev. W., Edmondbyres Rectory, Blackhill, Co. Durham
Fenwick, Miss, 36 Percy Gardens, Tynemouth
Fiedler, Dr. Georg, Hawkesley, Kings Norton, near Birmingham
Fieldhouse, Wm., Home Lea, Handsworth, Birmingham
Flower, Mrs., Avonbank, Stratford-on-Avon (2 copies)
Foot, Chas., Preston, North Shields
Forster, John R., C.E., Water Co.'s Offices, Newcastle (3 copies)
Forster, Alf., Water Co.'s Offices, Newcastle (2 copies)
Foster, Robt., The Quarries, West Clifton Road, Newcastle
Franklin, W. E., Newcastle

G.

George, Chas., Artist, North Shields
Gilzean-Reid, Sir Hugh, Warley Abbey, Birmingham
Glendenning, William, 4 Lovaine Place, Newcastle
Greene, Thos., 12 and 14 Dean Street, Newcastle

H.

Halliwell, Geo., Seaham Harbour
Harrison, Thos., 3 Otterburn Villas, Newcastle
Harvey, Dr. Jno., Handsworth
Haswell, Lieut.-Col. F. R. N., Monkseaton, North Shields (2 copies)
Haswell, Geo. H., Highfield, Queen's Park, Chester
Haswell, Miss, 38 Park Crescent, North Shields
Haswell, Fred., Ashleigh, Handsworth, Birmingham
Haswell, Henry, North Shields
Haswell, Prof. J. T., Edinburgh
Haswell, W. C., Linskill Terrace, North Shields
Haswell, William, St. Mary's Road, Smethwick, Birmingham
Heslop, R. Oliver, Corbridge
Hewett, Frank, Acock's Green, Birmingham
Hill, Alfred H., Cleveland, North Shields
Hill, Wm., 15 Dulke Road, Leathwaite Road, Clapham Common, S.W.
Hills & Co., 19 Fawcett Street, Sunderland
Holt, Miss A. K., c/o Miss Delaplaine, Madison, U.S.A.
Horton, Geo., Artist, South Shields
Howitt, Dr. F., Nottingham
Hudson, Thomas, Vine Cottage, North Shields

I.

Ingledew, J. P., Cathedral Road, Cardiff

J.

Jobling, Robt., Artist, North Shields
Jordon, John R., Secretary Working Men's Institute, Cornsay Colliery, Durham

K.

Kegan Paul, Trench, Trübner & Co., Ltd.
Kidder, Miss, Eau Claire, Wisconsin, U.S.A.
Kingston Public Free Library, Kingston-on-Thames

L.

Literary and Philosophical Society, Newcastle (6 copies)
Logan, Wm., Langley Park, Durham
Lupton, Banister, Beechcroft, Gosforth, near Newcastle (2 copies)

M.

Martin, N. H., 8 Windsor Crescent, Newcastle
Martyn, Hy J., Newquay, Cornwall
Maudlen, William, Salters Road, South Gosforth
Mears, Dr. F. C, 11 Northumberland Square, North Shields
Melbourne Public Free Library, Victoria (2 copies)
Miller, Jno Ed., 97 Howard Street, North Shields
Mills, Simeon, Madison, Wisconsin, U S A
Mitcalfe, J Stanley, Tynemouth
Mitchell, Chas., Jesmond Towers, Newcastle
Mitchell Library, The, Glasgow, per T. T. Barrett, Esq.
Morrison, Sam A., Morton House, Tynemouth

N.

Newlands, C. W, Homer Villa, Jarrow-on-Tyne
Newquay Reading Room, Newquay, Cornwall
Nicholson, Geo., 8 Barrington Street, South Shields

O.

Ogilvie, Frank, Artist, North Shields
Oliver, Jos. W., Ladywood, Birmingham

P.

Park, Jno., Artist, North Shields
Park, Septimus, North Shields
Parker, G F, U.S Consul, Birmingham
Parkins, W. J., Murdock Road, Handsworth, Birmingham
Pattinson, Jno., Shipcote House, Gateshead (2 copies)
Pendlebury, Chas, 16 Holyhead Road, Handsworth, Birmingham
Pepper, F. H., 34 Waterloo Street, Birmingham
Pepper, J. F., Shirle Hill, Handsworth, Birmingham
Pickering, Thos., 42 Osborne Road, Newcastle
Porteus, R. J., & Co, Lim, 19 Grainger Street West, Newcastle
Purvis, Robt, Broughton House, South Shields
Pyke, Thos., Public Library, South Shields

R.

Retallack, J. A., Melbourne, Victoria
Reynolds, Dr Frank, Eau Claire, Wisconsin, U S A
Richardson, Miss Alice M., 3 The Esplanade, Sunderland
Richardson, Mrs Bessie, Red Cloud, Nebraska, U S A
Ridley, T. D., Willimoteswick, Coatham, Redcar
Robinson, Geo, Eden House, Gosforth, Newcastle

S.

Scott, Clifford C., 4 Osborne Terrace, Newcastle
Scott, Walter, Holly House, Sunderland
Smith, George, Brinkburn, Gosforth, near Newcastle
Society of Antiquaries of Newcastle, per Robt Blair, Esq, F S A, South Shields
Spence, Ald. J. F., Chirton, North Shields
Spence, Wm., 29 Northumberland Square, North Shields
Spence, Mrs. R, Grosvenor Road, North Shields
St. Columb Minor Reading Room, Cornwall
Steel, Thos, J P, Kensington Esplanade, Sunderland
Stephens, Rev. Thos, Horsley Vicarage, Otterburn, R S O., Northumberland
Street, Rev. J. C, 180 Bristol Road, Birmingham
Strong, Hugh W, *Daily Argus*, Birmingham
Sutherland, Dr. C J., Dacre House, South Shields
Sydney Public Free Library, Sydney, N S. W. (2 copies)

T.

Tangye, Arthur L, 34 Waterloo Street, Birmingham
Tangye, Ed, Redruth, Cornwall
Tangye, George, J P, Heathfield Hall, Birmingham (5 copies)
Tangye, James, Chicago, U S A
Tangye, Joseph, Shallsburg, Wisconsin, U. S A.
Tangye, Richard, Ohio, U S A
Tangye, R. T. G., Malcolm Street, Cambridge
Tangye, Sir Richard, Kingston Vale, Putney, S. W (5 copies)
Tangye, James, Aviary Cottage, Redruth, Cornwall
Tangye, Alderman Jos, Bewdley, Worcestershire

Tangye, H Lincoln, Smethwick Hall, Birmingham (2 copies)
Tangye, Wm., Madison, U S A.
Taylor, Hugh, J.P., 57 Gracechurch Street, London
Taylor, Rev. Edw. J., F.S.A., St. Cuthbert's, Durham
Thomas, J. Henwood, London
Thwaites, R G, Historic Library, Madison, Wisconsin, U.S.A.
Timmins, Sam, J P., F.S.A., Arley, Coventry
Towers, M G., Clementhorpe, North Shields
Turner, Thos., Shelton, Stoke-on-Trent
Tynemouth Free Library, Tynemouth
Tynemouth Book Club, Tynemouth

U.

University Library, Madison, Wisconsin, U.S A (2 copies)

W.

Walker, Rev. Jno., Whalton Rectory, Newcastle
Waller, F. J., Sydney, N.S.W.
Welford, Richard, J.P., 25 King Street, Newcastle
White, W. R., Post Office, New Quay, Cornwall
Williamson, Thos, 39 Widdrington Terrace, North Shields (3 copies)
Wilson, Jno. N, 50 Percy Gardens, Tynemouth
Wilson, Dr., Salisbury House, Wallsend-on-Tyne, R S.O.
Winter, Frank, c/o J. M. Winter, Newcastle
Wood, Lindsay, The Hermitage, Chester-le-Street
Woods, Jas J, 45 Wordsworth Road, Smallheath, Birmingham

Lightning Source UK Ltd.
Milton Keynes UK
UKHW022158050922
408362UK00006B/1320